The Tragedy and Comedy
of Resistance

Penn Studies in Contemporary American Fiction
Emory Elliott, Series Editor
A complete list of books in the series is available from the publisher.

The Tragedy and Comedy of Resistance

Reading Modernity Through
Black Women's Fiction

Carole Anne Taylor

PENN

University of Pennsylvania Press

Philadelphia

10 9 8 7 6 5 4 3 2 1

Published by
University of Pennsylvania Press
Philadelphia, Pennsylvania 19104-4011

Library of Congress Cataloging-in-Publication Data
Taylor, Carole Anne, 1943–
The tragedy and comedy of resistance : reading modernity
through Black women's fiction / Carole Anne Taylor.
Black women's fiction / Carole Anne Taylor.
    p.   cm. — (Penn studies in contemporary American fiction)
Includes bibliographical references (p.   ) and index.
ISBN 0-8122-3510-X (alk. paper)
1. American fiction—Afro-American authors—History and criticism.
2. Women and literature—United States—History— 20th century.
3. American fiction—Women authors—History and criticism.
4. American fiction—20th century—History and criticism.
5. Modernism (Literature)—United States.   6. Afro-American
women in literature.   7. Afro-Americans in literature.
I. Title.   II. Series.
PS374.N4T38   1999
813′.5099287′08996—dc21   99-29489
                                                            CIP

to those who leave the story unresolved

Contents

In the death in which she had lived, she had been totally forced to pay attention to the dominant, raucous demands of Medusa. It did not matter there if flowers grew or women had children. Nothing mattered but the power of Medusa and her plans.

Bessie Head, *A Question of Power*

She would not have cut Medusa's head off, she is thinking, watching the mud come up worms between her toes. She would simply have told the sister to go and comb her hair. Or gotten a stick to drive the serpents out. Serpents or snakes? She drew a line in the dirt with her big toe.

Toni Cade Bambara, *The Salt Eaters*

Prologue: Ideologies of the Terrible and the Funny

All the old worlds die and become radically other from us at the moment of the birth of true modernity. The moderns, thus, with their religion of the new, believed that they were somehow distinct from all the other human beings who ever lived in the past—and also from those non-modern human beings still alive in the present, such as colonial peoples, backward cultures, non-Western societies, and "undeveloped" enclaves.

—Fredric Jameson, *Postmodernism, or the Cultural Logic of Late Capitalism*

. . . both European and non-European cultures were transformed by their "new" and closer relationship to one another in the "New World." For the most part, the relationship was one of exploitation, appropriation, oppression and repression. But it is also true that something came into and is coming into being: something neither "primitive/tribal" nor European modern.

While the most concrete sign of that something new is generally referred to as Postmodernism, unfortunately this move usually carries along with it the reinscription of Modernism's apartheid.

—Michele Wallace, "Modernism, Postmodernism and the
Problem of the Visual in Afro-American Culture"

The act of naming anything as tragic or comic calls on a network of cultural relations with implicit connections between what can or cannot be known or felt and what can or cannot be done. Since theories about tragedy and comedy, in Raymond Williams's words, "sound, insistently, like propositions about contemporary life," such theories always imply judgments about how social relations work or should work in the world. And because ideas about the tragic and the comic fit ways of knowing the world, they help to explain why particular ways of reading have produced—in this era named as postmodern—a preference for comedy as parody or pastiche and tragedy as dying, dead, or somehow debased. Tragic theory commonly refers to character and action that has about it something of awe or grandeur, just as comic theory commonly refers to the temporary or only mock transgressions of a rightful social order. In either case it remains difficult even to conceptualize valued representations of suffering or laughter outside a language that implies unacknowledged social distance. If "grandeur" refers back to what it means to be "grand," then "stature" and even the metaphors of "worth" and "value" themselves (turning people into implicit commodities) lead always back to the social measures—commonly named as ideologies—that mark one human being as somehow better or more important than another.[1] For those marked as lesser, the capacity for feeling or thinking in ways that acquire moral and aesthetic value resists the inadequacy of description.

The overt forms of resistance—expressing anger, hostility, or mockery; breaking the laws; transgressing the customs—have all taken their place within literary worlds most conceive as tragic or comic. But those forms of resistance that involve more doubleness, more covert negotiations with power, and more struggle with the complicit values that come with how one *must* live or speak, these modes have enough of paradox about them that they have had little place in discussions of the tragic or the comic. If the "nervous conditions" described by Fanon in *The Wretched of the Earth* characterize the iterative force of all that cannot *not* be experienced, then the necessary social contexts of that experience demand a revisionary aesthetics, one that acknowledges, as does Fanon, the interrelated troubles of oppressor and oppressed. The critical problem, that of understanding how the tragic or comic in literature means in relation to the tragic or comic in life, concerns how to recognize and value as potentially artful the capacity to feel and act upon human solidarity, a solidarity that resists the naturalized connections between social and moral judgments, between markets (or marketability) and morality.

However much the solitary writer and reader may value such solidarity, they already share in what I call here the paradox of resistance, that is, that any resistance necessarily participates in what it resists. A lowercase theory, either already marginalized or not yet acknowledged *as* theory, has frequently addressed the problematics of overlapping oppressions and has explicated the conflicted positioning of the writer who writes from below or outside, whether conceiving her trouble as disrupted processes of creation or production, multiple or fragmented identities, or conflicted (and therefore conflicting) subject positions.[2] These interrogations of how cultural memory remembers and how it represents what cannot be represented often have elaborate and complex awareness of the paradoxical role of a writer for whom writing itself does not have primacy of value. But if these writers inhabit paradoxical spaces, so must their readers. In terms of readerly desire, those struggling to affirm an endangered sense of identity may want art to act as a guide to how to live, whereas those accustomed to the presumptions and habits of unchallenged identity may see such a concern as irrelevant to discussions of aesthetic value. In the longing for solidarity, both writers and readers mirror the paradox of social desire itself (reduced here but not reducible to opposition): from below, one may want for oneself or one's children to climb out of hardship and injury, and yet not want to be either like those above or different from one's own; from above, one may admire the bonds that link others in hardship and isolate oneself in lonely achievement or the status of exclusion, and yet want to evade those lives' conditions. Understanding the relational paradox of such desire will help to understand tragedy and comedy as literary modes that may call into question what relations of power in life have to do with what and how we read, modes that may then come full circle to give primacy of place to resistances not in texts.

The fictions of black women writers, and concomitantly the contexts framed for them by (primarily) black feminist criticism, have relevance to whole bodies of Euro-American Theory (capitalized here to indicate its imperial sway) that tend to exclude these fictional worlds from theoretical discussion *as such.* In negotiating this terrain, I try not to ignore and yet not to dwell on my own positioning, wishing not to lose sight of the paradox of a critic writing about theory that values direct human relationship above the mediation of print; yet I will no doubt fall into participating in what I resist, unable to avoid reinscribing through habitual language (inaudible to me) the positions rejected as Theory.[3]

Although much of literary theory about tragedy and comedy presumes their definition as genres, I am less interested here in naming a work as tragedy or comedy in any generic sense (as names for works as a whole) than in elaborating the complexity of readerly/writerly relations as they imply a correspondence to social relations in actual worlds. For this, I have chosen the term "mode," connected since Aristotle with moral and social judgments about whether characters in fictions appear as better or worse than readers or audiences presume themselves. My use of the term takes as part of the problem that criticism does not have (and will not have in any foreseeable future) any consensual way of referring to multiple, split, or fragmented audiences, much less to the multiple identities or subject positions belonging to a single reader.

Written before the sometimes murky extension of generic terms to reach "beyond genre" or to combine and rename generic categories, the universalizing paradigm of Northrop Frye provides helpful clarity in understanding that genre always implies some distinction about presentation, with the foundational distinction among dramatic, lyric, and epic affiliations reflected in rhetorical distinctions about words acted before spectators, sung or spoken for a listener, or written for readers. By the time of debates about modernity and postmodernity, many critics claimed that these distinctions did not very well serve, and most of my own past work has labored toward a better understanding of works with more multiple, fluid, overlapping, and sometimes only implied or masked relation to particular readers' social positioning. Literary works negotiating plural rather than unitary selves, as well as diversely positioned and equally plural readers, tend to move in and out of tragic and comic modes. In doing so, they importantly address not only many of the issues commonly raised in theorizing tragedy and comedy as genres but also the parameters of what fictional worlds have to do with actual ones, with readerly/writerly relations themselves recognized as also multiply positioned relations of power.

To provide a context for my own readings and theorizing, I want to briefly survey the ways in which some of the most important ideas about tragedy and comedy as Euro-American genres have precluded engagement with the paradox of resistance and with those aspects of modern texts most relevant to it. In doing so, I foreground how diverse senses of power relations—how they do and should work—necessarily hover behind dominant explanations drawn from Euro-American Theory.[4] Such Theories offer explanations of tragedy and comedy that attribute stature in accordance with differing conceptions of the modern and the postmodern, and, although diverse in their ideological positioning, they create ellipses that will help explain why the fiction as theory of particular black women writers of the 1980s calls for a more critical modernity, a modernity conceived through a recursive reading of modern texts in the light of resistances once avoided, denied, tamed, universalized, or claimed as a privilege.[5]

Festivals to Bear with Living

Conceptions of tragedy and comedy allied with conservative ideologies have had such intimate connection with Aristotelian Theory that the festival performances of Greece and Rome provide the originary site for any public spectacle affirming a public history. Such Theory gives us dramatic performances that move forward to climaxes whose closure represents the return to a social and metaphysical order figured in the lives of those who remain on stage. And it gives us an audience that emerges with its social distance intact, an audience superior to the characters who behave in accordance with flawed knowing, feeling, or doing. Later conceptions supplant the stage audience with a readerly one and yet reinscribe this social distancing. Even in narrative extension, such tragedy purges an audience of felt connection to the dangerous excess of a now safely Other and such comedy purges any threat of otherness in the fools, buffoons, clowns, and dupes who so easily and so rightly become a disappearing act.[6] The troubled courtship of tragedy works toward death and the troubled courtship of comedy works toward marriage. And if tragedy is something wrong in Argos or Denmark that must be set right by purging a protagonist (who must die or disappear), then comedy is something wrong in Athens or Arden that must be set right by a reconciliation of nature and culture, forest and hall. Both give us worlds made right again, a moral authority shared by dramatist and audience, writer and reader. There is no room here for a tragedy that might find something ultimately wrong with the social order itself or a comedy that might refuse the venal bargain of nature brought back into culture.

Locating loss in concepts of order dominant within Euro-American traditions, a conservative sense of tragedy makes appeal to ideals of order and truth linked not just to Aristotle but to a cultural history finding tragedy's greatness in its response to uncertainty, to times "when cultures and societies have felt their values, most especially their religious values and articulated conceptual schemes, to be no longer stable, absolute or coherent" (Woodfield 194). Consistently, this perspective mourns the loss of a "genuine moral consensus" forever embedded within a chosen history and its chosen literature. One might read Alisdair MacIntyre and George Steiner as exemplars, for both elaborate a kind of cultural nostalgia that denies the possibility of contemporary tragedy, much less a tragedy of resistance.

MacIntyre's Theory of tragedy focuses on "rival allegiances to incompatible goods," where the rival claims possess equal authority because "accountable" to an order deemed simply true or false. With no sense of relationality, the values of the good or the true do not differ depending on the vantage point. Understanding that "belief in the virtues being of a certain kind and belief in human life exhibiting a certain narrative order are internally connected" (144), MacIntyre posits the *rightness* of success attending virtue and failure attending vice. Frightening when viewed from elsewhere, such a conception carries within it a faith in consensual virtues; and such faith, thought to have passed from modernity, accompanies Aristotle as the primary icon for value. The tragic self of Greek society and the contemporary search for rational justification merge, so that the Sophoclean protagonist embodies MacIntyre's own litany of such favorite values as order, accountability, and truth.

In a related vein, George Steiner's lament for *The Death of Tragedy* chides critics for allowing a "real" sense of tragedy to die.[7] Rather than interrogating the social foundations of aesthetic judgments, this criticism seeks out the essential traits of the "masters" and deplores a world of "secondary values" in which humanist individualism loses ground to mass culture on the one hand and to the promotion of lesser arts and artists on the other ("artists whose intrinsic stature remains arguable,"

Real Presences 26). Indeed, the highest tragedy has about it the aura of an "absolute" both extraordinary in its rigor and unendurable in its fatality: "Absolute tragedy is very rare. It is a piece of dramatic literature (or art or music) founded rigorously on the postulate that human life is a fatality." As tragedy moves away from the absolute ("*the performative mode of despair*"), it allows no greater relation to therapy for a disordered or unjust social world than "the therapy of discourse, be it philosophic or aesthetic" ("A Note on Absolute Tragedy" 147). Such a movement away from the absolute occurs in a Shakespeare seen as closer to a "tragicomic motion of spirit and of plot" than to the "wholly tragic" plot and spirit of Greek drama. Modern drama moves even further away in the form of Brecht and Claudel, the only dramatists "whose poetic means, stagecraft and choice of themes make comparison with Greek tragedians and with Shakespeare legitimate," but whose "messianic" visions Steiner names as melodrama rather than as tragedy. And of course, the rhetoric of the sacred surrounds a canon crumbling because of failures both critical and religious: "The contact with transcendence cannot be empirically validated. Its guarantor is theological" (" 'Critic'/'Reader' " 28).

A conservative sense of comedy projects a social world concerned primarily with the aggressive and defensive functions of humor, one that always returns to a prior order however much interrupted by a comic protagonist. In this, it mirrors Henri Bergson's sense of humor and difference: "Laughter is a social reaction which punishes and puts down deviant elements in man's behavior and in various events."[8] The belief that humor-as-coercion has a kind of therapeutic social function thrives on comic characters as scapegoats, those who take on embarrassment, foolishness, the ridiculous, or the absurdly malevolent in order to become scapegoats for social correction. A comedy thriving on aggressive and tendentious humor always casts them down, whether with vengeful relish in the darker forms of satire and parody or more benignly in romantic comedy's integration of a now powerless comic protagonist into a world stripped of critique. From this perspective, the laughter of the oppressed cannot attend meaningful resistance or even a vision of a better world. Rather, "laughter shared by the oppressed at the expense of the oppressor reduces fear and helps people to go on living under the regime with more ease" (42).[9]

The focus on preserving an extant social order or returning to an order lost when threatened by difference emerges full-blown in the *mythos* of comedy outlined by Northrop Frye in *Anatomy of Criticism*, which still informs most maps of the comic with its spectrum of comic kinds. They range from those in which a social order triumphs or remains undefeated (connected to birth) to those in which it dissolves or threatens disintegration (connected to death).[10] From satire and irony to romantic comedy, Frye's comic kinds simulate the growth of an organism, with different comic plots analogous to the ages of man. Comic fiction stands in the line of direct descent from an originary dramatic comedy (as opposed, for example, to any line of descent from the humorous tales of oral traditions).[11] With no troubling social reference to scapegoating rituals in actual social worlds, Frye's scheme implicitly naturalizes such rituals.

T. G. A. Nelson's recent overview of literary comedy follows Frye's generic distinctions and therefore begins with categories drawn from life stages (procreation, marriage, and death) and from already distanced comic protagonists: fools and rogues, the dupers and the duped. This view of comedy allows a conception of "the proliferation of trickery and mystification for their own sake, with a climax when the victim is brought (or apparently brought) close to death" (108). A comedy "for its own sake" distances its victims, such that even Tom Sawyer's play with Jim bears no taint from the cruelty of "play" with a freedom Jim does not know he possesses (arguably part of Twain's own auto-critique). Conservative readings here parallel the moves described by the misattribution Theory of humor as characteristic of an in-group's declaration of immunity from charges of cruelty. This comedy, like such in-groups, claims "only joking" status for its humor by attributing positive desire for "just good fun" to negative social behavior.[12] This comic play distances itself from any reference to a real world's suffering with its surety about what constitutes the "savage" and what the "civilized," or what the natural and what the cultural. And it does not worry about the social implications of who laughs, or when.

Unlike many liberal and transgressive perspectives, conservative views of the tragic and the comic do not separate arguments about art from those about life (or portray artists as the necessary mediators of cultural values). Because no distinctly formal realm of art separates the aesthetic from the moral, both tragedy and comedy become inseparable from the closed nature of a moral universe necessarily framed by unacknowledged power relations. In narrative, the problems of complicity become the problems of representation, and the "fit" of literary genre grows slack. Instead of valuing an artful building to a dramatic climax, narrative may move among tragic and comic modes that cohabit with often multiple and hybrid generic affiliations. Yet for narrative too, critical descriptions couch praise for effective "climax" in the "natural" figures belonging to the festive values presumed shared by writer, world, text, and reader. Such description depends on biological and organic metaphors, natural cycles (especially death as a cycle necessarily leading to rebirth), and the individual protagonist as central to *re*affirmations of values only temporarily in jeopardy. A tragedy purged of any impulse to sustained resistance finds its soulmate in comedy with only pretend or already disempowered revolt. With safely distanced transgressions, the "natural" cycles so vital to vitalism do not need to negotiate alternative space-times or the identities of any Others. They are already taken into account in characters portrayed from the outset as doomed, illegitimate, or powerless.

The Avoidance of Power

Although informing some of the most compelling extant interpretations of canonical works with clear generic self-presentation as tragedy or comedy, liberal theories tend to avoid issues of social justice, and avoid, too, the duplicitous and often involuted distance between any particular language-use and its hook-ups to a social world. More often psychological than psychoanalytic in orientation, liberal Theory delimits the contexts and definitions of Theory by practicing a suspension of ethical judgment in description seemingly without positioning. This seemingly neutral or value-free description of social contexts may isolate distinctions that seem irrefutable as far as they go, but they may not go very far toward any relational sense of ideological presumption.[13]

Unlike conservative conceptions that refer back to consensual notions of order and truth, liberal conceptions sympathize with tragic protagonists *as victims*. Rather than identifying with the social order that purges the tragic hero's rebellion, or with the rightness of that catharsis, liberal tragedy identifies with the tragic hero as a universal representative of human vulnerability. Such sympathy involves an only temporary identification that bypasses relations of power because after all, "We are all victims." That is, the tragic figure as the extraordinary representative of social disorder serves to enrich ordinary lives by disappearing in such a way as to allow them a form of compassion requiring no necessary changes in their conceptions of themselves (whatever the change in understanding the relation of the human to the sacred or the necessary). A liberal tragedy reliant on solidarity without commitment views the outcome of tragedy in terms of "win, draw, or lose,"[14] even while focusing on tragic conflict that occurs amid distortions of chance or that profound sense that "*the dice are loaded*" (Pavel 240). With the social status of characters and the death or catastrophe that befalls them understood as the "exterior" features of the tragic situation, the complicity of the social order itself merely coincides with the arbitrary, God-given nature of suffering. As such, tragedy belongs to a sphere of specifically aesthetic (or aesthetic-epistemological) acknowledgement, for which Stanley Cavell and Michelle Gellrich provide examples in an interpretive richness that has primary relation to a universalized human condition.

Looking closely at the processes of identification attending readerly response, Cavell nevertheless flattens responsiveness to the universal subject of "every man," a "we" of whom it can be said for certain that "we are severed; in denying that, one gives up not only knowledge of the position of others but the means of locating one's own" (337). Neither natural nor accidental, the death in tragedy is inflicted, and therefore "a punishment or an expiation (like an execution or a sacrifice). But if the death is inflicted, it *need* not have happened. So radical contingency haunts every story of tragedy" (341). With no answer to any "why" behind the death or disaster befalling tragic figures, their sacrifice begins and ends incomprehensibly "to maintain us in a present" (342) that speaks of "radical contingency" as entirely outside of any social world in need of radical change. For Cavell, the awe appropriate to tragedy, closely related to Kantian sublimity, relies on a very particular answer to the question: "Why do I do nothing faced with tragic events?":

. . . if I do nothing because there is nothing to do, where that means that I have given over the time and space in which action is mine and consequently that I am in awe before the fact that I cannot do and suffer what it is another's to do and suffer, then I confirm the final fact of our separateness. And that is the unity of our condition. (Cavell 339)

Relatedly, Michelle Gellrich finds the rebellion of tragedy *within* its own performance and not in any ideal of struggle, *phronesis*, or push to action that survives the performance. Consistently, she lauds a tragic subversion that stays limited to the dramatized world or that levels the suffering of characters in relation to the cathartic responses of an undifferentiated audience. Explication often ends on a self-repudiating note about the necessary limitations of Theory itself, perhaps because like other liberal critics of tragedy who sympathize with or mourn the tragic protagonist's condition (mourning before Electra?), she offers no alternative to the habits of a tragedy bound up in mental or aesthetic states.

The tragedy that makes us all equal victims, making all tragedy about a generalized human condition, finds its corresponding comedy in a seeming reconciliation of whatever opposites separate a universalized "us" from a comic "them." This comedy works toward reifying the distance between those within comic worlds who take the world's foolishness upon themselves (not just fools per se, but also dupes, clowns, buffoons, all humorists in spite of themselves) and those who watch or read, even while it admits to the foolishness "in all of us." Liberal humor Theory consistently derides any suspicion that humor may itself participate in the social construction of inequitable power relations,[15] favoring a comedy characterized by not taking human difference too seriously; after all, we are all fools sometime or other and comedy helps us to "keep it on the light side." And just as liberal Theory may provide a strong sub-textual criticism of those who do not laugh (the racial, ethnic, and female butts of jokes, for example), so it customarily makes of tragedy and comedy an opposition with tragedy the more profound, awe-inspiring purging of feeling for taboo-breaking Others and comedy the lighter expulsion of make believe (or at least safely Othered) difference.

Liberal opposition makes tragedy deep and comedy superficial, even if finding some connection in the relentless presentness of characters about whom one may ultimately say, "They are there and I am not." In this view, tragedy and comedy share actions that put "society back in touch with nature" (Cavell 330), and neither has any vision of resistant interconnections. Liberal theories promote for tragedy a compassionate identification presumed neutral or value-free and for comedy a suspension of self-reflective ethical judgment. Viewed thus, modern consciousness suffers because "we find ourselves at the cause of tragedy, but without finding ourselves" (349). A popularly mourned apathy becomes applicable to tragic response and the problem of "whether we have it in us always to care about something" becomes primary. This description of tragic response allows identification to take place even as a staged world removes the scapegoat-protagonist from the social order; and it corresponds to a frequent description of catharsis as inseparable from a kind of staged ostracism:

The sufferer in tragedies is typically moved from the centre to the margins, from the main-stream of human discourse and experience to the scene of the taboo and the unknown. "Solidarity of plight with diversity of state" is how Frank Kermode describes the "conditions of tragedy." Paradoxically, however, this description is appropriate to us all: singular loss is the certainty in a world perceived as unstable and multiple. (Woodfield 197)

Similarly, a modern sadness within comedy relies on a surface-core opposition:

The tragedy is that comedy has its limits. This is part of the sadness within comedy: the emptiness after a long laugh. Join hands here as we may, one of the hands is mine and the other is yours. (Cavell 341)

If liberal tragedy mourns "hav[ing] it in us always to care about something," then liberal comedy celebrates an absence of care found in psychological otherness taken as a given. And if we understand suffering as universal and laughter as marking our necessary separateness, then we can acknowledge or appreciate without doing anything else at all.

Medusa at the Carnival

Ideological predispositions that label themselves transgressive tend to alliances with postmodern reclamations of the negative, and therefore disavow tragedy (read as conservative) and claim resistance for parody, pastiche, and other ironic, often metafictional modes. This emphasis often values extreme positions that make intellectual nonconformity somehow equivalent to material oppression of the kind inscribed on bodies. Accordingly, an anti-tragic bias favors the forms of resistance found in writerly claims to extravagant subversion and readerly claims to an infinitely extended play with language. While avowing a leftist ideological desire to subvert dominant or official power, transgressive ideology looks to travestying forms of humor as important images of liberation. This Theory values the laughter of the disempowered, but only *in extremis*, and its highest value often inheres in the mediated laughter brought to us by the abstracted creative intelligence of the artist-writer who identifies with actual disempowerment.

Self-consciously formal writerly play and its chosen, "textualizing" readers afford the highest value to a modernity represented by Joyce, Kafka, and Beckett and to a postmodernity represented by Grass, Heller, Nabokov, and Pynchon. Together, such writers and readers inhabit possible worlds made of language, valuing such qualities as "entropic irony" in which "the obligation to decide is the central necessity and the central impossibility" (O'Neill 215). Such transgression finds frequent critics among those who live with a marginalization that they have not chosen, who argue that the willful adoption of outsider status does not in fact constitute significant transgression, but rather a too-easy, elite form of resistance easily coopted by institutions (the academy and the publishing industry among them).[16] For those on the underside of power, the yearly spring festival will not suffice as a model for social change any more than theoretically infinite extensions of carnival spirit apply to everyday social life. However much transgressive ideology (re)presents itself as strong social critique, it finds scant responsibility for social action or struggle for social justice in the carnival of language: its possibilities tend to remain abstracted or linguistic.

The play of transgression that disallows tragedy finds perhaps its most explicit theorists in Deleuze and Guattari when they pronounce schizophrenia and paranoia the oscillating forms in which desire must express itself in the age of late capitalism.[17] In their reading, tragedy itself—in the form of the family romance, the state, or whatever regulatory mechanisms circumscribe the taboo—sets up the parameters of desire that lend themselves to repressive means of enforcement (the discipline and punish that always follows the expression of desire). Beckett's

Unnamable—along with Murphy, Watt, and other character-states—replace both the tragic and the psychoanalytic as the forever decentered subject, a subject *"defined* by the states through which it passes" (20). Thus, the suffering in Beckett belongs to characters deprived of agency altogether, and produces startled recognition in audiences who laugh because they have no idea what to do about such a state of affairs. The excitement of such transgression seems characterized by a heady, euphoric irony, attended more by witty, bemused appreciation than by any imperative to social change.

As the foremost theorist of transgressive comedy, M. M. Bakhtin represents the difficulty both of his own complexly evolving views and of diverse uses of an appealing populism that overtly links the folk carnival of the middle ages to the creative, mediated transgressions of writer-artists. Expressly valuing the laughter of those without social power, the early Bakhtin emphasizes the carnival's ritual, public inversion of "official" power.[18] He sees the carnival's liberating laughter in the images of rogue, clown, and fool, those who in everyday life, as "outside" figures, enact "the right to be 'other' in the world, the right not to make common cause with the existing categories that life makes available" (*Dialogic Imagination* 159). The humorous kinds invoked by this idea of carnival rely on a sustained, often ritual inversion of already existing forms that presumably releases carnival participants from fear, whether the fear of death or authority or abusive power. In his favorite comic writers (Rabelais and Gogol, for example) Bakhtin finds inversions of ritual spectacle (tied to the church calendar or seasonal agricultural rites), vernacular parodies (of prayers, sermons, scholarship, any institutionally sanctioned forms), and even mimicry of the verbal abuse in the marketplace. Bakhtin sees travestying forms as "ever changing, playful, undefined" because they direct themselves at an order that includes the one who laughs. Read positively by those who accept meaningful relation between public carnival and mediational artist, Bakhtin's carnival laughter has strong alliances with Foucault's madman's laughter and Cixous's laughter of the Medusa, all representing a liberation available through literature.[19] Read negatively, carnival's temporary inversions cannot be arbitrarily sustained through the mediation of writers asserting the power of a discourse, a subject position, or a textuality only figuratively related to actual social worlds.[20]

Hélène Cixous's renowned "The Laugh of the Medusa" (1976) has particular relevance here because of her identification with a Medusa figure whose transgressions change the grotesque to laughter, something Cixous calls on all women to undertake through writing and through changes in identity made possible by writing.[21] For "a universal woman subject who must bring women to their senses" (875), the Medusa represents whatever remains unrepresentable, horrific—all the "dark continents" charted in their absence by phallocentric discourse.[22] Women's writing, says Cixous, must "look at the Medusa straight on," express the "otherness" presumed inexpressible in men's writing, in order to see that she is laughing and beautiful. As though crossing Bakhtin's grotesque parody with psychoanalytic sublimation (despite Bakhtin's own Marxist critique of Freud),[23] Cixous makes the Medusa's beauty and laughter a matter of creative and imaginative will.

The difficulty in sustaining the Medusa's laughter as a positive model remains the distance of these privileged conceptions from those who actually live on the borders of breakdown. In general, the mad or hysterical laughter claimed by postmodern sensibility rings as solo performance, a gesture of rebellion that asserts solidarity with other "outsiders" but does not seem to care much about the worldly relations of power within which writer-analysts also stand. For however good with humor at the boundaries of intuitive definition, transgressive Theory often makes this move from carnival conceived as subverting official discourse in people's lives to a representational subversion confined to literary or artistic representation. The wild, extreme laughter of disembodied texts "seems almost too ferocious to be believed. . .too disappointed with the world which is changeless only in the comic versatility which is still resistant to change" (Blau 39). And although Bakhtin remains the vital source for conceptions and readings of both popular and elite culture, readings attentive to both celebration and critique, he also remains the source of a cultural problematics that has not yet resolved the tensions between sentimentalizing a popular consumer culture and sharing the apocalyptic despair of privileged representations. And the revisionary psychoanalysis affirming laughter in extremis risks complicity with the "cynical ideology" that sees ironic laughter as "part of the game" (Žižek, *Sublime Object of Ideology* 28).

Yet transgressive ideology does allow room for theorizing more fluid modes of tragic and comic resistance, modes that possess a vision of normalcy and wholesomeness alterior to abstracted values. In difference from the Medusa-as-transgressor, Bessie Head and Toni Cade Bambara portray Medusa as the received, constructed "Other" who becomes a part of one's own identity-struggles and who, whether as horrible unconscious or a human projection, only ceases to "petrify" through the strenuous social struggles inseparable from those of identity-formation itself. Françoise Lionnet, writing about the historical contexts of the cross fertilization among women writers from Africa and the African diaspora, includes among other common characteristics "the negative mythic images of women—such as Medusa, Jezebel, Salome, the Furies, the Amazon, the mad woman, the hysteric, etc.—which they [black women writers] exploit and translate into powerfully subversive fictions" ("Geographies of Pain" 209). By extension from the Medusa's paradoxical doubleness, Morrison, too, positions her characters in complex relation to figures who haunt as part of oneself and whose exorcism involves, first, the strongest form of identification and, second, a cathartic form of action. All my chosen fictions posit the distinction between the rational and the irrational as coming from the direction of power and violence, and all reject the extraordinary artist-transgressor as mediator and hero in favor of those who must in their daily lives carry on multiple negotiations with both worldly and otherworldly power.

The Long Revolution

In "Living Memory," Toni Morrison aptly brings the actual, material experience of black women to bear on cultural definitions accustomed to more amorphous, metaphysical reference: "From a women's point of view, in terms of confronting the problems of where the world is now, black women had to deal with postmodern problems in the nineteenth century and earlier" (178). She reminds us that to live in a postmodern age is not, after all, to affirm any particular set of beliefs, but rather to engage, whether consciously or not, in the construction of whatever modernity precedes it.[24] Morrison names a limitation of even the most progressive theorists of tragedy and comedy, for even when Euro-American Theory has linked tragedy and comedy to contemporary dialogue about how to act in an unjust world, what one might call transformative Theory, it has not been *inter*cultural enough to find the literature such theory postulates. Potentially transformative ideology acknowledges the difference-in-relation of art and life, refusing to take the rituals of art as a surrogate for actual relationship or social action. And it acknowledges that the comic impulse, just like the tragic one, can be beaten out of anyone, since both take the energy, will, and solidarity with others that oppressive circumstances may defeat. The twentieth-century literary theorists perhaps most important to theorizing the dialogical interplay of tragedy and comedy, Raymond Williams and the late Bakhtin (and at least certain strains of the earlier) came closest to caring about what the tragic and comic in literature have to do with the tragic and comic in life. And yet, perhaps necessarily, both framed a somewhat inchoate transformation still looking for its literature.

Aware of the tendency to link progressive social thought with the non-tragic, Williams saw the reduction of tragedy to a single violent action as analogous to the reduction of revolution to single critical conflict and its resolution. In either case, "To limit violence and disorder to the decisive conflict is to make nonsense of that conflict itself" (65). For Williams, to call any rebellion against an oppressive social order "revolution," in the common sense of violent and disorderly acts, reflects an inability to see the systematic, institutional disorder and violence that comprise part of social process. (Or, as in the ease of references to "riot" or "rebellion," it projects onto a present-tense resistance the long-term causes of disorder.) Williams protests tragic Theory's preference for "the fault in the soul" over the faults of the social order, abstracting its subject such that even when no longer about any nobility, tragedy still links high genre to high class in the primacy it gives to a dominant order. (And of course, those with lives borne down by material need have no "purchase" in such order.) The "long revolution" about which he wrote so eloquently, comprised of the long-term, cumulative resistances of daily life as well as of more dramatic struggle, makes possible a conception of tragedy in which the separateness of those who witness becomes not the positive "unity of our condition" but the impetus to auto-critique and a social desire to undo the structures of one's own complicity.

Williams ends his description of the defeatist "structure of feeling" implied in modern tragedy with a paean to Bertholt Brecht's "rejection" of tragedy, for only in Brecht does he find a sensibility able to recognize the tragic in history even if unable to transform that vision into tragic drama. In Brecht's poem "An die Nachgeborenen," Williams finds the recognition of "a very complex kind of feeling" able to hold in paradoxical juxtaposition the brutal realities of social struggle and the affirmation of human possibility:

For we knew only too well:
Even the hatred of squalor
Makes the brow grow stern.
Even anger against injustice
Makes the voice grow harsh. Alas, we
Who wished to lay the foundations of kindness
Could not ourselves be kind. (Brecht, Williams 203)

When the struggle for fulfilled life thrusts people into fixed, hardened positions, those once alienated find themselves creating new forms of alienation; and at such moments, revolution arrests itself and becomes "a tragedy halted and generalised at the shock of catastrophe" (203). A new sense of tragedy finds affirmation in the generational metaphor of the future children of the revolution, those "who because of the struggle live in new ways and with new feelings, and who, including the revolution in their ordinary living, answer death and suffering with a human voice" (204). Following the call, Williams even tried to produce his own revolutionary tragedy in his two-act drama *Koba*, a work whose heavy symbolism and strained dialogue represent a thing apart from the narrative skill he often showed in his fictions. Perhaps representing the kind of work that all critics fear they might produce were they to turn their hands to primary acts of creation, *Koba*'s characters speak in dialectic almost as though Brecht's folk idiom has fallen into caricature. (A Stalinesque character named "Joseph" has lines like, "I will not die. I am Koba. I will master death.") But, however limited, the play represents the intensity of Williams's felt need for some example of a tragedy in which revolution does not refer to the crisis of a conflict, but to a whole story in which systems and institutions that once seemed neutral, or even innocent, come to be seen as themselves constitutive of tragic order.[25]

In a corollary way, the highest values throughout most of Bakhtin's life and work accompany the mediated laughter brought to a readerly audience by the abstracted, creative intelligence of the artist-writer. Yet because of his clear populism Bakhtin's early focus on even the very transient rituals of carnival dramatizes how provisional and vulnerable are the assumptions of power, and in so doing contributes to models of more long-term transformation (even if returning power to its customary site). And his late extension of comic genres, contained in unfinished ruminations on "speech genres," move back toward the orature behind the rituals of carnival, acknowledge the diversity of "intimate genres," and clearly link them to more sustainable efforts at social transformation than the mediations of writing or reading. For the late Bakhtin, humor became inseparable from thinking about what one cannot change *except through one's own spoken responses.* Given a life's work in which Rabelais and later Gogol represent the apex of comic genius, it remains unclear whether or not Bakhtin would have acknowledged that those who do not think of themselves as artists (whose motivations for talking or writing have nothing to do with producing "literature") may also produce this humor. And yet, the "everyday festival" Bakhtin mentions in his last notes moves in the direction of valuing a daily humorous rapport that needs no artist-writer for its expression. Even more importantly, such a festival moves toward "the erasure of boundaries between the terrible and the comical," "between the mediocre and the terrible, the ordinary and the miraculous, the small and the grand" (*Speech Genres* 154).

I want to argue that the transformative ideological correspondences circumscribed by Williams and the late Bakhtin come as close as that of any Euro-American literary Theory to a desire for a literature that now exists, and that the diaspora of black women writers of the 1980s, here primarily from the United States but not necessarily so, provides a provocative example of a literature of resistance fully engaged in the problematics of tragic and comic paradox.[26] In so doing, I want not to flatten a sense of the complex cross-cultural negotiations among African and non-African diasporic literatures, whose contexts generate a rich intertextuality. Yet, however contextualized, these works raise issues that "have compelled the human imagination since Sophocles and Euripides entertained fellow Athenians with tragic tales of murder and suicide," issues reflecting "the paradoxical desire to communicate, in the most honest way possible, the most radically subjective, and thus generally incommunicable, experience of pain" (Lionnet, "Geographies of Pain" 211). Perhaps because they implicate readers' own positioning, the fictional worlds of these writers have only rarely influenced the traditional categories of literary discussion, even though they have often informed debates among African American, Africana, black feminist, and postcolonial theorists. Such theorizing remains diverse in its sundry perspectives but linked by concerns about how social power and positioning inhere in both aesthetic and moral judgments. Not necessarily antithetical to all Theory that calls itself postmodern, although frequently critical of the implications and consequences of such Theory, this body of theory nevertheless finds itself often accused of the ideological predisposition it tries to reveal as part of a more general problematics of reading. Certainly, it has not significantly influenced discussion about tragedy and comedy, as though the "high" Theory that belongs to a "high" (post)modernism carries on a conversation with itself. That conversation may have much liberal tolerance, even approbation for literature and scholarship confined to elsewhere, or it may admit to failings seen as somehow necessary or inevitable; but it has not wanted to know how to get out of its ballroom or how to risk the clumsiness of beginning again. Taking up such clumsiness, I want to respond to the compelling charge that Euro-American Theory lives in spheres arbitrarily separated from *located* investigations, such that even those aligned against sundry hegemonies have "failed to investigate, frame, and contribute to a praxis or ideology of resistance and struggle" (Omolade 225).

The chapters in Part I focus on reconceiving the interrelation of tragedy and comedy through readings of the storytelling as theory of black women writers of the 1980s, who write in an era named by so many as postmodern in the act of excluding them from discussion about which postmodernity follows upon which modernity. Such writers as Toni Morrison, Alice Walker, Gloria Naylor, Toni Cade Bambara, and Bessie Head interrogate relations of power from vantage points that theorize both *intra*cultural and *inter*cultural difference—themselves paradoxically interrelated—while never losing sight of the possibilities in a common humanity. Head, writing of both her adoptive Botswana and her native South African, matters to this work on writers otherwise within United States borders because her view from elsewhere places itself in dialogue with a gendered African American diaspora and because she sees so clearly that Americans will "just remain big, stupid Americans" unless they engage in dialogue beyond their national and cultural borders (figured here in a Euro-American [post]modernity).

Taken together, these works necessitate learning to read the complicities seemingly within fictional worlds and yet inseparable from the complicities readers bring to them. Their dialogical interrelations mark as oppressive a modernity at ease with the bounded opposition of tragedy and comedy, nature and culture, oral and written, self and other. And they imply a therapeutic preference for that open "skid" among modes figured in Head's and Bambara's understanding of the modern Medusa —both her terrible demands and what activities transform her horror into felt human relationship. Born out of diasporic traditions and yet also in opposition to dominant Euro-American versions of modernism, Part I's chosen fictions differ widely in the forms of resistance they represent: whether Baby Suggs's taking to her bed to think of color, Celie's sewing of comfortable pants, Elizabeth's work in a collective garden, or brick-throwing women intent on tearing down, if in dream only, a wall that symbolizes arbitrary, oppressive power. Yet the fictions have in common a difference in process from the stories traditionally associated with tragedy or comedy: the rhythms of experience as told in these narratives rarely have a dramatic movement towards a singular or conclusive crisis and resolution. Far from the notion of power relations affording sure outcomes (Snyder's "win, lose, or draw"), these narratives relate experience as cumulative, contingent, imperfectly cyclical, and yet as unexpected as weather. ("The rest is weather," *Beloved* ends, "not the breath of the disremembered and unaccounted for, but wind in the eaves, or spring ice thawing too quickly. Just weather" 275.) In gendered contexts linking diasporic experience to movements characterized variously as anti-modern (Jameson), modern black (Rampersad), or countercultural (Gilroy), these works represent negotiations with narrative form allied with the strongest critiques of dominant (post)modernisms.[27] As such, they help to theorize the critical modernity of tragic and comic modes better than do the conventions of looking for tragic models to *Oedipus* (Deleuze and Guattari), *Lear* (Cavell), *Hamlet* (Derrida), and *Endgame* (Williams, Cavell) or for comic ones to the traditional fools, clowns, buffoons, and comedic performers of Western tradition (Nelson, O'Neill), a laughing madman (Foucault), or even carnival inversions of the Medusa (Cixous, Suleiman).

Rather than belonging to the social movements and contexts that have defined a "resistance literature" (Harlow, JanMohammed, Parry, Said), often explicated in relation to meanings that may seem to reside *in* texts or writers, these works remain difficult because they set up very different resistances (or do not) depending on which social meanings take priority and on how those meanings (often given such names as race, class, gender, or sexuality) do or do not cohere for particular (and particularly placed) readers. Because of their complex positioning and a multivocality that disallows singular or authoritative readings, most of these texts—whether adopted into a sense of canon or not—are already constituted as controversial.[28] When read as important to revising extant tragic and comic Theory, they elaborate a paradox that takes the spiritualist world as part of any material, actual one and they offer provocative testimony about what the tragic and the comic have to do with each other and with social transformation. Taken as neither specific genres nor forms but rather as dialogically interrelated—and sometimes simultaneous—modes, tragedy and comedy make meaning out of the terrible and the funny even as they offer conflicted relations to power and conflicted sites for readerly response. Indeed, the works in Part I reject the premise behind Cavell's question about why one does nothing in response to tragedy, finding instead the strongest imperatives to action in both witnessing tragic action and sharing comic laughter. After all, the rules of Euro-American tradition belong to "the conflict game," and the rules only change when someone resists—and provokes others to resist—the idea of a game and the power relations that sustain it.

The theory generated in Part I looks backward recursively to inform the readings of Part II, readings that address problems sometimes deemed formal, structural, or generic, yet incapable of disentanglement from the concerns of diverse modernisms' competing or conflicted representations of social identity; these readings view modern texts as enmeshed in a loss or lack articulated in resistance by those who "reject the 'modernization' project which is being imposed by the West to the detriment of the whole of nature and most of the world's people in all regions" (Miles 165). Texts read as precursors of the postmodern (William Faulkner's *Absalom, Absalom!*), as a prescient formalism (Gertrude Stein's *Melanctha*), or as a confusion of genres (Zora Neale Hurston's Vodou texts) variously inform a (post)modernism that commonly espouses a terror and an irony merely intellectual, merely textual. Read instead under the influence of Part I's theory, they bear complex relation to the matrices of social and aesthetic judgment so troubling to contemporary thought.[29] The dialogical interrelation of a tragedy inhering in the social order itself and a critically, comically utopian vision of a healing with strong ties to tradition suggests both the difficulty and the promise of reading against the grain of what Michele Wallace has aptly called "Modernism's apartheid" and against its postmodern legacy.

Reading backward recursively leads toward a more inclusive, critical modernism as progenitor to a more critical postmodernism that some have called a "postmodernism of resistance" in recognition that the metanarrative labeling as modernity the rupture from both a Western past and its cultural Others also labels as postmodern a "post-European modernism." And many critics have begun to explore the interconnections between a black modernism's crises of representation and the last decade's crises.[30] Ultimately, I argue that the repression of certain tragic and comic modes in theorizing how and when the modern becomes the postmodern, and therefore attitudes toward aspects of each, corresponds to the repression of intercultural dialogue on a much broader social scale, and that a transformed sense of tragedy and comedy should remain at the heart of cultural controversy precisely because they challenge the definitions of what constitutes responsible human relationship. Without a vision of how a "community without unity" might work and of what it would demand of any "us,"[31] the ideologies that neutralize or acommodate such challenges hold sway against resistances that are never "pure" and never simply *there* in worlds, or texts, or people. And out of such negotiated, paradoxical resistances comes the long revolution, the one already begun in what has actually happened.

Part I
Revising Postmodernity

Storytelling as Theory

Chapter 1
The Tragedy of Slavery and the Footprints' Fit

Vicarious Witnessing in *Beloved*

The histories of slavery and colonialism that create the discursive conditions for the projective past and its split narratives are tragic and painful in the extreme, but it is their agony that makes them exemplary texts for our moment. They represent an idea of action and agency more complex than either the nihilism of despair or the utopia of progress. They speak of the reality of survival and negotiation that constitutes the lived moment of resistance, its sorrow and its salvation—the moment that is rarely spoken in the stories of heroism that are enshrined in the histories we choose to remember and recount.

—Homi Bhabha, "Freedom's Basis in the Indeterminate"

Down by the stream in back of 124 her footprints come and go, come and go. They are so familiar. Should a child, an adult place his feet in them, they will fit. Take them out and they disappear again as though nobody ever walked there.

—Toni Morrison, *Beloved*

White Imagining and the Slave's Voiceless End

The problem of our own relation to Others' suffering finds an extreme case in slavery, because it presents an oppression so absolute that in its present tense, it has no recorded voice to speak to those outside it. For writers delimited by what Morrison has called "the whiteness of the imagination," accounts of slavery simulate this distance from slavery's present with corresponding gaps in agency and individuation.[1] Thus Melville's Babo can speak only mutinous deception and when returned to the status of slave submits to a "voiceless end," and Faulkner's types of blackness still have about them the obscured silences of slave ancestors. Even when symbolizing a great wrong, such literary depictions reveal a slavery possessing the abstracted quality of an injustice done to people en masse and producing necessarily speechless, often undifferentiated victims. As such, the impossibility of the slave's tragedy has an irrefutable logic: slaves as victims have no voice, whereas tragic characters live for us through speech.[2] Morrison addresses this delimitation by putting the slave's experience in the memories of ex-slaves and its legacies in present lives, and in doing so she creates a focus on witnessing itself absent from the theoretical progenitors of the voiceless Babo or the howling Jim Bond (wordless even in sound). The slave's tragedy can finally be read as the tragedy of slavery (even before *Paradise*, in which the primary impetus for an ex-slave community's judgmental exclusions inheres in *watching from outside*).[3]

If Hegel and Nietzsche constitute the poles of modern tragic theory, they do so while sharing the explicit certainty that the slave cannot possess tragic stature. Despite the difference in Hegel's insistent historicity and Nietzsche's equally insistent metaphysics, such certainty finds implicit endorsement in most Theory that highlights either a character's individual challenge to systems of belief or the necessary resolution of conflict in the return to some prior social or metaphysical order. If Hegel has relevance to subsequent theory because he posits a worldview always tied to history, Nietzsche has continued relevance because of his evocation of a world of ritual and mystery as the context for an audience's identification with tragic character. And the contemporary theorizing of René Girard draws from both in describing a history of ritual sacrifice with its origins in the tragic scapegoat. The initial juxtaposition of Hegel's absent slave, Nietzsche's contemptible one, and Girard's slave-as-scapegoat will provide a backdrop for studying how Morrison, with the tradition of slave narratives on which to signify and in the form of a story's theorizing, relates contemporary questions about representing the slave's experience to questions about vicarious witnessing.[4] Read with this focus, *Beloved* provides the theoretical impetus to redirect the problematics of the tragic, revealing the remarkable mystery in the social leveling that makes the witness's catharsis possible and yet undermines claims that the act of watching or reading tragedy imaginatively crosses the boundaries between an observing (reader's) subjectivity and that of the subject-characters in fictions (and by extension that of the people who live and suffer in actual worlds).[5]

Hegel considers tragic feeling in "the man of nobility and greatness" and asserts that the ethical claims of tragedy cannot be "excited by ragamuffins and vagabonds"; thus it should come as no surprise that he also associates tragic action with "the principle of *individual* freedom and independence, or at least that of self-determination, the will to find in the self the free cause and source of the personal act."[6] For Hegel, however repugnant the practice of slavery, its spectacle cannot arouse the

requisite pity and fear in an audience because it represents only the barbarism of those who in addition to usurping unjust power have "a bad
character into the bargain."[7] Thus the slave appears in Hegel's tragic
theory only as absence, either as a victim whose condition may arouse
disgust and indignation (but nothing of the required awe) or as a character over whom the false rights of slavery lift of their own just accord
(as when Iphigenia escapes sacrifice in Aulis and among the Tauri).

For Nietzsche, who castigated Euripides for abandoning the high language and characters of Greek tragedy and therefore its mystery, the
death of Greek tragedy necessarily culminated in a later comedy's glori-
fication of the cunning slave, whose "cheerfulness" depended on being
"without responsibilities or aspirations."[8] In an elitism that links mystery
and status, Nietzsche prized an audience's vicarious identification with
tragic character, the phenomenon of

projecting oneself outside oneself and then acting as though one had really
entered another body, another character. . . . [W]hat we have here is the individual effacing himself through entering a strange being. (*The Birth of Tragedy*
55)

Astutely, Raymond Williams characterizes such views of tragic suffering as dependent on differentiating the tragic from the ordinary. For
Williams, merely to ask "ordinary to whom and by whose standards?"
exposes the extraordinary nature of the presumption that slavery represents a dull round of passive servitude rather than a struggle foregrounding a resistant will to survival. Such assertion suggests the ease, then
as now, of linking servitude to necessary failures in will and "self-determination."[9] These views from above, where only slave-master relations
matter, disallow either that harmonious resolution of "one-sided" views
that for Hegel characterizes tragic closure or that grand and higher
unity, contemptuous of "slave morality," that characterizes Nietzsche's.

The several books of René Girard comprise perhaps the most replete
contemporary version of an originary story that seems to take account of
the slave as a tragic figure bound up in communal history. But although
Girard's explication of the tragic figure as sacrificial victim makes room
for the slave, it does so in conceptions that involve the dramatic and killing spectacle of collective violence against a chosen victim, not the sustained, institutionalized violence enacted as a way of life against those
structurally locked in the grip of a sacrifice required daily.[10] In tragedy,
the story goes, the hero or protagonist becomes the sacrificial victim
by committing the act whose difference demands punishment, whether
death, ostracism, or exile; the audience or community purges itself of
violence by placing it on this liminal surrogate. Girard's discussion of
"stereotypes of persecution" focuses on the collective aggression of some

dominant group against marginalized victims, an aggression he associates with times of great cultural crisis.[11] Plagues, famine, war, and other society-wide disasters set in motion the search for scapegoats because such crises level human difference and therefore undermine the logic of hegemony. Weakened institutions and weakened hierarchial differences among people generate a search for surrogate victims to relieve the pressure on the social order as a whole. And because they cannot assume their individual difference as easily as those with power or privilege, those in the weakest social positions are more vulnerable to overt prejudice and, therefore, more likely to become sacrificial victims in times of crisis.

Regarding the tragic *pharmakon* on the model of the sacrificial victim focuses on the cathartic function of casting violence outside the community, and consequently moves beyond a concern with both the "fall" of a tragic hero and the affirming "harmony" of a reconstructed order to a concern with the communal function of scapegoating; as such, it replaces interest in a single tragic figure with interest in ritual communal process, a concern more common to Greek tragedy than to Elizabethan. Following through the suggestive connection between the root of the Greek *krino*, which means both to judge (distinguish, differentiate) and to accuse or condemn a victim, Girard sees beneath the fear of difference to persecutors' obsession with the *lack* of difference: "In all the vocabulary of tribal or national prejudices, hatred is expressed, not for difference, but for its absence" (*The Scapegoat* 22).[12] Girard's sources reinscribe the tragedy that belongs to dominant communities by linking Judaeo-Christianity in its European developments with indigenous myths, often crossing without comment the gap between the oral and the written. Thus his cross-cultural comparisons unsettle because they so easily slip into progressive stages as distances traveled from originary myths. This makes the modern Western world the site of the most "distanced" problems, the place where the whole of Judaeo-Christian history makes possible a modern analytical superiority "capable of deciphering a causal sequence and revealing it to be one of arbitrary violence—whereas in the history of all humanity this causal sequence has never appeared in any form other than that of mythology" (Girard, *Things Hidden Since the Foundation of the World* 126). Girard claims that he does not confuse the reality of persecution with its representation in myth, and yet his chosen historical reference gives the sanction of universality to how those with favored lives *necessarily* create and protect the differences that both explain and justify their social roles. Although not a history of progress in the clear teleological sense, Girard's overview has something of Yeats's gyres about it, a system in which the "spiral" of history makes the Western "us" both better at analyzing and desacralizing the scapegoat story at the same time that it makes the scapegoating process both more brutal and less "efficacious."

The ongoing trade-off of belief and analysis (or effective and ineffective ritual) makes the story from the perspective of the persecuted impossible in any present; it exists only as a projective future existing as ellipsis somewhere between two phases: "a world in which texts are written from the point of view of the persecutor—a phase that, unfortunately, has not yet run its course—and a later universal deciphering of these texts, a time when their meaning grows increasingly clear."[13] Viewed as an "achievement of the modern and western world," the awareness of persecution replaces myth in a "demythification of which we ourselves are capable," where an advanced "we" stands separate from "the sacralizing misinterpretation of primitive societies" (Girard, *Things Hidden Since the Foundation of the World* 130). Thus the analyst or reader of tragic scapegoating reads from the perspective of a distance that *necessarily* accompanies brutal if ineffective scapegoating in her world. (And this implicit distance from the sacrificial victim finds itself in tragedy read ever again as a release that always evades "the real of desire.")[14]

Girard's suspended projection of the persecuted's story reflects the legacy of Hegel and Nietzsche in that he can ultimately, like them, care about slaves only as defined by their subjugation or sacrifice. Since Girard's narrative places the tragic *pharmakon* as scapegoat and tells the story in terms of the ritual use made of scapegoats by a dominant community, it fails to acknowledge—except as a future imaginary—that slaves, too, have communities not the same as either the community of masters or each other, lives that they do not conceive as marginal, and experiences not understood as sacrificial victimization.

Problems in Representation

Beloved's "social crisis as tragedy" (Williams) responds not just to a tradition from Hegel and Nietzsche through Girard, the white imagination as Theory, but also to the accommodations and negotiations of slave narratives as interpreted in an ever-expanding scholarship. That scholarship has particular relevance here because it demonstrates that, although African American slave narratives diversely record the impossibility of representing slavery's present, they enter the problematics of representation from positions unimaginable to tragic Theory still under the influence of Hegel and Nietzsche. In their recounting of slave experience, slave narratives represent suffering already shaped into written form, replete with ways of testifying to a prior oral telling and to a consciousness that preceded writing.[15] But any easy opposition between oral and written forms has given way to an increasingly sophisticated understanding of how both slave narratives and "fictive" neo-slave narratives mean through an indirect mediation of the oral and the written.[16] In all their diverse and problematized positioning, both slave and neo-slave narratives underscore a resistance within writing to written forms; they also make a resistant, vernacular orality the touchstone of a nonrecuperable, negative "history of illegibility that leads to the unavoidable problematics of narrative representation entailed in thinking about writing as being emancipatory" (Judy 98).

This resistant orality has specific presence in the slave narratives of women, whose difference from men's narratives also matters to *Beloved*'s genealogy of telling. Mae Henderson's "Speaking in Tongues: Dialogics, Dialectics and the Black Woman Writer's Literary Tradition" explains the connection of women's slave narratives to *Beloved* as a common multivocality and a negotiation of racial and gendered oppressions that affirms spiritual, intuitive, nonlinguistic values.[17] As Frances Smith Foster early noted, women's slave narratives did not portray themselves as the defenseless victims they so often became in narratives by male slaves. Because women write slave narratives from positions of strength and moral certainty, they tend to focus more on experiences that mold character than on scenes of a brutalizing oppression. Enslaved women of African descent, both within Africa and throughout the diaspora, took as goals "developing survival strategies and encouraging self-reliance through female networks."[18] Thus in her narrative, Elizabeth Keckley, eschewing any exceptional status for herself or other individuals, can assert that "through me and the enslaved millions of my race, one of the problems was solved that belongs to the great problem of human destiny."[19] Indeed, Valerie Smith has shown how the narratives of slave women resist the characteristic development of slave narratives by men, chronicles in which the passage from slavery to freedom incorporates a passage from slavehood to manhood. Writing primarily for an audience of Northern white women, ex-slave women as narrators record their dependence on others and their becoming a "self-in-relation" in part through gaps and ellipses marking the strained inadequacies of both the masculine slave narrative and the sentimental novel as formal models.[20] But women's slave narratives also mark the impossibility of narrating the violations and mutilations that, as Hortense Spillers ("Mama's Baby") has explained, call into question the very terms of womanhood and motherhood.[21]

Fully aware that changes in knowledge or discourse alone do not guarantee or even necessarily imply social transformation, Morrison participates in the project "to think the work of history, the subject, in a way that does not reclaim representation."[22] Sethe makes the ink that allows Schoolteacher to line up her "animal characteristics" on paper, not for her own story; and Paul D. with the bit in his mouth embodies the effectively silenced slave. *Beloved* acknowledges this distance of the slave's experience from written records, but by placing conflict within the community of ex-slaves and within individual memories it does more than provide multiple perspectives on experience once denied articulation. The slavery that appears as "rememory," not just an expressively redundant term but the name of memory in the act of a strenuous and threatening revisioning of both oneself and one's Others, paradoxically invokes a material presentness that compels readers to consider their own relation to it. Baldwin's assertion that Faulkner could depict slaves and their descendants "only as they related to him, not as they related to each other" (47) recommends a corollary that concerns me here, which is that by focusing on conflicts among ex-slaves about how to deal with the slave past *Beloved* asserts its relevances to very diverse audiences.[23] Like all slave narratives, *Beloved* addresses the distance between speaking and writing, between living slavery and bearing witness to it. But like women's slave narratives, it also takes up the self-in-relation, the collective story that replaces individual heroism with communal process.[24] Many readings focus on how *Beloved*'s reconfiguring of the relationship between the slave mother and her child also reconfigures the relationship of the black community to its history, and Mae Henderson, in particular, stresses the historical and psychoanalytic processes through which "Morrison redefines notions of genesis and meaning as they have served to constitute black womanhood in the dominant discourse" (76).[25] Building on these readings' explication of both historical and psychological process (especially as figured in the trinity of Sethe, Denver, and Beloved), my reading will take up how *Beloved* explores both the complexity of rememorying a slavery that defies representation and also the second-order, vicarious nature of the reader-observer as witness.

Witnessing, Catharsis, Action

As though in response to Girard's projection onto the future of a tragic story told from the position of the persecuted, the consciousness of *Beloved*'s ex-slaves provides a kind of choric backdrop for gradually revealed and interwoven stories. In this it takes up issues raised by the choric frame of Greek tragedy, models Morrison once identified as "extremely sympathetic to black culture."[26] Here the slave's suffering has primacy, but it does not end with either the literal escape from slavery nor the violence of the infanticide; the legacy of slavery dominates much of the suffering in *Beloved*, belonging to those now outside it who struggle with terrors they want now to forget and yet must, for their own communal salvation, remember. In a structural logic both related to and different from that of Greek tragedy, the terrible infanticide has already occurred, yet it occurs narratively after the cumulative violences of the slavery system that made death or capture a viable risk. In Greek tragedy the bulk of developmental structure foregrounds the protagonist or hero whose action is talk only until he or she commits an action (usually a killing) threatening the socio-moral world of witnesses. Unlike *Medea*, where tragedy builds from the conflicted emotional logic that leads Medea to kill her own children, *Beloved* does not take the emotional turmoil that leads to the infanticide as its primary problem, starting as it does with the act as a given of historical and literary necessity.[27] Rather than serve as the center of a moral dilemma, the infanticide serves as the occasion for crises in relationship and relational understanding. As such, *Beloved* portrays the processual character of an understanding that implies a recursive view of one's own relation to Others and of the social function of such process. As a work whose literary qualities emphasize the sense in which readers act only as vicarious witnesses to what those within witness more directly, *Beloved* revisions both the originary story ("In the beginning there are no words") and history itself so that tragedy may envision more than an endless and necessary repetition of the first violence.

Before considering the plural moments that resemble catharsis in their moral attention but broaden its possible meanings, let me describe how *Beloved*'s complexities of narration set both Sethe's and Baby Suggs's forms of resistance in relation to paradox often named as tragic.[28] *Beloved* opens in a domestic world intimate with the presence of the dead baby, a world in which Sethe attempts "to remember as close to nothing as was safe." Starting with the master's story from the view of Schoolteacher and the Sheriff, narration weaves together the stories of those like Stamp Paid, Paul D., and Ella who work toward reconstructing some normalcy, and those like Baby Suggs and Sethe, who spurn it—and of course Denver, who will represent its promise. Understandably the best explicated character in *Beloved*, Sethe resists by struggling toward "a counternarrative that reconstitutes her humanity and demonstrates the requirements of motherlove" (Henderson 79). Subsequent accounts of the infanticide embed it in so many narrative contexts that they constitute a textual refusal to scandalize the event. It appears not as dramatic spectacle but as an ongoing challenge to communal relationship. Sethe's alienation belongs to both her and the community since she walks past community members "in their silence and hers" (152). An estranged chorus, the onlookers neither speak to her nor sing for her, not because of the infanticide but because of her demeanor. Yet even in this, narration refuses certain attribution of cause and effect, resorting instead to speculative probability: "Was her head a bit too high? Her back a little too straight? Probably. Otherwise the singing would have begun at once" (152). Long before Sethe's own internal voice remembers the humming in her ears that drove her to the shed, we hear a communal response in "Humming. No words at all" (152), reminiscent of all those other contexts of humming as an ominously suppressed threat.

The gradually revealed stories that circle one another's telling pay constant attention to the gaze, its angles of vision and how they affect both witnessing and self-witnessing. From the focus on the desire of the Sweet Home men as they watch cornstalks moving in the field where Sethe and Halle make love to the gaze of Ed Bodwin as it rests on Beloved's pregnant image rather than on Sethe's coming toward him with an axe, scenes in *Beloved* place readers in the second-order position of vicarious witness as they watch characters watching. (Even marked bodies—the lash's design on Sethe's back, Baby Suggs's limp, or Beloved's neck—provoke alternative readings dependent on the viewer's gaze.) Accordingly, images become turning points as Sethe acts on the sight of Schoolteacher's hat, Paul D. struggles with the picture of Halle with butter on his face, Stamp Paid becomes ill over a red ribbon attached to a piece of scalp, and Baby Suggs goes to bed to concentrate on color. Indeed, revelations of witnessing tend to coincide with climaxes of telling, giving special narrative pull to scenes that involve the terror of a disembodied self-witnessing: Sethe seeing the brutal theft of her milk as watched from above by the paralyzed Halle and Paul D. with the bit in his mouth seeing himself as watched by a rooster. By the time characters work through to a reconstruction of their own stories, it will be in the terms of seeing themselves differently through different eyes, as a self-in-relation to the gaze of others.

Both the positioning of gaze and narration's multivocality set Sethe's story in relation to others, so that *Beloved* seems not only "her story,"[29] but one that commonly passes among figural perspectives without losing its own rich voices and textures. As Sethe lies in bed with Paul D., for example, Baby Suggs's phrase "A man ain't nothing but a man" spurs on her memory. She remembers her early life at Sweet Home and how she sometimes watched the men without them knowing. As so often, narration passes from following her watching a past self in the act of watching others to a narrative overview that moves toward another character's consciousness and beyond:

Hidden behind honeysuckle she watched them. How different they were without her, how they laughed and played and urinated and sang. All but Sixo, who laughed once—at the very end. Halle, of course, was the nicest. Baby Suggs' eighth and last child, who rented himself out all over the country to buy her away from there. But he too, as it turned out, was nothing but a man.

"A Man ain't nothing but a man," said Baby Suggs. "But a son? Well now, that's *somebody.*"

It made sense for a lot of reasons because in all of Baby's life, as well as Sethe's own, men and women were moved around like checkers. (23)

Partly narrative authority and partly Sethe's memory, narration moves from here to description that simulates Baby Suggs's own voice ("What she called the nastiness of life was the shock she received on learning that nobody stopped playing checkers just because the pieces included her children") until it returns to judgment on Sethe's youthful defenses against what Baby Suggs knows. Authoritative judgment asserts that Sethe's attempts to act in Mrs. Garner's house "as though Sweet Home really was one" made her "a bigger fool" than ever lived, and the judgment belongs in part to omniscience, in part to Baby Suggs's own view, and in part to the Sethe who remembers back on both Baby Suggs and her own youth. Cumulative actions before and after the infanticide may center around Sethe's story, but cumulative narrative perspectives suggest that narrative voices themselves have much further reach. As characters think of each other, the voice of internal consciousness frequently merges with that of both the character thought of and omniscient narration, itself multivoiced. Even the four lyrical chapters at the center of Part Two, the only chapters using first-person personae, merge Sethe's voice with Denver's and Beloved's and the "unspoken" voices of the women of 124 are themselves "mixed in" with the mumbling voices of all "the black and angry dead" (198).[30]

It is important that no one actually witnesses the act, even though the infanticide accumulates accounts and moves from the master's narrative through Sethe's attempts to "reread or reemplot her own experiences" (Henderson, "Speaking in Tongues" 77). As potential witnesses, Stamp Paid and Baby Suggs are closest in the sense that they stand outside and watch the shed much as characters onstage watch outside Agamemnon's gory bath or hear from without Willy Loman's suicidal shot. This difference from actual witnessing reminds us that vicariousness as an imaginative act stands as metaphor to a literal vicariousness in the suffering endured by one person in place of another. Of this, Baby Suggs has the most intimate knowledge because Halle purchased her freedom at the expense of his own. Perhaps because of this experiential foreknowledge, a child "who bought her future with his, exchanged it, so to speak, so she could have one whether he did or not," she intuitively feels "it" coming, like weather, as though she were a part of "it" even before the fact. Thus Baby Suggs's contiguity has about it an intimacy that Stamp Paid's lacks, and unlike the response of Baby Suggs, whose prior experience of the vicarious suggests both what it means and what it costs, Stamp Paid exercises a moral judgment that justifies his subsequent withdrawal. Initially, Stamp Paid's position stands closer to that of readers, whose even more vicarious gaze on an act both terrible and unseen makes them even less likely to recognize a scapegoat disguised by righteous judgment.

After the infanticide, both Sethe and Baby Suggs stand outside the terrible unanimity of communal judgment, Sethe because of her refusal to be cast down and Baby Suggs because she cannot participate in a restorative order and refuses "to either approve or condemn." Both refusals exist in dialogical relation to diverse communal failures, including the initial failure to warn of Schoolteacher's coming. Though Stamp Paid will retrospectively speculate that "whitefolks had tired her [Baby Suggs] out at last" (180), he also understands the blow attendant on having the community she so well loved and served "step back and hold itself at a distance," a distance that keeps them from either suspending judgment or understanding Sethe's action as human. Correspondingly, narration refuses to accept Sethe's self-justification, her proud refusal to acknowledge the horror of her own action or even to move beyond considering Beloved still a part of the family; but narration also refuses to accept the community's defensive ostracism, its clear, easy condemnation. Already ostracized by the community in narration's present, Sethe lives through the consequences of wanting some barriers inviolable (her own body) and others not (life and death), which explains the vulnerability of her lovemaking to Paul D. and her sense that one letting go connects to others.

Narrative structure juxtaposes Sethe's refusal to regard Beloved as dead rather than "safe" with Baby Suggs's refusal to accept her former role in a world where even her own good works can end by doing harm; and both use an exclamatory syntax that asserts itself as resistance both to white power and to communal accommodations of the past. (It is impossible here, perhaps even tediously mimetic, to detail the art with which successive chapters accumulate, almost like iterative refrains, the moments when communal lack comes up sharply against these resistances.) Sethe's "They took my milk!" parallels Baby Suggs's "They came in my yard!" as they reflect an insistence on inviolable boundary, with Baby Suggs's invocation of the yard that Halle's sacrifice defined as "free" a parallel for Sethe's invocation of the mother's capacity to nurture. The reiterative "falling," not "*the* fall" and only tangentially the fall of Sethe into infanticide, invokes a participial present in a world of sensation and agency not even "heard" by a world viewing it as liminal, outside. When Sethe's internal consciousness finally does focus on the infanticide, her rememory sticks on the sight of Schoolteacher's hat, the whir of hummingbirds' wings, and her simple, spontaneous flight to anyplace "outside this place" where her children would be safe. She knows what narrative art has also stressed, that "she could never close in, pin it down for anybody who had to ask. If they didn't get it right off—she could never explain" (163). The form in which narration (re)presents Sethe's internal resistance ("And if she thought anything it was No. No. Nono. Nonono" 163) testifies to that negative "illegibility" theorized by Ronald Judy. For however much Sethe lacks agency as a mother, and however much Baby Suggs withdraws from the community she has served, another angle of vision reveals how judgment itself stands judged. Importantly, even the first-person lyrical personae in Chapter Two are not the voices of slaves and claim no representation of a "story to pass on." Rather, present-tense voices of liminal subjectivity, "unspoken, unheard voices," "mix in" with "all the black and angry dead," the historical voices unremembered and therefore cast outside the community. (Others have well explained this ontological penchant for "negotiating the tenses."[31])

Sethe refuses the tragic by regarding her daughter as "safe" rather than dead, and by devoting herself to the living experience of her incarnation in the form of Beloved. But Baby Suggs's resistance has been less well explicated and bears even more specific reference to the tragic. In particular, her work with imaging responds to a communal lack itself linked to the idea of rememory as imaging. In the center of the work lies the chapter whose present tense occurs eighteen years before the 1873 present in which the work opens; it begins "in the back of Baby Suggs' mind" and immediately invokes a freedom reliant on the material basis of the vicarious: "If only this final son could do for himself what he had done for her and for the three children John and Ella delivered to her door one summer night" (135). For Baby Suggs, Schoolteacher stands as a known terror, but the lapse in her neighbors' goodwill and in their solidarity against such known terrors gnaws most at her understanding. Other characters think they know that Baby Suggs has given up, withdrawn into a kind of terminal tiredness, refused to "like herself anymore" (251), and much critical commentary has taken their view. But Baby Suggs's own words have nothing to do with disliking herself or passive withdrawal. Rather, they attest to her conviction that no amount of reason, foresight, or planning can defend against white people's oppressive power: "there was no defense—they could prowl at will, change from one mind to another, and even when they thought they were behaving, it was a far cry from what real humans did" (245). And narrative language reveals a connection between Baby Suggs's refusal to "either approve or condemn" Sethe's action, though the "salvation" offered by either worldly or metaphysical systems demands some choice, and her taking to her bed to think on color. Far from passivity or apathy, Baby Suggs commits herself to "think," and the "peace" she declares does not concern quitting an internal resistance, but rather quitting the social world of those "strangers and familiars [who] were stopping by to hear how it went one more time" (177). Baby Suggs experiences, long before the assertion of the final chapter, that this is *not* "a story to pass on," not a story to satisfy the passing interest of not only friends but *strangers*, those for whom Sethe's story invites approval or condemnation rather than more profoundly paradoxical responses. (I have had students, usually white and female, who declare that however good this book, *they* simply cannot understand how a mother could do such a thing, thereby demonstrating how sagacious and full of reference to readers' positioning is the task Baby Suggs sets herself.)

Despite others' misconstructions and her bone tiredness, Baby Suggs actively thinks about color and works away at the spectrum such that "By the time Sethe was released she had exhausted blue and was well on her way to yellow" (177). Mae Henderson has explicated how rememory starts from imagery not in one's own control, more like "something which possesses (or haunts) one, rather than something which one possesses" (67). In an explicitly imagistic form of thought, Baby Suggs undertakes an alternative form of resistance, one grounded in a struggle involving control on the level of bodily experience. Neither forgetting nor repressing in the manner of others' attempts to achieve normalcy, she undertakes an alternative project "to fix on something harmless in this world" (179). Paula Cooey's explanation of oppositional routes for bodily resistance helps with the contrast between Sethe's and Baby Suggs's chosen routes:

Like socialization, resistance is not necessarily conscious in those involved; however, resistance, whether intentional or unintentional, produces a range of possible responses marked with respect to an experiencing subject, at one extreme, by the transformation of the body into a weapon turned against the subject and, at the other extreme, by the transfiguration of pain and pleasure into a resource for changing the material conditions in which the subject finds herself. (92)

Sethe turns herself into a weapon against her own, but Baby Suggs turns to the most basic level of sentience to seek some form of control. Giving up on systems of meaning and order, and giving up especially on notions of a beneficent God, she turns to her own body as a primal site of resistance. In doing so, she seeks something she can control, some aspect of experience invulnerable to the power of others. Most important, she turns against language itself, both the word and the Word, as an instrument already formed by its social contexts and therefore complicit in abuses of power. No one has been more in touch with others, more aware that touch itself stands as a metaphor for how shared experience may represent anything from intimacy to menace. She has tried mapping experience "from the outside in," and now tries "from the inside out" (Cooey 92). She starts from something she can imagine as *harmless* pleasure prior to social meanings ("I like yellow"), with what can be acknowledged as meaningful sensation at all.

Even what Baby Suggs "quits" needs particular reference, since she does not "quit" immediately after Sethe's infanticide. Only when the vicarious interest of others reduces what has happened to a good story, one they suppose she will participate in elaborating, does she undertake her explicitly internal labor. Baby Suggs's end does not *only* signify withdrawal and defeat because it also evinces the genius of understanding both the complicity of language and the most basic level of cultural struggle, her own body's capacity for imaging. At this level, the symbolic value of her resistance catches hold of both racial and gendered myths of dominance. The color line, after all, has determined her role and her own body has been taken as the passive female receptacle for engendering children subsequently taken from her. Thus a clear bodily logic demands that active resistance start with color itself, a reworking of the most basic cultural constructions that have construed black women as both passive and servile. Recognizing the formative nature of language itself, Baby Suggs evinces no naïveté about some supposed purity of sensation or even about its alterity to discourse. Rather, she understands the concentration, even the struggle, necessary to carry on the discipline she sets herself, a discipline she dignifies with a somehow gracefully resilient form of resentment.

The radical nature of Baby Suggs's form of resistance has appealed to many readers less than has Sethe's tenacious, heroic resistance to both white power and black ostracism. Sethe retains a passionate hopefulness for her daughter, a hopefulness that relies on her own determination that the daughter will escape what haunts the mother's memory. But note that her refusal to acknowledge the vulnerability of such maternal control attributes to Baby Suggs an exceptional capacity not understood in the community's perception—often the critical community's as well—of a Baby Suggs who has "given up":

> And no one, nobody on this earth, would list her daughter's characteristics on the animal side of the paper. No. Oh no. Maybe Baby Suggs could worry about it, live with the likelihood of it; Sethe had refused—and refused still. (251)

What does it mean to live with the likelihood that the humanity of oneself and one's children, friends, and community can be willfully, arbitrarily, cruelly denied?

Baby Suggs cannot *not* know the probability that Sethe "refuses," and this refusal complicates the relation of resistance to tragedy. If Sethe's refusal bespeaks her ongoing resistance to a white world, Baby Suggs's more global refusal encompasses the inescapable surplus that tragedy's merger of *epistemai* and *technai* implies: the refusal to forget a contamination that includes herself in order to bear once more with living. Although leading toward death in refusing to compromise with either worldly or spiritual power, a characteristic of the tragic protagonist in Western tragedy, Baby Suggs's form of resistance rejects compromise and acts as a standard against which to measure such compromises. She simply lies down where all the ladders start, and refuses to ascend any rung not worked through on the level of the implications and consequences of the desire to do no harm.

Catharsis traditionally refers to a climactic purging of feeling, or felt cognition, that returns characters or audiences or readers to an order that allows them to take up once again some normalcy of living.[32] The subject of catharsis passes from that surplus of identification which connects formerly opposed categories to some normalcy made more replete by the experience. In Baby Suggs, Morrison creates a character drawn to catharsis but unwilling to forgo the implied consequences by returning to a world with separations at least provisionally intact. To Eliot's question, "After such knowledge, what forgiveness?" Baby Suggs resolutely responds, "None, not even for myself." Instead, she sustains the resistance that makes shared language, anything resembling the word or the Word, irrelevant. She does not go through a cathartic reentry into communal life, but undertakes a bodily resistance to systems of power—both metaphysical and social—in her attempt to separate the image from the word. Outside the logic of tragedy—and yet like a critique of that part of the conception most at ease with hegemonies—she catches tragic resistance at its height in a consciousness resolutely fixed on the paradox that freedom realized becomes freedom compromised, that shared language means tainted language, and that even choosing the radically delimited sphere of the sensible world implies working hard, and with no guarantee of success, at conceptions that "do no harm." Other characters' processual moves back to communal life stand in stark contrast to her refusal to participate in either a language or a world in which one can do harm even against one's will.

The work's longest chapter follows the consequences for Baby Suggs of that refusal to either approve or condemn, her commitment to a paradoxical resistance with tragic implications, but it also foregrounds the consequences for others in the community who come to witnessing only eighteen years later. As the structure of narrative and figural consciousness pulls toward *re*memory, the continued presence of Baby Suggs instigates all self-interrogations that lead toward the most overtly transformative forms of catharsis: the purging of felt distance from Sethe's haunting by Beloved and the removal of Beloved from 124. Because of Baby Suggs, first Stamp Paid, then Paul D., then Ella, and finally, by extension, all those who help in the exorcism of Beloved are drawn to action through felt realizations about their own connections to what they formerly named and judged as Other. What stands purged in this alternative form of catharsis is not feeling, some variant of pity and fear, but rather the distance from an outcast-other than enables an Othering judgment.

For Stamp Paid, "the memory of Baby Suggs" and "the honor that was her due" (171) stirs up a chafing self-questioning about whether it really was as a "Soldier of Christ" that he told Paul D. about Sethe's history and that he has shunned 124. He rememories his final conversation with Baby Suggs that significantly turns on his plea for her to return to her "calling" and preach the Word. The entire conversation pits her rejection of language against his reliance on it, and in the act of making a harsh judgment on himself for "the high tone he took," he turns inevitably to his own "marrow weariness" and its connection to "a red ribbon knotted around a curl of wet woolly hair, clinging still to its bit of scalp": "He kept the ribbon; the skin smell nagged him, and his weakened marrow made him dwell on Baby Suggs' wish to consider what in the world was harmless" (181). The connection between his own weariness and that of Baby Suggs undoes the self-protection of a former security that all was done "for a clear and holy purpose":

Mistaking her [Baby Suggs], upbraiding her, owing her, now he needed to let her know he knew, and to get right with her and her kin. So, in spite of his exhausted marrow, he kept on through the voices and tried once more to knock at the door of 124. This time, although he couldn't cipher but one word, he believed he knew who spoke them. The people of the broken necks, of fire-cooked blood and black girls who had lost their ribbons.
    What a roaring. (181)

And so, as though now called on to bear witness to her having been in the world, he acts to undo what he has done and not done, first with Sethe and subsequently with both Paul D. and Ella, plying them with the same relentless standard of humanity exercised by Baby Suggs.

A more complex catharsis surrounds Paul D.'s self-protecting separation-plus-judgment. When he tries to save himself from Beloved's demands, he does so by asking Sethe to have their child, understanding on some level that committing himself to Sethe means taking up again the affective development of his own "red heart," the depth of feeling against which he has protected himself ever since seeing Sixo lynched, Halle covered in butter, and himself watched by a rooster. With the insight that hostile attention to difference masks the more terrible threat of sameness, Morrison's narration understands how persecutors' obsession with the lack of difference drives them to treat men like animals in order to *make* a difference. (Schoolteacher's monologue about how his nephew abused Sethe is riddled with horrendous animal analogies.) And in dialogical relation the slave's obsession becomes how to free oneself from those images of oneself as animal.[33]

Paul D. has trouble speaking of himself with the bit in his mouth, not because of the pain but because he cannot rid himself of the image of the mobile, unfettered rooster looking at the captive, broken man. Thus an irredeemable necessity moves him to condemn Sethe in an animal figure at precisely the time he feels most self-repudiating in terms of his own animality, the uncontrollable pull to Beloved reminiscent of his uncontrolable vulnerability with the bit in his mouth. Both make him regard himself in relation to animals, casting down his difference as a man. And both make him see himself as acting against the integrity of human relationship, figured instead in Chanticleer as lord of the barnyard family. Chanticleer's lording it over his family of hens parodies a masculinist version of manhood, defined by a strutting gender monopoly of barnyard power. Yet the scene within Paul D.'s memory explains that he has stifled his own "red heart" because of suffering witnessed by no other human beings, without the human empathy that true witnessing implies. At first he resists knowing that Sethe killed her baby girl ("That ain't her mouth," he keeps repeating when Stamp Paid shows him the newspaper photo of Sethe). But he finds even more difficult her adamant self-justification that she was trying to make her children "safe" from the horrors of slavery. An entirely coherent logic mandates that his fearful response to Sethe, as well as his rush to leave, should take the devastating form of an animal analogy: "You got two feet, Sethe, not four." After admitting his own betrayal and abandonment of the woman he loved, raped by the master, Stamp Paid asks Paul D. all the hard questions, including the one about whether he left because of "what I told you 'bout Sethe" or because of Beloved. Narration describes Paul D.'s internal response in language replete with a cathartic connection between the images he tries to forget and his own judgment on Sethe:

A shudder ran through Paul D. A bone-cold spasm that made him clutch his knees. He didn't know if it was bad whiskey, nights in the cellar, pig fever, iron bits, smiling roosters, fired feet, laughing dead men, hissing grass, rain, apple blossoms, neck jewelry, Judy in the slaughterhouse, Halle in the butter, ghost-white stairs, choke-cherry trees, cameo pins, aspens, Paul A.'s face, sausage or the loss of a red, red heart. (235)

As in Stamp Paid's earlier crisis, the complicit nature of his own judgment on Sethe—necessary to "the loss of a red, red heart"—overwhelms him, so that he can say only, "How much is a nigger supposed to take? Tell me. How much?" And to Stamp Paid's "All he can," a final voice— Paul D.'s in part, but also all the testifying voices, and all narrative authority—answers with the outraged question (and Lear's four echoes): "Why? Why? Why? Why? Why?"

Just as Stamp Paid's and Paul D.'s cathartic moments cause them to act, so too does Ella's form of catharsis move her to engage that chorus of women capable of exorcising the haunting nature of Beloved, able to do so because she exists now for them too. When Ella asserts her judgmental distance from Sethe ("I ain't got no friends take a handsaw to their own children"), Stamp Paid responds, "You in deep water, girl," to which she answers "Uh uh. I'm on dry land and I'm going to stay there. You the one wet." Her response relies on a separation made explicit in the metaphor of land and sea, and therefore as vulnerable to erosion and sea-change as all coastlines. In narration that interweaves the exorcism with her own cathartic rememory, Ella acts on others as Stamp Paid has acted on her. Initially, when Janey Wagon forces the story of Beloved's presence out of Denver, she views it with easy superiority and judgment. Remembering Sethe's pride, she receives confirmation of Beloved's haunting presence with, "Well, I guess there's a God after all" (254). Left to Janey and the grist of gossip, the story of 124 would play itself out as just retribution, not so much for the desperate act of infanticide but for Sethe's subsequent distance from a community, seen by them as her problem rather than a mutual one. But Baby Suggs has reached Stamp Paid who in turn has reached Paul D. and Ella. So as legacy it falls to Ella to confront the truths inside the spreading rumors about 124:

It took them days to get the story properly blown up and themselves agitated and then to calm down and assess the situation. They fell into three groups: those who believed the worst; those that believed none of it; and those, like Ella, who thought it through. (255)

Because "whatever Sethe had done, Ella didn't like the idea of past errors taking possession of the present" and because her own past gave her something "very personal in her fury," Ella adopts a version of Baby Suggs's refusal to either approve or condemn in order to defeat a logic of judgment:

"Guess she had it coming."
"Nobody got that coming."
"But, Ella—"
"But nothing. What's fair ain't necessarily right." (256)

A vernacular tonality reminiscent of Baby Suggs's resentment and insight characterizes Ella's focal consciousness, suddenly free of its former distancing: "Slave life; freed life—every day was a test and a trial. Nothing could be counted on in a world where even when you were a solution you were a problem" (256). Purged of judgment and tranformed by her identification with Sethe's haunting, Ella rouses the women to action.

Not knowing what they will do when they get there, the group of thirty women envision themselves as young and happy in Baby Suggs's yard on the day of the party. The vision provokes rememory because it wipes away "the envy that surfaced the next day" (258). Only now do we discover that Ella, too, has committed infanticide in resistance to a grotesque sexual captivity. And a primal holler comes out of her empathic fear of such a child, like Sethe's, "coming back to whip her too." With ironic relation to "In the beginning was the Word," a phrase that above all others locates the logocentric authority of Judaeo-Christian traditions, narration documents how Ella's holler takes the group back to felt origins:

Instantly the kneelers and the standers joined her. They stopped praying and took a step back to the beginning. In the beginning there were no words. In the beginning was the sound, and they all knew what that sound sounded like. (259)

Here narration has about it a scriptural authority but without a script, since it comes from a richly oral spiritualist tradition in which ritual invocations of primal stories rely on affect and empathy rather than on words. Such active empathy-plus-sound differs radically from the mere absence of words, the "no words" from the community to warn of Schoolteacher's arrival and the "no words" from onlookers after the fact. In rememory, Stamp Paid believes that the failure of neighbors or townspeople to warn of Schoolteacher's and his nephew's arrival comes from something like the evasionary distancing that also allows for judgment, something "like, well, like meanness—that let them stand aside, or not pay attention, or tell themselves somebody else was probably bearing the news already" (157). Here, because of the nature of Beloved, the exorcism leaves them changed, as though the integration of the moral and the affective life in action leaves a kind of transformative value.

Now narration breaks to Edward Bodwin, riding along the road in the direction of 124. It will follow him until, following the primacy of sound over sight, he "heard the singers before he saw them." This time, racing away from Beloved's naked, pregnant image, Sethe turns the ice-pick toward the white man; and this time, the group of women act together to save her. Although she has occupied the position of scapegoat for seventeen years, Sethe draws out of others the communal restraint to keep her from killing, something that can only happen when others empathize enough to be able to act in solidarity against both worldly and otherworldly oppression. Bodwin's nostalgia for his childhood toys and his compelling ignorance of systemic horror give Sethe's gesture a felt logic. Yet Ella, having been "beaten every way but down," knows that distinctions among white men must be made, that Sethe's vision of Bodwin as Schoolteacher—based on the sameness of the hat and the look of a man "without skin"—will not hold. For this moment at least, she extends Baby Suggs's principle of suspended judgment to working out what to do about the dead daughter who has come back in the flesh to "fix" Sethe. The exorcism of Beloved from Sethe's home might itself seem a cathartic purging of a past that refuses to assume its pastness. Yet multiple, internal catharses make the exorcism possible and these occur in dialogical relation to witnesses' memories of their own experiences with slavery. Tragic conflict inheres in the fragility of the negotiations that allow ex-slaves' lives to proceed as though normal because such normalcy hides behind self-protective social distance. Unlike the choric observers of Greek tragedy, this choric group acts and comes to bear witness in the manner of all such witnesses, that is, by learning to see their own complicity in what they have too easily judged as Other. To sustain such self-abnegation would imply slipping, like Baby Suggs, in the direction of death. And yet tragic knowing and supportive action lead to an altered state, one that forever affects felt identifications—even the ease of social judgments. In tragic extension of Janie Crawford's "you got tuh *go* there tuh *know* there," witnessing implies not just one's presence as an observer with its implied passivity, but bearing witness, giving testimony, providing supportive *action.* And it does so whether applied to the inward testimony of memory and conscience or to subsequent deeds on behalf of the outcast.

The witnessing that characterizes tragic experience begins in some vested position from which the conflicted nature of tragic action threatens the separations, oppositions, and concomitant orders on which a social fabric or a personal identity seem to rely. If catharsis does not mean witnessing a specific tragic action, it at least means attaining some consciousness that will ever after change the unconscious and, therefore, how one lives with other people in the world. Here catharsis does not imply a purging of affective identification with a tragic figure; rather, the process brings quite different characters toward both acknowledging and acting on the equivalent humanity of those once too easily judged as Other (the purging of distance, judgment, separation). Importantly, these are not just any witnesses—and therefore not as vicarious as either a chorus on stage or a readerly audience—because they each come to the capacity for transformative catharsis by undergoing a process that links Sethe's experiences to some aspect of their own. Stamp Paid understands his refusal to understand Baby Suggs and how he has himself practiced exercises in forgetting; Paul D. understands how the horror of seeing himself as an animal lies behind his animal analogy for Sethe; and Ella understands her refusal to nurse a child born in captivity to "the lowest yet." In suspending some easier and more judgmentally self-protecting view of Sethe, each of the three experience a form of catharsis that draws them to "invest" in Sethe's present, a revisioning not only of her past but also a *re*memorying of their own pasts that serves as a call to action.

The legal sense of a "witness action" has relevance here, since it refers to a judicial process in which witnesses are called rather than legal principles argued; as such, it values personal experience over abstracted arguments. In *Beloved*, experience represented in images and not-language — and from multiple angles — shows the insufficiency of any normalcy that does not acknowledge its link to experience once too easily felt as Other. Against any claims of mere reason, only an embodied, affective understanding displaces prior judgments on Sethe. Drawn into "imaging" their own pasts and that past's relation to complicitous evasion, Stamp Paid, Paul D., Ella, and the chorus of women act in support of Sethe rather than in judgment on her. Concomitantly, Paul D. and Stamp Paid have a renewed capacity to laugh, not the "chewing laughter" related to Baby Suggs's allusion to the whitefolks who "chewed up her life and spit it out like a fish bone" (177), but the laughter that responds "Ain't we all?" to "That woman is crazy": "As the scene [the exorcism] neither one had witnessed took shape before them, its seriousness and its embarrassment made them shake with laughter" (265). Accordingly, as Paul D. remembers — is now able to remember — how he saw himself differently through Sixo's and Garner's eyes, he comes to understand something about the relational nature of the gaze itself. And in this the logic of his most terrible moment stands revealed: when seeing himself through the eyes of a rooster, how could he possibly see himself *as a man?*

Earlier, the narration presenting Sethe's outing with Beloved and Denver, a riotous skating and slipping on the ice, repeats with lyrical authority that "nobody saw them fall," invoking in its difference all the resonance of both the fall from grace and the tragic fall so omnipresent in Western symbology. Here the participial falling is both joyous and murderous, glad and perverse, familial and grotesque, unlike the normalcy attending the fall of a stressed community out of moral and affective identification. Before Ella's choric action, the community cannot even see Beloved because they have so successfully repressed the terrors of "rememory"; their order and respectability refuses to suspend judgment without suspending moral fervor. Beloved's ghostly presence puts this refusal in bodily form, since she exists to awaken unspeakable desire: in Sethe, for bodily, maternal relation to a dead child; in Paul D., for bodily, sexual relation without the entanglements of love; and in others in the community, for the necessary distance from a presence so intense that it threatens the very senses. Such presence demands more than merely vicarious witnesses offer. If, as Homi Bhabha puts it, Beloved herself symbolizes "the furious emergence of the projective past" ("Freedom's Basis" 57), then her strident demands correspond to the truth that she can only disappear into timelessness when those who have held themselves separate bring themselves to felt relationship.

Many readings take "This is not a story to pass on" as self-referentially ironic since the story has just been told, and in so doing ignore the potentiality embedded in the paradox as somehow secondary. Marianne Hirsch's reading of *Beloved* as "maternal narrative," for example, passes over Morrison's most emphatic and global assertion as worthy of only a dependent clause: "Although the novel reiterates that Sethe's story 'is not a story to pass on,' *Beloved* is the story of the mother, and narrative is hers."[34] And some commentators use "rememory" as a synonym for the history that has not been written and yet is somehow written here. But to the degree that *Beloved* implicitly theorizes the gap in extant tragic theory, the paradox refers more precisely to that revisionary working through of one's own relation to Others' suffering (felt differentially by those coming to slavery's imaging from disparate positions). Such experience may resemble identification or empathy or what Nelson Goodman has called "felt cognition," but it reveals itself in what Lawrence Grossberg names "affective practices," those particular investments in feeling, commitment, energy, and volition "that give 'color,' 'tone,' or 'texture' to the lived" (81). The individual character of the self-revisioning undergone by Stamp Paid, Paul D., and Ella reflects the diverse forms of their experience, but they have in common an affective agency directed toward someone formerly separated and judged. The closing chapter suggests why catharsis is theirs, and may or may not be the reader's.

The last two-page chapter of *Beloved* provides the best contemporary expression I know of the effects of a tragic consciousness that works not through the scapegoating mechanism of a community but, rather, through a community's undergoing a revolution that makes the scapegoat's problem a communal one, and therefore purges the need for a scapegoat. And the chapter explains, too, why such effects cannot be sustained, and why—once experienced—they may "come and go" as often as one risks suspending individual, bounded identity in favor of felt relationship. The most lyrical chapters in the book prior to this final chapter belong to the successive monologues that follow Stamp Paid's failure to enter 124 and confront the voices he hears. Narration identifies the commotion very explicitly: "Mixed in with the voices surrounding the house, recognizable but undecipherable to Stamp Paid, were the thoughts of the women of 124, unspeakable thoughts, unspoken." The first three chapters identify themselves clearly as the "unspoken" thoughts of Sethe, Denver, and Beloved herself, all difficult in the density of their figurative interrelation and all belonging to what Stamp Paid cannot decipher. But the last of the four lyrical chapters has a larger self-reference, which includes the women but also "mixes in" the voices of "the black and angry dead" that Stamp Paid hears as "undecipherable language clamoring." In prose that tells a story but reads like a lyric poem, a taut structural logic moves forward through a figurative, scenic coherence within a narrative frame that addresses the paradox of what "everybody" knew and yet did not know. In doing so, it passes strong judgment on what the "forgetting" of the last chapter implies, a forgetting explicitly linked to Sethe's earlier explanation of rememory to Denver:

"Some things go. Pass on. Some things just stay. I used to think it was my rememory. You know. Some things you forget. Other things you never do. But it's not. Places, places are still there. If a house burns down, it's gone, but the place—the picture of it—stays, and not just in my rememroy, but out there, in the world. What I remember is a picture floating around out there outside my head. I mean, even if I don't think it, even if I die, the picture of what I did, or knew, or saw is still out there. Right in the place where it happened."
    "Can other people see it?" asked Denver.
    "Oh, yes. Oh, yes, yes, yes. Someday you be walking down the road and you hear something or see something goin on. So clear. And you think it's you thinking it up. A thought picture. But no. It's when you bump into a rememory that belongs to somebody else." (35–36)

Although part of Sethe's warning exercise in "keeping the past at bay," rememory itself involves that "bump" into the most intense images that belong "to somebody else," an idea strongly allied with tragic agency.
    To begin, as the chapter does, that "bump" implies loneliness, and not the garden-variety loneliness that can be assuaged by rocking. The rocking variety, "an inside kind—wrapped tight like the skin" (274), belongs to some relatively secure sense of personhood, so that one can hold onto it as though it were something containable. But tragic loneliness troubles even personhood and cannot be contained. This loneliness roams, "a dry and spreading thing that makes the sound of one's own

feet going seem to come from a far-off place." It involves painful self-distancing, a dangerous merger with things more safely experienced as outside the self, *un*familiar.

In language that reiterates Beloved's fear of disintegration or consumption, the second section reveals that when Beloved is forgotten she "erupts into her separate parts, to make it easy for the chewing laughter to swallow her all away" (274). This image of a violent, explosive dismembering and a festive cannibalism (consumption plus laughter) does not resemble Bacchic rites for nothing: what Beloved represents must be somehow "swallowed whole" in order to be consumed. Thus ingested, she becomes part of lives that can accommodate a "chewing laughter."[35] Narration has recorded, after all, none of Beloved's internal consciousness except her desire to monopolize Sethe and her fragmentary fears that she is somehow bodily "coming apart." Beloved fears that she may "wake up one day and find herself in pieces" (133) whenever she is alone. When her tooth comes out, she fears that the process may have started and she suffers from two dreams of dissolution: "exploding, and being swallowed." The consumption figure also helps explain the meaning of Beloved's swelling up, as in pregnancy, to precisely the extent that Sethe herself withers: "Beloved ate up her life, took it, swelled up with it, grew taller on it" (250). Like a past taking over a present, Beloved, as the merger of life and death, mother and daughter, explains how and why Paul D. succumbs to the painful merger of lover, husband, and father, and why only acts of resistant self-confronting enable that forgetting (the knowing and then "forgetting" of repressed and forbidden desires) inherent in the paradox: "Although she has claim, she is not claimed."

The next sections circumscribe the forgetting that does not entirely forget, or at least paradoxically forgets while retaining the capacity for rememory. Usually, people do not touch that hovering "familiar" (a pun here on the African "familiar," as in Alice Walker's *The Temple of My Familiar*):[36] "They can touch it if they like, but don't, because they know things will never be the same if they do." Witnessing the tragic may be "forgotten" in order to repress those forever troubling connections between oneself and those on whom one passes judgment. But for those who once "touch," the connections become available, even if they present themselves only "occasionally" ever after. The play on "familiar" applies both to something that moves besides the image itself in a photograph looked at too long and to the footprints behind 124 that fit anyone willing to put their feet in them. It moves and then disappears just as footprints disappear once the feet are taken out of them; both senses of the familiar function as metonyms for an affective agency able to enter into a formerly unbearable, self-distancing story only to "quickly and deliberately" forget it in order to live as an individuated self in a differentiated world. But this forgetting has nothing of permanence about it, but rather an openness to felt connections to the marginal and the out- cast—and to whatever Otherness tempts the relative ease of judgment.

The last section names what "they" who have forgotten do *not* remem- ber for the moment: the footprints, what is down in the water, "the breath of the disremembered and unaccounted for," and "clamor for a kiss." The focus on the not-remembered in previous sections culminates in the reiterated "not" of this section, which builds with the rhythm of desire, the desire of the forgotten Other to be not only remembered but remembered lovingly, *as* the beloved. In life, "things that just happen, like the weather" naturalize a terrible inhumanity, one denaturalized in *Beloved* as a whole and made unnatural in this section's lyricism. Fulfill- ing the earlier paradox, "Although she has claim, she is not claimed," this ending's self-reference says much about stories that can and cannot be told, or that must be told but whose significance requires unbear- able knowing and therefore a kind of forgetting. Here narration has that global authority which sees beyond both public history and pri- vate struggle to the wisdom inherent in the four single lines linking the five stanza-sections. The repeated refrain "It was not a story to pass on" builds to the more immediate variant, "*This* is not a story to pass on," and then to the personal embodiment of that story caught in the last, isolated word-line: "Beloved." This story's paradox inheres in requiring witnesses willing to put their feet in footprints that imply a profoundly existential loneliness, restlessness, uncontainability of a kind that must be *already lived.* Memory becomes "rememory" in *Beloved* because it in- volves forging connections with such painful implications and conse- quences that they cannot be sustained, even though they remain forever "familiar." Such rememory implies what tragic knowledge implies, that "things will never be the same" after it passes and hovers outside con- sciousness as a once-experienced possibility (rather like "an unpleasant dream during a troubling sleep").

The last section ends with desire, the story that is not to pass on merged with "no clamor for a kiss," and the final, lyrical "Beloved" links the tragedy of slavery with all the forms of desire invoked in *Beloved*— maternal, sexual, matrimonial, funereal, narrative. Diverse characters reveal how a vulnerability in agency is all bound up in the vulnerability of desire. This is not to say that sexual desire stands in some metonymic relation to other desire, but rather that without desire—some passional relation to the terror of Others' experience—there can be no specifically tragic agency. Beloved as process represents both the "something more" that Denver knows she meant and the "something missing" that Paul D. feels in 124. Because he comes to join his story to Sethe's, and there- fore looks toward a future, he senses only for a moment the "something more": "just beyond his knowing is the glare of an outside thing that embraces while it accuses" (171). Vicarious witnessing of the kind that takes place here calls in the direction of actively bearing witness, even if it too must retreat from tragic witnessing toward only momentary senses of "the glare of an outside thing that embraces while it accuses" (271). Different from the formal development of tragedy as genre, this mode of tragedy focuses on the relationality of moral judgments, their embedding in social and cosmic positioning, and their inadequacy to any vision of social life that recognizes the primacy of human relationship.

As affirmative as are Denver's newly socialized health and Sethe's embarking on life as her own "best thing," *Beloved*'s final reverential awe hangs on an intimate familiarity with those in troubled or marginal relation to communal life whose irreducible relation in difference reveals the fragility of any constructed normalcy. On the model of Hegel rather than that of Euripides, dominant views of tragic understanding have often implied a tension resolved in favor of the superiority of witnesses and the nontragic, hegemonic world they create, the world seen as closure to tragic action. Morrison's art allows no such superiority, since narration ultimately allies itself with a perspective still tragic in import but looking as though from a distance on the move away from tragedy toward laughter and forgetting. As in all tragedy, the vision threatens individual identity, linear time, moral rectitude, and all those certainties that secure any life in its bounded difference and distance from its Others. But just as no singular "fall" and no univocal authority claims primacy here, so Beloved's footprints "come and go," with the capacity to become the same as whatever foot dares the fit of specifically human relationship: "They are so familiar. Should a child, an adult place his feet in them, they will fit. Take them out and they disappear again as though nobody ever walked there" (275). The "should" of hypothesis does not precede the expected, declarative "would"; rather, textual authority affirms what *will* necessarily follow after the first gesture toward that "something more familiar" that remains of an intimacy with the projective past. *Hamlet*'s "The rest is silence" becomes *Beloved*'s "The rest is weather," and a changeable, familiar, hovering paradox of felt relationship supplants any absolutes of social good.

In an irony taken up again in a reading of Hurston's writing on Vodou, this text's spiritualist frame of reference enables a focus on very human forms of agency. I do not want to suggest that *Beloved* does not ask difficult questions about the slave's agency, only that it does not explicitly answer them, in the manner of Baby Suggs, through either the approval or the condemnation criticism commonly adopts.[37] Questions about what the physical body can endure and what moral behavior means merge in the site of the tortured body; but here the questions concern a torture made chronic. How much can one endure and still exert an effort of will or resistance? What are the qualities that enable some to withstand a chronic oppression and hold out against the oppressor? What does "holding out" mean when lengthened to a lifetime? What comprises morality with choice so constrained, when the stealing of a mother's milk means the stealing of her children into slavery? *Beloved* tells its story through the processes of rememory, or rememory as affective agency, and therefore theorizes a perspective aware of the implications and consequences of such imagining, even for those whose return to normalcy depends upon a paradoxical forgetting.

Rather than regard the persecution of slaves as a form of "generative violence" that protects the community from turning violence inward, as in a white imagining's ultimate focus on the dominant community, *Beloved*'s protagonists resist the ease of communal constructions even in the act of working toward communal health. For although Sethe in some ways serves the role of scapegoat for the black community, her violent action directs itself against the world of Schoolteacher, not against the world of ex-slaves. Resistance comes from points of view that mark and remark the analogy between limitations in personal and communal judgment and limitations in the reader. Thus the strongest moral judgments in *Beloved* are not on Sethe, who once Ella and the community reaches out can have horror exorcised, but on the vicarious witnessing of those who consider themselves apart from what she has done. In them, multiple catharses take place dialogically: the one that Baby Suggs refuses (along with the compromises of normalcy) in dialogue with the ones that take place in Stamp Paid, Paul D., Ella, and the community of women. Here healing does not happen until other characters recognize their own failures in Sethe's and connect them to a need to act. When that happens, Sethe can recognize her own humanity, her links to those from whom her act seemed to separate her, and she, too, can face the problem of enforced complicity: "I made the ink, Paul D. He couldn't have done it if I hadn't made the ink."[38]

Importantly, narration never answers the question about whether some other choice besides the untenable one was available to Sethe, avoiding framing the problem in terms of rational choice as surely as does Baby Suggs. Here the slave's tragedy belongs to the tragedy of slavery, which variously positions the reader-observer-rememberer in a shared history of forgetting. The witnessing in *Beloved* may seem to merge, finally, into some identity reconstituted as normalcy, but the difference remains in the footprints' fit, the fact of their familiarity to those who have come through judgmental distance to supportive action. That is, they are only familiar to those who have already walked there by undergoing the strongest identification with some formerly repudiated Other. We explicate away this paradox at our own peril.

Daily Life and Tragic Paradox

The dynamics of tragedy as imagined by Hegel or Nietzsche and as re-imagined by Girard refer us to a genre whose sense of an ending would seem to disallow *Beloved* for inclusion; after all, the story begins rather than ends with its horrors and projects a hopeful future. Yet any generic sense of *Beloved* as tragedy seems less important than recognizing that it shares the moral concerns of Western tragedy while resisting certain hegemonic takes on tragic meaning, and therefore spurs a revision of the values that inhere in the stature afforded the tragic. As a work riddled with precise paradox, but neither ambivalent nor amorphously indeterminate, *Beloved* extends the paradoxes of the slave's written story about which so many have usefully thought; this tragedy acknowledges its continued life outside the written form it takes in the paradox of a forgetting that allows rememory because it abandons the *struggle* to forget (as in Morrison's more propositional phrasing of intent: "The struggle to forget which was important in order to survive is fruitless and I wanted to make it fruitless" ["Living Memory" 179]).

But what does the disappearance of the struggle to forget mean to those who nevertheless still live their daily lives in states of forgetfulness? How does the tragic matter to both the lives the story projects beyond its pages and the lives of readers? In the Prologue I found sympathetic impetus for such questions in Raymond Williams's insight about a tragedy inherent in the social order and, more indirectly, in Stanley Cavell's exploratory investigations of what it means to acknowledge others. There I suggested reasons why Williams's frame of reference urged him to find his ideal tragedy in historical vision rather than in imaginative literature and why Cavell's, however much grounded in *Lear* and other tragic drama, sticks so close to the matter of knowing other *minds* (both, therefore, involving a deep sense of outsiderness very much inside Western traditions). Here I want to pull together some connective links between the paradox of a forgetting that allows rememory and a sense of the tragic less reliant on "the claim of reason," more finely attuned to readerly positioning, and more insistent on the value of bearing witness over any merely vicarious witnessing (whether a matter of social, aesthetic, or analytical distance).

The last chapter of *Beloved* lyrically invokes a certain timelessness belonging to the effects of what I have here called catharsis, even in its difference from that catharsis after which all worlds—metaphysical, social, aesthetic—return to some normalcy bought at the cost of dramatic iden-tification with a sacrificial scapegoat-figure. Conventional catharsis pulls the observer away from vicarious witnessing and back to some consen-sual dominance, however forcefully a tragic figure has articulated dis-ease with worldly and cosmic orders. The power of tragedy as genre in-heres in its play of danger and safety: remembering felt identification (or Cavell's "empathic projections") from the position of having moved be-yond it leaves one with an appreciative, abiding sense of the temptingly transgressive but also with a certain repletion and relief that the danger of melting one's own affective agency into that dangerous Other's has passed. Interestingly, many of the negative or uncharitable readings of *Beloved* engage in a kind of witnessing or identification fallacy by presum-ing that a fiction must somehow draw its readers into a world with the strongest identity between reader and character. Charges of sentimen-tality or melodrama practically always accompany descriptions of *Beloved* as a story about women as victims, part of a "family romance," for ex-ample, guilty of "some of the excesses Nietzsche objected to in Wagner":

She [Morrison] doesn't eschew melodrama in her big, violent scenes, or weep-ing in her domestic ones. There is a chorus of stock characters—good neigh-bors, evil prison guards, a messenger of the gods called Stamp Paid, and even a tree named Brother. The prose is rife with motifs and images that the narration sometimes orchestrates too solemnly. Paul D.'s last speech to Sethe is not the only one that trembles on the edge of pathos. (Thurman 190)

With Stamp Paid as a stock character and a chorus reduced to the speechless passivity of a tree, what *besides* pathos could result? Or note Stanley Crouch who, in a particularly mean-spirited misreading, faults *Beloved* as tragedy because of what he decides it should include in order to have "a true sense of the tragic": "In *Beloved* Morrison only asks that her readers tally up the sins committed against the darker people and feel sorry for them, not experience the horrors of slavery as they do" (40). Crouch presumes aesthetic identification *can* simulate feeling "as they [slaves] do," even though *Beloved* very carefully does not claim to represent slavery's "lived moment of resistance, its sorrow and its salva-tion" (Bhabha, "Freedom's Basis" 57) any more than it invites readers to identify readerly witnessing with bearing witness.

In a multivoiced narration ever conscious of positioning, *Beloved* claims no representation for a slavery that cannot be represented. No assumptions about appropriate readerly response inhere in a sense of an ending with fulfilled relationship and new beginnings, and yet insis-tent upon the value of the risk so rarely taken, the daring to place one's own feet in footprints whose fit guarantees that "things will never be the same." For the characters within the story who undergo the affective difference of a catharsis leading to action, the life that comes after changes forever, even though a seeming forgetting necessarily follows within the linear life. Very different from the intellectual knowing of other minds, this internal relation to others carries within it the potential to rememory one's own connections to comunally constructed Others. Here not struggling to forget does not exactly mean remembering, only an openness that brooks the possibility of a self-revisioning leading to active relationship with any who occupy the position of *pharmakon*. Just as this forgetting has none of the repressed or obsessive tenacity of a *struggle* to forget, so the state-related, affective acknowledgement that comes upon one "like weather" implies a continuing capacity intimately connected to what it means to bear witness. Instead of purgation leading away from feeling toward the tragic Other, it leads toward an identification that suspends judgment and enables action.

All tragedy reveals that human beings cannot plot their lives with any security in reason or foresight. But a tragedy showing *witnesses* moving from the vicarious through catharsis to the action of bearing witness reveals any vicarious relation as lack. Rather than discovering what one could not have known, this tragedy discovers, even if to "forget" it again, that we are both different and the same, even if frighteningly so to those habituated to positions of privilege, power, or dominance. Minimally, to bear witness implies the capacity to avoid conceiving oneself as superior to victims, who in the act of being beaten down necessarily expose failures in agency and understanding (that characteristic lack of "perspective" so dear to Hegel and all views from above).[39] *Beloved* formally represents the processes that bring witnesses to a felt cognition, for the moment of tragic vision, that they have themselves defectively imagined the agency of those whom they have presumed defective. But the characters in *Beloved* who come through to bearing witness also reveal a more complex set of values named too patly and too disjointly by such terms as emotion, perception, intuition, spirituality, identification, empathy, and intimacy. The achievement of bearing witness as a kind of affective agency and practice relates them closely to Bhabha's "freedom as indeterminacy," an interested stake in reality that relies not on a neutral freedom from value but on a distance from fixed or judgmental values, a freedom that allows a more "efficient" intervention into a social reality taken by most tragic theorists as given. To pass from vicarious witness to the act of bearing witness means to act as a self-in-relation to whoever and whatever seemed formerly Other. And the tragedy inheres in the focus on the process of response itself. Without experiencing the consuming threat of felt connections, some familiarity with the terrible vulnerability and relationality of systems of value (including one's own unwilled complicity in doing harm), no responsive act can move beyond "the nihilism of despair or the utopia of progress" (Bhabha, "Freedom's Basis" 57).

Yet if even characters who undergo the affective transformation of catharsis eventually forget (even when they retain the capacity for re-memory), what of the reader's affective engagements? The effects of Morrison's tragic modality belong not so much to some generalized audience response as to readerly positioning. That is, *Beloved* is not a naive call to experience that none would choose, but a contemporary and complex reworking of Hurston's "you got tuh *go* there tuh *know* there," one relevant to why it matters that readers come to reading as witnessing from very different positions. Readings from feminist posi-tions emphasizing maternal narrative necessarily differ in focus from readings, often by black feminists, emphasizing the specific defilements of black motherhood under the slave system. When Carole Boyce Davies finds *Beloved* wanting in models of maternal agency, she brings to the work her own vital concerns and expectations, as do readers concerned with a seemingly omnipresent heterosexuality that has, for example, the Sweet Home men turning their longings to Sethe or animals but never to each other.[40] Similarly, my own reading here catches at what intra-cultural relations might mean to cultural outsiders and finds resistance in communal characters seen by Davies as implying "that slavery and racism wiped out resistance except at a very personal level" (142). But issues of focus and readerly relation do not divide up neatly in accor-dance with the social categories available to analysts or to the multiple and interconnected processes of self-identification. For example, if the authority of the chorus's "they all knew what that sound was like" still has about it a ring of distant and occult ritual, then it reads differently than if the reader thinks that she, too, knows what it sounds like, could even make it herself. This view of history and of tragedy moves beyond "win, lose, and draw" as the only relevant power relations and recognizes that even a trinary logic (and even the categories of race, gender, class, and sexuality) exclude much that has happened here.[41] In this tragic mode, the reader may not herself bear witness, yet may feel the spur to move beyond the vicarious to the rigorous difficulty of becoming a self-in-relation who rememories how a community makes its outcasts and, more particularly, how the present tense, experiencing self is complicit in maintaining the lack of connection inscribed in communal represen-tations.

Those with the habits of judgment, including those who have lived in the domain of analyst-observer-critic, may have particular tenden-cies to believe in differences that explain or justify their own position-ing, which is why they in particular, perhaps, need to understand that scapegoating processes work not just in moments of crisis but also in those everyday acts of differentiating cruelty (usually so institutionalized and internalized as to seem natural) that respond to a more generalized, ongoing threat of sameness-in-difference. If the social order itself owns the tragedy, then tragic vision must imagine a cultural wholeness in which differentiation does not imply self-justifying hierarchy and in which sameness loses its threat. As such, it counters that *doxa* of postmoderns and Lacanians alike, however different the referents for otherness, that "intersubjectivity is founded upon the fact that the other is phenomenologically experienced as an 'unknown quantity,' as a bottomless abyss which we can never fathom" (Žižek, *For They Know Not* 199). *Beloved* as theory betrays the coldness of such easy futility, revealing even the bits of cynical ideology that impress us with our own cleverness but suggest no responsible action toward those we reduce through distanced analysis. As though in precise resistance to the Western alterity described by Lacan as grounded in language,[42] *Beloved* consistently counters relationships in language with active, embodied connection, as in Paul D.'s cathartic body spasm or Ella's and her chorus's making "the sound that broke the back of words," reminding us in its own *para-doxa* that Beloved is both symbolic and actual, an embodied, human connection in the form of a spirit-girl who even as she disappears resists any place on the scrap heap of Western metaphysics.

For this tragedy, even vicarious witnesses must consider what it means to act where before mere judgment felt itself justified as principled or righteous (or where the act of reading could itself constitute the appropriate response). Vicarious witnessing cannot expect to frame a way of living with Others that values difference yet finds no threat in human sameness. An aporia in much literary discussion, this difference between the cathartic self-revisioning of figure-characters' and reader-observers' responses often informs debates about power and responsibility, as when Joy James aptly characterizes the evasionary quality of liberal, usually white racial attitudes convinced that being an enlightened spectator is enough. Discussing a confusion very much like those cited in readings faulting *Beloved* for a generic failure to achieve tragic stature, James cautions that readers often ask of a text (or of a discourse, a performance, any call to "bear witness") to make her a responsible actor through the act of reading (or seeing) alone, thus promising "comforting closure to and containment of human barbarism and tragedy":

The language of the horrified spectator is not necessarily the language of the antiracist activist. "Identification" through viewing a spectacle, no matter how horrific, does not necessarily lead to analysis, moral commitment, or political organizing. (122)

An asserted collapse between vicarious experience and the lived moment of resistance reinscribes the long tradition of vicarious supremacy and makes exaggerated claims for a witnessing that avoids the complexities of human relationship and social responsibility.[43] Understandably, claims for the value of the vicarious, with their too easy imaginative identifications, tend to justify those who connect tragedy to regressive social thought, as in Joseph Napora's global attribution of necessary limits to tragedy: "The culture of exploitation is the culture of tragedy. Tragedy is used to substitute for recognition of real suffering" (157).

The dialogue about tragic meaning taken up by *Beloved* does not foreground the movement beyond catharsis as either a return or a progression, but rather as a focused interrogation of how difficult and fragile are the processes necessary to feel and rememory our human connection to the suffering of any outcast. Through such processes, better described as belonging to affective agency than to reason, this tragic mode requires quite different positioning for different readers. If critical fashion tends to blur discursive formations and lived experience, then it only participates in a now commonplace blurring of fictive and actual crisis (often radically more strange than dominant fictions). Any attempt to find representations not already "taken into account in advance" by social fantasy must contend with how habituated one becomes to a daily spectacle that merges seamlessly with the disturbing social vision of overtly fictional popular series.[44] An addiction to dramatic stimulation naturalizes the terror and gives audiences a taste for the vicarious as the excitement of danger-plus-distance, commodified in the estranged intensities of *911, Cops,* and *Eye/I-Witness Video* ("When tragedy strikes, ordinary people become heroes").[45] In artful difference, *Beloved*'s tragic mode does not "strike," as though from elsewhere and at an always Other; it belongs to any "us" in direct accordance with our every assumption about who we and our Others are—and what to do about it.

Chapter 2
Humor, Subjectivity, Unctuousness

The Case of Laughter in *The Color Purple* and *The Women of Brewster Place*

They crush and crush
your heart;
your humor
escapes.

—Alice Walker, "Ndebele"

Postmodernism for postmodernism, politics for politics, I'd rather be an ironist than a terrorist.

—Susan Suleiman, *Subversive Intent*

Indeed, irony in the face of actual torture is arguably less worthwhile than terrorism in the face of a text. And we don't, in any event, always get to choose our contexts or our adversaries.

—Lillian Robinson, "At Play in the Mind-Fields"

The Context of Adversaries

Perhaps no text more dramatically demonstrates how differently diverse communities of readers construct literary meaning than does Alice Walker's *The Color Purple*, the locus of ongoing debate about interlocking systems of oppression and their representation in literature. Even among generally appreciative critics, some have found a clear model for the organized struggle against oppression and others have found a wish-fulfilling romance, such that both problems of representation and problems of genre inform estimations of value. What does the seemingly polarized distance between Celie's distinctive personal voice and Nettie's "essay on the history of the Olinka tribe" *mean*?[1] Is the ending too utopian to address the difficult tensions between the material oppression that writes itself on actual women's bodies and the fictional oppression that either disappears or ennobles its victims somehow too easily? Where is resistance in a world replete with incest wiped away, abuse forgiven or transformed, and a propertied Celie surrounded by extended family? Relatedly, the framing lyricism of Gloria Naylor's *The Women of Brewster Place* becomes part of the problem in a work that, in Jacqueline Bobo's useful formulation, readers construct as controversial. Critics may point to this work's sympathy for middle-class characters and values, its seemingly doomed sexual relationships, its heterosexual take on lesbian life, its approval for a marriage to a "responsible" white man as a way out of the impossible stresses on black marriage, implied insults to black manhood, and more, even in the act of appreciating the artfulness of its unfolding stories. What relevance have these fictional worlds—where black women always get up again no matter how beaten down—to actual social worlds? Such questions matter to debates about resistance in literary texts and how such resistance hooks up—or does not—to the sociopolitical world. Read as art-with-theory, these fictions help clarify how adversarial contexts belonging to the social order itself contribute to the paradoxes of critical reception, that is, to the paradox of how resistance is never *purely* resistance nor simply *there* in a text, but always multiply, relationally situated in terms of what it resists.[2]

Defiant, aggressive laughter and festive comic inversions exist abundantly in both Walker's and Naylor's fictional worlds; and such laughter assimilates easily into the dominant theories that identify humor as a form of resistance with a focused attack on specific butts or targets. Yet a humorous rapport among characters also celebrates a healthy normalcy and ultimately merges the subjectivities of its characters, placing the comic tonalities in these texts outside dominant formulations. For storyteling in *The Color Purple* and *The Women of Brewster Place* does not entirely return to an older, western realism nor does it entirely adapt the conventions of comic romance or entirely abjure speech as a postmodern play among ontologies.[3] Rather, interrogations of subjectivity itself attribute value to an intersubjectivity that has multivalent relation to readerly desire.[4] That is, when a character-in-process comes to see herself as becoming more like a subject rather than one who has been the object for others' manipulation, or when she must confront how she has affected others and begins to relinquish her hold over them, then changes in subject-positioning accompany an ideal of merged subjectivity, or intersubjectivity, inseparable from changes in power. By exploring the interrelations between humorous rapport and an ideal of intersubjectivity among characters, I want, ultimately, to consider these works as having instructive relation to a dialogical form of comic resistance that privileges the "unctuousness" that Walker herself found in Hurston's writing and that has everything to do with where readers enter relations of privilege or power.[5]

And so I start with what does not console or comfort my own reading position(s) in any way: an unheard laughter, a laughter that refuses any easy desire for inclusion, a laughter that upsets any hold on the security of writerly-readerly relations. Neither ironists nor terrorists, Walker and Naylor create worlds in which characters achieve the possibility of sharing in the laughter by changing who they are: those with oppressive power must relinquish it and those without it must achieve new power over themselves, a kind of empowerment without the negative connotation of "power over others." The comic rapport so important to these works asks no less of readers whose responses must in some way confront the ideal of a leveling intersubjectivity and its critical relation to the assumptions of a happily-ever-after comic romance.

Intersubjectivity and Characters-in-Process

Most of the characters in *The Color Purple* ultimately share the capacity for humorous rapport, and the work's sense of an ending relies in large part on a vision of happiness that incorporates a robust, vernacular humor into daily life. Yet the way humor accrues value in *The Color Purple* has little to do with funny scenes, humorous lines or narratives, or some overarching comic structure. Rather, humor develops as an interaction that in its implied normalcy provides the daily context of value. The development of this interaction mitigates the generic security of both Molly Hite's attempt to reconcile feminist and poststructuralist concerns in a reading of *The Color Purple* as a comic romance and, more supplementally, Henry Louis Gates's postmodern emphasis on an epistolary transformation of "speakerly language which no character can ever speak, because it exists only in a written text" (250).[6] In comic romance, the impulse of a sympathetic humor works through the involuted exigencies of disguise and disorder until at the close, a united couple represents the unthreatened norms of a society returned to its rightful order. And in an epistolary text where writing protects the reader from Gates's "tyranny of the narrative present," a sense of resisting agency resides primarily in the act of writing.[7] Deborah McDowell's conception of character-as-process helps focus on the value of humorous rapport because it usefully supplants Hite's sense of characterization and supplements Gates's emphasis. This conception affords humor greater importance precisely because it helps differentiate characters with fluid or merging identities from either unitary, ego-centered selves defined in contrast to some Other or characters subsumed by their existence in writing.[8]

A humor integral to the experience of interconnected relationships, dramatically presented in dialogue form, structures all Celie's developing interactions with women, but her letters about Sofia's imprisonment and subsequent release focus on a humor contrasted to any humor "normative" to social health. Celie recounts how Sofia, at the beginning of her jail term, can still laugh, albeit with the quality of a blues expressivity.[9] When her extended family visits her in jail, no one present can bear the emotive force of her condition, which exists outside ordinary language:

Mr. _____ suck in his breath. Harpo groan. Miss Shug cuss. She come from Memphis special to see Sofia.
I can't fix my mouth to say how I feel. (88)

Context connects this lyrical, expressive sadness with laughing alone:

I'm a good prisoner, she [Sofia] say. Best convict they ever see. They can't believe I'm the one sass the mayor's wife, knock the mayor down. She laugh. It sound like something from a song. The part where everybody done gone home but you. (88)

In several subsequent letters, Celie tells of the scheming to release Sofia, a scheming cleverly relying on white vengefulness. Then, suddenly, Sofia reappears as a participant in Celie's daily life, with a narrative ellipsis of three years marked by her presence in a relationship that once again allows mutual laughter. The absence of three years from Sofia's story, then, becomes not just some imaginary expansion of a terrible time in jail followed by a slavelike existence as resident "maid" to Miss Millie; rather, it becomes the absence of mutual, if not yet intersubjective laughter, a laughter whose disappearance and reappearance signals a gaping ellipsis in human as well as narrative time.

The capacity for this laughter marks Sofia's return to human interaction after her grotesque imprisonment, but the invocation of humor frames the opening and closing of Celie's letters rather than providing some humorous content. The first letter, telling us that the scheme to release Sofia to a servitude outside the jail has worked, begins with Celie's reported discourse that acknowledges the legitimacy of Sofia's rage but transforms it into a humorous comment on the politics of power:

Sofia say to me today, I just can't understand it.
What that? I ast.
Why we ain't already kill them off.
Three years after she beat she out of the wash house, got her color and her weight back, look like her old self, just all time think bout killing somebody.
Too many to kill off, I say. Us outnumbered from the start. I speck we knock over one or two, though, here and there, through the years, I say. (98)

To argue that this reported dialogue represents Celie's "control" of another's speech (Gates's generalization about the primacy of writing) undervalues the dramatic immediacy of the exchange and the context specific focus on a sustaining, resisting humorous rapport. Even though Celie asserts "Us outnumbered from the start," her attitude has nothing of impotence about it, especially since her consoling figure ("I speck we knock over one or two, though, here and there, through the years") has literal as well as figurative resonance: Sofia went to jail, after all, for knocking over "one." Internally, the letter recounts the spiteful, self-injuring kick of Miss Millie's Billy and the more needy demands of Eleanor Jane, the daughter-outsider. At the close, Sofia ponders, "I wonder why she [Eleanor Jane] was ever born," and the chapter-letter ends:

Well, I say, us don't have to wonder that bout darkies.
She giggle. Miss Celie, she say, you just as crazy as you can be.
This the first giggle I heard in three years. (99)

Sofia's giggle marks the (re)created possibility for the humor taken up in the next letter. Here Walker frames Sofia's story about Miss Millie's abusive driving experiment with explicit references to humorous rapport. Celie remarks at the outset that "Sofia would make a dog laugh, talking about those people she work for" and Sofia herself closes her narrative with "White folks is a miracle of affliction," yet the narrative itself does not represent some in-group narrative humorously targeting an out-group. The humor here, in fact, has nothing to do with the narrative per se, which has a bitter irony but nothing that invites laughter. Rather, the frame refers to a manner of telling, a humorous context in which even narratives of the most disturbing events—here Miss Millie's teasing petulance with Sofia's enforced separation from her family—become occasions for laughter. Humorous rapport, here, grows out of mutual assumptions and responses within this world, and the changing humorous subject/object resides in an attitude, a tonality, a shared pleasure. Such pleasure inheres in the verbal assertions of characters resisting both others' definitions and, indeed, any easy self-other parameters. Because, as hooks rightly observes, Sofia never participates in her own oppression and most radically enacts physical resistance, her return to humor does not merely introduce her once again into a world where "us giggle"; rather, it locates resistance in a laughter intimately related to suffering, yet powerfully critical precisely because of the absence of any didactic, authorial assertion surrounding it.

This humor does not avoid or deny anger, but, perhaps more important, its interactive rapport specifically disallows any normative view of an identity differentiated from others by greater power. Sofia's tales that "would make a dog laugh" end in her outright rejection of Eleanor Jane's desire to take part in her family's life as the still-privileged other. Subsequent invocations of humor cumulatively emphasize that relations of unequal power make humorous interaction impossible. Value accrues to the intensity and intimacy of a rapport that comes from a mutually felt pain and can only attend equitable power relations.[10] Such humor supplements rather than displaces the more aggressive wit with which women as often as men resist domination.

Walker's debt to Zora Neale Hurston may suggest some parallel between the "rebellion" of women characters in *The Color Purple* and in *Their Eyes Were Watching God*. Janie Starks certainly devastates Joe when her verbal wit improves on the sexual insults he's grown accustomed to heaping on her, and when Walker's women characters stand up to men they may do so with similarly tendentious wit. But the intimate, humorous rapport primary to my argument here, explicit in supportively embracing difference however jocular the tonality, comes much closer to Susan Willis's overall sense of the difference in black women's writing: "black women's writing imagines the future in the present. It sees the future born out of the context of oppression" (159).[11] Such laughter as the trope for the values of improvised, spontaneous rapport, meaningful domestic activity, and a future imagined in the present—all in the context of daily activity—supplements Gates's attention to more overt rebellion and more aggressive wit. It also more closely reflects Walker's own concern for how the loss of compassion marks the end of any hopeful strategies, "whether in love or revolution," elsewhere glossed by the poetic vision of a Christ who walks with "His love in front. His love and his necessary fist behind" (Walker, *Her Blue Body* 289).

The daily normality of humorous rapport suggests a value at least supplemental to that placed on writing. Indeed, to take writing as the primary metaphor of value somewhat obscures Mae Henderson's insight that "Walker's use of the epistolary form allows her to transpose a formal tradition into a vehicle for expressing the folk voice, so her emphasis on material and popular modes of expression allows us to revise our conventional notions of 'high' art and culture" (17). To transform all emphasis on *voice* into emphasis on *writing* passes over how the power of the written word, here distinct from elite culture, takes its place among such other daily art forms as sewing, quilting, cooking, and singing. Each of these art forms redistributes power, so that, for example, only men who have undergone transformation can participate in them. Writing as exclusive value also disregards the text's own emphasis on resistance within speech. Celie reports that Darlene aspires to correct her speech because, on grounds she reports in her own vernacular, "colored peoples think you a hick and white folks be amuse" (193). The depth of tradition inherent in that vernacular accords with Celie's frustration in trying to change it:

> Every time I say something the way I say it, she correct me until I say it some other way. Pretty soon it feel like I can't think. My mind run up on a thought, git confuse, run back and sort of lay down. (193)

To Darlene's assertion that Shug would love Celie more if she talked "proper," Shug gratifyingly responds, "She can talk in sign language for all I care" (194). Such explicit attention to speech and its vernacular meanings rests somewhat uncomfortably with Gates's assertion that "no one speaks in this novel," despite that assertion's reliance on a fine analytical accuracy about Celie's reportage:

> Celie only tells us what people have said to her. She never shows us their words in direct quotation. Precisely because her written dialect voice is identical in diction and idiom to the supposedly spoken words that pepper her letters, we believe that we are overhearing people speak, just as Celie did when the words were in fact uttered. We are not, however; indeed, we can never be certain whether or not Celie is showing us a telling or telling us a showing, as awkward as this sounds. (251)

Certainly, the awkwardness of explanation corresponds to the awkwardness of engaging both the primacy of Celie's speech and the voyeurism of reading another's intimate letters. Yet the intimacy of speech (just as direct, perhaps even more so, as if it were within the constraints of quotation marks) formally coincides with an intimately shared humor as an important contrast between Celie's and Nettie's (re)presentations.

That Celie's writing compels associating her with voice underscores how strongly the presentness of characters within her epistolary narration (e.g., Shug, Sofia, Mary Agnes, Harpo, Albert) differs from that of characters within Nettie's (Samuel, Adam, Tashi).[12] Writing does not *necessarily* transform the writer, which matters to the dramatic contrast between Celie's voiced, intimate writing and Nettie's more academic, distanced letters. As Gates notes, Celie's framing of Nettie's letters may merge voices in the manner of free indirect discourse. But the letters also give direct experience of voice that differs markedly from Celie's perceptions, especially from the character-as-process she will become toward the end of the work. Certainly, Nettie's letters establish the similarities between the condition of black women in the rural south and black women in Africa, giving an alternative context for female bonding; "It is in work that women get to know and care about each other," writes Nettie. But the absence of humor or anything like the humorous rapport so important to Celie's developing relationships, suggests that

Nettie's letters serve as much a judgment on missionary sensibility as on black patriarchal culture, despite her own suspended judgment on Samuel's hopes and expectations.

In the portrayal of Samuel's missionary activity, Walker's authorial juxtapositions remove any sense of Celie-cum-character, signifying more in the manner Gates describes when showing her relation-in-difference to Zora Neale Hurston and Rebecca Cox Jackson. Samuel's latent bitterness about his own failure erupts just after his anecdotal tale of how Aunt Theodosia (the name says much) found herself rebuked by a young Harvard scholar named Edward DuBoyce ("or perhaps his name was Bill") for pride in a medal given her by King Leopold, a medal that symbolizes to him her "unwitting complicity" with a brutal white despot. The tonality and passionate impatience of DuBoyce wittily alludes to William Edward B. DuBois, also young at Harvard, whose alter sensibility here contrasts uncomfortably with that of Samuel. Recounting DuBoyce's outrage at Aunt Theodosia's misplaced pride, Samuel uses the story to identify not with DuBoyce but with "poor Aunt Theodosia." Like Samuel, Aunt Theodosia found little gratitude among Africans who "hardly seem to care whether missionaries exist" (210). In a form of humor very different from the intersubjective humor of the Celie sections, this authorial humor signifies a joke in which Nettie as narrator does not share. Nettie's report of Samuel's disillusioned outburst, not in quotation marks but clearly representing his voice, captures with precision the reasons why humorous rapport necessarily absents itself from the African letters:

We love them. We try every way we can to show that love. But they reject us. They never even listen to how we've suffered. And if they listen they say stupid things. Why don't you speak our language? they ask. Why can't you remember the old ways? Why aren't you happy in America, if everyone there drives motorcars? (210)

Samuel's focus on an altruism from above, and on "our" suffering, prepares for the litany of "stupid" responses that so effectively undermine the missionary's presumption of superiority; and it explains, too, the formal justice of the text's most mystified distance: that between Nettie's story and the compellingly absent, invisible *mbeles*. (Indicatively, the *mbeles*' "place" rests "so deep in the earth" that it can only be seen "from above.") The hope for Samuel lies less in the vision of a new church "in which each person's spirit is encouraged to seek God directly," than in his entry into a world of work challenging hierarchial power relations and opportunities for dominance. Here, even Samuel might become "us" and learn to laugh.[13]

Walker takes pains to link both Celie's late developing camaraderie with Albert's and Sofia's hard-won equity with Harpo to the possibility of an already leveled humor. Celie describes her reflections on the African renaming of Adam, with Albert as participant-observer, and closes:

> [Albert] So what they name Adam?
> [Celie] Something sound like Omatangu, I say. It mean a un-naked man somewhere near the first one God made that knowed he was. A whole lot of the men that come before the first man was men, but none of 'em didn't know it. You know how long it take some mens to notice anything, I say.
> Took me long enough to notice you such good company, he say. And he laugh. He ain't Shug, but he begin to be somebody I can talk to. (241)

And when Sofia and Harpo discuss Eleanor Jane's likelihood of continuing to work for them despite the disapproval of her "menfolks," Celie reports:

> Let her quit, say Sofia. It not my salvation she working for. And if she don't learn she got to face judgment for herself, she won't even have live.
> Well, you got me behind you, anyway, say Harpo. And I loves every judgment you ever made. He move up and kiss her where her nose was stitch.
> Sofia toss her head. Everybody learn something in life, she say. And they laugh. (246)

Sofia's "Everybody learn something in life" well captures the solidarity necessary to a laughter that represents a principled resistance to white judgments and values, a laughter initially associated with women in *The Color Purple* but held out as possibility to any who sustain no felt superiority-in-difference. Celie's acceptance of Albert attends not only his abandonment of dominance but also his participation in humorous rapport, evident in the little purple frog he carves for Celie as an emblem of his acceptance of her sexuality. (She has told him earlier: "Men look like frogs to me. No matter how you kiss 'em, as far as I'm concern, frogs is what they stay" [224].) When Shug returns and senses a new intimacy between Celie and Albert, she questions the implications of their "idle conversation." Celie puts down the impulse to provoke:

> What do you know, I think. Shug jealous. I have a good mind to make up a story just to make her feel bad. But I don't.
> Us talk about you, I say. How much us love you. (248)

Despite Shug's weakness for men and Albert's former abuse, the three achieve an intimacy without power inseparable from a prose that merges these characters-as-process.

In the prose of the last pages, not only do couples disappear, but a generally shared humorous rapport effaces any individuated points of view. Thus, the ending undermines any critical argument that simply exchanges periphery for center, still trapping explanation in critical oppositions. Note, for example, how Molly Hite's sustained attempt to explicate *The Color Purple*'s dismantling of hierarchial oppositions still finds its closure in a center:

On the basis of such redrawn lines the entire immediate society reconstitutes itself, in the manner of Shakespearean romance, around a central couple. This couple is not only black, it is aging and lesbian. Yet clearly Celie and Shug are intended to suggest the nucleus of a new and self-sustaining society: the triply marginalized become center and source. (117–18)

Such description finds a central couple in narration that blurs the couple out of existence; for repeatedly, in the last pages, Celie's presentation disallows either a female-centered or a couple-centered world. In the last section, often cited as the microcosm of a romantic idyll, Albert speaks first, followed by Celie's reference to "me and him and Shug." Parallel syntax foregrounds "Shug mention . . .," "Albert say . . .," and "I talk . . .," followed by the reiteration of sitting on the porch "with Albert and Shug." Even the rhythms of dialogue seamlessly incorporate the vantage points:

Could be the mailman, I say. Cept he driving a little fast.
Could be Sofia, say Shug. You know she drive like a maniac.
Could be Harpo, say Albert. But it not. (249)

And in the many times Celie mentions Shug and Albert in the first part of the last letter to God and "Everything," they always occur together, linked in syntactic symmetry:

Shug reach down and give me a helping hand. Albert press me on the arm.
I stand swaying, tween Albert and Shug.
I point at my peoples. This Shug and Albert, I say.
Then Shug and Albert start to hug everybody one after the other. (250)

This letter loses the sense of one-way communication that formerly characterized Celie's letters and substitutes what Trudier Harris aptly calls "religious relationship."[14]

The last part of the letter, the book's close after Nettie and her family have arrived, begins on July 4th as the day "us can spend celebrating each other." It invokes a panoply of characters who finally merge into an "everybody" and an "us" in a gesture that, following the global inclusiveness of the letter's address, includes everyone as subjective agency, even in contexts not normative to do so. When Tashi names her favorite African food as "barbecue," "Everybody laugh and stuff her with one

more piece." Clearly, not everyone reaches for the "one more piece";
the collective gesture and the collective laugh put the closing frame on
the sequence that begins with the first letter's address to an exclusionary God, followed by an opening subjectivity insecure as presence (with
"I am" under the erasure of "I have") and a prose inundated in singular
personal pronouns. (It also intertextually plays on Hurston's celebratory
sense of "barbecue" at the end of *Dust Tracks on a Road*.) After the last
laugh, and before the final "Amen," comes only the felt sense of distance
between how the children see them and how they feel themselves:

I see they think me and Nettie and Shug and Albert and Samuel and Harpo and
Sofia and Jack and Odessa real old and don't know much what going on. But I
don't think us feel old at all. And us so happy. Matter of fact, I think this the
youngest us ever felt. (251)

With a focus that revises a traditional comic closure's generative renewal
in the young, the prose does not differentiate among the older cast of
characters, and the repetition of the fluid "us" creates an expressively
merged identity of characters renewed in the process of intersubjective
relation.[15]

Hite's notions about reversing hierarchial oppositions or exchanging
periphery for center, especially some center "couple" consisting of Celie
and Shug, ill describes such process and overlooks the importance of
laughter as value to resisting self-other distinctions with dominance as
a defining difference. Remember that Nettie-as-writer does not recount
episodes of laughter, nor does her standard English capture the "presentness" of humorous rapport. Only Celie's narration has used language
that mitigates a constant readerly transformation of dialogue into something written, something mediated by her own "control." In fact, the
language of "control" supports a reading where characters have unam-
bivalent agency, not a more processual characterization where dramatically presented dialogue does not threaten a "tyranny of the narrative
present" precisely because "presentness" does not imply fixed identity.

And "romance" or "comic romance" suggests a teleology alien to this
sense of an ending foregrounding how "us feel." No "Edenic norm" ever
existed here in a world always constrained by power relations (and with a
graphic, non-Edenic enthusiasm for sexuality), and therefore no nostalgia for its return. Both Harpo and Albert must literally make themselves
sick with the desire for dominance before they revive into an intimacy of
work and care that allows laughter. And although the gendered tensions
provide a model for "the recognition of conflict and pain, for the possibility of reconciliation,"[16] a dominance ignorant of its own presumptions
still persists in the white world. Eleanor Jane helps Harpo look after

the children and creates yam-dishes in artful disguise for Henrietta, but must yet outlast the judgments of both her parents and "menfolks." The fact that she has learned to *sound* a little like Sofia augurs much, given the cost of Sofia's resistance:

Do her people know? I ast.
They know, say Sofia. They carrying on just like you know they would. Whoever heard of a white woman working for niggers, they rave. She tell them, whoever heard of somebody like Sofia working for trash. (246)

And "celebrating each other," with a laughter attendant on "working together," can take place only because, as Harpo tells us, "white people busy celebrating they independence from England July 4th . . . so most black folks don't have to work" (250). This celebration has neither turned the authority of the white world upside down nor, in this instance, broken its rules. Nor has it simply inverted white norms, though "us feel" has about it the "*joyful relativity* of all structure and order" that Bakhtin locates in such inversions (184).

The model for this celebration-in-resistance has much to do with the spiritual reclaiming of nature in Celie's last address and the expressive work in which all engage, a communal work that in its very form disturbs T. G. A. Nelson's claim that modern comedy may not end in idyll, but must in any case return us to "the awareness that life is a struggle in which nobody can always be on the winning side, and where each of us will sometimes fill the role of victim, scapegoat, or fool" (186). To be sure, Celie inherits a house and gets her extended family together, but Harpo's reference to July 4th as providing only temporary relief from working for white people carries dissent within it.[17] *The Color Purple* rejects the terms of romantic acceptance both because it rejects the construct of "winning" and "losing" sides, and because it posits as value a felt merger among different characters' multiple subject-positions, whether as male/female, lover/loved, employer/employee, manager/worker, et al. Such bonding feels stronger than empathy because one's own health *depends* on not accepting as "natural" the process of alternating victims and victimizers.

The merger of individuated characters into a replete intersubjectivity at the end of *The Color Purple*, does not necessarily refer us to an uncritical new age spiritualism; rather, celebration takes place in the midst of a gap named by Harpo as a respite from white people's work.[18] An overtly "happy ending" invokes values inseparable from a resistance as real as Sofia's stitches and as demanding as learning to tear dominance or the comforts of privilege out of one's own life; and he who formerly most dominated, Albert, has most radically altered his position in order to participate in the merged, intersubjective identity characteristic of the closing pages.[19] The fantasy language, the trappings of generic sentiment, the closeness of characters to stereotype, all stand undermined by an intersubjective laughter that acknowledges in its very representation the pain of past and future oppressions. Analogously, the metaphysical, distancing values of romance occur within a context that harshly implicates any idealized wish-fulfillment; indeed, it implicates all difference felt as privilege. Thus a text with felt relation to realism, to epistolary romance, to comedy, and to comic romance closes with precisely relational recognitions and refusals, with some necessary complicity in the structures its values reject.[20]

Overlapping subject positions engage readers in multiple, contradictory responses to Celie's and Nettie's sections or to the judgment on righteous altruism—and by extension on the missionary venture in Africa as a whole—implied in the "DuBoyce" passage. *The Color Purple* merges issues of subjective agency with cumulative expansions and combinatory identity that exclude those set apart by privilege or power. An intersubjective humorous rapport moves toward an inclusive suspension of individuated subjectivity, one that bears little relation to the more likely sentimental picture of beauty born again as fairy tale: "fanciful, heartrending, and uplifting."[21] Oppressive power in *The Color Purple* does not recede into some abstracted, depersonalized evil. But because the text assigns yet does not essentialize blame, it proffers the possibility of transformation on the model of those specifically undergone by Harpo and Albert. The intense difficulty of such transformation inheres in the grave, embodied consequences of turning away from the abuse of power. Each has to earn a subsequent inclusion in intersubjective humorous rapport through traumatic and self-repudiating realization, through relinquishing power, and through taking up, in James Snead's phrase, "a shared awareness of shared energy" (245). The case does not offer anything so simple as some affirmation about humor as a kind of therapeutic transformative (a sort of Norman Cousins theory of resistance). Rather, humorous rapport becomes the textual embodiment of value, the value of an intersubjectivity that most forcefully undermines the subject-object relations on which power relies.

Just as this humor as value helps differentiate Walker's text from the several genres she uses as frames of reference, so too it addresses the presentness, as opposed to presence, of characters whom readers engage as analogous to embodied selves, even when fluid in construction and merged in identity. Neither a comic romance with a utopian ending nor a postmodern fiction that celebrates writing as *the* figure of resistance, the very incompleteness or partiality with which *The Color Purple* fulfills generic expectations addresses a debate about textual resistance both as conceived "inside" texts and as a negotiation made by readers "outside" texts.[22] Texts are no less resistant by virtue of double or mediated social locations than are readers interested in bringing subjectivity back to human form without unifying or psychologizing it.

Whether thought to address a primarily white female audience or to address an intimate sisterhood figured in the two sisters' letters,[23] the text demands self-reflective responses about readerly positioning itself, and its humor addresses any perceived evasions into either fantasy or didacticism. *The Color Purple* confronts in the transformation of Albert and Harpo—and the possible transformation of Eleanor Jane—the impossibility of consoling notions of resistance "from above." Because it does not console or comfort distanced reading position(s)—though of course it may be read in this way—this intersubjective humorous rapport refuses any easy desire for inclusion and upsets any hold on the security of writerly-readerly relations. In this context, laughter belongs to an artfully represented intimacy which, while not itself transformative, comes to formally represent the value of an intersubjectivity already achieved. However targeted the humor of particular characters in moments of assertive self defense, this humor's intersubjectivity has less aggressive and more "other-aligning" impetus. Therefore it has multivalent relation to readerly desire for either identification or wish-fulfillment, for either a realistic security in character-as-person or a postmodern play among ontologies that abjures characters and speech altogether.[24] This comic mode certainly exists before Walker, but its "newness" here lies in its relevance to cultural debates surrounding the tropes chosen for value. Displacing the subject has so often meant either overlooking the subjective agency of the oppressed (conceiving of victims as *only victims*) or theorizing it "for them," "from their position," as though the felt experience of all people's lives could find articulation in figures most applicable to those who write. Celie may write, but the works ends with a very particularly positioned kind of laughter.[25]

Positioning Violence and Humor

The Women of Brewster Place, too, develops an interactive humor as value in successive stories' relationships among women, relationships within a fictional world differentiated from realist models in part through that humor. And like *The Color Purple* it provokes readings troubled by conflicted political impulses.[26] Containing one of the most overt scenes of protest in contemporary women's fiction, it nevertheless contains portrayals of black women that come dangerously close to stereotype, to some expressive futility about women's communal treatment of lesbians, and to a consoling faith in black women's resilient caring and endurance. Yet, here, character-as-process and the literary context of women's laughter raise issues that affect how to read the devastating sense of an ending for individual characters. In *The Women of Brewster Place* laughter and merged identities have explicit connection. Miss Eva's hearty laughter accompanies a blending of her life with Mattie's such that "what lay behind one and ahead of the other became indistinguishable" (34). Kiswana's alienation from her mother cannot survive such humor: "She stared at the woman she had been and was to become" (87). Miss Eva and Mattie, Mattie and Etta, and Kiswana and her mother all stand mutually revealed through a humor that allows the blurring of identity, with the humor itself imagined as charged interaction: "Each time the laughter would try to lie still, the two women would look at each other and send it hurling between them, once again" (59). All the tropes about territorial imperatives, including the imperative of a self to assert its identity on another, serve to elaborate the central symbol of Brewster Place itself in the context of a narrative where humorous repartée dramatizes the possibility of suspended judgment and merged identity. Without such repartée, the possibility of resistance would dissipate into the tendentious factions of Kiswana's Block Association. With it, those who have taken "totally different roads" to Brewster Place find themselves drawn into "a conspiratorial circle" against hostile exigencies. And the extent of failed resistance has felt connection to the extent of failed humor.

The playful humor among women contrasts to the territorial games played by males, games cumulatively linked to forms of domination in the wider, white world. Initially, narration describes Etta in the positive terms of resisting the "game" of restrictive social expectations: "Rock Vale had no place for a black woman who was not only unwilling to play by the rules, but whose spirit challenged the very right of the game to exist" (59). But when the game figure appears in her contact with Moreland (More-land) Woods, its corrupted form depersonalizes human contact with the "game" of making a conquest of Etta:

Let her win a few, and then he would win just a few more, and she would be bankrupt long before the sun was up. And there would be only one thing left to place on the table—and she would, because the stakes they were playing for were very high. But she was going to lose that last deal. (71–72)

The callousness of reducing sexual relationship to winning or losing at poker coincides with Etta's almost fated sense of living out the rituals of what would be for her "the same as all the others." In Eugene, narration introduces a male whose inability to control territory—a job, a woman—represent to him failures in a masculine assertion of power. And finally in Ben, the man with no power at all and hence emasculated in the narrow male view, masculinity without power nurtures Lorraine like a daughter, a daughter who brutally and ironically kills him in terrible response to her own brutalization. Like Mattie, Ben understands the timing of silence, as when he listens to Eugene's pathos and, with Mattie's sanctioned logic, says "yup" when he clearly intends not agreement but support.

The last section's scene, in which C. C. Baker and his gang rape and destroy Lorraine, provides the most grotesque elaboration of a violence born of disempowerment. Given all the stereotypic distortions of black male sexuality that inform the mythic black rapist, one might ask, why offer up yet one more dehumanized band of black teenage thugs who represent the danger in "human males with an erection to validate"? But the frame of the rape, an excursus about power as an aggressive masculinity at the beginning and a slow motion view of Ben's death at the end, reveals a focus on the necessarily brutalized masculinity that attends the identification of maleness with power, certainly not on some danger inherent in black maleness or in gender relations at large. The whole scene enacts an analogy between territorial conquest—seen as a birthright of male prerogative—and the localized violence in this alley:

> She had stepped into the thin strip of earth that they claimed as their own. Bound by the last building on Brewster and a brick wall, they reigned in that unlit alley like dwarfed warrior-kings. Born with the appendages of power, circumcised by a guillotine, and baptized with the steam from a million nonreflective mirrors, these young men wouldn't be called upon to thrust a bayonet into an Asian farmer, target a torpedo, scatter their iron seed from a B-52 into the wound of the earth, point a finger to move a nation, or stick a pole into the moon—and they knew it. They only had that three-hundred-foot alley to serve them as stateroom, armored tank, and executioner's chamber. So Loraine found herself, on her knees, surrounded by the most dangerous species in existence—human males with an erection to validate in a world that was only six feet wide. (169–70)

The catalogue of violences legitimated in all those "nonreflective mirrors"—social constructions of these women's reality—moves from the most directly physical act to acts increasingly distanced from their agency: from the thrust of a bayonet into the body of the Other, to targeting a torpedo, to scattering destruction from a plane, to pointing the finger that orders the aggression, to the global "nationalization" of the moon. Phallic aggression characterizes all these acts ("thrust," "target," "scatter . . . seed into the wound of the earth," "point a finger," "stick a pole"), yet the greater the actual power the more distance the aggressor achieves between himself and his victims. (I am reminded of Gayatri Spivak's "Socialized capital kills by remote control" [*In Other Worlds* 90].) In this context, the terrible physicality of the rape only enacts on this local level, with a single victim, a violence with increasingly greater scope the more "hidden" and absolute the power. The fact that the rape represents the only form of violently territorial masculinity available to them in no way explains it away. Rather, the text focuses analogically on a terrible identification of power with masculinity. Consistent with the placing of Brewster Place itself as a street designed by the powerful for easy exploitation, and subject to increasingly more remote absentee landlords, the scene's frame of reference reinvokes all those other places in *The Women of Brewster Place* where local action invokes global analogy, as when Mattie rocks Ciel

on and on, past Dachau, where soul-gutted Jewish mothers swept their children's entrails off laboratory floors. They flew past the spilled brains of Senegalese infants whose mothers had dashed them on the wooden sides of slave ships. And she rocked on. (103)

Thus the rape—described in such devastatingly graphic detail and with such painstaking physical reference—reveals the direct, exposed nature of a violence "most dangerous" to the individual victim when surrounded and entrapped "in a world that was only six feet wide."

The horror stands exposed in a language that embodies destruction in skin and hair, eyes and throat, cell after cell of the brain, yet in a context that asks us to read connections beyond this violence. Ben's death, which parallels Lorraine's in its physicality, occurs immediately after his drunken, rhythmic "singing and swaying" incites Lorraine's destroyed mind to violence because of the almost "perfect unison" it has with her own pain. As she slowly crawls toward him, "side to side" in concert with her pain, narration interrupts with a paragraph about how Mattie comes to see the scene outside her window, and then returns to Lorraine's slow crawl, repeating the "side to side" that encapsulates her dislocations of inside and outside worlds. Just as Ben's rocking recalls Mattie's former, restorative rocking, so his last words take up the suggestion of Mattie's "Merciful Jesus!" and remind us of his nurturant role in Lorraine's life: "My God, child, what happened to you?" Mattie's screams "went ricocheting in Lorraine's head," and Lorraine "joins them with her own" at the same moment that she joins her own destruction to that of Ben; for she repeats the blows "rendering his brains just a bit more useless than hers were now." For the first time, a passage of self-conscious connection links identity across the genders, as though to reinforce the idea that Lorraine's destruction cannot happen to her alone. Nor need maleness imply aggressive and destructive power. Indeed, that Ben has not been seen as a counterexample to phallic aggression, nor as any part of a counterargument to "anti-male" portrayals, suggests a reluctance to find any affirmation in a *man* without power.

The collapse of inside-outside, self-other in narration's most painful moment prepares for the merger of dream and reality in "The Block Party," a last scene in which fictional logic relates humorous possibility and collective resistance. A first section ends by referring to the women's and Mattie's troubled dreams, troubled explicitly because of their avoidance of the implications *for them* of Lorraine's death: "they feared asking how or why and put open Bibles near their bed at night to keep the answers from creeping upon them in the dark" (176). But "answers" do creep up on Mattie, nonetheless, in the form of a dream that students frequently misconstrue as reality because its descriptive prose does not differentiate it form the text's "normative" mode of narration; it even contains within it Ciel's description of a dream of her own with the vague, surreal contours and meanings conventional to dream. The dream begins with Mattie's and Etta Mae's vital, humorous repartée, soon interrupted by the return of Ciel, who prior to Lorraine has suffered the worst loss in the book. Returning with news of a white fiancé, she fears disapproval. But now, in this dream reality, what's "good for you" stands as the only criterion of approval. She gives us a dream within Mattie's dream in which she identifies with Lorraine's death as that of a woman "who was supposed to be me," an identification blurry in its detail, in the manner of dreams, but specific in its focus: "I felt it was me." A relatively superficial meaning of such a merger connects Lorraine's assimilationist strategy, her denial of difference on the grounds of lesbianism, with Ciel's former strategy of placation and appeasement with Eugene. But more importantly, this changed experience—Ciel experiencing Lorraine's death as her own—enables her to draw Kiswana out of a resistance entirely compatible with bourgeois liberalism: petitions, Shakespeare in the park, middle-class organizing among the poor. Mattie's efforts at community, on the other hand, follow in the tradition of the communalism she has learned from Miss Eva. (Michael Awkward's intertextual reading in *Inspiriting Influences* rightly observes that Mattie Michael's efforts at community "can be profitably viewed as her attempt to establish in the urban North the patterns of unity and communalism that had existed when the black American population was located primarily in the agrarian South" 133.)

In stark contrast to Mattie's and Etta's laughter, and to Ciel's dream of perfect merger with Lorraine, the scene turns to Kiswana's failure in laughter and her frenetic attempts to superimpose "reason" on those who first deny the rain and then see it turn into a stain inseparable from Lorraine's blood on the wall. The women laugh at their own construction of landlord reasoning:

"Guess he figure niggers don't need no heat."
"Yeah, we supposed to be from Africa, anyway. And it's so hot over there them folks don't know what oil is." (182)

But Kiswana does not laugh, failing to understand either the humor's focus or the primacy of mutual, collective laughter among women and how it matters more than a point of geographical accuracy:

Everybody laughed but Kiswana. "You know, that's not really true. It snows in some parts of Africa, and Nigeria is one of the most important exporters of oil in the world."

Similarly, the women themselves stop laughing when Theresa comes out of the building, laughter failing once again when group solidarity fails. When Kiswana tries to convince Ciel that the "blood" on the bricks is really rainwater, Ciel responds, "Does it matter? Does it really matter?" This different Ciel, who has felt the dream of a "me" who is a "her," realizes that the presence or absence of specific evidence for oppression matters less than the women's felt merger, their collective sense of agency. At Ciel's insistent provocation, Kiswana overcomes the difference that keeps her correcting and chafing "from above" and shares the felt cognition that makes protest possible: "She wept and ran to throw the brick spotted with her blood out into the avenue" (187). Kiswana's Block Association organizes for social change "from above" in a combination of coalition and identity politics consistent with the extent to which she herself cannot laugh among women nor accept Lorraine's and Theresa's lesbianism (witness her lame "Why can't good friends just live together and people mind their own business. And even if you're not friends, even . . . well, whatever").

Perceived as a "riot" by the taxi driver, the women's following protest affirms not only Kiswana's transformation but also Theresa's necessary inclusion. Confronted with a brick to throw, Kiswana at first "looked as if she had stepped into a nightmare." Mattie, on the other hand, who has come closest to appreciating Lorraine's and Theresa's love ("Maybe it's not so different. . . . Maybe that's why some women get so riled up about it, 'cause they know deep down it's not so different after all" 141), starts the chain of women throwing out the bricks with their oppression figured upon them: "Come on, let's make sure that's the only one." Dream reality revisions Theresa's cynical separatism from the community of women when she assists Cora with a load of bricks and demands that Cora not say "please": "Now, you go back up there and bring me some more, but don't ever say that again—to anyone!" She refers, of course, to Lorraine's pathetic confinement to the last word she uttered in futile appeal and cannot get past ever after, but she also refers to any attitude of supplication. Theresa participates in the protest, (in fact the others bring the bricks to her to throw), and in so doing enacts both the general rejection of all submissive strategies and her own participation in communal identity. As Theresa throws her umbrella away so that she can "have both hands free to help the other women," narration offers a contrasting "almost in perfect unison"—that of the rain and the women's beating hearts—to the last "almost in perfect unison" of Lorraine's pain and Ben's rocking, the horrific blending of Ben's movement with "the sawing pain that kept moving inside of her" (172). The ending of Mattie's dream reality in this moment "almost in perfect unison" envisions the inclusionary logic of women merging with each other and the rain, but that it remains a dream also comments on the felt differences that earlier prevented Kiswana from laughing and the women from including Theresa in their laughter. The cumulative wisdom of the stories has demonstrated that only the laughter casting out difference has potential for resistance. Mattie's dream may fool us because it has none of the blurred edges of dream and none of the images awaiting interpretation, but its framing humor acts as context for the failed internal humor, identifying why struggle "*almost* in perfect unison" (my emphasis) wakes up outside the shifting boundaries between dream and reality, between signifier and signified, between Brewster Place as symbol and Brewster Place as city street. At the end of "The Block Party," when Mattie really does awake, Etta's last line refers to a "party" that both has and has not taken place, in the form of desire inseparable from the jocular mode of her address: "Woman, you still in bed? Don't you know what day it is? We're gonna have a party" (189).

The lyrical last chapter of *The Women of Brewster Place* places the street as both dream and reality, an enduring protest of a specifically black, specifically female kind, with broad implications for a politics of resistance grounded in revelatory connections between local, domestic scenes of personal hurt and increasingly more global systems of oppression. When women characters *in their best moments* throw their laughter off one another and meld into each other as subjects, they enable the "dream" of difference without power, solidarity without assimilation, and subjectivity with fluid, dialogical boundaries (not some "melting pot" sense of community). With characters neither constituted as ego-centered selves nor valued for any easy, instrumental agency, such subjectivity—though not explicitly excluding a racial or a gendered other—validates no comfortable readerly desire for altruistic interrelations among women and, by extension, among all people. Rather, the symbolic suspension of time at the work's close coincides with a specifically plural, collective sense of agency among these women, based not on altruism but on a sense of survival that disallows any felt sense of difference. Readings informed by particular subject-positions—the black, the feminist, the lesbian—understandably chafe against a level of action that may seem a romantic, passively enduring response to grotesque social injustice, yet the romance comes without the trappings of romance, in a dream protest with real bricks and real laughter. How trivial or meaningful the protest has much to do with how any "I," as reader, positions a self in relation to when laughter works and when it fails, one's own position in the relations of power invoked here, the capacity to take up the bricks and see one's blood upon them. And readerly positioning affects, too, whether symbolic primacy attends the "death" of Brewster Place or its projected rebirth as figured in the phoenix rising from its ashes.

A Critically Utopian Mode

Both *The Color Purple* and *The Women of Brewster Place* purposely blur issues of subjective agency with cumulative expansions that exclude from value those whose positions include the privileges attending power. Though not explicitly excluding a gendered or a racial other, both move toward an inclusive suspension of individuated subjectivity, one that bears little relation to the somewhat smarmy picture of born-again women that would make of *The Color Purple* something in the direction of comic romance and of *The Women of Brewster Place* something in the direction of either an older, devalued realism or an equally devalued sentimental utopianism. Neither case offers anything so simple as some affirmation about resistance requiring humor. Rather, a humorous, intersubjective agency itself becomes the textual embodiment of value, the value of a responsiveness most forcefully undermining the subject-object relations on which power relies.

The relation-in-difference of these texts addresses the difficulty of imagining equitable power relations without imagining what must happen to different forms of difference. The exhilaration of *The Color Purple*'s sense of an ending sets it far apart from the more horrific images that remain with us at the end of *The Women of Brewster Place*. Yet the quite different strategies of each address what Andrée Nicola McLaughlin calls "multiple jeopardy," all those differentials in power relations that constitute the specificity of oppressions. *The Color Purple*'s ending has clear relation to a utopian vision, yet remains unwilling to relinquish its critical ties to actual social worlds. *The Women of Brewster Place* has more ambivalent relation to the actual because the inclusionary logic of women merging with each other and the rain remains a dream. Yet the difference between the celebration crowded into a white holiday at the end of *The Color Purple* and the merger of dream and reality at the end of *The Women of Brewster Place* should not mask a similarity in a utopian vision that retains—however differently as read from different subject positions—its critical reference to the real. *The Women of Brewster Place* may well take its present from the space-time of black urban removal, with the decay of the inner city its backdrop. But as a migration narrative, its affirmations rest firmly in the values Mattie and Miss Eva bring with them from the South as they adapt to the forms of resistance required by Brewster Place.[27] Without the literary signs of the wish-fulfilling dream of romance, this dream bears every descriptive imprint of the real; and therein lies its difference from either an older, Western realism or a sentimental utopianism. It has neither a nostalgic view of a prior state nor a context of wish-fulfilling changes in status that might diminish the cost of becoming "us" to dominant subjectivity.

Both texts bring subjectivity back to human form (not just for discourse anymore) and affirm a laughter thrown among "us" as the normalcy of a subjective agency felt as merger, a normalcy that resists the dominance implicit in both subject-object relations and the discourses of power. If such laughter comes closer to essentialism, to positing some chosen, constructed reality (black women's laughter and community) as a first-order one, then it does so only to the degree that "presentness," as opposed to presence, implies both a readerly penchant for engaging characters as analogous to embodied selves, however fluid in construction, and the importance of real-world constructions to just about everyone who lives in one.[28] These texts address any estrangement from the value of a laughter that a dominant critic could only possess by changing her place among power relations (and among the expressive traditions they create). And what better a substitution than a resistant laughter—as focus and as trope—for marking the self-elevating abstractions of any critical distancing?

This humor's invitation to the reader involves not so much either the identifying empathy of realism or the intellectual/spiritual desire of romance. Here interaction works more on the model of generative call and response, where each response acts as another call at the same time that it comments on a responding, regressive resistance to answering fully, that is, by laying down the book and changing one's life. The comic wit of John Barth, Thomas Pynchon, or even Leonora Carrington relies on distancing strategies with roots in the ironic fragmentations of fantastic, apocalyptic, or abstracted modes. A humor embodying "a form of power that is exercised at the very limits of identity and authority" may well *not* take place in contexts fulfilling generic expectations;[29] humorous intersubjectivity acts as a context for storytelling that begins from an angle of passionate engagement with interlocking identities, and as such, its treatment of subject-object relations refuses to engage Susan Suleiman's question about whether black women writers regard race or gender as priorities.[30] Remember that when Sofia helps Eleanor Jane she does so because Eleanor Jane has begun to see through white altruism and has begun to understand that no less than her own "salvation" depends on finding a work not imbued with assumptions of privilege *of any kind.*

If resistance is not simply *there* in a text, but produced and reproduced through the constitutive codes necessarily embedded in genre, trope, figure, and mode (Slemon 31), then readers who read from different subject positions will have quite different responses to this textual call. From my own reading position, the response of "I want to be like that" or "I want to have those values in my life" carries with it the cognitive dissonance attending much white, privileged admiration of black culture, the unsaid "But not at that cost, not living like *that,* not relinquishing the 'I' who moves in the world as a separate, individuated self, and not—especially not—giving up the privilege that allows me to read from this position, the one reading, speaking, writing, thinking now."[31] (Again, Walker's poetic voice serves as gloss: "Their envy of us / has always been / our greatest crime" [*Her Blue Body* 435].) The case of laughter here mitigates any appropriative presumption of utopian inclusion, for its roots lie in a history specific to a felt repudiation of the mythology, indeed the metaphysics, of a unitary self.[32] As readers, our own positions regarding privilege in the world—as well as our diverse ways of resisting, repressing, or evading them—affect the degree to which the implications of intersubjective humor seem threatening or comfortable. Readers made aware of white, male, class, or heterosexual privilege will find themselves caught, I suspect, in unlikely combinations of desire, intimacy, and fear.

The Color Purple and *The Women of Brewster Place* engage readers in reflective responses about implied analogies between how characters relate to each other, how speech relates to writing, and how writers relate to readers. The intersubjectivity in both, however differently situated from the identity formations of readers, demands only *some* readerly relation to "what authentic solidarity with the oppressed demands" (hooks, "Writing the Subject" 188). But for reading positions of privilege, caught in the tension between desire and quite literal self-repudiation, the humorous rapport that formally links flexible, processual characterization with a valued intersubjectivity has much to teach: it teaches that, as long as theory privileges tropes "from above," it will not undermine the subjectivities it likes to declare obsolete; that resistance need not be conceived *only* in the conflictual terms of weapons, targets, and combat—or indeed any instrumentality—but also in constructions of value resisting an ego-centered, individually-achieving and performing self; and that only relinquishing *actual* social power—not just that in discursive formations—affords any hope of salvation.

Chapter 3
Tragedy and Comedy Reborn(e)

The Critical Soul-Journeys in *A Question of Power* and *The Salt Eaters*

That is the partial tragedy of resistance, that it must to a certain degree work to recover forms already established or at least influenced or infiltrated by empire.
—Edward Said, *Culture and Imperialism*

This terror of power and an examination of its stark horrors created a long period of anguish in my life and forced out of me some strange novels that I had not anticipated writing.

It was almost as though the books wrote themselves, propelled into existence by the need to create a reverence for human life in an environment and historical circumstances that seem to me a howling inferno.
—Bessie Head, "Notes from a Quiet Backwater II"

It pleases me to blow three or four choruses of just sheer energetic fun and optimism, even in the teeth of rats, racists, repressive cops, bomb lovers, irresponsibles, murderers.
—Toni Cade Bambara, "What It Is I Think I'm Doing Anyhow"

The Need for Reverence

Since tragedy and comedy thrive on their paradoxical relation to both systems of order and seductions of disorder, they have potentially meaningful relation to any artful placement of human experience in paradox large enough to include cosmic myth.[1] Yet several contemporary voices argue that dominant conceptions of tragedy and comedy have always mediated resistance (personal, philosophical, or literary) and brought it ultimately under the control of some higher order recognizable within Western philosophical and religious traditions.[2] And this mediation, its importance in describing what constitutes higher order, determines whether and how one sees the awe or the solidarity necessary to a complexly situated, paradoxical resistance. If the forms of representation necessarily differ as much as other cultural constructions, then dominant predispositions tend to level the moral ambiguities that trouble both identity-formation and such values as the good, the just, the necessary, and the true.[3] For any resistance under severe duress must confront whatever dominances separate the tragic from the comic as surely as the female from the male, nature from culture, self from other, and so on. In this chapter, I want to turn to the interconnections of tragic and comic resistance, interconnections linking "the choice word, the chosen silence," in Morrison's phrase, "whether it laughs out loud or is a cry without an alphabet."[4]

As stories of suffering and healing that grow out of the troubled interconnection of intracultural and intercultural struggle, Head's *A Question of Power* and Bambara's *The Salt Eaters* create reverent, processual responses to the hurt of dominant myths. And they offer different but related interrogations of a set of moral, spiritual, and aesthetic presumptions often attending tragedy's opposition to comedy. Most descriptions of blues consciousness emphasize an experience of tragic worlds as "not without laughter" (in Langston Hughes's phrase), yet critical theory has not taken seriously a healing that undermines the separation between tragic catharsis and comic release. The healing rituals central to Head and Bambara help elaborate the solidarity and the moral connections linking pain and humor; and such healing makes possible a conception of tragic and comic modes more dovetailed or merged than easily oppositional.

In provocative narrative art difficult to place within Euro-American genres, *A Question of Power* and *The Salt Eaters* together suggest a revisionary, expansionary view of both tragic awe and comic rapport as potentially permeable, even simultaneous modes.[5] And they elaborate a movement of spirit that takes both worldly and cosmic systems of order more seriously and yet more critically and more provisionally than do dominant ideologies of the terrible and the funny.[6] In doing so, they ask readers to locate the position of their own (com)passion, or its lack, in relation to the mocking smile of Head's Medusa (the parodic tormentor in a social tragedy taking place both without and within) and to the humanized Medusa of Bambara's mental landscape (the sign of a comedy able to heal from within in a tragically divided world).

As with all the texts in Part I, neither *A Question of Power* nor *The Salt Eaters* provides a mimetic view of resistance (in which case Head's Motabeng village and Bambara's Claybourne would seem to have confused, rather than mythic, reference to actual places). Rather, narrative representation serves to reveal subjective complicity in characters' struggles against totalizing systems of power. In *Beloved*, vicarious witnesses come to bearing witness through a rigorous unraveling of their own complicities and a cathartic identification with something formerly judged as separate from themselves; and they do so through an intersubjective process related to but different from merely tragic *knowing* because it leads to supportive action. In the tragic/comic modes of *A Question of Power* and *The Salt Eaters,* two women, both made sick by their worlds, struggle to achieve some normalcy of work and relationship despite systems of power already bound up in who they *are.* In both cases, complex narrative strategies reveal processes neither clearly "internal" nor "external" but always involved in how to live in a world "where even when you were a solution you were a problem." That they must do so remains the social tragedy of these worlds' "dominant, raucous demands," where these characters as protagonists find effective resistance, as in Morrison, in intersubjective moments when the psyche, indeed the whole affective world, does not seem at the service of already constructed power. In these moments, they do not necessarily change their worldly position, but they imagine themselves on a scale in which—in the words of Obioma Nnaemeka—"victims are equally agents, and oppressors are also victims; [and] violence is not a male but a human problem" (Nnaemeka, *Sisterhood* 21).

Exalting the Ordinary

In its focus on the ethical and spiritual parameters of violence, *A Question of Power* bears relation to the Dionysian violence so central to Euripides, though in less oppositional terms; here the "liberating forces of nature" do not triumph over the "repressive forces of culture."[7] Rather, the given divisions between mind and body, nature and culture, female and male refuse to stay separate within the central character, Elizabeth, for whom cycles of madness ritually enact the terrible consequences of a social domination validated by every level of experience, from the local authorities to the gods.

The stages and character of the violences suffered by Elizabeth concentrate in symbolic form "the profound complicity between morality and the amoral, between civilized existence and violence."[8] Neither blameless except for failures in knowing, like Oedipus, nor caught up in a world with no way of validating any truth, like Hamlet, Elizabeth's much more ordinary life embodies a combinatory relation to epistemology: she does not exist separately from the man-gods who torture her, and her felt cognition of "truth" struggles to reconcile the contaminated discourses of spiritual and social order with the positive experiences that hold together communal life. Elizabeth must negotiate for her own sanity with figures both mythic and "vividly alive," figures derived in part from multiple religious traditions and in part from witty, contemporary reference to sociohistorical power.

Usually any emphasis on tragic suffering as an ordinary part of life accompanies a deemphasis on tensions between order and disorder of cosmic proportions; a problematics of what comprises moral virtue overtakes a focus on human agency.[9] On the contrary, the narrative art of *A Question of Power* places even the simplest acts of working, mothering, and loving within a mythic depiction of "forces hostile to human virtues."[10] Moral ambiguity pervades what Elizabeth undergoes in a "madness" clearly inseparable from the tragically mad world that engendered her. Complex narrative perspectives and juxtapositions artfully suppress or displace information about when or whether Elizabeth shares a narrative overview, and narrative art suspends, too, any readerly security about the precise nature of forms both "intangible" and "vividly alive." A narrative voice, for example, frequently asserts judgments about what passes for sanity and humanity in her world, but only in passing, and only as an almost allusive suggestion to alternative possibility. Thus, after Elizabeth hears from her foster-mother about her white mother's incarceration in a mental hospital for having borne a child by a native, she thrills to the story of her white grandmother's stubborn insistence on visiting the familial outcasts: "It was such a beautiful story, the story of the grandmother, her defiance, her insistence on filial ties in a country where people were not people at all" (17). Clearly Elizabeth, too, found it a beautiful story, but reference to "the grandmother" distances the locution from some easily mimetic mirror of Elizabeth's consciousness. Elizabeth's own story proceeds according to the linear logic of external action: Elizabeth worked, lived, married, broke down, all in a past-definite modality where she *had* to treat people as though they existed, even those male figures who represent alternatively seductive and brutal oppression in visions always linking worldy and otherworldly systems of power.

The question of narrative voice and multiple tonalities in *A Question of Power* corresponds to the inadequacy of Euro-American distinctions between fictional and non-fictional genres to describe its dominant mode. The events in *A Question of Power* roughly approximate the events Head describes in her own life, yet take place in a fictional world where personal narrative acquires mythic resonance. As Carole Boyce Davies has demonstrated ("Private Selves and Public Spaces"), Euro-American feminist models of autobiography do not necessarily address the most characteristic modes of African women's writing, modes strongly in the tradition of oral lifestories. These modes shift among a self described as synonymous with political struggle, a self presented in dialogue with family and/or sociocultural history, and a self identified in resistance to patriarchal/racial order. Davies portrays each self as in constant dialogue with its Others, in common with some of the strategies of African women's autobiography.[11] Such processual shifts among multiply positioned narrative selves in African women's writing, Davies suggests, frequently stress both the unreality of autobiography and the self-revelatory nature of fictions.

Understandably, a conception of tragedy that begins with any oppositional sense of cosmic myth and personal history may make judgments presuming much, judgments that devalue the connective artistry of writers for whom such distinctions do not serve. Unlike the stories by African men writers that so often begin after a struggle and that speak retrospectively and collectively for a nation or group, often "African man," African women's modes of narrating often struggle toward negotiating personhood and make as few gestures toward representing African women at large as they do toward belonging to *either* real or imagined worlds. That Bessie Head should consider the art of *A Question of Power* "a kind of . . . autobiography book" (Dovey 33), despite its fictionalized constructs, seems mandated by the intensity of the title's question as it figures in the most strenuous psychic interrogations of power relations. Here, rather than refer to already formed myth, character, and history, the personal history/fiction of *A Question of Power* interrogates the very framing of the mythic systems that give shape to history and definition to character.

Relatedly, Head's nonfiction essays stress the difference between the position of those who speak of resistance from the sure ground of already forged identity and her own troubled position as a displaced person within an African diaspora. By extension, she understands that any America able to resist the raucous demands of dominance would also be able to "[take] note of the future greatness of the African continent" (72). Accordingly, in tandem with her criticism of American arrogance, she positions herself as someone who learns "deep compassion" from an African American friend who merges in her mind with a created, feminine counterpart of God: "It seems to me that I shall never forget her big, flashing, black eyes and her universal compassion for the Sudras or underdogs of the world" ("God and the Underdog" 46). Sometimes resenting her friend's "battering and bashing" ("I always seemed to have my mouth open and she always seemed to be bashing something down it"), Head describes the nature of her own psychic violences, specifically differentiated from her African American friend's capacity to focus on "who was going to feed the poor":

There's nothing neat and tidy about me, like a nice social revolution. With me goes a mad, passionate, insane, screaming world of ten thousand devils and the man or God who lifts the lid off this suppressed world does so at his peril. (*A Woman Alone* 47)

Accordingly, the progressive forms of Elizabeth's illness correspond to her degree of enthrallment to forms flatly asserted as "there," and yet intangibly linked to her lack of control over her own subjectivity. Her illness makes it impossible to sustain the simplest and most rewarding forms of work and relationship precisely at those moments when visions neither internal nor external, neither self nor other, reveal her complicity in the systems that make identity possible. Like the initially vicarious witnesses in *Beloved*, Elizabeth purges a judgmental alienation from systems of power that include herself, and her mode of tragedy belongs to those systems' continued power and to their demand that she feign accommodation.

Elizabeth undergoes the horrors of upbringing under apartheid in South Africa and subsequently moves to Motabeng, a village in Botswana where—although still ostracized by many local people for her difference—she finds humane acceptance among those working for a nonracist society and for economic independence from South Africa: the principal of the Motabeng Secondary School, the head of the "local industries" project (Eugene), a Peace Corps volunteer (Tom), and a woman who works under Elizabeth's tutelage in the village garden (Kenosi). Elizabeth's breakdowns in this period of self-exile to Botswana project the terrifying legacy of racist, sexist, classist, and heterosexist myths onto the healing work she undertakes in the postcolonial context. Though often explicated by critics within either the tensions of autobiographical (re)presentation or psychopathology, Elizabeth's "soul-journeys" proceed not according to the logic of some sequential "plot," but according to the dramatized logic of a self constructed under multiple oppressions and de/reconstructed through powerful self-interrogations.[12] Even when narration presents seemingly external action straightforwardly, it often merges matter of fact presentation of Elizabeth's psychic misery with the mythic expansion of that misery in the form of her spiritual struggle with Sello and Dan, two men-gods who walk in and out of her consciousness in accordance with her experience of liminal, marginal identity. Because of this frightening intermeshing of Elizabeth's sense of self with that of the men-gods who threaten her, her mind races within a kind of foreshortened present where she symbolizes more a problem in self-conceiving than some personality disorder. However particularized in its luminous detail, her suffering consistently takes on the highest level of abstraction as it confronts cruelties that exist always in the plural as only one "of a kind."[13]

Even the manner and tonality of narration elaborates a problematics of how both consciousness and conscience depend on relations of power. Declarative sentences take Elizabeth from explosive detail to explosive detail in her struggle *not* to become the subject made by "prophetic" systems. Without emotive pause in the telling, seemingly in prose without affect, narration asserts the most terrible experience as a painfully ordinary sequence; appalling events follow each other in almost methodic rhythms, such that sudden, startling displacements present themselves as normalcy. Note, for example, how iterative declarative syntax reinforces Elizabeth's failure to face the events that seem to acquire an assertive power of their own:

Women were always complaining of being molested by her husband. Then there was also a white man who was his boy-friend. After a year she picked up the small boy and walked out of the house, never to return. She read a newspaper advertisement about teachers being needed in Botswana. She was forced to take out an exit permit, which, like her marriage, held the "never to return" clause. (19)

And shortly following, note how the word "just" carries the daily weight of a white hatred so normative, so naturalized, that it can only suggest new periods of pain:

It was like living with permanent nervous tension, because you did not know why white people there had to go out of their way to hate you or loathe you. They were just born that way, hating people, and a black man or woman was just born to be hated. There wasn't any kind of social evolution beyond that, there wasn't any lift to the heart, just this vehement vicious struggle between two sets of people with different looks; and, like Dan's brand of torture, it was something that could go on and on and on. (19)

Like "Dan's brand of torture," narration continuously provides a stark interweaving of a "normalcy" characterized by "not-people," an insane "sanity," with Elizabeth's mental nightmares enacting the explicitly mythic dimensions of her resistance. Thus even Sello's "good" prophecies deny Elizabeth any personal autonomy; she finds herself with "no distinct face of her own" and included in religious prophecies that will destroy her when Dan defeats Sello and assumes "directorship of the universe." Always, Elizabeth finds herself in the position of one forced to use the categories that threaten to destroy her, and the socioreligious constructs that order her nightmare also contaminate the world of daily experience.

Thus *A Question of Power* does not *only* (re)present some African response to the Manichean legacy of colonialism, though familiar dualisms sometimes inform both the prose and the criticism.[14] Rather, Sello-Dan's tyrannical superimposition of prophets and visions dramatizes Elizabeth's vulnerability to a spirituality that validates who she is, yet in terms dangerous to coherent subjectivity (only loosely caught in a singular sense of "identity"). Elizabeth's internal questioning interrogates the reasons for her suffering, but it does so from within a frame of reference where "sanity" and "insanity" derive from the contingencies of power. Accordingly, Elizabeth's ordinary life, most importantly her work as mother, gardener, and community member, finds itself part of a mythic interrogation of personal choice: both social and divine constraints problematize the very notion of choice, so that she feels compromised by her own victimization. Elizabeth's terror emanates from a developing certainty that she has chosen, without knowing or willing it some complicity in her own destruction. This seems reminiscent of Berke's tragic formula, "A mythical self-annihilator annihilates himself with an instrument of self-annihilation" (24), except that Head renders obsolete any such easy instrumentality in subject-object relations. With narrative perspectives reiterating paradoxical truths, Elizabeth experiences both victimization and agency, both complicity and resistance. Her soul-journeys take her in and out of madness in the form of visions that do not exist separately from living and do not behave like nightmares. Rather, like daymares of a waking self, they specifically threaten any sustaining or affirming identity of herself as woman, as mother, and as African.

A magical, surreal torture invokes mythic identifications with female sexuality and motherhood (both the actual mothering of a child and the symbolic mothering that secures a human future). Sello's idealizations of a future, indeed a whole discourse of goodness that Elizabeth accepts as her own, becomes compromised by his introduction of a sexuality where manipulative power relations compromise all sexual engagement. It does so in a conflictual drama where Medusa, representing an unbridled female sexuality, makes perverse and raucous sexual demands and where an ideal madonna figure stands for perfection but fills Sello with murderous instincts to kill whenever confronted with actual, earthly sexuality. When in the thrall of Medusa, Sello's lust extends to child abuse and a whole panoply of perversions; when crying out for the beauty and perfection of the madonna, he cannot keep from killing instincts toward ordinary women: "when the mind of the monk was turned down towards earthly things he became a grotesque murderer" (99).[15] Sello's and Dan's homosexuality raises the whole question of how to take a homophobia so essential to Head's description of perversion that it has clear culture-wide sanction; in her cultural vision of men turning to homosexuality because deprived by force of their manhood, male homosexual relationships take on metonymic force for all perversions. But this homophobic vision does not represent the only possible form of love between men, just as Medusa's is not the only form of heterosexual love; rather, socioreligious oppression enforces these haunting specters of the perverse.

In fact, a densely figurative language sets up as metonymies all the relations implied by Sello's vision, suggesting an infinite process of flexible and extending power relations: Sello is to Elizabeth as father to daughter, as doctor to patient, as man to woman, as European to African, as any dominant to any subordinate. In this, Head's literary, symbolic space does not represent, but nevertheless bears relation to, the diverse (post)colonial experience of African women as represented in the writings of Africana feminisms. These feminisms, despite a corollary diversity in strategies for negotiating multiple forms of oppression, consistently articulate a refusal to foreground gender in colonial and postcolonial contexts characterized by the racist economic institutions that make poverty a way of life for the majority of black men and women in Africa and the African diaspora. Relevantly, these feminisms also describe dangerously achieved forms of women's resistance as the legacy of empowering traditions often concealed in postcolonial or nationalist institutions, traditions making women powerful both as spiritual presences and as active participants in production and economic life.[16] Here the Medusa's torments range wildly, but not allegorically, among master narratives' oppressions.[17] For the Medusa tries not only to alienate Elizabeth from her own sexuality, but also to alienate her by extension from all the forms of belonging that rely on identity (to community, nation, or the African continent).

Since Elizabeth plays participant-observer in a mythic drama enacting mutually conflicting demands on women (to be both sexually desirable and a soul-symbol of purity, to be both child and yet mother to the child she cannot protect, to both belong to Africa and yet escape the negative connotations of Africanity), she undergoes her first breakdown into a "madness" characterized by classification systems breaking down, not just in facing conflicted sexual feeling but in trying to reconcile the weight of mythic systems—signed by Medusa or an Egyptian priesthood—with her own experiential values.

Similarly, Dan's more explicitly perverse, more spectacular array of sexual experiences sets Elizabeth up in competition with a series of women as extraordinary sexual performers, all humiliating to watch, but most humiliating in the elaborate way Dan engages her own sexual feelings in the act of watching. Dan carefully orchestrates how his female symbol-characters enact their names' suggestiveness: Miss Wriggly-Bottom, The Womb, Miss Body Beautiful, Miss Pink Sugar-Icing, Miss Chopper, Madame Loose-Bottom, Madame Make-Love-On-the-Floor (where "anything goes") and so on. With particular focus on how they play to Elizabeth, Dan then interrupts Elizabeth's daily life with superim-

positions of his scenes, making even her least tainted relationships grotesque. With the visions taking over, Elizabeth withdraws from her child
and finally attacks a white woman in the village who has made of her a
"silent listener" (170). She feels herself become mad again with the incapacity to reconcile any of Dan's horrors with what she knows of value.

The helplessly "feminine" nature of her place in received myths of
good and evil brings on a bout of "madness" when Dan's subtleties manage to "leave nothing that was not tainted with perversity" (119). Thus
the Medusa accuses Elizabeth both of belonging to the debased, victim-
ized Africa of European consciousness and of failing to belong to Africa
at all (because ignorant of African languages).[18] Such madness implies
a resistance to Sello-Dan's version of Africa and African gods, a conflict bound up in figures of "the Father," often old men who warn her
that Dan "does not want the new world" (118). The Medusa's terror links
terrible sexual contradictions with African contradictions that oppose a
dislike for self-importance (witness the chosen proverb "Be ordinary")
to a lust for power:

The wild-eyed Medusa was expressing the surface reality of African society. It
was shut in and exclusive. It had a strong theme of power-worship running
through it, and power people needed small, narrow, shut-in worlds. They never
felt secure in the big, wide flexible universe where there were too many cross-
currents of opposing thought. (38)

The "monstrosities" of the world's mythologies—power-hungry, dominating gods—override both Sello's attempts to keep control of the "God
show" and Elizabeth's own vision of a "mythology without power," where
"philosophies were spun around the everyday events of people's lives
and included the animals, the flowers and the occupations of mankind"
(41). But as Dan threatens to defeat and kill Sello's soul, the performances of Sello-Dan overpower "the compassion and tenderness with
which people regarded each other, the uncertainties of questing within,
the lack of assertion and dominance" (42). Sello's convictions that many
of the gods are white corresponds to Dan's attitude toward the poor; and
the assertions of both convict Elizabeth in her own eyes because they
come too close to her own unconscious or unacknowledged feelings, as
when Dan maligns the poor:

"I don't like them. They're so stupid and cruel." Again Elizabeth was taken off
guard. Didn't she know some unpleasant details about tribal life, a basic cruelty
and lack of compassion that was a part of the African personality? (108)

Just as she rejects Dan's lovers as "shut in and exclusive, a height of
heights known only to the two eternal lovers," so Elizabeth resists both

the Africa of Sello-Dan and that of the white world. On the one hand, she screams to Sello,

I'm not the dog of the Africans, do you hear? I'm not the dog of these bloody bastard Botswana, do you hear? It's you, you and Dan, you who are so weak you don't care where you put your penis. Why must I be the audience of *shit?* (175)

On the other hand, she screams to the white hospital's enforcers of regulations for Africans, "I'm not an African. Don't you see? I never want to be an African. You bloody well, damn well leave me alone" (181). Her "madness" involves the liminal condition of resisting both European and African forms of violence, both the colonialism of South Africa and the colonial legacy in postcolonial Botswana.

Elizabeth's mythic boundary crossing appears most climactically in her resistances both to Sello-Dan's visions and, by mythic extension, to all dominant systems of the spiritual and ethical; and it appears most tragically as well, since her own idealizations keep getting corrupted by the models of worldly power inherent in "the gods within who compete for her soul." Cumulative, carefully interwoven mythic allusions to richly cross-cultural systems work against any cumulative, universalizing sense of belonging. Although none of the received gods and figureheads "took into account a situation with a total lack of compassion" or "recorded seeing what she saw on this nightmare soul-journey," the beauty of sundry religious systems corresponds to her own awakening "love of mankind" (35). The socioreligious systems that make up Elizabeth's frame of reference may inspire her to say, " 'Oh, what a world of love could be created!,' " but they do not help with her soul's dependencies on the hierarchial conceptualizations of "types like Sello [who] were always Brahmin or Rama." Sello's prophecies involve her in complicity with contaminations of the good that lead to death, and Dan's prophecies dramatize her inability to sustain an image of the ideal that can withstand History, Power, and Africa-as-It-Is. Nor can she sustain those parts of her that exist because of what these things have made her. When she bodily enacts how contaminations of the good leave the soul coopted and self-defeating in confronting actual evil, her final bout of madness interweaves the implications of both Sello and Dan.

Having experienced through madness the processual interrelatedness of Sello and Dan, Elizabeth's last soul-journey takes her through something very much like catharsis, but within the terms of the mythic dream about suspending the link between power and identity. The *agon* within emerges in a peace not unlike earlier releases from madness, and, not unlike them, still showing the legacy of entrapments—and yet with a difference. Elizabeth has fought the legacy of hubristic mythologies within herself, in the act of finding her language, her imagery, even her states of feeling already contaminated with first order essence/presence. The end of the work refuses the conservative impulse so often noted within both tragic theory and tragedies themselves to provide a closure that mediates either the particularity of challenge to a moral system or a more generalized moral ambiguity; rather, it foregrounds resistances to authoritative morality within the ongoing tensions between the desire to "belong" to a people, a land, or a moral order, to love one another's humanhood, and at the same time to use the language, the symbol-systems, even the internal discourses that imply power relations anti-thetical to such desire.[19] Cumulatively, the tensions between collective and individual speech become the most brutally conflicted language: both Sello's elevated, prophetic, oracular style and Dan's cynically witty aphorisms and formulations war with Elizabeth's imagistic states of feeling for which narration uses an almost folk simplicity.

How the end means depends on how it juxtaposes reminders of the soul-journeys and their legacy with Elizabeth's communal, worldly joy in once again taking up both personal relationships and the now ailing garden. All those parts of the book with stunningly straightforward narration describe Elizabeth's felt wholeness in relation to nature, to other people, and to her own spirituality. But the spiritual health of these re-lationships—as in her personal relationships to Eugene, to Tom, and to Kenosi—finds no analogue in the mental, linguistic discourses that rely on received systems. Relieved to find that "the world had returned to normal again" (204), Elizabeth nevertheless "could never do anything normally" (203). After her last and most annihilating bout of madness, she has "a permanently giddy head," and she suffers constantly from the ongoing, internal tension of values outside mythic sanctions. When Sello appears once more, she understands, this time, how he has "in-cluded her in his prophecies, which endangered human life," and, even though she still feels the intimacy "of two companions who shared a per-manent joke," she has no way of reconciling daily affirmations with any authoritative moral vision. When she offers him the status of brother, she does so with a canny vision of protecting her own future (or rather, some open slate on which to imagine a future):

"I'll look around for suitable parents for us," she said cunningly. "I'm much better than you at organizing family affairs, and once I find the parents you will always be my favourite brother."
She simply meant she wanted parents who did not believe in prophecies. They boiled down to bugger all, and they made a normal happy person, who loved birds, insects, vegetable gardens and people, the victim of Dan. (201)

Thus, when Sello's laughing response is to open his traveling bag and release an "incandescent light" with "the message of the brotherhood of man," "she left the story like that, unresolved" (201). Because Sello's history, past and future, belongs to the dominance of Old Father Time, even its idealizations can never fully satisfy. In a passage usually ignored, narration frames the context for the book's final vision. Sello says to Elizabeth, " 'You have my wife,' " and "the wife of Buddha" emerges from Elizabeth to settle herself at his feet, knowing "she'd travelled a journey with a man who had always deserted her in a pursuit after things of the soul" (201). Not the sister, as in her own vision, but "the wife of Buddha," this ideal keeps reminding us of its origins in Sello's gambler's heart, always out somewhere "spinning coins."

The work ends with a "gesture of belonging" to an Africa into which she "had fallen from the very beginning," one with "no direct push against those rigid, false social systems of class and caste" (206). Having rejected "god show[s]" at such dire cost, she must experience even peace and joy from within a narration whose irresolution expresses the rich ambiguities of tragic paradox.[20] For Elizabeth, this "happy ending" fulfills the promise of an expanded joy to match a prior expanded pain. A "belonging" inseparable from sleep and thought relates in difference to all those other bursts of cosmic self-reference in which she feels suddenly free of the tormented visions that even her language indicates will come again. The madness is not over yet, and the deal with Sello about parentage and prophecy (surely no less than a negotiation for a past and a future) relies on an intersubjectivity achieved at terrible cost. It depends on an internal suspension of all belief systems and the intensity of desire for a provisional normalcy that does not come with a given cosmic and social order, but must be achieved. She rejects the hierarchy implicit in all the Father-figured dominances linking spiritual and social systems, regarding Sello now "as though they were two companions who shared a permanent joke" (200). A sense of private, personal agency transforms such assertions as "There is only one God and his name is Allah. And Mohammed is his prophet" to "There is only one God and his name is Man. And Elizabeth is his prophet"; the context affirms "the brotherhood of man" but places the language as belonging to the kind of "slippery resolution" characteristic of totalizing systems.[21] Elizabeth as her own prophet may fall asleep in "a gesture of belonging," but does not pretend to be able to sustain a story beyond that of "the clamour of horrors" precisely because she has not the power of the prophet to envision a future: "Whatever would happen next she could not say, because her mind retreated to its own privacy" (201). Her own "private thought" shimmers with light, necessarily reminding us of Sello's bag of light and its control of the public discourses from which thought must pluck its personal story.[22] Elizabeth's hard-won "gesture of belonging" does not close the work in an idealization of some monolithic Africa;

rather, the gesture suspends false holinesses as negotiable, especially in those moments not relegating "all things holy" to unseen worlds but subverting the holy to present, ordinary experience.

Made in the context of "private thought," such affirmation remains paradoxical because also a part of a dominant, public history's discourse surrounding "the brotherhood of man." In Caroline Rooney's apt terms, such paradox both embraces Head's understanding of "the inexplicability of the experience—that is, the impossibility of the attempt to transcribe it further—and at once demonstrates that the process of writing, or writing up, is simultaneously one of speculative interpretation" (118). Read thus, *A Question of Power* does not most fundamentally elaborate a thematic focus on the evil and corruptibility of human nature (Goddard) or, alternatively, on the ultimate "goodness of mankind" (Gover); rather, it explores what it means to "belong" to a world in which one's most joyous, healthy, and spiritual moments find themselves bound up in the power of oppressor-others and oppressive systems. The work's structural, stylistic rhythms capture readers not so much in a prison house of language as in a prison house of power, while simultaneously elaborating both the strategies and the costs of resistance in such a world.[23]

Head's difficult and magnificent work suggests a way of theorizing the mythic in the modes of women's imagining close to oral traditions, and by extension in any of those modes felt closer to the rhythms and actions of life on the underside of power. Here grandeur does not depend on spectacles of public performance, the larger-than-life actions of the empowered that bring them to the experience of powerlessness. When autobiography, oral narrative, or mythic realism creates "ordinary" characters with tragic resonance, such characters do not fling themselves headlong into tensions between the moral order they think they enact and some higher moral order they cannot or do not see at the time of action. Rather, the seeming normalcy of received moral systems dramatizes their liminal positions, and "action" or "development" often comprises a kind of discovery that comes only from overachieving a dominant moral code. Horrific fantasms or experiences reveal characters as both victims and agents in framing subjectivity, demonstrating the implications and consequences of values both false and contrary to an achieved sense of relational spirituality (without power dominance). In this case, tragic knowing means "choosing" what one did not choose, an alternative spirituality sustained despite its costs, a paradoxical resistance that accepts the fact of a processual, always-becoming "self," but not the processes themselves, not the machinations of power. This alternative tragic mode rejects a theological value system that makes tragedy possible only because of some divine rationale, thus mediating horror into some higher order. Rather, a spiritualized sense of belonging gets born in struggle with how the world is; here, characters find themselves even if they must "suspend" the problem of how to narrate themselves (that is, how to sustain themselves in any of the extant discourses of public history). Far from the stature of Euro-American tragic protagonists who become extraordinary through speech, they come to resistance through the horrors of experience presumed ordinary and only an achieved sense of agency asserts continued, visionary resistance with *phronesis* (practical wisdom embodied in work) as its highest value, usually in the context of a redefined community exalting the ordinary, the poor, and the powerless.

Bessie Head's *A Question of Power* taps many of the forces widely associated with powerlessness and gender across the cultures—the liminal, the irrational, the emotional, the mad-hysterical—and in so doing endows her central character's suffering with a grandeur evident as such only within the context of a mythic struggle against that part of herself coopted by power relations.[24] She suggests that however diverse or multiple the tragic positioning of such characters, their moral crises work themselves out in terror that lies precisely in the fact of an already complicit subjectivity (Judith Butler would say *produced* through the effects of power rather than internalized [*The Psychic Life*]); and such work has explicitly subversive relation to public history. Recent feminist interest in Euripidean tragedy suggests a related interrogation of gender and value, one reliant on a necessary link between women's myths and internal crisis.[25] Yet for the marginalized, "playing the other" may involve internally conflicted values, and tragic possibility growing out of such marginalized suffering may well foreground problems of complicity, terrible identity trouble, and concomitant self-disgust, exactly those things Head elaborates through Elizabeth. Most significantly, Head, perhaps because of her marginal relation to a number of traditions' hierarchial models, elaborates how *peripeteia*—the move from mastery to weakness, from control to surrender—takes very different form for any Other who begins by experiencing the underside of power and control.[26] "A shared awareness of shared energy," James Snead's phrase for the African conception of universality, captures the motivation behind reversals that affirm without prophecy or resolution. Appropriately, when Snead associates African universality with a nonexclusive "contagion" ("recoverable *affinities* between disparate races of people" in opposition to a western "collection" of differences), he finds the best western counterpart of such metonymic "invasion" (*con+tangere*= "touching together") in Euripides' *The Bacchae*.

This alternative tragic mode relies on a particular kind of dislocation, that which occurs when what has seemed natural or normal becomes suddenly revealed as a social construct, vulnerable even in the very processes of identity formation. Despite attempts to fulfill socioreligious expectations, characters without initial status or power find themselves engaged in the moral ambiguities of a felt critique of virtue, life lived liminally with the tensions of margins, the forces against mediation to higher order, and the strongest resistances to the logic of authority and power. The concomitant tragic mode implies specifically paradoxical forms of resistance, which may or may not have clearly instrumental value as resistance to those viewing work and relationships from outside such systems. No pure resistance exists in either actual worlds or literary texts, suggests such theory, and resistance will always reveal in some way its partial complicity with what it resists.[27]

This tragic worldview does not inhere in the "fall" of a unitary self, but in the continued power of a world that mandates entering a state resembling madness and illness—and yet of one's own choosing and making—as the only means to wholeness. Thus these tragic forms are full of strategies that catch the reader-spectator in a frightening/pitiful complicity for which no final resolution emerges and from which no final detachment is possible.[28] With no myth more prevalent than that of the autonomous self, and nothing more "self-annihilating" than the knowledge that what one thought one chose was unknowingly already chosen, many of these fictions find themselves interrogating from within the "always already" chosen.[29] What looks like self-annihilation from one perspective may from another look like wholeness, since what comprises *intelligible* cause within the realm of human action changes with positioning. A protagonist who begins on the underside of power may not die, but rather undergo successive deathlike attempts at understanding and resistance (deathlike because attendant on a concept of self that by definition precludes acceptance in the world in which one thinks one believes).[30] Head's soul-journeys challenge which definitions stand for reason and intelligibility, whose myths have communal sanction and, after finding much of the spiritual world in cahoots with worldly powers, whose resolutions create the public discourses of time and history. "Rebirth" in this context implies the most extreme suffering, a death-surrogate figured in madness, isolation, or mythic entrapment, but may or may not suggest some alternative "self" that survives the fiction. Rather, it posits an alternative way of conceiving the agency that creates value, especially spiritual value, not as part of some received system with others as prophets, disciples, and patriarchs, but as forged through *phronesis* (here a communal work), supportive interpersonal relations, and a soul imagined as active presence.[31]

"Choices Tossed into the Street like Dice"

Always willing to "[lift] the lid off this suppressed world," Toni Cade Bambara's robust "wholesomeness" avoids no one's screaming and makes possible a dialogical understanding—as in the African/African American dialogue described by Head—of how resistance works through paradoxical interactions and changes with its positioning. Related in difference to *A Question of Power*, Bambara's *The Salt Eaters* also makes a Medusa figure represent crises in a central character's soul-journey. Set in the town of Claybourne (the bourne of clay), the narrative present focuses on a black woman brought to a healing at a progressive local Infirmary, one combining the good offices of the traditional healer Minnie Ransom, who presides over this healing, with the medicine of local doctors. Velma Henry comes to the healing stool after an attempted suicide, and her internal, affective processes have no clear separation, narrative or spiritual, from the crises of others. Fragmented stories create sustained correspondences between the black community's factions in the face of oppressive power and Velma's fragmented self; indeed, the space-time of Velma's healing coincides with the community's preparation for the reenactment of the Crispus Attucks Rebellion, a communal holiday, and a growing storm-music. In a sustained symbolism, a disordered music corresponds to the disordered body:

Calcium or lymph or blood uncharged, congealed and blocked the flow, stopped the dance, notes running into each other in a pileup, the body out of tune, the melody jumped the track, discordant and strident. (48)

Throughout the healing, Minnie plays recordings and hums and croons in a music made possible by shared suffering (and always linked to black musical traditions). She calls out the loas, the Vodou spirits who aid healing through a possession of the spirit-guide herself, in a process of identification so strong that Minnie must also plead for help from her own spirit-guide, now deceased but present *in spiritu* as Old Wife.

Because Velma's disorder does not narratively disentangle itself from that of others, much of *The Salt Eaters*, like *Beloved*, follows a woman's crisis as inseparable from that of the community who has sloughed off her trouble as belonging to her and not to themselves. But if at the beginning the community, in this case that represented by the audience of onlookers at the infirmary, see themselves as different from "that Henry gal," the cumulative stages of her healing correspond to cathartic moments for these communal others, their gradual acknowledgement of the myriad ways in which Velma's hurt belongs to them too.

In a narrative transition mirrored by the logic of interwoven stories,

Sophie (M'Dear) Heywood looks at Velma's forlorn figure on the healing stool, but remembers the dragging and beating of her own son Smitty. In keeping with her processes of identification,

Sophie Heywood closed the door of the treatment room. And there was some-thing in the click of it that made many of the old-timers, veterans of the incessant war—Garveyites, Southern Tenant Associates, trade unionists, Party members, Pan-Africanists—remembering night riders and day traitors and the cocking of guns, shudder. (15)

The presentness of shared adversaries and horrors comes back to those in the position of witness, making them shudder for themselves as much as for Velma. Such intersubjective moments provide the backdrop for the ongoing intersubjectivity of spirit possession, the basis of the overtly humorous rapport between Minnie (who speaks out loud) and Velma (who responds internally). This dialogue becomes itself part of another dialogue, the other interchange between Minnie's internal speech and the words of Old Wife that appear in the text as spoken dialogue, given the quoted reality of spirit-speech. Humorous banter revolves around each healer-mentor's willingness to share the suffering and her chiding awareness that the responsibility of agency can be borne together, but must be borne nonetheless.

The humor and spirituality of the healer have much to do with the nature of the healing, and the extended dialogue between Minnie Ransom and Old Wife shows these women-as-healers to be scapegoats with a difference: they voluntarily take suffering upon themselves for the sake of those who come for healing. Self-love, never much good at humor-ous rapport, opposes the relationship of spiritual possession, which is why Doc Serge can do nothing for Buster whereas watching Minnie with Velma does much for him. (Doc Serge has "long ago stumbled upon the prime principle as a player—that self-love produces the gods and the gods are genius" [137].) The "gift" passed on from Old Wife to Minnie involves both the terrible and the funny: each has experienced a deep, obsessive trouble by the time she hears the call to witness the tragic and respond with rituals of healing involving interaction, intimacy, and felt relationship; and each comes to a spiritual bonding characterized by a tough but humane humor. Narration remembers Minnie herself, "full-grown, educated, well-groomed, well-raised Minnie Ransom down on her knees eating dirt, craving pebbles and gravel, all asprawl in the road with her clothes every which way" (51), before being healed by Old Wife, "the teller of tales no one would sit still to hear anymore" (52). Under the instruction of Old Wife, whom she once called a witch and regarded as crazy, Minnie acquires the ceremonies, the loas, and builds "the chapel in The Mind."

Many have seen the belief in a single all-powerful God as the most important distinguishing characteristic of cultures validating hierarchic models of social organization. A truism of sorts, it misses that other, related characteristic of monotheism: in a spiritual world with so much concentrated power in a single figure, humor plays little spiritual role, either as part of spirits' interaction or as a human response to oppressive power. For those accustomed to the distancing privileges of monotheistic religious authority, the conjurer whose status as healer has nothing to do with social privilege may seem anomalous. That such healers may also possess a specifically humorous rapport with spirits coincides with their penchant for sharing the labor, speaking the language, and facing the same oppressions as do those they heal. However much they invoke hardship or poverty, the stories of Job or Christ have something of both epic and romance about any tragic ethos, since they suffer an oppression peculiar to heroic individuality. A humorous rapport with even the spiritual world makes power relations negotiable, suggesting that no authority, however absolute it deems itself, can totally triumph:

> "What ought I to do about that Henry gal, Old Wife?"
> "Don't you know?"
> "Don't you? Ain't you omniscient yet, Old Wife? Don't frown up. All knowing. Ain't you all knowing? What's the point of being in all-when and all where if you not going to take advantage of the situation and become all knowing?" (49)

The two "signifyin sisters" might seem to act like midwives to Velma's rebirth, except that their role is more than mediational: they take on themselves any suffering too much for Velma to bear and their combination of willing surrogacy and humorous intimacy cooperates "to take up the yoke and pull toward life" (61). With spirit figures made in such a human, leveling image, both coalition politics and world-traveling is borne. As Old Wife has done before her, Minnie heals the young as a way of passing on the tradition although failing in physical strength.

The final stages of Velma's healing-process revolve around her attempt "to neutralize the serpent," figured for her, as for Head's Elizabeth, in a horrific version of the Medusa as the black woman, or rather, as the black woman's internalized, mirror image of negative visions of herself. Thinking about how she had thought, prior to her breakdown, that she knew how to "build resistance," Velma remembers thinking that she knew how to

> stay poised and centered in the best of her people's traditions and not be available to madness, not become intoxicated by the heady brew of degrees and career and congratulations for nothing done, not become anesthetized by dazzling performances with somebody else's aesthetic, not go under. (258)

The "amnesia had set in anyhow," and the "something missing" of 1960s political and social movements merges with the amnesia of more global history as Velma remembers having once, combing her own hair, seen the answer

come tumbling out of the mirror naked and tattooed with serrated teeth and hair alive, birds and insects peeping out at her from the mud-heavy hanks of ancient mothers' hair. (259)

Velma recognizes herself in a figure combining Medusa-like features with the mythic maternal ancestors, such that she flees the horrible connection between herself and this nightmare of the primitive: the serrated teeth connect her to recurring images of African circumcision, the black woman's sexuality under assault both intraculturally and interculturally. And as Susan Willis has well explicated them (*Specifying* 154–55), these "tribal initiates in a muddy bath" resemble both dominant ideological representations of the primitive and Hollywood's more spectacular exotics.

With an image of the past that bears down on her as strongly as Elizabeth's mythic torturers, Velma sees herself barefoot in the park unable to look up at anything and therefore fixated on her own swollen feet. The Medusa appears as a woman sitting next to her "trying to get familiar," a woman whom Velma thinks she ought to know but *dare not look at* even though she steals a glance at her "extravagant" appearance. Although not looking, Velma nevertheless imagines inviting the unnamed woman over to "share with her how she herself had learned to believe in ordinary folks' capacity to change the self and transform society" (260), and this thought begins the upward swing in Velma's self-conception. The effort of not looking at the Medusa or at the mud-mothers, both taboo because relegated to a terrible and "primitive" version of the ancestral past, prevents Velma from looking at the woman on the park bench, much less recognizing any common sisterhood.

Still with a gaze paralyzed by the dominant Medusa story, and therefore thinking on serpents, Velma remembers a scene that glosses an important difference between snakes and serpents and explains the figurative frame of reference for "salt-eating." She remembers how M'Dear ministers to Daddy Dolphy's snakebite, explaining as he swallows salt and she packs it on the slit she has made in his shoulder, "Helps neutralize the venom." Daddy Dolphy's winking response reveals the healing of a snakebite as an easier, more clearly physical task than the healing of the serpent's bite: " 'To neutralize the serpent's another matter,' Daddy Dolphy had winked, taking deep breaths" (258). The serpent's bite "[turns] would-be cells, could-be cadres into cargo cults," whose divisive baggage has brought her to this stool. She also remembers the visit of one Barbara Watson, superior since her removal to Washington, D.C. and glad to find Velma "crazy as ever" in the town she's so glad to have left. But Barbara is tired and looking for something, whereas Velma is not tired and has more to say than she manages.

Minnie now puts on the music "Wiiiiild women doan worreeee, wild women doan have no bluuuuzzzzz," which brings back the woman in the park at whom Velma dared not look, this time connected to the desire to "get real wild." Feeling as though she "could be coming apart, totally losing her self," Velma undertakes a world-traveling that takes her through both the traumas of the diasporas as well as through her own personal trauma, the divisions of history merged with the factions of sixties activism. In this, Velma relies on Minnie's internal capacity to become part of that soul-journey and Minnie relies on Old Wife's fulfilling that same function for her:

"She's off again. Take care, Min, you don't lose her."
"Time to hit the yellow-brick road, is it? Stay close, Old Wife." (251)

And Velma's "dancing" needs the surrogacy of Old Wife through the surrogacy of Minnie, who calls her spirit-mentor with: "And what about my legs? My legs. We might lose her. Give her your legs, Old Wife." The complexity of artistic improvisation figures the complexity of the processes of identification as singer, dancer, healer, "signifyin sister," and herself all merge into a Medusa-woman no longer unbearable to see. Velma feels an intersubjectivity in the synesthesia of the arts (appropriate to the Academy of the Seven Arts, where music, spinning, dance, theater, pottery, and more provide trans-artistic tropes for the processes of healing).

Now, the Velma eager for "balance and kinship" becomes the Velma able to transform even the power of those centuries-old constructions of black women as the perversely erotic Medusa: "She would run to the park and hunt for self. Would be wild. Would look." Rehearsing a litany of all the times she might have died, Velma's final "glow aglow" partakes of the "glow" of the woman in the park, no longer a terrible kinship. Like Paul D. beginning to feel his own "red heart," Velma begins to feel "a wind in the rib cage, a tremor in the lungs rustling the package straw in the floor of the heart" (257). (To Paul D.'s assertion " 'That woman is crazy. Crazy,' " Stamp Paid responds, " 'Yeah, well, ain't we all?' " [*Beloved* 265].) Amidst the richly imagistic lyricism of Velma's journey as it nears healing, the dialogue between Minnie and Old Wife inserts the humor and the tenacity of their participation:

"So what do I do now? Iz you iz or iz you ain't my spirit guide?"
"Loan her some of yo stuff, Min. And don't be stingy."
"I'm bout worn out." (252)

Bambara's critical, negotiated spirituality provides a very different answer to Cavell's question: "Why do I do nothing faced with tragic events?" From the vantage point of Bambara's fiction, doing nothing would imply the answer: "I do nothing faced with tragic events because I *only* see them in the responses to drama that I designate *as* tragic. My acknowledgement of others is only that and relies on an abstracted analogy between the worlds represented on stage or in print and my own ethical relation to other human beings." A world reborn(e) not as fixed, settled, or made whole again requires more responsible intervention on the model of those within tragedy who take responsibility for the conditions dealt them with loaded dice.

Bambara's lyricism understandably calls attention to the whole behind the "wholesomeness." Minnie Ransom's question, " 'Are you sure you want to be healed?' " and its corollary understanding that with wellness comes responsibility makes Velma's interior processes inseparable from problems of social responsibility. A structure more complex than its description here dramatizes how Velma's internalization of social struggle turns the forces assaulting her from without into a part of self-assault. The tragic here inheres in whatever deprives people of their freedom and makes of responsibility a struggle and a conflict forever imbricated in issues of social justice. Students sometimes project onto Velma a language drawn from popular psychology about how she needs to "take time out to take care of herself" or "stop trying to solve everything," thus misconstruing both the nature of her illness and the processes of its healing. She has not lost her way fighting the world and, thus, now needs to change her focus; rather, a terrible world has made her sick in ways that only internal struggle can address. In Velma's case, being responsible for her own health means not just some narrowly conceived connection between herself and the mud mothers, but achieving a presentness in her relation to the ancestors. Such sacred connections do not mitigate tragic paradox because Velma's disease belongs to her *and* to the social world, and Minnie Ransom experiences in her body the intricacy of the interconnections (in classical terms, an *ananke* or necessity that constitutes a personal fate only in conjunction with personal choice).

As with Elizabeth's provisional sense of rebirth, in which she proclaims herself a prophet yet knows her prophecy must leave things "one-sided" and "unresolved," Velma's start "back toward life" does not participate in a comic genre's sense of an ending, but rather looks forward to a time when "years hence she would laugh remembering she'd thought *that* was an ordeal. She didn't know the half of it." Similarly, narration directly incorporates Sophie's forward-looking certainty that "what had driven Velma into the oven. . .was nothing compared to what awaited her, was to come." As in the exorcism that draws Sethe back into a community's struggle to make some normalcy without creating scapegoats for a tragic past, this healing involves others in new periods of struggle: "Sophie vowed to concentrate more fully and stay alert and be at hand, for Velma's next trial might lead to an act far more devastating than striking out at the body or swallowing gas" (294).

Just as the tragic action of *Beloved* precedes a narrative focused on responses to divisions in the social order that are themselves the cause of tragedy, so the tragic action of Elizabeth's bouts with madness and Velma's attempted suicide precede narration's present. Despite the difference of Bambara's more broadly comic narration and dialogue, the fact that catharsis attends healing rather than self-destruction does not do away with tragic import. In the final pages of *The Salt Eaters*, the felt legacy of the mud-mothers as ancestors and seers gives way to the more immediate, but corresponding, legacy of one priestess, mentor, or conjure-woman to another: the last pages merge Old Wife's humorous rapport with Minnie Ransom with that of Minnie and Velma Henry. Minnie feels the danger in this night but also the charity of women preferring their men safe "with some other woman" than "on the prowl searching out disaster" (295). The intimacy of the two living women with each other mimics an intimacy with the spirit of Old Wife, all necessary to the resurrection of Velma, who now "turning smoothly on the stool" has clearly outrun disaster. She throws off her shawl-cocoon to reveal a nakedness in full achievement of its own presentness:

No need of Minnie's hands now so the healer withdraws them, drops them in her lap just as Velma, rising on steady legs, throws off the shawl that drops down on the stool a burst cocoon. (295)

Traditionally, tragic theory has suggested that such a rebirth belies the structure of tragic development and closure, and comic theory has suggested a much more replete resolution than the narrative projections of Velma's future struggles allow. And yet here a tragic mode matters importantly to the nature of the suffering and a comic mode matters importantly to the nature of the healing, neither separable in the formal and structural separations of the genre named as tragi-comedy (or those that necessitate playing *The Merchant of Venice* or *Endgame* as primarily *either* comedy *or* tragedy). The healers here treat each other and their patient as a "signifyin sister" even as they suffer; and as she heals, she too adopts that "unctuous moral agency" that merges pain and laughter.[32] Velma's future will remember back to no longer resisting the healer's touch; instead, resistance now involves imagining herself surviving "some low-life gruesome gang bang raping lawless careless pesty last straw nasty thing ready to pounce, put our total shit under arrest and crack your back—but couldn't" (278). The suffering and the healing, the tragic and the comic, are simultaneously borne—both in the sense of birth and in the sense of what one must continue to bear and fight— and therein lies its exaltation and awe, its intimacy and connection, and its impetus to social action.

In the healing-through-narration of both Elizabeth and Velma, artful narrative juxtapositions take as "truths" both the sudden, embodied forms of spiritual attack and the central character's coherent, retrospective presentation of internal processes and affective states. Perhaps only fantasy, among western genres, sustains both supernatural and coherent (or "rational") explanations of sudden occurrences. But there is nothing of fantasy here in tales with "realistic" narrators who assert with authority the presence of powerful mythic figures from many traditions (African, Vodou, Greek, Christian, Hindu, and Buddhist among them). These healing stories focus not on which spiritual system has value or status, but on how anyone can be brought low by a malignant, unsupportive community or by a sustained, spiritually-supported (in)difference. Caroline Rooney understands this when she describes Head's spiritualism as "complexly contradictory," a function of a world in which events happen that do not *literally* happen and in which even when they do not literally happen, "they are more than just metaphoric situations" (117). Head both "understands the inexplicability of the experience—that is, the impossibility of the attempt to transcribe it further—and at once demonstrates that the process of writing, or writing up, is simultaneously one of speculative interpretation" (Rooney 118).

Both *A Question of Power* and *The Salt Eaters* end on this note of provisional normalcy, an achieved normalcy that bears little resemblance to that of the world-as-backdrop when tragic characters act upon essential selves or when comic ones possess a "natural" vitality. Here both writers and their characters value "wholesomeness," but such health stands forever in dialogue with what it excludes; it has none of the givens belonging to any absolute "we who are healthy and therefore know what that means." An identity under terrible stress achieves a spirituality as reliant on a gendered interconnection with other women, both ancestors and living comrades in labor, as ongoing critique of a spiritual world holding on to hierarchy. Here, a still-problematic identity affirms values that both resist any reduction to "win, lose, or draw" and also acknowledge the oppressive character of continuing power relations (hence, a paradoxical resistance). This paradox occupies a position as much spiritual as logical: relational but not relative, provisional but not skeptical.

The Black Medusa

Most theorists acknowledge tragedy's overlap with systems of belief, understanding how the backdrop of the gods (and if not the gods, some sustaining, shared *ethos*) matters to the teleology of tragedy even when a human focus keeps the spiritual-ethical frame of reference elusive. Yet the current tensions and modalities of moral discourse in Europe and America often forgo at the outset any felt relation between imagined or spiritual worlds and actual human suffering.[33] Speculative discourse that does not think to turn to the created worlds of writers like Head or Bambara for the most profound treatment of human suffering, "the most prestigious form of art," fails to recognize how this form of spiritualism differs from the foundational or the essential. The location of suffering in entrapping worlds makes the extremes of disorder and dislocation terrifying and dissociates social resolution from the pain of suffering. The state of such dissociations of moral sensibility suggests, in contrast to Faulkner's famous insight about a past neither dead nor even past, a forward-looking corollary, perhaps, "The future will not wait; it has always already started." It has already started in the expressive forms of suffering and humor elaborated here by Head and Bambara, forms that resist the ease of self-other categories.[34] The tragedy that Euro-American theories keep on killing and reviving is already reborn(e) in writers whose cultural forms do not abjure 1) the depths of *critical* soul-journeys, 2) the purposive vision of suffering unresolved and yet transformed by shared energy in shared work, and 3) the paradoxical affirmations of subversive but spreading alliances among the poor and disempowered. Also reborn(e) is the comedy that finds wholesomeness in the intimate rapport centered around a struggle inseparable from social justice, with that struggle's commitments toward a transformed, leveling work, a liberatory sexuality, and a spirtualist imagination.

The cultural traditions that frame scholarship as impersonal intellection maintain their skepticism about testimony from life about art, especially in the case of writers talking about either of their own. Yet something of the intracultural wisdom and intercultural charity in *The Salt Eaters*, combined with the subsequent loss of this underread writer, spurs a relevant memory. On a night in 1993 after a dinner with Mama Helen (to whom *The Salt Eaters* is dedicated) and her children (Toni, Walter, and daughter-in-law Leslie), I asked Toni if she knew of Bessie Head's use of the Medusa as a figure of terror-with-wit and if her own Medusa in

The Salt Eaters might not be a comic mirror in a figure of wit-with-terror.
She said something typically funny and affirmative, and offered the insight that neither tragedy nor comedy comes so separately to blackness
as it does to whiteness, but rather as moving gestures in the same dance.
(Later, in a reading of Hurston's Vodou texts motivated by Head's and
Bambara's spiritual worlds, I hope to show that this spontaneous figure
fits the case of Vodou precisely, and in the same manner that the feet
of the priestess possessed by the spirit of humor and death [Gede] must
differentiate her own rhythms while under the spell of the beat of different drums.) Even her performance that evening, with "Goldilocks
and the Three Bears" in transformed variation cajoling a largely white,
middle-class, customarily hung-up New England collegial audience into
wildly enthusiastic call and response, bore the imprint of the tragic context that made such humor possible. She performed a humor clearly reliant on struggles and intimacies that much of her audience had not had.
Yet even in inviting a general participation she privileged the black rapport inseparable from the radical contingency of experience that none
had chosen, and everyone knew and felt this. As artist, she had created
not the sloppier version of an ideal, unified whole that so often informs
the rhetoric surrounding community, but rather a finely differentiated
inclusion that placed different segments of her audience-as-community
in carefully provisional relation (that is, in the context of differing relations to power and therefore differing forms of resistance).

Both Head and Bambara create fictional worlds intimately interrelated
to actual ones and both depict an intracultural terror and humor that
helps theorize the intercultural problems attending the construction of
a Medusa who paralyzes. Head's tragic understanding of the Medusa's
horror (with its paradoxically comic vision of the monstrous Other)
and Bambara's comic insight about how humanizing the Medusa makes
one's own healing possible (with its paradoxically tragic understanding
of power relations) together reinvent the Medusa's meanings. Without
the disjoint separations that characterize Euro-American tragi-comedy,
these writers invoke this serpent-bedecked figure as a symbol of the
Other constructed as monstrous, a site for the complex and spreading
hurt that occurs when we can see no connections between another's
humanity and our own everyday selves and lives. Such fiction as theory
argues persuasively that we have not understood how to unpetrify ourselves in part because we have not engaged the Medusa's ordinary humanity, neither the meaning of suffering that is not our own nor that of
laughter that we cannot share. Across the power relations, reimagining
the Medusa's humanity means searching out those values of tragic and
comic consciousness most resistant to constructing her as the unnatural
Other (even in positive, carnivalesque inversions) and therefore most re-

sistant, too, to dominant vengefulness, cynicism, and apathy. Conceived as such, both tragic and comic modes have more permeable boundaries and more dialogical interrelation than previously theorized; and as such, they inform an ideology and a praxis of a resistance that changes with its positioning.

Different from her role as character in dominant genre theory, the Medusa of both Head and Bambara appears as an internalized—or already produced—construction of oneself as horrific, a construction that the healing self must exorcise, tame, or negotiate. From the perspective of traditional genre theory, the Medusa belongs most readily to romance and not to tragedy or comedy (Frye 196). A sister of Jung's "terrible mother," this Medusa embodies a moral antithesis to heroism and acts to reinscribe a romantic certainty about good and evil. The *essential* type of a perversely sexual hag, the Medusa takes upon her own body a tradition's fear of specifically erotic perversion. In a particularly female hideousness used by Minerva on her shield to turn men to stone, Medusa represents the most horrible thing: to be female, old, ugly, and still sexed. Her body represents a fearsome mix in constructions of gender and sexuality (those phallic snakes writhing in female hair), and relies on a story of origins: she lost a formerly beautiful, virginal body for the transgression of defiling Athena's temple (with its many connections to virginity and warfare).

Both Head and Bambara recognize in the Medusa a figure internalized from a mythic history with which black women must contend in order to survive. Unlike Frye, they do not confine her significance to the essential categories of romance, but rather show her as a social construction personifying inner torment or as a woman healed into humanhood. And, unlike Cixous, they do not desire to *become* the Medusa-in-her-horror or make her a symbol of liberation. A suggestive argument surrounds the black Athena, who exists in the iconographic interconnection between Athena as a "shield-goddess" and the Egyptian Neït, portrayed in pre-dynastic times as a cockroach on a stick and later taking her place on the shield of a goddess.[35]

This revisionary story suggests a strong identity between the goddess herself and the nonhuman figure on her shield, rather than Medusa as the punished Other. And rather than the mix of species and race combining with sexuality and gender to construct the perverse, this story suggests a figure willfully chosen to frighten and protect, a symbol of female power taken up with the shield rather than as an essential characteristic of the feminine made hideous. Head's Medusa exerts the power of oppressive constructions of race, sexuality, and other modern "demands" for difference-as-perversity, a power defeated only when understood as in cahoots (or complicity) with both worldly and cosmic authority. Bambara's Medusa loses her power to paralyze when the internalized/produced serpent becomes only a snake whose poison allows treatment as surely as Sophie Heywood cuts the venom from a shoulder and administers the healing salt. Understanding Medusa's raucous demands as coming from the mirror of power and not from familiar and intimate relationships with women's actual differences makes possible her transformation from paralyzing serpents to snakes to merely hair in need of a comb.

Part II
Reading Recursively

Against Modernism's Apartheid

Chapter 4
Who Owns the Terror in *Absalom, Absalom!*?

Quentin's Marriage and Clytie's Fire

The notion that we can transfer our guilt and sufferings to some other being who will bear them for us is familiar to the savage mind. It arises from a very obvious confusion between the physical and the mental, between the material and the immaterial. Because it is possible to shift a load of wood, stones, or what not, from our own back to the back of another, the savage fancies that it is equally possible to shift the burden of his pains and sorrows to another, who will suffer them in his stead. Upon this idea he acts, and the result is an endless number of very unamiable devices for palming off upon someone else the trouble which a man shrinks from bearing himself. In short, the principle of vicarious suffering is commonly understood and practised by races who stand on a low level of social and intellectual culture.
                                    —J. G. Frazer, *The Golden Bough*

[Social] fantasy is a means for an ideology to take its own failure into account in advance.
                                    —Slavoj Žižek, *The Sublime Object of Ideology*

Hearing, Listening, and Narrative Trouble

In *Absalom, Absalom!* the narrative voices of Mr. Compson, Rosa Coldfield, and Shreve McCaslin, often disturbingly imbricated with textual narration, articulate some of the most appalling constructions of the female and the black to be found in Faulkner.[1] And yet in a significant body of important criticism, Quentin Compson has emerged as *Absalom, Absalom!*'s most easily distanced sensibility, either because he has no identity separate from other tellers or (by extension) because he fails *as narrator*. Both judgments rely heavily on a reading of Chapter 8 as a "marriage of speaking and hearing" that merges characters with their story in textual affirmation that self-referentially embraces Faulkner's own storytelling.

On the one hand, readings with postmodern or poststructuralist affinities describe Chapter 8's narrative union of Shreve and Quentin as
"transcendent," with narrative speculation taken by Brian McHale (following Peter Brooks, John Matthews, and others) as the site best dra-
matizing the shift from modernist to postmodernist narration. A fascination with "incredulous narration" privileges this absence-as-climax,
where "the signs of the narrative act fall away and with them all questions of authority and reliability,"[2] and harshly judges the Quentin of the
final chapters for falling out of a transcendent narration. On the other
hand, readings that contrast Quentin's "sorry means of self-defense" to
the epic story of Sutpen (like those of Eric Sundquist, Karl Zender, and
Philip Weinstein),[3] take the merger of voices in the "marriage of speaking and hearing" to include that of the implied author; such readings
foreground a story with the literal bloodline at the center and make the
text as a whole represent a generalized, if conflicted, nostalgia for the
Old South.[4] Across the readings, Quentin's failures coincide with failures
of mind and imagining tantamount to a flawed masculinity (incapacities
in agency, action, and assertion).[5] Reference to the idealizing genres of
epic and romance tend to merge into a singular, coherent story all about
race, class, gender, and sexuality created by two white men at Harvard,
even though one has no affective attachments to the story at all and one
must repress them utterly in order to play the telling game.

Read under the influence of the mode of social tragedy elaborated
in *Beloved*, where the strongest moral judgments fall on the vicarious
nature of experience that never achieves the status of actual relationship, *Absalom, Absalom!* reveals its own paradoxical positionality: it may
itself represent terrible social crisis but it does so artfully enough that
social tragedy emerges not solely as elegaic or nostalgic loss, but more
importantly as the inability to act upon a felt humanity. Such a tragic
modernity locates the loss, both here and in many other cultural stories,
inherent in devaluations of both affective lives and the actual, embodied
connections among human beings; and it relates Quentin's narrative
subjugation, and his resistance to it, to the appalling accommodations
of the female and the black, as well as to the loaded silence about
homoerotic possibility that narrators describe but never name. Read as
such, *Absalom, Absalom!*'s characters have less identification with epic or
romantic idealizing and more with a resistant but self-conflicted mode
of the tragic, characterized by what Morrison articulates as Faulkner's
"brilliantly intricate" forays into "the failed maintenance of the past" ("A
Conversation" 7).

In a work that repeatedly invokes the tragic, what does tragedy have
to do with its renowned narrative involutions? I want to draw out *Absa-*

lom, Absalom!'s moral problematics of narrative in part as a revisionary response to readings that value the play of language over the concern with social relationship, but also in response to the related charges that the work belongs to a formal aestheticism removed from significant social engagement or that it necessarily bequeathes to a singular "us" as readers a kind of patriarchal male romance caught in "the story of racial turmoil as the heartbreaking poetry of filial outrage."[6] Because others' stories work on Quentin with both emotive and visceral, physical effect, his final outbursts offer minimal support either for ideas about "a reader freed to speak the text" or for an aestheticized, elegiac tragedy with primacy on "the monumentality of the culture that has been lost."[7] An alternative focus on Quentin's affective life, his internalizations, passions, and resistances, suggests that the play either affirmed or read as representing "a single epic narrative told in more or less the same voice" stands negatively judged in the context of its own suppression of social history, albeit a social history with complex linkages to the terror and tragedy recurring as motifs throughout. In the telling of both Rosa Coldfield and Mr. Compson, Clytie, like her namesake Clytaemnestra, takes up herself a kind of genealogical terror, here a legacy stemming from the initial corruption enacted when Thomas Sutpen mingles his blood with that of her slave mother. And like her namesake she enacts a supporting role in a work named for a leading man, and yet a role embodying all the tragic taboos at once a matter of race (those ancient bloodlines again defiled), gender (a manlike will in a female body), and sexuality (the inherited taint of woman with woman, black with white, half-sister with half-sister).

The narrative complexity of *Absalom, Absalom!* in many ways resembles that of *Beloved* because its multiple tellers may or may not merge with a multivocal textual narration that often reiterates characters' language. Cumulative narrative contexts set up Quentin's particular relation to the storied past, a past shown us from within an imagination dependent on others' narratives, their ghostly world of appearances. Yet however dependent on such recapitulations, successive narrations take place within a textual emphasis on Quentin's relation-in-difference to other tellers and tales. However many narrators share pieces of the telling, *Absalom, Absalom!* does not present itself as a work made of indiscriminately piled up "rag-tags and bob-ends of old tales and talking" (303). Rather, its fabric juxtaposes and measures others' modes of narrating against Quentin's processes of mind and feeling, processes often transcribed in the merged languages of others but always carrying signs of his own difference. That difference relies in part on his manner of hearing and listening, which always suggests a troubled sense of the passive social roles that determine how he acts, but not how he feels. But it also relies on his relation to textual narration which, though not omniscient, takes careful, frequent limitation from what the community knows or thinks or remembers. This textual narration, separate from all *personae*, frames the context in which all other narrations take place, even though narration as direct or indirect discourse comprises much of *Absalom, Absalom!*.[8] Quentin's listening and hearing acquire increasingly troubled relation to all affective structures (Williams's "structures of feeling") long before the equally troubled "marriage of speaking and hearing."

Characteristically, the opening pages of *Absalom, Absalom!* foreground a moral problematics of narrative in Quentin's listening to Miss Rosa. Describing Miss Rosa in words that Peter Brooks and others have taken as applicable to the work as a whole, the textual narrator sees her

talking in that grim haggard amazed voice until at last listening would renege and hearing-sense self-confound and the long-dead object of her impotent yet indomitable frustration would appear, as though by outraged recapitulation evoked, quiet inattentive and harmless, out of the biding and dreamy and victorious dust. (8)

When Rosa prescribes Quentin's function as reconstructing a family romance "out of the biding and dreamy and victorious dust," she recapitulates her own narrative entrapment. The passage does not assert that Miss Rosa's telling *is* "quiet inattentive and harmless," but rather describes Quentin's manner of listening her voice into a silence where subject-object relations *appear* harmless because disassociated from actual reference.

Quentin himself, in "the long unamaze" of his own internal recapitulations ("as if it were the voice which he haunted where a more fortunate one would have had a house"), hears in and out of her voice according to the "two separate Quentins," the one who must, perforce, listen to the "ghosts" tell their versions of the storied past, and the other who

was still too young to deserve yet to be a ghost, but nevertheless having to be one for all that, since he was born and bred in the deep South the same as she was—the two separate Quentins now talking to one another in the long silence of notpeople, in notlanguage, like this: *It seems that this demon—his name was Sutpen—(Colonel Sutpen)—Colonel Sutpen. Who came out of nowhere and without a warning upon the land with a band of strange niggers and built a plantation—(Tore violently a plantation, Miss Rosa Coldfield says)—tore violently. And married her sister Ellen and begot a son and a daughter which—(Without gentleness begot, Miss Rosa Coldfield says)—without gentleness. Which should have been the jewels of his pride and the shield and comfort of his old age, only—(Only they destroyed him or something or he destroyed them or something. And died.)—and died. Without regret, Miss Coldfied says—(Save by her) Yes, save by her. (And by Quentin Compson) Yes. And by Quentin Compson.* (9)

Quentin thinks of "notpeople" because they exist only in fictive reference, and in a "notlanguage" because his own thinking does not differentiate itself from the composite, merged words of others. Despite the
introductory idea of the "two Quentins," Quentin's thrice-negated mental speech (a "long silence," "of notpeople, in notlanguage") dramatically confounds the Quentin who must listen to ghosts and the Quentin
who himself becomes one. The parenthetical voice, sometimes belonging to Miss Rosa and sometimes to a more generalized other, stands
always repeated in the "other" Quentin's thinking. By the end, the regret
for the passing of Sutpen felt across the parentheses stands juxtaposed
with the pronounced moral ellipsis of any storied certainty ("Only they
destroyed him or something or he destroyed them or something"). A received romantic language introduces Sutpen as a seeming "demon" and
describes his aspiration and disappointment in the heroic terms explaining both Miss Rosa's and Quentin's regret. If anything, these opening
pages focus less on the motivation for narrating than on the convolu-
tions of Quentin's manner of listening (when listening "would renege
and hearing-sense self-confound").

The language theory and practice of both Miss Rosa and Mr. Compson, however different as characters, fully fit Peter Brooks's sense of
narration with an empty center, but not without almost ritual reminders that narrating stands bracketed by a certain performative falsity, the
shadowy enactments of characters always distinct from "actual people."
After the framing scene with Quentin listening to Miss Rosa, the two
senior narrators share this second-order telling until the point where
Henry breaks through Judith's door to exchange verbal "slaps," an exchange in a reduced language formally equivalent to Quentin's exchange
with Henry when Quentin breaks through the same door in the last
chapter. Whenever Miss Rosa narrates, she enacts narration in the manner of a frustrated novelist. As "the country's poetess laureate," she
summons Quentin as a figurative amanuensis for her own storied life-in-
death with "maybe you will enter the literary profession . . . and maybe
someday you will remember this and write about it" (9–10). Yet Quentin
senses "Only she don't mean that," and the textual narrator offers alternative reasons why he does not recognize Miss Rosa's request as "revealing a character cold, implacable, and ruthless," a due warning about the
harm imminent in only *apparently* harmless narration.

The Detachment of Role

Miss Rosa's penchant for portraying herself and others as doomed to
play the shadowy roles bequeathed them as Sutpen's legacy overtly links

tragedy's commingling of sexual and racial horror (Oedipus and Medea as the *foreigners* who commit heinous acts) in what, although she does not name it as tragic paradox, carries all the terror and the mystery of Clytie as "perverse inscrutable and paradox":

Clytie, not inept, anything but inept: perverse inscrutable and paradox: free, yet incapable of freedom who had never once called herself a slave, holding fidelity to none like the indolent and solitary wolf or bear (yes, wild: half untamed black, half Sutpen blood: and if "untamed" be synonymous with "wild," then "Sutpen" is the silent unsleeping viciousness of the tamer's lash) whose false seeming holds it docile to fear's hand but which is not, which if this be fidelity, fidelity only to the prime fixed principle of its own savageness;—Clytie who in the very pigmentation of her flesh represented that debacle which had brought Judith and me to what we were and which had made of her (Clytie) that which she declined to be just as she had declined to be that from which its purpose had been to emancipate her, as though presiding aloof upon the new, she deliberately remained to represent to us the threatful portent of the old. (156–57)

As sure as Aeschylus that fate checks all excess, Miss Rosa invokes Clytie's role as an abstract necessity that must fall on the house of Sutpen as surely as on the house of Atreus.

Since for Rosa Clytie exists as an invincible, immutable "it," the touch of Clytie's hand upon her shoulder, staying her from seeing Charles Bon's corpse, generates a crisis out of all narrative proportion in a chapter ripe with marriage contracts and violent, homicidal death. The touch of "flesh on flesh" has traumatic effect on Rosa precisely because it disallows the habitual distancing, that separation of categories on which her identity rests. Rosa recognizes that "let flesh touch with flesh, and watch the fall of all the eggshell shibboleth of caste and color too." With the shibboleths falling around her, she moves from the terror of a taboo racial and class connection to the terror of taboo sexual connection. The terrible sameness that makes Rosa "twin sistred to the fell darkness that had produced her [Clytie]" (140) haunts Rosa's telling about her youthful obsession with an imaginary Charles Bon, a time when, even then, she shrank in recoil from fleshly contact:

As a child, I had more than once watched her and Judith and even Henry scuffling in the rough games which they (possibly all children) played, and (so I have heard) she and Judith even slept together, in the same room but with Judith in the bed and she on a pallet on the floor ostensibly. But I have heard how on more than one occasion Ellen has found them both on the pallet, and once in the bed together. (140)

This contact threatens the boundaries of sexuality and gender, such that the screaming "ostensibly" and the vicarious "have heard" hide a sexuality so forbidden that it emerges only in narration that conceives of Charles Bon as the dream lover of her adolescence. Yet the story only pretends an obsession with Charles, revolving in fact around this four-teen year-old's _vicarious_ obsession with the Judith imagined in bed with Clytie, a vicariousness that justifies desire for the actual body of Judith with an elaborately transferential logic. She locates herself as "child enough to go to her and say 'Let me sleep with you'; woman enough to say 'Let us lie in bed together while you tell me what love is" (148). She cannot go to Judith, however, because she would also "have had to say, 'Don't talk to me of love but let me tell you, who know already more of love than you will ever know or need.'" Protesting a great deal too much, especially given the sequential logic that moves from Judith imag-ined in bed with Clytie to this summer's sexual awakening, Rosa insists on Charles as the final object even though she gives her awakening love "not to him, to her" in a form designed to remain a secret kept from him:

it was as though I said to her, "Here, take this too. You cannot love him as he should be loved, and though he will no more feel this giving's weight than he would ever know its lack, yet there may come some moment in your married lives when he will find this atom's particle as you might find a cramped small pallid hidden shoot in a familiar flower bed and pause and say, 'Where did this come from?'; you need only answer, 'I don't know.'" (149)

No wonder, then, that Clytie's touch stops her "dead" and provokes in her a "shock which was not yet outrage because it would be terror soon" (140).

Related in difference, Mr. Compson's narration also keeps its careful distance from any felt relation to the actual or even to his own life. His version of Henry's "seduction" by Bon, for instance, speculates upon Henry's idealization of his sister's virginity in language that might well self-refer to his own narrational absences. Given his instinctive nature, speculates Mr. Compson, Henry only _may_ have been conscious that "his sister's virginity was a false quantity which must incorporate in itself an inability to endure in order to be precious, to exist, and so must depend upon its loss, absence, to have existed at all" (96). Characteristically, the thought spurs a metaphysical sense of what may have gone on not in Henry's mind, but in his soul, a tenacious idealist's version of

"the pure and perfect incest: the brother realizing that the sister's virginity must be destroyed in order to have existed at all, taking that virginity in the person of the brother-in-law, the man whom he would be if he could become, metamor-phose into, the lover, the husband; by whom he would be despoiled, choose for despoiler, if he could become, metamorphose into the sister, the mistress, the bride." (96)

As so often, Mr. Compson's story assumes the language of idealization, a narration in which climaxes correspond with sustained divagations on the inexplicability of "volatile and sentient forces" (101). In his "shadowy attenuation of time possessing now heroic proportions," characters "perform" their actions, but as though in a chemical formula where "something is missing." Within a theory of language that postmodernity takes for the text's own, Mr. Compson speaks fatalistically of the impossibility of reading human actions:

"you bring them together in the proportions called for, but nothing happens; you re-read, tedious and intent, poring, making sure that you have forgotten nothing, made no miscalculations; you bring them together again and again nothing happens: just the words, the symbols, the shapes themselves, shadowy inscrutable and serene, against that turgid background of a horrible and bloody mischancing of human affairs." (101)

For Mr. Compson the actual becomes background and the "shadowy inscrutable and serene" word-symbols foreground. Thus the "mischancing" bears no very personal threat and the "serene" stands inseparable from the "shadowy inscrutable." The pejorative quality of the description may invoke something like the structuralist's prison-house of language, but the way in which human behavior affords presumably endless meanings corresponds to critical description of *Absalom, Absalom!* that always moves in the direction of infinite-speak. Yet self-reference here refers us back to Mr. Compson's telling and not to narration in *Absalom, Absalom!* as a whole.

The degree to which Mr. Compson embeds his story in his own sense of "corruption" highlights a textual self-reference to his own detached narration, as when he imagines Bon's working upon the innocent Henry in a scene where he himself works upon Quentin in tellingly similar fashion. Imagining Bon's talking, Mr. Compson envisions (among other "inscrutable and curiously lifeless doorways"):

the calculation, the surgeon's alertness and cold detachment, the exposures brief, so brief as to be cryptic, almost staccato, the plate unaware of what the complete picture would show, scarce-seen yet ineradicable—a trap, a riding horse standing before a closed and curiously monastic doorway. (111)

Similarly, when Quentin reaches the doorway that he cannot pass, the door that Henry crashes in to announce to Judith that he has killed Bon, he imagines their dialogue in his father's terms as "brief staccato sentences like slaps," arising from a brother and sister "curiously alike as if the difference in sex had merely sharpened the common blood to a terrific, an almost unbearable similarity" (172). Mr. Compson's narration repeatedly inscribes differences in gender and sexuality as threatened by similarity. At the same time, textual narration focuses on the terror of such felt similarity to Quentin, for whom the blows *are* unbearable: "He (Quentin) couldn't pass that" (172). Critical description of Mr. Compson's "noble but slightly futile epic evocations" reveals an approbation not evident in Faulkner's text, where the harm of such narrating—linked to the "design" of Sutpen and its legatees—grows on us. And it grows upon us in part because of complex reference to tragedy, both Greek and Shakespearean, both performed and lived.

Mr. Compson's emphasis on a history of corruption—found in those doomed as female and black and the "threatened similarity" of binary opposites—finds a receptive figure in Greek tragedy, to which he frequently refers. He describes, for example, how Rosa as a child comes to know Sutpen not as a person but as though he were

just that ogreface of her childhood seen once and then repeated at intervals and on occasions which she could neither count nor recall, like the mask in Greek tragedy, interchangeable not only from scene to scene, but from actor to actor and behind which the events and occasions took place without chronology or sequence, leaving her actually incapable of saying how many separate times she had seen him for the reason that, waking or sleeping, the aunt had taught her to see nothing else. (62)

So, too, in Mr. Compson's tale does the racial story embed itself in a fated tragedy that might as well have the Eumenides hovering over its mystery (especially in combination with his own distance as choric observer). Sutpen uses his material wealth to force himself on white respectability without regard to suspicions that "there was a nigger in the woodpile somewhere" or that his Haitian journeys have taught him how to "juggle the cotton market itself," his success associated with a conjuring trick all the more feared for its association with the "wild niggers" he has brought back with him.[9] As though from a cosmic perch, Mr. Compson observes

that while he was still playing the scene to the audience, behind him Fate, destiny, retribution irony—the stage manager, call him what you will—was already striking the set and dragging on the synthetic and spurious shadows and shapes of the next one. (72–73)

Mr. Compson's Greek tragedy gives way to Elizabethan tragedy at precisely the moment of Quentin's blocked passage. In textual present time, Quentin's inability to "pass" the "brief staccato sentences like slaps" exchanged between Henry and Judith immediately precedes his inability to read to the end of his father's letter about Miss Rosa's death. And both stoppages exist in the context of his father's and Shreve's insistent detachment, the older's more eloquent, speculative hypotheses ending always in the unknown, and the younger's more crass, emotionally-detached assertions in Cambridge heckling. The textual narrator repeatedly asserts that Quentin does not listen to his father, but marks a turning point at the beginning of Chapter 6 when Quentin

walked out of his father's talking at last . . . not because he had heard it all because he had not been listening, since he had something he was unable to pass: that door, that gaunt tragic dramatic self-hypnotized youthful face like the tragedian in a college play, an academic Hamlet waked from some trancement of the curtain's falling and blundering across the dusty stage from which the rest of the cast had departed last Commencement, the sister facing him across the wedding dress which she was not to use, not even to finish, the two of them slashing at one another with twelve or fourteen words and most of these the same words repeated two or three times so that when you boiled it down they did it with eight or ten. (174)

From this moment, Quentin's participation in narrative will represent a struggle to "pass" the second-order, somehow strained tragedian enacted in his father's telling and, later, the romantic idealization of his own and Shreve's making. This entrapment in a reduced language does not simply happen to all the characters across the narrations. Rather, it places Quentin throughout the section between the two doorways (172–375) in the ontologically unique role of thinking thoughts he recursively shrinks from as sounding too much like others' narrating or as having only a shadowy, enacted quality that makes him, the thinker-rememberer, into a kind of disembodied ghost living among much-reconstructed ghosts. Narration's falterings and silences do not simply attend a passive Quentin who becomes a more active teller later in tandem with Shreve; rather, they foreground Quentin's sustained resistances to others' telling in the form of interior interventions that insistently comment on the passive audience others make of him (whether to his father's epic tragedy, Miss Rosa's romantic tragedy, or Shreve's romance). Since criticism harshly judgmental of Quentin's passivity largely fails to see this position as a "feminizing" of a male character, it also does not note the resistant nature of his internal responses.

After the turning point at the beginning of Chapter 6, narration returns to direct discourse in a sequence emphasizing how Quentin's thinking both submits to his father's language and yet moves beyond it. Here, as elsewhere, complex narrative juxtapositions repeatedly demonstrate how Quentin's thinking incorporates the language of others without losing the displaced sense that what others know they know through him. Others *know* without the experience that differentiates mere language from language with reference to an actual world. After a ritually acquiescent "yes," Quentin thinks of Shreve's narration, "*He sounds just like father. . . . Just exactly like father if father had known as much about it before I went out there as he did the day after I came back*" (181). That is, he sounds like the authoritative, albeit reductive, teller his father would have been had he not had the benefit of Quentin's experience earlier. The italics that follow "think" along with Quentin, but in the received language "exactly like father," a language so distanced from identity that "Yes, Quentin said" inserts itself into his own thinking in precisely the way it punctuates his responses to his father's or Shreve's narrations. And Shreve interrupts Quentin's thought (long before the two begin to invent in tandem) as though the interior world were as available to him as to the reader: "'How was it?' Shreve said. 'You told me; how was it?'" Without pause, narration then moves outside what characters saw to what Mr. Compson said on that occasion and Quentin, who at first thinks he sees Sutpen's return so clearly that he "might have been there," then corrects how remembering works within another's verbal envisioning: "*No. If I had been there I could not have seen it this plain*" (190). Quentin's acknowledgment that plain seeing attends his father's description more readily than it would direct experience matters to Quentin's continuing dependence-in-difference on his father's assumptions.

Quentin's feminized role forces him to live the distinction between felt experience and the received language available to describe it.[10] With even a developmental analogy, he acknowledges that processes of mind entrap thought in experience accumulated like that of children rather than like the knowledge that one person imparts to another. Without differentiation from the storied focus, the fusion of thinking and remembering ritually reflects Quentin's benumbing relation to the actual words of his father, to which he does not need to listen:

But you were not listening, because you knew it all already, absorbed it already without the medium of speech somehow from having been born and living beside it, with it, as children will and do: so that what your father was saying did not tell you anything so much as it struck, word by word, the resonant strings of remembering. (212)

By the time of Quentin's italicized thinking (211) and following, his thinking has become a remembering that both overtly parallels Mr. Compson's language and yet covertly resists itself. With tired forbearance, Quentin bemoans the telling of a Shreve, so like his father's in its "wisdom." At the same time, thinking/remembering merges sensory memory with the abstracted fatalisms so characteristic of the other tellers' overt dismissal of female or black significance and their covert avoidance of homoerotic passion.

When Mr. Compson describes Charles Etienne de Saint Valery Bon's return to Sutpen's Hundred with his black wife, his description of the couple's identity repeatedly invokes the separations with the force of taboo on which all aspects of the story rest: those between man and woman, black and white, human and animal. Charles Etienne, who like Joe Christmas in his years of evasion invites a self-repudiating violence, appears again at Sutpen's Hundred with, in Mr. Compson's words, "a coal black and ape-like woman," "an authentic wife resembling something in a zoo," "a black gargoyle." Mr. Compson's perverse description juxtaposes this "ape-like body of his charcoal companion" with the man's body, "almost as light and delicate as a girl's" in language that both engenders and racializes social values. Importantly, whenever Quentin mouths these others' distancing reductions of doomed gender or race, often in tropes referring to the enacted, performed roles of the storied characters, he does so in the context of an insistent protest against having had to think "*too much, too long*." Complaining yet once again that Shreve sounds "just like father," Quentin "thinks" his father's precise thought (everything following the colon) in the act of noting the grim necessity such thought entails:

thinking *Yes, too much, too long. I didn't need to listen then but I had to hear it and now I am having to hear it all over again because he sounds just like father: Beautiful lives women live—women do. In very breathing they draw meat and drink from some beautiful attenuation of unreality in which the shades and shapes of facts—of birth and bereavement, of suffering and bewilderment and despair—move with the substanceless decorum of lawn party charades, perfect in gesture and without significance or any ability to hurt.* (211)

So, too, when a by now conventional language describes Clytie as "*a little dried-up woman not much bigger than a monkey . . . her bare coffee-colored feet wrapped around the chair rung like monkeys do*," the textual narrator immediately inserts twice the "'Yes,' Quentin said" that so forcefully indicates his mental removal from the language he can no more expunge from his head than he can from Shreve's narrator's sensibility. Italics internalize, self-reflectively, the father's own language at the same time that they signal the processes of internalization, the alienation of a passive hearer from the story already remembered "word by word" in "the resonant strings of remembering" (213). The terrible bending of others (Henry, Charles, and Clytie herself) to Sutpen myths that give them all a "repressed fury" (198) casts in relief Quentin's forms of resistance, evident in the italics that offer a record of intensely felt, though failed resistance to others' imagining: Miss Rosa's, his father's, and Shreve's at different points in the book. For although Quentin in no way escapes the habits-of-mind that characterize their terrible dehumanizations, narrative attention focusses on his struggle to resist being formed by their stories, to experience something of the past for himself.

Thus Quentin's "yes" (215), directly after the italicized "narration" (in fact an interior monologue made up of bits of remembered speech and reflections on remembering) does not bespeak affirmation but rather acquiescence, as it will when it becomes his single most iterative response to Shreve in play whose repudiated homoeroticism is never acknowledged by either narration or characters. Quentin's "yes" means, in effect, that although Quentin does not listen because he "knew it already, had learned, absorbed it already without the medium of speech" (212), he nevertheless has an affective life apart from such narration. In fact, Quentin's "yes" appears as a non-sequitur used to put off an annoying interlocutor, despite Shreve's (and frequently criticism's) insistent assumption that Quentin's monosyllabic responses confirm his own narrative direction:

"and you said You see? and she (the Aunt Rosa) still said No and so you went on: and there was?"
    "Yes." (216)

Quentin's forbearance here logically precedes no answer at all to Shreve's subsequent vicarious, adolescent excitement: "Jesus, the South is fine, isn't it. It's better than the theatre, isn't it. It's better than Ben Hur, isn't it. No wonder you have to come away now and then, isn't it" (217). Both Shreve's rhetorical repetitions and his cultural frame of reference belong to a performative mode as oppressive as Mr. Compson's strained, academic Hamlet and Miss Rosa's incredulous narration.

When Quentin narrates, rather than thinks, he does so with constant reference to those masculinist stories fascinated more with patriarchal origins than with actual, felt experience (his grandfather's, Thomas Sutpen's, his father's, and Shreve's); but as he does so, textuality embeds the storied concern with Sutpen's "old morality" within a complex self-reference. Quentin struggles with the moral implications of his own conception of what actually existed and therefore now exists at the same time that textual authority reinforces interconnections between the morality of Sutpen, his storied sense of self, and that inherent in others' sundry reconstructions. Always, the furthest removes from reality, the most pronounced "attenuation of unreality," imply the most falsely performative modes. When Thomas Sutpen narrates his own story to Quentin's grandfather, he reveals what Grandfather Compson calls "the old morality,"

that innocence which believed that the ingredients of morality were like the ingredients of pie or cake and once you had measured them and balanced them and mixed them and put them into the oven it was all finished and nothing but pie or cake could come out. (263)

Importantly, Grandfather Compson understands that Sutpen's version of morality emerges in the detachment of his telling; according to him, Sutpen's "pleasant faintly forensic anecdotal manner" derives from a still-functioning moral "innocence" that enables him to view his own story as a form of spectacle or theater.

When Quentin reaches into such abstracted genealogical theorizing, Shreve accuses him, in his turn, of sounding like his "old man." Quentin's thinking affirms Shreve's insight, and expands upon it in a powerful figure about anyone's sense of whatever "happens":

Maybe nothing ever happens once and is finished. Maybe happen is never once but like ripples maybe on water after the pebble sinks, the ripples moving on, spreading, the pool attached by a narrow umbilical water-cord to the next pool which the first pool feeds, has fed, did feed, let this second pool contain a different temperature of water, a different molecularity of having seen, felt, remembered, reflect in a different tone the infinite unchanging sky, it doesn't matter: that pebble's watery echo whose fall it did not even see moves across its surface too at the original ripple-space, to the old ineradicable rhythm. (261)

Quentin's figure focuses on the interconnectedness of pools/persons, the way in which neither a simple sense of an event (a pebble's sinking) nor the passage of time (*"feeds, has fed, did feed"*) alters how the immediate effect (the rhythmic, spreading ripples) links all subsequent tellers and hearers in an involvement in the initial event. Such interconnectedness leads Quentin, with perfect logic, to observe how we are made by the stories we make:

thinking *Yes, we are both Father. Or maybe Father and I are both Shreve, maybe it took Father and me both to make Shreve or Shreve and me both to make Father or maybe Thomas Sutpen to make all of us.* (262)

This passage does not presage some fusion of all tellers without moral consequence; rather, it provides a dramatic context for the moment when textual authority likens Quentin's and Shreve's mutually created *morality* of telling to Sutpen's or Rosa Coldfield's.

The Text of Disembodied Sex

Chapter 8 begins "There would be no deep breathing tonight" and ends with Shreve's "Let's get out of this refrigerator and go to bed." The dialogism of merger and detachment explain why Quentin's and Shreve's "marriage of speaking and hearing" should end before the unilateral orgasmic jerks that begin Chapter 9's focus on Quentin's embodied desire for actual relationship. The quality of a detached amazement attributed in turn to Sutpen, Miss Rosa, and Shreve rests upon a morality whose logic from the outset ignores actual hurt. In Chapter 8, the young men adopt such logic by dedicating themselves to

that best of ratiocination which after all was a good deal like Sutpen's morality and Miss Coldfield's demonizing—this room not only dedicated to it but set aside for it and suitably so since it would be here above any other place that it (the logic and the morality) could do the least amount of harm. (280)

Phrases like "the best of ratiocination" and "the least amount of harm" have ironic resonance in a passage comparing the romance-making of Shreve and Quentin to the story-telling of Sutpen and Miss Rosa. Even the "after all" captures an ironic distance from the young men. And yet, postmodern readings affirm this telling in a language idealizing the Shreve-Quentin and Henry-Bon merger as climax-in-absence. Such "fulfillment" replaces any dialogism and any mutually embodied sexuality with a reader who speaks the text and a novel which constructs itself.[11]

At the point where Shreve and Quentin as interlocutors think together, creating shadows "who were not of flesh and blood which had lived and died but shadows in turn of what were shades too," textual authority that exists outside their thinking repeatedly comments on the perceptual mistakes that do not "matter" to them and on the adolescent nature of their mutual dream of a ubiquitous father and a "perennial" brotherhood. The shifting identifications among the four young men open up a circle of self-reference, where Shreve's attribution to Henry of a world "like a fairy tale" applies as well to his own and Quentin's imagining. All of Chapter 8, including the much-touted "happy marriage of speaking and hearing," has for predicate a context of adolescent, self-mythologizing romance (with Bon "the silken and tragic Lancelot"!) and an often ironic textual self-reference. The textual narrator tells us that the actual scene took place in night and winter, but that this does not matter to Shreve and Quentin "because it had been so long ago" (295). Because the story represents "the heart and blood of youth," it does not matter to them

what faces and what names they called themselves and were called by so long as the blood coursed—the blood, the immortal brief recent intransient blood which could hold honor above slothy unregret and love above fat and easy shame. (295)

They create out of a young nostalgia, "youth's immemorial obsession not with time's dragging weight which the old live with but with its fluidity: the bright heels of all the lost moments of fifteen and sixteen" (299).

And yet, as readers, we stand frequently reminded of both the identity of names and "time's dragging weight." Like a refrain, the textual narrator says of *their* narration that "Neither of them said 'Bon'" (305), "Never at any time did there seem to be any confusion between them as to whom Shreve meant by 'he" (311), or "But he didn't need to say that either [that the subject is love], any more than he had needed to specify which he meant by he" (316). But the text, the presenter of their narration, frequently identifies "he (Bon)" or "she (the octoroon)" and differentiates Quentin and Shreve with reference to what "Shreve had invented" or to what "were (to one of them at least, to Shreve) shades too," as though in separate address to a reader who stands outside an idealized relation specifically avoiding moral "faultings" in favor of an unreality "conserving what seemed true, or fit the preconceived—in order to overpass to love, where there might be paradox and inconsistency but nothing fault nor false" (316). Outside of their world, "where nothing else save them existed," exists a narration intent on identifying which parts of their tale were "probably true," repeatedly marking the hovering, absent actuality that took place in historical time.

The narrative fusion of Quentin-Henry and Shreve-Bon does not simply merge heterosexist romance with a homoerotic ideal. Rather, Quentin's bodily responses (a blood "quick to cool, more supple to compensate for violent changes of temperature perhaps, perhaps merely nearer to the surface") accompany bodily difference. Quentin assumes postures "fragile" or "delicate" or "hunched" as opposed to the "cherubic burliness" of Shreve, all those bodily gestures of dominance in a body that "looked huge and shapeless like a disheveled bear." Quentin's repeatedly feminized speechlessness plays hearer to Shreve's speaker's dominance as they "together" reconstruct the *unnamed* sexual passion of Henry for a Charles Bon described frequently in "feminine" aspect. But the "happy marriage" founders repeatedly as Shreve redirects the story to accommodate Quentin's objection "But it's not love" (322) and a later "But it's still not love" (328). In addition to all Shreve's demands to "wait" or "listen," even though he has been narrating, the textual narrator calls attention to the experience differentiating Quentin's part "in the creating of this shade" from Shreve's. Typically, textual narration notes that the speaker "might have been either of them," but focuses in ironic indirection on the "slight difference" between them in "turns of phrase and usage of words" (303). This (in a work highlighting "unbearable similarity") seems expressive understatement in a section where Shreve's radical woman-hating and his easy reference to Charles as "that black son of a bitch" or Charles's mother as "the old Sabine" make us painfully aware of his penchant for crude-speak. Shreve offers this aside on women, for example:

"Because you can't beat them: you just flee (and thank God you can flee, can escape from that massy five-foot-thick maggot-cheesy solidarity which overlays the earth, in which men and women in couples are ranked and racked like nine-pins; thanks to whatever Gods for that masculine hipless tapering peg which fits light and glib to move where the cartridge-chambered hips of women hold them fast)." (312)

Shreve's insistent, tale-loving excitement ends on an exuberant, "Ain't that right? Ain't it? By God, ain't it?" to which Quentin responds "Yes" and nothing else, reminiscent of all those other "yes"'s that acquiesce in the context of felt distance. Even in passages most frequently cited as evidence of the narrative "falling away," syntax or parenthesis undermines idealized fusion:

the two of them creating between them, out of the rag-tag and bob-ends of old tales and talking, people who perhaps had never existed at all anywhere, who, shadows, were shadows not of flesh and blood which had lived and died but shadow in turn of what were (to one of them at least, to Shreve) shades too, quiet as the visible murmur of their vaporizing breath. (303)

Such parenthetical attention to differences in sensibility and experience, in addition to all the distancing strategies of the textual narrator, mitigate any readerly "speaking the text" as some limitless merger of reader, teller, and tale. This tale, too, stands undermined in the act of its own making.

Happy only in the sense of narrative wish-fulfillment, then, the "marriage of speaking and hearing" dramatizes a youthful attempt to avoid the implications of the "old morality," a morality present as variation in this version of the story. In accordance with a protective, idealizing motivation for telling, the youthful identity of the four young men ends with the italicized climax of pages 351–58. As announced, this section "overpasses" to love by envisioning Henry's motive-in-honor for shooting Charles and Charles's motive-in-love for replacing Judith's picture with that of his octoroon mistress. Thus the "marriage" begins with a textual distancing from fairy tale imagining and ends with an abrupt and emphatic commentary on what "the least amount of harm" means for Quentin.

John Duvall lucidly explicates the interrelated and often homoerotic gender reversals in *Absalom, Absalom!*, but he follows Brooks, Matthews, and others in taking "the happy marriage of speaking and hearing" as an "overpassing to love" authorized and validated in the text. Certainly the textual narrator involves Shreve's and Quentin's imagining in a homoerotic reenactment of Henry's and Bon's engagement; in this they merely follow Dante's Paolo and Francesca in the long tradition of would-be lovers who look up from a love story with "something curious in the way they looked at one another." But such a transcendent *over*passing disembodies sexuality, such that only a critical idealizing can affirm a moment when "the death of Charles Bon consummates homo-erotic desire at the level of both story and discourse."[12] The fact that Henry shoots Bon disappears for those who wish to make a homicide into a consummation; and the alternative endings conceived by a critically undifferentiated narration take on the fatalism of Rosa's "might-have-been which is more true than truth."

With bodily and narrative climaxes dramatically juxtaposed, the orgasmic homicide precedes Quentin's jerking uncontrollably with the cold in the "orgasmic" beginning of Chapter 9:

now he began to jerk all over, violently and uncontrollably until he could even hear the bed, until even Shreve felt it and turned, raising himself (by the sound) onto his elbow to look at Quentin, though Quentin himself felt perfectly all right. He felt fine even, lying there and waiting in peaceful curiosity for the next violent unharbingered jerk to come. (361)

The only place in the text where Quentin "felt fine," this moment of autoeroticism occurs after the marriage, when Shreve and Quentin occupy entirely disparate, divorced narrational realms. The positive view of Chapter 8 as narrative climax-as-absence represents a masculinist sense of climax, ignoring what actually happens to bodies: during the marriage, a homicide worked up to in the doubly-nuanced language of "do it now" and panting breath, and after the marriage, a solitary jerking watched by the other who asks "what are you doing that for?" in the midst of his own narcissistic ramblings. Yet Duvall takes Quentin's and Shreve's "happy marriage" as a textual reminder that "good narrative is like good sex and . . . it is metaphorically appropriate that formalists label the moment of greatest dramatic intensity of a plot its climax" (115). To make either transmission itself or a Shreve-Quentin's "mutual" construction of unreality the book's affirmation requires that we either foreground flaws in Quentin's character or censure a later Quentin failing to acquire any version of himself to narrate. Such judgments make the Shreve-Quentin couple advocates for an affirmed love, even though it relies on asymmetrical involvement in telling and feeling, disembodied sexuality, and a transcendently adolescent idealization of love (a love subsequently brought down from imagining to Quentin's entirely auto-erotic experience of reified orgasmic shudders).

In Chapter 9's postmarital context, Shreve glibly asserts his difference from Southern sensibility ("or have I got it backward and was it your folks that are free and the niggers that lost?"), an appropriate tonality for one who has thrilled over mulatto man-sacrifice to the cult of white aristocracy and womanhood. Quentin responds with, "You can't understand it. You would have to be born there," and Shreve continues to taunt Quentin with what he does and does not know by virtue of his Southern heritage. Both Shreve and totalizing affirmations of the marriage ignore the embodiment of gendered and sexual difference. Now, in Chapter 9, Quentin must object yet again to Shreve's reference to "the old dame, the Aunt Rosa." In prose inundated in the language of perception (*taste, feel, smell, hear*), Quentin begins to reexperience what has actually happened to him in a form most like a collage of others' narrations. Yet no textual narrator now comments, as it did in Chapter 8, on what "was probably true enough" and no textual distancing places us as readers outside Quentin's internal discourse.

Quentin's postmarital narration reconstructs the trip to Sutpen's Hundred with Miss Rosa that reveals Henry's corpselike existence behind the door Quentin's memory has taken so many pages to cross. In climax related to "the marriage of speaking and hearing," this door swings inward, representing a symbolic mental passage marked formally by the frame surrounding pages 172–373 in the short bursts of dialogue, the earlier between Henry and Judith and the latter between Quentin and Henry, and by the two halves of Mr. Compson's letter describing Rosa Coldfield's funeral. Like Hightower, Quentin looks for mental escape into a past made different through narration, looks with the same mental accompaniment of galloping hooves and the same invocation of storied retreat in "Now. Now" (363). But such storied "peace" only works for Quentin "for a time" (364), as he reconstructs his actual trip with Miss Rosa out to Sutpen's Hundred to find Henry. Immediately before he determines to ascend the stairs and pass the door himself, he bends to help Clytie up from the ground where Miss Rosa's fist has placed her. The Clytie constructed by others' narration, and therefore with only putative agency, becomes for Quentin *the* figure of a tragic terror experienced by Quentin as such, without reference to the performed, artificial, distanced genres providing the tragic frame of reference for Rosa, Mr. Compson, and Shreve. As earlier when Rosa shrank in terror from the touch of Clytie's flesh, it is the actuality of Clytie's body as he lifts her that forces Quentin to acknowledge both consciousness and intentionality amidst the terror he sees in her eyes:

When he reached her he saw that she was quite conscious, her eyes wide open and calm; he stood above her thinking, "Yes. She is the one who owns the terror." (369)

Earlier Shreve's narration said of Clytie that "she didn't tell you in actual words because even in the terror she kept the secret" (351), and yet Quentin's invocation of Clytie's terror and his later vision of the fire she sets demonstrates a very different affect behind different "turns of phrase and usage of words." (When criticism glosses over such differences between Shreve's language in Chapter 8 and Quentin's in Chapter 9, it treats everything from the "marriage of speaking and hearing" on as though it belongs to "the boys.")[13]

Clytie's only line, a plea for nonintervention based on her own self-sacrifice, asks of Quentin that he take away Miss Rosa because "Whatever he [Henry] done, me and Judith and him have paid it out." Quentin's narration moves in contrast from Clytie's light body ("like picking up a handful of sticks concealed in a rag bundle") and that "feeble movement or intention in her limbs" to Miss Rosa's bloodless, "sleepwalker's" face returning from Henry's room. Quentin realizes he "must" see what lies behind the upstairs door, and does so in a remarkable narrative ellipsis. The actual experience of seeing Henry takes place somewhere between Quentin's "but I must see" and the following "So when he came back down the stairs" (371). Narration only provides us the action of that ellipsis in the form of memory as Quentin's internal discourse fights off the implications of what he/the text/we have avoided. In the act of comparing Miss Rosa's "fixed sleep-walking face" to his own, Quentin tries to talk down fear: "He was twenty years old; he was not afraid, because what he had seen out there could not harm him, yet he ran" (372). Quentin's response to the terror in Clytie's eyes protests too much and he thinks suddenly of a purification ritual: "I need to bathe." As fear overtakes him, he mentally acknowledges that he too has been asleep, that the sight of Henry beyond the door he has forced himself to open, a mental door in memory-narration here, was the same whether "waking or sleeping." Such language remembers the process by which Miss Rosa herself became a ghostly presence, for at the beginning of Chapter 3 she could not tell how many times she had actually seen Sutpen, since his "ogreface" occurred in all narrations: "waking or sleeping, the aunt had taught her to see nothing else" (62).

Howling Through History

Invoking again the textual relation between felt harm and storied evasion, Henry's corpselike physical inaction embodies Quentin's own feared entrapment in remembered/narrated experience. And the palindrome in couplets that follows perfectly links this identity and death:

And you are———?.
Henry Sutpen.
And you have been here———?
Four years.
And you came home———?

To die. Yes.
To die?
Yes. To die.
And you have been here————?
Four years.
And you are————?
Henry Sutpen. (373)

Such cyclical repetition dramatizes the ultimately empty center of a self predefined by language and therefore outside one's control because of its given form.[14] But the futility evident in the palindrome's cyclicity does not simply apply to some abstracted narrativity; rather, it marks Quentin's mental passage into narration/memory describing the return of Miss Rosa to Sutpen's Hundred "though he had not been there." However much Quentin may here become the ghost others have made him, he retains a panting sensation that follows on his feared identification with Miss Rosa and Henry. Now he intones a Learlike "Nevermore of peace. Nevermore of peace. Nevermore Nevermore Nevermore," which like the passional denial of the book's last sentence signifies his affective distance from others' telling even as their language subsumes his own.

After the palindrome, no mention of the tragic or of its all-too-visible paraphernalia attends the story of Rosa's last trip to Sutpen's Hundred and its role in sparking the fire Clytie sets to keep her from intervening in the Sutpen destiny (perhaps with ironic reference to Mr. Compson's conjecture that Sutpen meant to name her Cassandra but confused his tragic women). And yet, the Quentin who emerges from the *actual* trip to Sutpen's Hundred and the actual touch of "flesh on flesh" now enters, once again, into forced and uncooperative narration-as-dialogue with Shreve about what he sees "though he had not been there." Now he cannot tell if he stares at "the actual window or the window's pale rectangle upon his eyelids," and what emerges has the "curious, light, gravity-defying attitude" of all those unrealities *Absalom, Absalom!* labels as such. And although he has avoided finishing his father's letter for over 200 pages, he works up to finishing it with the same dire slowing of narrative time: "in a moment; even almost now, now, now" (377). Appropriately, for Quentin's avoidance forebodes such a finish, Mr. Compson's ruminations on Miss Rosa's death concern evasion itself, taking up the thought on "the ultimate escape" mid-sentence:

And if there can be either access of comfort or cessation of pain in the ultimate escape from a stubborn and amazed outrage which over a period of forty-three years has been companionship and bread and fire and all, I do not know that either————. (174)
————or perhaps there is. Surely it can harm no one to believe that perhaps she has escaped not at all the privilege of being outraged and amazed and of not forgiving but on the contrary has herself gained that place or bourne where the

objects of the outrage and of the commiseration also are no longer ghosts but are actual people to be actual recipients of the hatred and the pity. It will do no harm to hope—You see I have written hope, not think. So let it be hope. (377)

Syntactically, Mr. Compson moves from "Surely it can do no harm to believe that perhaps" to "It will do no harm to hope," reinforcing how necessary it is for him to push to the afterlife any possibility of *actual* engagement. And even "hope" stands undermined by his refusal to use "think," his refusal, even, to let "hope" pass without comment. Fixed on the transmogrified amazement and outrage of Miss Rosa, Mr. Compson's letter reveals his own personal detachment, figured forcefully in his final figure about the living-then-frozen redworm in the clods of earth displaced for the grave (a frozen field as fitting end for Rosa Coldfield).

Quentin's fearful experience of potential selves in the "all of us" made by Thomas Sutpen's story disallows the ease with which his father and Shreve retreat to doomed others: doomed women, doomed races, doomed sexualities. Quentin's responses-in-progress to sundry narrative motivations show him painfully aware of narrative manipulation, although ultimately trapped by narrations whose assumptions he can neither accept nor exorcise. Unlike Morrison's characters' undergoing the processes of rememory, Quentin's narrating others fix all personhood within the historicized conventions of genre, making a false analogue of Morrison's use of "love" and the adolescent, romanticized love of Chapter 8.[15] Possessing almost "unbearable similarity" to prior narrations, Quentin's final "seeing" nevertheless distinguishes itself through "turns of phrase and usage of words" (303) and a dramatized emotion. However many details his account shares with others, Quentin's sensibility still differentiates itself by his engagement in an actuality felt most forcefully in its absence.

The Clytie who remains doomed to tragic mystery in already narrated stories appears in Quentin's figural consciousness in similar language, and yet his and a textual narrator's final version reveals an affective agency that distinguishes his engagement from their sloughing off of terror onto the tragic mulatto. Without pause after the final words of Mr. Compson's letter, Shreve launches into his grotesque racial accounting, ending, "So it takes two niggers to get rid of one Sutpen, don't it?" (378). Without answer or response from Quentin, Shreve "clears the whole ledger" except for "the one nigger Sutpen left." Quentin responds "yes" to Shreve's first question about Jim Bond: "You still hear him at night sometimes. Don't you?" And although he responds "no" to Shreve's "Do you want to know what I think?" Shreve barges on with his flippant vision of a miscegenation made harmless, where as they spread out toward the poles they will bleach out again like the rabbits and the birds do, so they won't show up so sharp against the snow. But it will still be Jim Bond; and so in a few thousand years, I who regard you will also have sprung from the loins of African kings. (378)

Then he asks Quentin, as though the logic of race here suggests it: "Now I want you to tell me just one thing more. Why do you hate the South?" By this time, Quentin's passional resistance can happen only as ellipsis, an ellipsis reminiscent of the panting cold characterized by some as "good sex":

"I dont hate it," Quentin said, quickly, at once, immediately; "I dont hate it," he said. *I dont hate it* he thought, panting in the cold air, the iron New England dark; *I dont. I dont! I dont hate it! I dont hate it!* (378)

Quentin's last words catch him flailing in denial, but the spontaneous and cumulative passion of that denial emanates from his sustained resistance to a self formed by others' harmful stories. The context dramatizes Quentin's engagement in an absent actuality entirely peripheral to Shreve's flip observations about women and blacks, an actuality outside the language of what he sees because "waking or sleeping" he has been taught "to see nothing else." Ricoeur's insight that we recognize ourselves in the stories we tell about ourselves has inverse application to Quentin, who recognizes himself in stories told by others, yet without recognizing his actual experience.

The work's end, with neither significance nor climactic value for many contemporary readings, relies on some readerly acknowledgment that Quentin's engagement in the dynamics of love and hate implicate him in tragic and haunting loss (modern now, and with only already internalized language as reference to Greek or Elizabethan tragedy), an estrangement from any *actual* human connections. In passing through framing doors inseparable from his father's "inscrutable and curiously lifeless doorways," he moves passionally beyond what prior narrations allow him to "see," even though narration confines itself to this second-order "sight." Quentin's actuality, different in its absence here from the easier "something missing" in his father's narration, posits a consciousness overcome by a Clytie who "owns the terror," a Jim Bond whose howling has no clear origin, and a history he/we cannot narrate into oblivion without ourselves becoming ghosts. *Absalom, Absalom!*'s power inheres in processes of construction and deconstruction that cannot merely accommodate a terrible history in speculation separate from passion and its embodied affects. Redemptive readings let us as readers off the moral hook by avoiding any identification with Quentin as the passive, feminized victim of narrations designed to accommodate and then absent such a history. And conceptualizing the "marriage of speaking and hearing" as a triumphant climax-as-absence to narration's foreplay only overpasses to idealizations valuing the masculinist version of a homoeroticism constructed from the salvage of heterosexist romance.

A model of narrative climax inseparable from romantic nostalgia for how "a youth and a very young girl" might look at each other "out of virginity itself" necessarily prejudges the Quentin of *Absalom, Absalom!*'s last chapter, who quails in self-reflexive horror at his resemblance to other failed sensibilities: Miss Rosa, Henry, his father, and Shreve. Quentin has no capacity to "bear with living," no remaining possibility of action, none of the detachment of his father, and no sustainable pleasure in narrative construction of a self. Against the unreality of Miss Rosa, "fighting like a doll in a nightmare," the death-in-life-in-death of remembered Henry, and Mr. Compson's penchant for pushing away the actual to the afterlife, Quentin's passional outburst at the end stands as another cry of outrage. Neither Clytie's terror, born of the most profoundly internalized self-repudiation, nor Jim Bond's howl ("only the sound of the idiot negro left"), nor Quentin's final, passionate assertion receive much critical attention, primarily because the activity of the play-within-language links value with the "incredulous narration" rather than with actual human relationship.[16]

The complexity of tensions within *Absalom, Absalom!* certainly informs the indeterminacy of its ending, but it also determines the primacy of concerns: the overwhelming power of these narratives to usurp memory of "the actual people to be the actual recipients of the pity and the fear"; the self-deluding innocence of any morality whose ingredients, like those of pie or cake, define an outcome (like the mix that makes up, say androgyny, from the ingredients of masculine and feminine); and the falsity of second-order experience when it subsumes both actuality and referential connection. Heretofore, even Shreve as the normative, "ratiocinative" Canadian has emerged more sympathetically from criticism than has the subjugated, feminized, emotionally wrought Quentin, who, after all, will confirm all moral opprobrium by committing suicide in an earlier text![17] Critical desire turns gladly toward Shreve's play, Miss Rosa's cyclic repetitions, and Mr. Compson's language theory precisely because they avoid the feminized Quentin, who, despite his virgin's role in a narrative marriage dominated by Shreve, is the *actual recipient* of narration's doublings, repetitions, and mergers. Such a marriage "overpasses" to a narrative of remarkably conventional romantic altruism, one whose miscegenation disappears in the ideal gesture of an idealized death/absence very much on the model of Henry's virginity and

Mr. Compson's language. Shreve becomes identified with a "lesson of love" and Miss Rosa has the "last word."[18]

The narrators originally associated with what only *appears* harmless also originate the actual harm done in *Absalom, Absalom!*, harm harkening back to the social institution of slavery. The slight instigating Thomas Sutpen's initial trip to Haiti involves the slight of not just class, but racialized class—that "marriage" of economic and racial injustice—in his knowledge that he has been treated "like a Nigger." (Patricia Williams aptly calls this sense of injustice based on the fall into a racially marked social position "the ethnic scarring of whiteness.") Shreve's ranting has seemed merely irrelevant to many contemporary readings, but its relevance inheres in its difference, in tonality and affect, from Quentin's passional response to the social crisis not recognized as tragedy (as opposed to the tragedy sloughed off onto the mulatto Sutpens). Quentin becomes what he wants not to become *except* for his difference in affective engagement: only Quentin remains haunted by Jim Bond's "directionless" howl; only Quentin intones "nevermore of peace" in thinking the thoughts that "waking or sleeping" entrap him in terrible accommodations of narrating mind. Whereas Shreve's crass interpretive sense of race, gender, and sexuality attends the heterosexual family romance in which Bon dies in a fit of self-sacrifice rather than in a mode of protest, Quentin's repetitions of others' views attend dramatic realization of his fears that the empty center of narrative truth may coincide with his own empty center. His final, passionate denial lives in the referential space between language and any actuality to which it refers, and his personal struggle—more sympathetically portrayed than either criticism or cross-reference to *The Sound and the Fury* suggests—engages difference that refuses to reduce "unbearable similarity" to the same old oppositions. Whatever the parameters of resistant readings of *Absalom, Absalom!* they would value Quentin's passional, buried life over the ability to find himself within a dominating narration, and they would fully examine the textual puzzles behind which stories do the "least harm," a very different thing than which stories subject-characters *say* do no harm.

Attention to the text's narrative involutions need not obscure Quentin's difference in affective practice from that of other characters. Critical distaste for the Quentin of *Absalom, Absalom!* resonates in part because it parallels the problem of any subordinated identity engaged in avoiding received, dominant constructions, yet cognizant of the construction inherent in "identity" itself. Quentin's affective life argues against some depersonalized equivalence between Quentin and the language others put in his head.[19] *Absalom, Absalom!* consistently calls attention to Quentin's material, embodied self, to his struggle to hold onto personhood and agency despite erotic involvement, and to the manipulative harm—indeed, a kind of power play—that inheres in dominant narratives moving to abstract and disembody her/him who does not narrate, the text's silenced (but not always silent) voices. Quentin's fictional resistances in *Absalom, Absalom!* constitute a tragic lack, tantamount to asking readers to identify with a passional life inexpressible in dominant discourse and to understand narrative involution as a critical commentary on detached, merely intellectual relation to actual bodies and to actual worlds. Such understanding sees the moral problematics of identity as social and fluid precisely because it does not see entrapment in language as absolute.[20] When criticism grants Miss Rosa or Mr. Compson or Shreve a moral superiority to Quentin on the grounds that each manages to "bear with living" by constructing a personal narrative, it privileges values of accommodating mind in the act of escaping precisely those connections outside language figured by Morrison's fulfilled tragic paradox in sound, or touch, or weather.[21]

Read as a site of social struggle, the tragedy hovering behind *Absalom, Absalom!* belongs to a history of terrible hurt that continues to reinscribe itself through the narrations of those for whom disembodied, abstracted discourse is all. Ironically, postmodern excitement over a dehistoricized absence—the metaphysical "marriage of speaking and hearing"—has overshadowed what reads equally well as a critique of postmodernity's penchant for talk disengaged from action. So too does attention to Quentin's sameness, especially if not seen as a second-order, resisted sameness, to other narrators, whether positively as part of "incredulous narration" or negatively as inevitably entrapped in a monumental South, allow readers to abstract themselves from values alternative to a fatalistic sense of tragedy. Not without its absences, this tragedy belongs to the linked and hovering absences informing the book's structure: the soundless howl of Jim Bond, the absence of either figural consciousness or agency in the carefully named Clytie, and the absence of the "actual persons" with whom only Quentin desires "actual" relationship. That novels cannot write the histories of *actual* bodies does not lessen the intensity of felt desire for a relation to the past that takes into account the past's ongoing presence-in-absence. If we have been taught to read the body as the inscribed surface for relations of power, then surely Quentin's shivering, impassioned body has as the subject of desire a more innovative relation to the past and a more embodied relation to the living.

Reading *Absalom, Absalom!* under the influence of *Beloved,* a recursive act, helps turn the Faulknerian question about tragedy, "Who owns the terror?" on itself. Why has no one read Shreve's racist phantasmagoria as a modern sequel to Poe's *The Narrative of Arthur Gordon Pym,* a fantasized miscegenation that permanently neutralizes the power of blackness?

Why has Quentin's sloughing off of his own terror onto the tragic mulatto—ancient, female, and "gnomelike"—had so little resonance as the vicarious sacrifice hidden from Frazer (yet revealed as self-reference in Girard)? Why has all that self-repudiating, disembodied sexuality been taken as "good sex" or even as a progressive homoerotic fantasy? Why has Jim Bond's howling been lost to hearing? In choosing to end analysis with Quentin's marriage, as opposed to ending as the work ends with Clytie's fire, readers both share and sacralize the wish-fulfilling fantasy of the scapegoat who volunteers her own purification by fire, immolating herself and all the "guilty" in a conflagration that accomplishes, via myth, the desire Baldwin saw in Faulkner himself: "He is seeking to exorcise a history which is also a curse. He wants the old order, which came into existence through unchecked greed and wanton murder, to redeem itself without further bloodshed—without, that is, any further menacing itself—and without coercion" (47). Considerable irony inheres in the theoretical consensus about a modernism demythologizing the sacred and a postmodernism "demythologizing the demythologizing." A certain logic has framed Judith into a tragic heroine out of a psychoanalysis worshipful of the phallus.[22] And yet she has no more real mystery about her than does Sutpen, who doggedly pursues an epic design from which he does not waver, or than does the narrative speculation of Chapter 8. Here, as elsewhere, dominant readings may repress that myth named by Baldwin and very much with us still: that an oppressive social order can be redeemed through the sacrifice of a tragic hero, one who willingly takes up a heroic self-immolation that negates any continuing menace to the social order and wipes the slate clean (or at least takes it back yet once again to a familiar story of origins). The same Faulkner who so convincingly represents the limitations in sensibility about which he writes has here the fictional, no doubt unconscious prescience to represent how readings intent on applauding "incredulous narration" emerge in a predictable outcome: "but nothing happens" (at least nothing beyond the creation of the social fantasy itself).

And yet, for the postmarital Quentin, something beyond conjecture does happen. Clytie burns down the Sutpen house with herself and others in it and Jim Bond escapes howling into the night. As though in fulfillment of Girard's premise that scapegoating rites lose their "effectiveness" as systems of belief falter, Clytie's fire does not wipe out the last mixed-blood Sutpen. Quentin retains a residual passion linking his own affective crisis to Clytie's eyes and Jim Bond's howl, and his only "original" lines, those "nevermore"s he gets from Lear and not from other narrators, take up aspects of a tragic tradition in which he cannot read himself. The dominant and dominating narrators of *Absalom, Absalom!* frame tragedy out of a Haitian revolution that becomes the mysterious origin for other terrors—sexual, racial, historical—for which it stands as the fearsome figure. When Quentin recognizes that "It is she who owns the terror," his projection of tragedy onto Clytie reveals precisely his own failures *in action.*

Reading backward from Morrison helps foreground the cost to Quentin of giving up on actual relationship and the degree to which he does not simply succumb to fatality, for his last words still have the passionate intensity of ongoing struggle that differentiate him not only from other narrators, but also from Bodwin's unknowing complicity— the white man who does not even know enough to see the terror in Sethe's eyes. Quentin's sustained struggle *not* to become like those whose voices dominate him gives way to a struggle not to hate the South, but neither struggle reduces to the elements of nostalgia and elegy found in tragedy as fated by history.[23] Rather than participating vicariously in Shreve's and Quentin's self-indulgent fantasizing, any "we" would do better to read more closely that moment that retains the tragic edge of a modernity whose social tragedy does not inhere in the loss of some monumental past but in precisely the incapacity to act upon felt connection across boundaries. Read under the influence of *Beloved* as such, Quentin stands as the character closest to the passional desire for actual relationshp and the action that might achieve it, even if on a level unconscious to himself or Faulkner; and readers stand differentiated in terms of how they might identify or not with that moment when Quentin looks in Clytie's eyes and knows at once, "She is the one who owns the terror." However much her diminutive name and formulaic reductions distance Clytie from the wronged and vengeful Clytaemnestra, what Faulkner-Quentin sees in the depths of her eyes is his own terror, the terror that somewhere within the house mulatto lurk the fires for which the Haitian revolution stands. Quentin's tragedy does not lie in a past overtaking his present, with its attendant sense of loss, but rather in his incapacity to understand or act upon the precisely positioned meaning of Clytie's gaze. And although the Quentin who hears Jim Bond and blurts his protest against the perversity of his world does not himself have the stature of a tragic hero, his white but feminized and homosexualized form of resistance testifies to the tragedy of a social order that can no more prevent Clytie's fire than it can own the terror of its own making. For all subject positions complicit not just in a generalized patriarchy but in explicitly white, gendered, and sexualized dominances, it is "we" who own that terror and we who remain unable to understand or act upon the presence articulated by Baby Suggs: "Here, in this place, we flesh" (*Beloved* 88).

Chapter 5
Literary Passing

Ida, "Melanctha," and the Andrew-gyne

A new theory of irony is called for, one that focuses not on productive intentions but on reception as a productive activity. However, this does not involve merely relocating the intentions that make a difference from the author to the reader. Any reliance on conscious intentions, even the feminist intentions one might assume are behind the production or perception of mimicry, needs to be examined. What has passed for "passing" for rather than being womanly—the parodic mimicry of femininity—may cover up certain unexamined notions of genuine femininity that are class-based and ethnocentric. Feminists must uncover the unintended effects of the mimic's good intentions through an analysis of the politics of the unconscious that subtend this politics of consciousness.

—Carole-Anne Tyler, "The Feminine Look"

But it was natural enough. Nature is not natural and that is natural enough.

—Gertrude Stein, *Ida*

The Lesbian Lie and the Racial Lie

Like Faulkner, Gertrude Stein stands as a giant of modernism now increasingly valued for her prescient foreshadowings of postmodernity. But just as celebrating narrative indeterminacy in *Absalom, Absalom!* threatens to overtake attention to the social meanings of Quentin's entrapments and resistances, so does celebrating Stein's linguistic "wandering" as textual resistance threaten to overtake attention to the implications of the social worlds she invents as liberation from those of the realist novel. In *Ida*, written late in her literary career, a focal character seems to overcome values identifiable as masculine, bourgeois, heterosexual, and white. Despite this, many critics have read *Ida* as "without external reference" even though a character may appear with dramatic suddenness to say, "I only like a white skin" or "She was not unemployed. She just sat and she always had enough. Anybody could" (28). In the

earlier "Melanctha," a mulatto woman stands defeated by roughly similar values in one of the most blatant modern examples of "playing in
the dark," in which Stein transfers a story about herself (unfulfilled
in *Q.E.D.*) to black characters whose sexuality she can then "unmask"
as controlled by convention.[1] Yet interpretations of "Melanctha" commonly either explicate away the racism or ultimately forget that Stein
chooses to set her own story in a black community of her own making.[2]
Perhaps this is because, however heralded the death of the author, reading Stein often follows her own self-conscious articulations of process
and purpose (for example, how *Ida* addresses her problems with Hollywood's image-making or how "Melanctha" works through her relation to
William James). Indeed, Stein's own emphasis on her identity as a woman
and a writer "taking the novel into the twentieth century" has validated
readings that foreground gender and genre, with authorial interventions
into governing cultural narratives seen as committing liberatory acts of
speculation that "make visible what the culture has agreed not to see."[3]
Yet the critical problem remains of how to distinguish such heady narrative intrusions from what remains unseen because so "natural" to Stein's
own cultural assumptions. And in a world of naturalization, it is only
natural that ways of reading often mirror the normative dominances.

Among the few critics to see some relation between Stein's treatment
of sexuality and race, Catherine Stimpson suggests that dissimulations
about lesbian identity ("the lesbian lie") help sustain Stein's capacity to
"anesthetize" black history. Indeed, narration in which complicity and
resistance seem so often inexorably linked greatly complicates judgments about what it means for a white lesbian writer to "lie" about her
positioning. Both culturally produced and producing culture, Stein's
experimental conflations of fiction and lifestory participate in cultural
meanings distinct from the enforced hiding, described well by Gloria
Hull, of black women writers of the period even tangentially linked to
a black lesbian network.[4] Though the tendency to be both sympathetic
and critical, to "denounce the lie while exculpating the liar" (163), seems
itself relational to one's positioning, I want to explore how the lesbian
lie of *Ida* provocatively differs from the racial lie of "Melanctha," despite
an often comic indeterminacy important to both. Comparative readings here will emphasize neither childlike "kitsch" nor postmodern pastiche, but will explore the relevance of the comic yet critically utopian
mode theorized in *The Color Purple* and the mode of social tragedy that
always threatens to disturb comic "wholesomeness" in *The Salt Eaters*. The
nature of the fictive worlds Stein constructs for the androgyne and the
mulatto should help sort out the processes of complicity and resistance
as they negotiate the permeable, often conflicted nature of the comic.

Nothing Natural About Nature

Until recent feminist attention, readers of *Ida* referred its level of abstraction to formal or cubist principles and tended to find in its form a
"freedom from fidelity to the external world as referent" (Dubnick 71).[5]
In this they followed the lead of early reviewers who found it a para-
gon of language laid bare of social meanings and contexts, or, as one
Time reviewer would put it, "The words in which it is told are stripped
of normal logic and totally cleansed of emotion. The result is something
as intricately clean as a fugue or a quadratic equation." The cleanliness
of a mathematics without social reference made obvious the comparison to Lewis Carroll's form of the comic: "As a story *Ida* makes no sense
in causal terms. The logic is the logic of fantasy. *Ida* makes the kind
of sense *Alice in Wonderland* does" (Dubnick 74). Since characterization
seemed to consist of only the most general or superficial traits, the comedy seemed naive or childlike and any praise focused on experimental
form, a play for its own sake with prior conventions.

Feminist and postmodern readings have paid more attention to *Ida*
as a figurative liberation from both social and artistic constraints. Ellen
Berry, for example, usefully reads *Ida* as a kind of postmodern melodrama in which the division of sexuality from sociality informs the restlessness of desire, making the work as a whole a parable about "the impossibility of expressing female desire while at the same time remaining
within social law" (158). And Harriet Chessman makes of *Ida*'s narrator
a "she" whose subversive role lies in undermining "the position of superior knowledge and certainty traditionally assumed by the narrative
persona." This Ida represents heroic attempts at forging an "authentic
self" to emerge from beneath all the simulations attendant on "women's
doubleness as a condition of life." For postmodernists, *Ida* becomes primarily about "strategies of appropriation and recoding," and its value
resides in its play with any number of genres (bildungsroman, melodrama, comic romance, and tabloid journalism among them). And in
the context of parody, Stein's own assertion about *Ida*'s treatment of
"publicity saints" supports readings that find a cartoonish or "kitschy"
celebration of a character who, presumably as Stein's alter-ego, finds a
liberation from the public, heterosexual world.[6] In these readings the
episodes that early readers found digressive serve primarily to simulate
the excesses of prior conventions. Read as such, *Ida*'s wit rests on the
play with language and genre, and its focus complements Stein's ongoing social geography of the United States in a lightly satirical view of
gender relations and national character. Read under the influence of revisionary comic theory, however, it emerges as a critically utopian mode
with the satiric or dystopian mode of the first half working toward the

second half's ideal of relationship, an ideal still under the social duress of the natural (or what "anybody" knows and "everybody" says).

The Ida of *Ida*'s first half lives in a narrative world that mimics the language and values of largely bourgeois social discourse and yet suppresses the sense of a narrative or authorial persona. This form of radical mimesis blurs any possible distinction between whether Ida actively creates herself to fit the social world narration provides her or passively conforms to social expectation. Narrative positioning overlaps with the indirect discourse (or figural consciousness) of Ida such that one might in a shorthand way talk about the "character" of Ida as though Ida's consciousness internalizes and represents as her own story what it has learned from prior scripts. One might equally well talk about a character reduced to the social languages that describe her as though narration reports the scripts that write Ida on an initially blank slate. Whatever the indeterminacy of a character more process than individual personality, the social values—and the often comic critique of them in the first half—have considerable specificity. Once understood as a conflation of internalized, figural consciousness and the language of social construction, the narrative discontinuity taken as the work's most salient characteristic comes to reveal both a logic internal to particular episodes and a more global logic relevant to the gaps between episodes.

Despite an ongoing present tense and an insistent (if surface) discontinuity, episodes in the first half of the work proceed within the structure of a kind of parodic bildungsroman. However, instead of the bildungsroman's affirmation of growth or maturation, the narration here follows a chameleon character whose changes come to mean in relation to the expectations that attend social roles, most notably those of unwanted baby, girl-child, sexual object, and the wife of successive men (a sort of typology of husbands) who have diverse requirements for wives. Within each episode, narration simulates how the processes of social construction "create" the Ida who goes from a split subject to one "lost" in an identity trouble named specifically as such.

Ida's birth happens in the third person yet in the language of the stories surrounding the subject of birth, corresponding to a consciousness simulating the processes of social construction; since the only thing any of us know about our births comes in the form of familial stories accrued over time, it makes no difference whether narrative consciousness belongs to early memory or to later story. "Its mother held it with her hands to keep Ida from being born" (7) signifies that the object-child is unwanted, and though we do not yet know what it means that she remembers having a "twin," we will find out later when she remembers "having" to have a twin (inventing a twin to fill a gap). The subject of an unwanted birth invokes familial lore about an old woman "who is no relation" but who keeps spreading it about that "the great aunt had something happen to her oh many years ago, it was a soldier." In this world, what happens to women is men, and what happened to this woman becomes a kind of family scandal: "and then the great-aunt had had little twins born to her and then she had quietly, the twins were dead then, born so, she had buried them under a pear tree and nobody knew." Narration cannot name the scandal as such (it being the nature of family scandals to be hidden) any more than it can name abortion (or who knows what kind of death), leaving only the suggestive, second-order reference to burial under a pear tree. The family record demands that nobody believe the old woman, but nonetheless her story continues to haunt, as scandals will. The episode pretends to tell about a birth, but its logic reveals how the birth of identity grows out of a world fraught with worries about respectability.

Similarly, stories of childhood and adolescence portray not the individual child but the way a social world inducts the child into its assumptions and values. Most overtly, gender and sexuality become a part of the "funny things" that happen to Ida, only to be assimilated into Ida-consciousness. Thus whatever is at first "funny" becomes simply what happens, a part of normalcy. As we read, the sociotextual world assimilates all "funny" things into the fabric of assumptions, a narrative certainty about the way "anybody" in the world *is*. The repeated "there was nothing to do" catches the passivity expected of females, as does all worldly talk about how to say and do. In a world that teaches girl-children passivity, new things frighten, especially boy-children who take action: "The first time she saw anything it frightened her. She saw a little boy and when he waved to her she would not look his way." Not much later, Ida learns a more sophisticated lesson about the attentions of men: "Once she was lost that is to say a man followed her and that frightened her so that she was crying just as if she had been lost. In a little while that is some time after it was a comfort to her that this thing had happened." This narrative sequence shows that men threaten loss (of self, virginity, reputation), but to be female means both to think of men as frightening and also to see their attentions as comforting signs of one's desirability.

Several episodes, most important those centered around her dog and her twin, demonstrate how a gendered competition marks the measure of this desirability. Displaced to the household of her grandfather, and in the absence of any adult responses to her child's need, Ida suddenly asserts the presence of a dog named Love. (As so often, narration operates on a symbolic level so overt that it dramatizes cliché: since "love is blind," the dog Love is of course blind.) And she confides to the blind dog Love the intimate details of the created twin whose name changes according to need in the manner of all the made-up constructions of childhood. That Ida "has to have a twin" plays on all the divided selves of fictional tradition, but reduces to assertion the function of an alter-ego who succeeds at everything only too well. As a split subject just beginning to learn about competition among women for love (unknown women appear in an automobile and abscond with Love!), Ida begins to experience her twin as a potential threat. Thus, in complicity with narration, Ida kills off Winnie just when she overtakes Ida in competitive designs of her own imagining. Taught that women compete for the attentions of men on the basis of beauty and that men impress with status, Ida of course meets men who show off before women ("If I were to give orders and everybody obeyed me and they do, said the officer, would that impress you"). But beauty does not mean love, winning the contest matters more than the thing won, and ending up on the top of a star system (winning "the beauty prize for all the world" 27) in no way assuages the fact of being "lost." Without self-definition except as a response to such facts of life, Ida has no trouble playing the absent other to the officer who insists on "conversing" by himself.

The episodic story of Ida's marriages parody both melodramatic form and the emptiness of gendered roles and conventions, but it also catalogues diverse ways of evading actual interaction with others. Having tried a projected twin-self and a sadly solitary self-centeredness, Ida turns to marriage; but narration foreshadows failure in advance by announcing that marriage will *not* mean "that never again would she be alone" (49). In a brilliant parody of the heterosexual marriage in its privileged forms, Stein takes Ida through a series of marriages that change men and locales but stay unfortunately the same in the loneliness and alienation of wifely roles. The husbands, of course, come with their own constructions. Her first husband, Arthur, has learned myths of sexuality and gender from other males, particularly myths about indiscriminate male sexuality (as in a parable about a dog who "would just go on making love to anything") and about the necessity of masculine adventure (as in a shipwreck so rewarding "that he tried to get shipwrecked again" 37). When married to the sentimental romantic who intones "Oh Ida," and who sighs over the water in Virginia as easily as over the snow in Montana (as long as he does not actually look at it), Ida dreams of white orchids and of longing for water. When married (in I.4) to the "selfish" and exclusive Bostonian Andrew Hamilton, she goes nowhere because "all who had anywhere to go did not go. This is what they did."

Normalcy as a wife means creating the self that conforms to both husbandly and societal expectation. But of course, the supposed normalcy protests too much: "Everything that happened to her was not strange. All along it was not strange Ida was not strange" (57). The prose records only what Ida "thought she was thinking," which includes the world-justifying "it was so important that all these thing happened to her just when and how they did." "Lost" as a child when most successful in competition, Ida the adult has the recurrent identity trouble attendant on overachieving others' expectations: "Everybody said to Ida and they said it to Frederick too. Smile at me please smile at me. / Ida smiled" (56). Whether in Washington, Ohio, or Texas, Ida and her husbands "were not there together or anywhere" (57). And in a chapter named "POLITICS" (I.5, 65), a "pleasant" Ida learns the political self-definition of a wife who "always saw everybody and said she saw them." She moves from intoning "oh dear" and "thank you" to the more elegantly empty "thank you very much, thank you very much indeed" (73). Moving between husbands and cities in a restless form of serial monogamy, Ida's marriages take her through sundry forms of invisibility and absence, a traveling in stasis that corresponds to the unfulfilling nature of attempting to fulfill womanly, wifely identities.

For many readers, the abrupt movement from episode to episode represents the arbitrary nature of language, yet the logic of Ida's going away or marrying again always relates to failures implicit in social worlds. For example, note how narrative logic comments less on language per se than on a social pathology that presents itself as normalcy: "She looked around her, she was not all alone because somebody passed by her and they said, it is a nicer evening than yesterday evening and she said, it was. Ida married again" (62). The abrupt announcement of marriage simulates the "natural" logic that responds to the effort of empty conversation with yet another attempt at marriage as the way not to be alone or sad or tired or depressed. The identity trouble inheres in Ida's perpetual need to make herself the shape that will fill the lack created by social naming: "They all said everybody said, never rather be Ida, it got to be kind of a song. / Ida never heard anybody sing it. When she heard her name she never heard it. That was Ida" (59).

What the gaps between episodes have to do with the general identity trouble of a character thus constructed and constructing has much to do with the overall progression of episodes, which does more than follow Ida through the stages of life from babyhood to wifehood. Readers have frequently suggested that *Ida* avoids all historicity. Yet if attention to how identity formation works constitutes merely a different kind of reference, one that simulates the very processes of social construction, then the transitions between episodes—although more gap than transition—suggest not so much the absence of historicity as the interruptive, intervening status of a repressed historicity. In the implied social world of *Ida*'s first half, other characters appear and disappear as sudden and seemingly inexplicable interruptions of a restless and troubled identity bent on making itself over to fit whatever environments demand. Thus whatever happens "to" Ida makes her first into a divided self and then into the nonself visible to public history or what "everybody" knows about Ida. However, what "everybody" neither sees nor wishes to see is a history so marginalized to Ida's world—in which the exigencies of obtaining food, clothing, rent, or work never appear—that it can only break into the more sustained episodes of through-composed history.

Almost any page offers evidence of how the internal leaps within sustained episodes relate to those abrupt disjunctures between episodes. Note, for example, an early scene in which the leaps may seem to evade any very particular social subject:

> She was walking and she saw a woman and three children, two little girls and a littler boy. The boy was carrying a black coat on his arms, a large one.
> A woman said to Ida, I only like a white skin. If when I die I come back again and I find I have any other kind of skin then I will be sure that I was very wicked before.
> This made Ida think about talking.
> She commenced to talk. She liked to see people eat, in restaurants and wherever they eat, and she liked to talk. You can always talk with army officers. She did. (28)

The passage gives apparently gratuitous voice to the lowest common denominator of racist myth; yet, read as a simulation of how a world's talk becomes internal logic, the passage joins others that allow a repressed, marginalized historicity to emerge in the only way it can: as an intervening blurb, an interruptive and unanalyzed allusion to race in a white and privileged world whose overt concerns and assumptions make race irrelevant. Here a black coat carried on an arm images forth a comment about the social meaning of skin color, a meaning articulated by a white woman sure that blackness and evil coexist. Because the woman's comment creates white skin as having both aesthetic and moral value, it demonstrates the power and importance of talk. A lesson not lost on Ida, she puts this lesson to use immediately in talk that affirms her own respectability and status. Thus a passage with three seemingly separate moments (and the overt lack of connection often named "surreal") has a social logic that reveals the interwoven constructions of gender, race, and class.

Immediately following Ida's responsive decision to talk with certainly white army officers, the parable of the gate introduces a theory about the relation of historicity (or history as memory) to the artificial barriers that define social categories:

> Once upon a time way back there were always gates, gates that opened so that you could go in and then little by little there were no fences no walls anywhere. For a little time they had a gate even when there was no fence. It was there just

to look elegant and it was nice to have a gate that would click even if there was no fence. By and by there was no gate.

Ida when she had a dog had often stood by a gate and she would hold the dog by the hand and in this way they would stand.

But that was long ago and Ida did not think of anything except now. Why indeed was she always alone if there could be anything to remember. Why indeed. (30)

That the frequently "lost" Ida moves abruptly away from men and locations may signify a general problem in identity, but the progression of episodes signifies the impossibility of someone with such trouble achieving anything like personal memory. Like the time when there were no fences, walls, or gates, a repressed historicity reveals itself only in the difficulty of having "anything to remember."

Cumulative episodes show Ida as she meets those who do not interest her, talks to people to whom she does not listen, and always goes away after the paradox of saying "yes and no" (the social come-on that says no to actual interaction). Caught in a kind of stasis-in-motion, Ida voices the paradox of the privileged, female self approaching its Others: the polite, formal relationships allowed do not fulfill, and yet more intense ones threaten the myths of individual identity and social distance, held in the fragile syllables of a name:

You see, said Ida, I do look at you but that is not enough. I look at you and you look at me but we neither of us say more than how do you do and very well I thank you, if we do then there is always the question. What is your name. And really, said Ida, if I knew your name I would not be interested in you, no, I would not, and if I do not know your name. I could not be interested, certainly I could not. Good-bye, said Ida, and she went away. (30)

The passage from "I would not" to "I could not" necessitates one of those abruptly discontinuous departures that only confirms the continuity of an alienation based on conflicted desires: for belonging and status, normalcy and self-aggrandizement, love and winning at all the competitions.

In general, the linked episodes of *Ida*'s first half entrap Ida in any number of social roles but also point to what narration-as-Ida necessarily leaves out. In the midst of episodes divided into successive men and husbands, short, often imagistic scenes that reveal the consequences of social privilege continue to intervene:

She saw a sign up that said please pay the unemployed and a lot of people were gathered around and were looking.

It did not interest her. She was not unemployed. She just sat and she always had enough. Anybody could. (40)

Here short, declarative assertions mimic the self-satisfied logic of privilege, how it presumes universality in the act of looking away from anyone in need. Ida may even cry over the gnomic words that name her alienation, as in: "How many of those yoked together have ever seen oxen?" But in the manner of the privilege she so unfulfillingly meets in others, she talks to herself and operates on the premise that "she would look at everybody and everything and she knew it would not be interesting. She was interesting" (44). In this mode, she mimes a role-playing modeled on individual performance, deciding "that she was just going to talk to herself. Anybody could stand around and listen but as for her she was just going to talk to herself" (43). As a talk that avoids concern with "anybody" who might themselves listen or talk, Ida's language appropriately responds to the characters represented in either direct or indirect discourse as mouths for the conventional, whatever the role (as "officer" or "husband," for example) or the world (political Washington or exclusive Boston, for example) requires.

The silent/silenced characters intensely trouble a privileged narration that turns so quickly from them because they are disreputable or poor or Arabic or black. Ida's learned conviction that "she was interesting" exerts a fraudulent sense of control based on forms of evasion and denial, most specifically denials of any concern with race, poverty, or any Others at all: "Ida knew just what was going to happen. This did not bother her at all. Mostly before it happened she had gone away. / Once she was caught" (45). When "caught," the alienated Ida (who never listens and who finds only herself interesting) goes away to a hilly country where she tries talking to others and not just herself. When one of two men respond to her talk by saying, "it is not interesting and I am not listening," she becomes angry and demanding in the manner of dominant sensibility suddenly confronted with the painful anomaly of its own exclusion: "You are not listening to me . . . you do not know what you are saying, if I talk you have to listen to what I say, there is nothing else you can do" (48). Individual episodes may show how Ida's internalization of social roles keeps her alone and moving, but the sequence of episodes and the disjoint gaps that separate them reveal a more global logic about fear and evasion as the price of this world's achieved respectability.

In *Ida*'s first half, the merger of a largely impersonal social discourse and the impersonality of Ida as a kind of symbol-character help refer excesses in narration to comic effect. But because the narration that overlaps with Ida's figural consciousness reveals what it leaves out and why, the parody hovering behind the melodrama of Ida's men and adventures has a more disturbing, potentially tragic side. Characters like the scandalous great-aunt or the twin Winnie play their part in the parody of manners and mores, and comic narration attends them much as it does the comic view of an Ida constructed according to the conventions of very privileged, very gendered, very white, very rule-bound worlds. But the narrative intrusions of the poor, the unemployed, the Arab, or the black have a fearsome edge appropriate to those who appear as imagined Others. Unable to achieve either interaction or solidarity even with other dominant rule-followers, Ida moves to and away at the cost of an even more absolute alienation from Other worlds unimaginable even as story.

The first half's story of identity trouble in a dystopian United States parodies story forms from the bildungsroman to popular melodrama, but it also affords a critique of the social alienations on which individual identity in these referential worlds rely. And though the logic of Ida's developmental stages of nondevelopment may suggest comedy, it is not without an intermittent and tragic chafing against the people and worlds outside this prisonhouse of constructedness. Interventions from a marginalized, repressed historicity break into the comic with the threat of divisions more tragic than those of a split (or splitting) subject. And Ida's appropriate fear evolves even as she discovers enough of agency to act beyond social expectation (even enough, later, to think in storied form).

In *Ida*'s shorter second half, such intervening reference to the social margins recedes to parable and a repressed historicity recedes to indeterminacy. That is, the critique of dominance becomes both more lyrical and more abstract; it hovers behind a paradoxical utopia in which actions do and do not happen, words are and are not said, and Ida does and does not free herself from the constructions of the first half. Such paradoxical affirmation means in relation to the interplay of the Ida-Andrew story with extended passages often read as extraneous "digressions" or simply as "surreal" (a word that has come to imply the absence of interpretive demands). Yet if the parts of the second half progress toward a relationship between Ida and Andrew specifically differentiated from marriage, one that works through any number of problems toward an increasingly successful interaction, they do so in a context where narration both frames and interrupts the development from identity to intersubjectivity with often lyrical parables about problems of perspective (or what I have called "constructedness"), its changeability and indeterminacy. Reading these seemingly digressive parables in context will inform a sense of an ending in which social divisions do not simply disappear behind celebration of the happy couple.

The beginning of the second half figuratively reinvokes the privilege associated with white skin ("I only like a white skin") and therefore addresses a fear of any difference not easily naturalized:

The road is awfully wide.
With snow on either side.
    She was walking along the road made wide with snow. The moonlight was
bright. She had a white dog and the dog looked gray in the moonlight and on
the snow. Oh she said to herself that is what they mean when they say in the
night all cats are gray.
    When there was no snow and no moonlight her dog had always looked white
at night.
    When she turned her back on the moon the light suddenly was so bright it
looked like another kind of light, and if she could have been easily frightened it
would have frightened her but you get used to anything but really she never did
get used to this thing. (93)

Ida's initial perception confirms something she has already heard in the
manner of "I won't see it until I believe it."[7] But she cannot entirely quell
a fear that she tries to sustain only as a hypothetical possibility. And how
frightening to see the familiar in a different light and from a different
angle, especially when it so changes what seems a natural trait (the dog's
color) and suggests that things are not as natural as they have seemed.
    The first instance of Ida's capacity to think in the sustained form of
parable also concerns dogs, the work's most consistent projections, and
attends changes in her self-conception. Actively listening to Andrew tell
about his walks and talks, Ida becomes someone who can herself identify with another and therefore both go for walks with others and talk in
a way that invites interaction: "she talked as if she knew that Ida knew
how to listen" (95). As she does so, identity trouble begins to recede:
"gradually . . . it was not so important that Ida was Ida" (95). The Ida who
has had many husbands but nothing resembling desire has also held out
against the "strangeness" of motherhood ("She was not a mother. She
was not strange"). When she thinks "about her life with dogs. And this
was it" (96), she thinks primarily about their sexual liaisons in ways related to herself.
    Despite the convention that stories about animals always mask stories
about human beings, and despite earlier coherence in Ida's dogs, most
critics read the parable of the dogs as an autobiographical interpola-
tion more about Stein's own dogs (it is) than integral to its placement in
the second half.[8] When the child Ida could not acknowledge the need
for love, the dog Love, always vulnerable to abduction by others, suddenly appeared. Later, when Ida begins to marry, "It was not she who
was blind, it was her dog Iris" (50). Those same fears about sexuality and
otherness enter the dog parable through the attention to "dirty" dogs,
especially to the temptress Mary Rose (replete as parody with all the metonymic associations attending virgins and church windows). Mary Rose's
sexual liaison with a "dirty" dog produces a brown puppy (Chocolate)
thought to be a "monster" and "ugly" (101), clearly attributes of sexu-

ality across social boundaries. This mulatto as puppy meets a socially sanctioned violence ("nobody meant it but he was run over") and is replaced by a "real" daughter named (what else) Blanchette. The virtuous white female replaces the dangerous mulatto male, even though Mary Rose loved Chocolate and has no particular interest in Blanchette, who "would live longer and never have a daughter" (101) in an emblematic sterility. So Mary Rose turns her attention to Polybe, the embodiment of transgression, who sucks table legs as though they were his mother and who can always be led astray. Here the classed social sanctions against both sexual transgression and miscegenation take on doggy form.

In this context, the forging of actual interpersonal relationship bears little relation to the metaphor of "falling in love," but rather becomes something "to do all over again." The second half's second part begins with Ida and Andrew "almost married," and as Ida indulges in imaginary wish-fulfillment ("dreamed well not dreamed but just dreamed"), the induction into the conventions of marriage threaten Andrew's life (as a sign-character for the capacity to cross boundaries, how could it not?):

> She was sitting and she dreamed that Andrew was a soldier. She dreamed well not dreamed but just dreamed. The day had been set for their marriage and everything had been ordered. Ida was always careful about ordering, food clothes cars, clothes food cars everything was well chosen and the day was set and then the telephone rang and it said that Andrew was dying, he had not been killed he was only dying, and Ida knew that the food would do for the people who came to the funeral and the car would do to go to the funeral and the clothes would not do dear me no they would not do and all of this was just dreaming. (111)

Andrew's imagined dying into marriage foregrounds his assimilation into festivals of largely undifferentiated commodity-exchange, but Ida fails to naturalize Andrew into a world of masculine, bourgeois value and he escapes the constraints of this imagining with his life.

Because life starts with identity, and Ida's identity has been so compromised by constructed worlds, she "begins" as someone who "almost never had been younger" and "was just as much older as she had been" (115). In II.4, where Andrew becomes "almost Andrew the First," Ida's beginning difference attends the first appearance of "Yes Ida" as a kind of iterative refrain, one whose indeterminate location suggests the merged affirmations of author, narrator, reader, Andrew, and even Ida's own figural consciousness. Yet episodes with all who are not-Andrew confront her newfound, processual sense of self with the influence (closer to the contemporary "reinscription") of the omnipresent stories of others, stories telling the constructions from which her relationship with an Andrew-gyne might free her.

In the paradoxical context of a change both sudden (in its narrative appearance) and not sudden (in experiential time), a "soothed" Ida undertakes a conversation in the terms of what "everybody" knows about her and everything else. Yet the two subsequent tales of what everybody knows about dogs, soldiers, and lineage plays on the double referent for sodomy: a sexuality involving wrong-gender and wrong-species categories. Reminiscent of the security of men in uniforms in the first half, the two tales concern soldiers who bring unique dogs home with them. One brings home not a sheep dog but a "shepherd dog different from any shepherd dog he had ever seen," presumably in its curious amalgamation of species and functions. The said dog parents a whole line of shepherd dogs and the tale moves abruptly to a man telling a tale about a sister-in-law with "the smallest and the finest little brown dog he had ever seen." In response to a question about "what race it was and where she had gotten it," the sister-in-law responds in what only seems a non sequitur: "Oh she said a soldier gave it to me for my little girl, he had brought it home with him and he gave it to my little girl and she and he play together, they always play together" (116). Easy to read over as empty conversational whimsy, rather like the earlier "digression" about dogs, the stories—like all stories—reveal in what they conceal. A fascination with dogs who have race and engage in intimate relations with human beings reveals not only an unacknowledged prurience but also a conflated fear of miscegenation and homosexuality, however displaced in sheep dogs or domesticated in household pets.

The more overt reference to such a fear occurs in the next part (II.5), where more stories about what people fear follow narrative assertion that Andrew acts as a "sign," since "the first of anything is a sign." And what he means as a sign has everything to do with his difference from Ida's (constructed as) "natural" world:

> Ida had not known he was a sign, not known he was a sign.
> Ida was resting.
> Worse than any signs is a family who brings bad luck. Ida had known one, naturally it was a family of women, a family which brings bad luck must be all women.
> Ida had known one the kind that if you take a dog with you when you go to see them, the dog goes funny and when it has its puppies its puppies are peculiar. (120)

The peculiar puppies result from an involuted familial story involving a woman who loses husbands and then finds herself spurned by men. Because men pay no attention to her without even asking "what for," they observe that she "could not bring good luck to any one not even a dog, no not even." Ever vulnerable to the influence of "everybody," Ida immediately responds by closing down:

> No really bad luck came to Ida from knowing them but after that anyway, it did happen that she never went out to see any one.
> She said it was better.
> She did not say it was better but it was better. Ida never said anything about anything. (121)

Staying in assures that the "anybody" who comes will never include either funny families or peculiar women with peculiar effects on dogs that produce peculiar puppies.

And in this context of an Ida protecting herself from the bad luck of the peculiar, Andrew "came he just came in." Andrew differs from Ida in many respects, but first and foremost in not believing in good luck and bad luck, either as gendered or as belonging to particular kinds of families or identities. He does not share the fears that make up Ida, though he listens with interest to the stories about what "everybody" fears. He does so immediately by engaging a man who frames the most extended parable of the Second Half about "spiders, cuckoos, goldfish, and dwarfs" as "the things anybody has to worry about" (122). (Even the list reads something like the "red, yellow, black, green, whatever" that one hears so often in white mouths asserting—too strongly and in anxious tonality—an equitable indifference to race.[9]) This man's worry takes the form of an injunction to "think of a spider talking," and proceeds to assume the voice of spiderness, certain that "to see me at night brings them delight, to see me in the morning, brings mourning." Andrew finds the spider's monologue "interesting," and asks if "they know any other superstition." "Yes," responds the man, "there is the cuckoo." "Supposing they could listen to a cuckoo," the man presents a cuckoo-persona sure that his own song acts as the harbinger of good or bad fortune. Subsequently, the goldfish argues that he is "stronger and meaner" than the others because he glories in never bringing good luck, only bad. Increasingly interested, Andrew listens as the man presents the voice of the dwarf who declares his "good luck and bad luck" paradigm as "eternal." A silence follows and then goldfish, cuckoo, and spider all erupt in objections to each other's mythologies, excluding the others from belief. Finally, the spider screams "I believe in me I am all there is to see" as prologue to an argument ending in, "it is so lovely to know this is true and not to believe in a fish or in dwarfs or in a cuckoo, ooh ooh it is I, no matter what they try it is I, I, I" (128). This fight for primacy ends when, once again assuming a position above the fray, the dwarf asserts his humanoid tendency to universalizing in an entirely utopian affirmation:

we are in the beginning we have commenced everything and we believe in everything yes we do, we believe in . . . everything that is mortal and immortal, we
even believe in spiders, in goldfish and in the cuckoo, we the dwarfs we believe
in it all, all and all, and all and every one are alike, we are, all the world is like us
the dwarfs, all the world believes in everything and we do too and all the world
believes in us and in you. (128)

This assertion of a liberal inclusion, claiming universality while elevating
the speaker's position to alpha and omega, rests not only on rules about
gender ("female dwarf bad luck male dwarf good luck") but also on the
necessary coupling of female and male (as though to neutralize the danger of unattached women): "if they see one of us and it is the female he
or she had to go and go all day long until they see a dwarf man, otherwise anything awful could happen to them" (126). Importantly, Andrew's
interest grows with the man's vicarious recitations, but it does so in the
context of tales he regards as "superstition."

Both dog and dwarf tales accumulate superstitions about identity,
each reliant on some presumed effect of a group on human "good luck
or bad luck." But whereas Ida's listening projects a debased but ex-
citing sexuality onto the Other, Andrew's listening names superstition
as such. Although narration refers to Ida and Andrew as separate characters, it does so in the context of a union based on Andrew's existence
as a "sign" and their increasing penchant for becoming more like each
other. From the Greek *andros* for man, Andrew signifies the "manly," but
as an Andrew-gyne (*gyne* for woman), Andrew and Ida signify precisely
the processes of negotiated identity that intersubjective relationship entails. The art of the first half inheres in narration that both presents
normalcy as such but also comments on its perversity, both by following through the implications of Ida's identity and gender troubles and
by allowing the interventions of a repressed historicity. In the second
half, Ida's troubles recede as artful changes in readerly/writerly relations
come to portray an androgynous ideal most notable for its peeling away
of the received constructions of both gender and sexuality. With a more
intimate narration moving toward a celebratory sense of an ending,
the second half has no narrative interventions by the unemployed, the
black, or the otherwise marginal. Rather, the more symbolic and lyrical
narration becomes, the more problematic self-other relations become
regarding the matter of perspective, the subject of all those parables
so frequently labeled "digressions." The "second half"'s shorter, more
numerous parts provide much more staccato narrative rhythms, associated with the complex negotiations between social positioning and
interior states, language and what cannot be represented in language.
With dominant consensus still ringing in the recurrent "everybody" and

"anybody," and Others reduced to "the rest of them," Ida learns to live *with* those who "come" but do not.

In the development of the second half, all the crossing of thresholds and barriers, all those comings in and goings out, take place in a language of sexual coding. The absence of punctuation makes almost every "coming" verb part of a coded narration increasingly more concentrated as Ida-identity and Andrew-identity merge while trying to stay separate or autonomous. Every page follows the difficult adjustments of these negotiations, with each adopting the new habits that make them different as two than they are as one. Andrew, for example, begins to "come in" in response to Ida's wishes:

To Andrew she had said yes come in and Andrew had come in.
It was not a natural life for Andrew this life of coming in and this was what had been happening to Andrew, he had commenced to come in and then he never did anything else, he always came in. (138)

Narration remarks of such negotiations that "It is not easy to lead a different life, much of it never happens but when it does it is different." As Ida becomes "more Ida" and Andrew becomes "less Andrew," their comings and goings become more problematic, and, as Peter Schall has noted, "As the codes become more complex, they permit Stein to discuss a variety of allegedly pornographic subjects ranging from cunnilingus to sodomy with a freedom that 'straight' narration would not have permitted."[10]

Passages with coded reference to desire build to the only affirmed event that "happens" in the second half, a kiss that has nothing to do with any fulfilled desire belonging to Andrew and Ida. The "something" that happens in the second half revolves around desire figured in a kiss, even though what those in this world "miss" refers to all absences (defined as whatever "everybody" can neither acknowledge nor know):

What happened was this.
Everybody began to miss something and it was not a kiss, you bet your life it was not a kiss that anybody began to miss. And yet perhaps it was. (148)

Repeated in a variant only a page later ("And it all began with everybody knowing that they were missing something and perhaps a kiss but not really nobody really did miss a kiss. Certainly not Ida" 149), the indeterminate "event" that fills the gap circumlocutes desire: "Everybody thought everybody knew what happened. And everybody did know and so it was that that happened" (149). Such happening by consensus refers to what does not happen for Ida: "When something happens nothing begins. When anything begins then nothing happens and you could always say with Ida that nothing began" (149). With "it" as the referent for an absent sexuality, a sexuality that has to come from somewhere emerges suddenly in women who "come":

Before it happened well quite a while before it happened she did meet women. When they came she was resting, when they went she was resting, she liked it and they did not mind it. They came again and when they came again, she was obliging, she did say yes. (152)

Because Ida does not relinquish any fixed hold on identity in such relationship, she returns to saying "yes and no" and "no and yes" to Andrew.

In a work that has just declared "Nature is not natural and that is natural enough," narration asserts both the affirmation and the limitation of conceptualizing freedom as indeterminacy: "It is natural enough that she said yes, because she did not catch up with anything and did not interrupt anything and did not begin anything and did not stop anything" (151). Ida's indeterminate subjectivity becomes so much Ida-Ida-Andrew that a bluntly declarative syntax presents as action those experiences that both shape Ida and provide the language of narration. Ida's pleasures and affirmations imply a potential (even probable) lack in the reader-observer, who has not undergone any of the identity-work undertaken by Ida and her Andrew-gyne.

If *Ida* ends on a celebratory note, it does so without the comic romance's universalizing homage to a world reborn in the happily married heterosexual couple. *Ida*'s sense of closure relies on a closing language so densely filled with paradoxes that no assertion passes without its opposite, including Ida's penchant for saying both no and yes. The negotiation of identity is itself a paradox:

Little by little there it was. It was Ida and Andrew.
Not too much not too much Ida and not too much Andrew.
And not enough Ida and not enough Andrew.
If Ida goes on, does she go on even when she does not go on any more.
No and Yes. (154)

The "there" here refers most overtly to the processes ("little by little") of social relations not reducible to relations of power. And yet, along with subsequent paradoxes, the language captures an imaginary of desire (always approaching a boundary of "too much" and yet always "not enough"). Whereas before, Ida's identity made itself into what men, places, and contexts required, here the presence of self-assertion (and our own readerly approach through Ida) explains the asymmetry needed for interactive balance ("not too much not too much Ida and not too much Andrew"). Narration asserts that when Ida says anything, she says "yes" (as utopias do), yet immediately asks "Why should she say yes. There is no reason why she should so there is nothing to say" (154).

Thus the final lines of witty second-person address to the reader end on a note of intimacy, both an intimacy with Ida ("Dear Ida" now part of narrative-authorial consciousness, not just a part of empty social discourse) and an intimacy with the reader (implied in the second-person address of: "They are there. Thank them. Yes."). Stein frames the last page with a "Dear Ida" and a "Yes" that do not come from any particular figural consciousness. Rather, they seem the intimate responses of authorial sensibility, or rather a sensibility that asks readers to first feel and then speak in solidarity with newfound feeling for Ida. Liberated from her problem with doors and thresholds, Ida occupies an explicitly relational geography: although she both goes out and comes in, she waits within for people to come, and her saying "yes" corresponds to "inside" activities (like resting, or dressing, or simply being there). The work's last "yes" responds to the authorial instruction to "thank them," and the second-person address of "Thank them" moves to the almost choric, and certainly antiphonal, "yes." The last "yes" has multiple reference: to the positive fact of Ida and Andrew being there (as opposed to Oakland), to the reader to "thank them" for so being, to what Ida says when she says anything, and to the most global affirmation conflating writer, narrator, characters, text, and reader in a syllable confirming finality, completion, totality. But in each case, the "yes" that seems determinate and certain has its hovering modifier: if Ida and Andrew are "there," then it is where neither narration nor we can go or see or hear or describe; if we thank them as readers for being "there," then we join narrator and character in an intimacy made of the most shallow social language (Ida has spent much constructed time, after all, doing necessary thanking); if saying "yes" suggests some cheerful positivity, it is because saying "no" has been defined as having nothing to say; and if the last "yes" has a utopian ring, it rings not with triumphant and infinite perfection but with a transient, negotiated, and changeable finitude always vulnerable to critique.

The Color Purple and *Ida* may seem to belong to entirely disparate comic worlds, yet *The Color Purple*'s sense of a happy ending relies on the analogical relation between how characters relate to each other in a textual world, how writers relate to readers, and how readers relate to others in actual social worlds. They have in common a "utopian" ending that does not relinquish its critical edge because as characters themselves cross barriers and discover selves-in-relation, writers withdraw from any felt distance from their characters in favor of sharing with readers an appreciation of some enunciated presence (whatever "being there" may mean by way of textual closure). The last "yes" is the one unequivocal statement of presence in *Ida*, and yet it follows two pages whose paradoxical celebration of relationship—relationality, even—argues that even this presence works as process (as an ongoing embodiment of processual relationship): "Gradually it was, well not as it had been but it was, it was quite as it was." Not a word-play without social reference, such assertion applies to relationships that continually change, making them never simply *there* as they were before. And yet, "it was quite as it was" testifies to a self-(re)presenting that abjures any fixed identity in favor of an enunciatory present, a present with implicit continuity to how "it had been."

Read in this way, Ida neither speaks her desire nor enters some "deep space of mind where harm cannot enter" (Berry, 24). Put most simply, feminist and postmodern readings tend to locate in *Ida* a value that belongs to writers and readers, not to the lived experience of those who may neither write nor read, a common tendency among academic readers who perhaps "naturally" value the kind of experiences they themselves have with texts. In my reading, the Ida of the first half exists as an effect of social relations, whereas the Ida of the second half struggles with causality, her own capacity to change and to cause change. Thus the union of Ida with her Andrew-gyne bespeaks comic representation as lack, where a character's presence in a very temporary, provisional utopia signifies that it is not Ida, after all, who says "yes," but narration and the reader. Ida remains caught in the paradox of "no and yes" and a language that moves between saying "yes," a requirement of social discourse, and having nothing to say.

Not "clean as a fugue or a quadratic equation," but a dirty book in the highest sense, *Ida* demonstrates that reading, like passing, may play out the surfaces while forever pulling toward affective depths affirmed only as indirection. Whether read as modern in its portrayal of a fragmented character in search of a self, or as postmodern in its emphasis on a plural self-in-process, *Ida* constructs a utopian yet critical mode in which neither the arrival of a unified self nor affirmations of indeterminacy quite capture the paradoxical sense of an ending. In Chapter 4, I argued that important contemporary readings of *Absalom, Absalom!* trouble, because they celebrate either an intersubjectivity that starkly avoids its dependence on a dehumanizing social vision or an aestheticized, elegaic tragedy with primacy on a lost culture. With so little of mimetic surface, *Ida* does not make race—or other marginalized social categories—important except as interventions from repressed worlds, those seemingly absent from the increasingly utopian vision of the second half. And yet, the second half addresses the problems of privilege and power in episodes about the miscegenation of black and white dogs; about the relationality of difference embodied in dwarfs, cuckoos, and spiders; about the self-fulfilling "superstitions" of social constructedness; and about the ongoing negotiations of selfhood undertaken by Ida and her Andrew-gyne, whose intersubjectivity across the social barriers reveal how "nothing is natural about nature." If *Ida* renders its Others as invisible and unspeakable, it does so in the act of paying much attention to its own alterity: the lie of individual autonomy, the relationality of identity formation, the social construction of difference, and indeterminacy as the basis of freedom (Bhabha). *Ida* has its visible ellipses, repressions, and fears intact, and the very differences in social reference (and therefore in readerly/writerly relations) between Parts I and II inflect the sense of an ending. Neither characters nor language ever entirely escape the bipolarity of female and male, black and white, rich and poor, inside and outside, feeling and thinking, telling and writing, yes and no.

The end of *Ida* chooses gender as the site for boundary crossing, with an indeterminate sexuality never far from the surface of narration. The sexual story, a passing addicted to coded, revelatory signs embedded in only seemingly heterosexual merger, differs markedly from the story about race or poverty, both more abstracted into generalizing parables about all difference and all boundary crossing. Yet race and class remain integral to *Ida*'s form, even if in an unconscious cultural logic that chooses gender over sexuality in entering any dialogue of difference and that relegates race and class to the abstraction of a generalized difference. *The Color Purple* may well fulfill some of the expectations of comic romance by rewarding its characters with property and well-being, but because those characters mean in intersubjective relation, and only under the constraints of space allotted by white power, their final, utopian mode of celebration formally reminds us of the actual constraints on black celebration that retains this mode's critical edge. So in *Ida*, the early satiric focus on the entrapping processes of the bourgeois mind and its attempts at meaningful relationship evolve into an increasingly abstract comic mode to affirm a relationship utopian and yet critical because ultimately caught in the repressive binary logic of its own elaboration. The focus of *Ida* begins and remains on the processes of identity-formation characteristic of privilege and on the costs of protecting any privileged self from interactions threatening received boundaries.

The Mulatto as Melodrama

Diverse interpretations of "Melanctha" make her a surrogate for others, either for Stein herself or for the "deepening" of the bourgeois, socially self-conscious Jeff Campbell. Whereas *Ida* draws readers into a problem of both privileged experience and its representation, "Melanctha," in cyclical fashion, distances its central character from a writer's and reader's increasingly conspiratorial superiority. Sonia Saldívar-Hull aptly characterizs the racism and classism of "Melanctha" on the level of story, but I want to examine here how this earlier text differs from *Ida*'s formal attention to its own limitations by entrapping readers in a tyranny of dialogue with nothing very dialogical about it. Without sociality, this one-on-one world exposes a radical absence of community in the act of largely comic representations of how social processes work. (And since characters reveal more than they know, only writer and reader are in a position to speculate about that revelation.) Those who credit Stein with a subversive critique of "realism and its social implications" rarely focus on how "Melanctha" negotiates the converging social meanings of race, gender, class, and sexuality. Rather, they see narration itself as "unstable" and Melanctha as a positive character who, despite an ultimately unfulfilled desire, represents Stein's own move toward a narrative liberation connected to liberation from both sex and gender roles (or even from racial ones, witness the well-known approbation of Richard Wright and Nella Larsen).[11] Here I want to build on the insights of extant readings by Saldívar-Hull, North, and Stimpson that focus on Stein's use of this fictive black and mulatto community as the context for a character's sexual and narrative transgressions. I want to argue that, although "Melanctha" may well represent "both adherence and critique" of an earlier realism, or the deployed yet resisted stereotypes of the naturalist text, its asymmetrical critique never takes up or fulfills either the comic critique of social roles or the tragic suggestiveness that hovers behind this melodrama.

Not merely double or "unstable," narration in "Melanctha" simulates the social discourse of the worlds it describes, with narration itself revealing a vested correspondence to the figural consciousness of Melanctha and to the succession of characters who judge her from the perspective of fixed identity.[12] Narrative structure shows how Melanctha's language increasingly mimics that of those who judge her negatively as both woman and storyteller; simultaneously, her sexuality becomes more and more repressed as her status improves, primarily in her newfound relationship with the young doctor Jeff Campbell. (Harriet Chessman thinks that Jeff tries to "rewrite" Melanctha, and yet his attitudes toward her merely reflect the fixed nature of the identity he superimposes on all "the colored people" from his own mulatto superiority and his traditionally patriarchal morality.) With often no narrative distance at all between narrative language and Melanctha's own internal discourse, "Melanctha" provides a narration not just unstable but complicit in others' successive views of her, such that differences in narration mean across the characters and narrative "episodes," those "moments" comprised of Melanctha moving up and then down the class ladder in opposition to a succession of others—most important Rose Johnson, her parents, Jane Harden, Jeff Campbell, and, finally, Rose Johnson again.

From the outset, narrative pity for "poor Melanctha" accompanies a largely ironic presentation of a search for "wisdom" that depends on a troublesome knowledge of the body. Harriet Chessman sees this quest as an "acquisition of a language and a narrative that could leap beyond the constrictions of social and literary convention" (45) and Marianne DeKoven characterizes it as "incoherent, open-ended, anarchic, irreducibly multiple . . . indeterminate, anti-patriarchal (anti-logocentric, anti-phallogocentric, presymbolic, pluridimensional)."[13] The story of Melanctha's childhood begins with a mother who "had always been a little wandering and mysterious and uncertain in her ways" and "never cared much for her daughter who was always a hard child to manage." The father, who is working class—and therefore virile, rough, and brutal—says things like, "Where's that Melanctha of yours?. . . If she is to the Bishops' stables now with that yellow John, I swear I kill her" (94). Granting Melanctha herself a kind of narrative empowerment when she shows her "tongue" against her father or in a coded lesbian relationship with Jane Harden, these readings make of "Melanctha" a kind of comic bildungsroman in which she gains empowerment as a woman in the act of speaking.

The "Melanctha" who "had been half made with real white blood," also stands in opposition to Rose, who "had been brought up quite like their own child by white folks." These essentialist constructions about nature and nurture have their sexual complement in Melanctha's later relationship with the better educated Jane Harden, who "loved hard" and who equates control of desire with power (with "world wisdom"). In this social world, love relationships work according to equations of need, with the "weaker" being she who desires, longs, or needs more. Jane becomes an alcoholic and Melanctha becomes the "teacher," the one with power over another because she needs less.

Wanting something that "should really wholly fill her" (108), Melanctha tries "a great many men," but ends by wanting Jefferson Campbell because "he held off." She feels that she can learn nothing from men who readily desire her. He helps her take care of the mother for whom she does "everything that any woman could," but for whom she cares little and who cares very little for her. The negotiated changes in Melanctha's and Jeff's relationship in some ways resemble those of Ida and Andrew, except that neither of these characters acts as a "sign" and both have personality and character outside of narrative language. A narrative voice "passing" as racial omniscience declares that Jeff "had never yet in his life had real trouble" and has "the free abandoned laughter that gives the warm broad glow to negro sunshine" (111). He likes Jane Harden—who abuses Melanctha to him—much better than Melanctha. When Jeff—like other characters before and after him—transparently subjects bodily desire to the indirection of social speech, his prolonged and repetitive speeches to Melanctha harangue about the virtues of helping "the colored people" live "just regular as can be" and the dangers of "excitements," reflecting a liking for his race based entirely on "what he could do for the colored people."

Jeff Campbell's own "progress" coincides with the silencing of Melanctha, as when he disguises sexual feeling as an approving assessment of mind while simultaneously interpreting silence as responsiveness:

Dr. Campbell began to read through the old papers that Melanctha gave him. When anything amused him in them, he read it out to Melanctha. Melanctha was now pretty silent with him. Dr. Campbell began to feel a little, about how she responded to him. Dr. Campbell began to see a little that perhaps Melanctha had a good mind. (116)

The good mind of the silent woman corresponds to a subsequent polarization of a decent, disembodied sexuality (defined in its absence):

One kind of loving seems to me, is like one has a good quiet feeling in a family when one does his work, and is always living good and being regular, and then the other way of loving is just like having it like any animal that's low in the streets together. (124)

It will be left to Melanctha to finally name what she wants as "real, strong, hot love," an admission that sends Jeff into paroxysms of retreat from "that kind of loving hard [that] does seem always to mean just getting all the time excited." And it is Jeff, not Melanctha, who knows of nothing more dangerous "than being strong in love with somebody." At best tender, "like a good, strong, gentle brother" (140), Jeff's version of sexuality brings Melanctha to exclaim: "How could you ever like me if you thought I ever could be so like a red Indian?" (141).

Interestingly, the autobiographical love story behind "Melanctha" validates some critics in reading the morally righteous and sexually repressed Jeff Campbell as Stein's own voice, with presumably self-ironic perspective on a language that reveals the "nature" represented by his desire for whatever is "just regular" (conventional, normative) and "nice and quiet." Although Catherine Stimpson identifies the period of *Three Lives* as that most characterized by a masculine self-identification, the character of Jeff Campbell serves an often comic role as mentor to Melanctha's necessarily futile and unfulfilled search for "wisdom" and "understanding," a search repeatedly linked to carnal knowledge. That is, Jeff reveals himself as a limited bourgeois subject with all his repressions intact. And, as with other characters opposed to Melanctha, he provides a foil against which Melanctha tries to escape seeing herself as these others see her, to find some way of "telling" herself outside the constructions that inhere in both figural consciousness and narration itself. It is as though narration adopts the language of whatever discourse dominates Melanctha in the textual present, and as though Melanctha herself internalizes that language.

When Melanctha returns to Rose Johnson's moralizing, she has worked her "wandering" and "restless" way though several different and pejorative ways of hearing herself in other's voices. A reading that takes Melanctha's desire for Rose as "the possibility of another form of narrative, one that will be fulfilled in Stein's later and more experimental writings" (Chessman 53), understands narrative self-reference as the link between sexual and textual desire without meaningful relation to the racial context. But if Rose is the "regular" or "correct" form of narrative to which Melanctha, in the end, returns, she is also the "real negress" who always makes sure she is engaged because she "had strong the proper sense of conduct," even before she decides "to get regularly really married" (88). Although Melanctha desires and Rose rejects desire, Melanctha desires in the context of Rose's penchant for the emotion of sentimental melodrama, with its taste for socio-moral certainty, racial as well as sexual and classed essences, and the dire consequences of transgression. Rose's refrains about Melanctha condemn her because "[s]he didn't do right ever the way I told her" and bemoan, with transparently fraudulent pity, the likely results:

"I certainly don't never want no kind of harm to come bad to Melanctha, but I certainly do think she will most kill herself some time, the way she always say it would be easy way for her to do. I never see nobody ever could be so awful blue." (235)

And narration, too, takes up the sing-song of melodrama before returning abruptly to the language and world of Rose Johnson. The return comes around to the opposition with which "Melanctha" started, caught in Rose, a black woman raised as white, and Melanctha, a mulatto with "white blood" (the childless Melanctha and the Rose incapable of sustaining offspring).

The identity of sexual and textual liberation sees Melanctha as working at intimacies that will "transform the discursive formation underlying realism through a process of disidentification with and thus displacement of the enunciative position from which the tenets of realism have been propounded" (Berry 39). This look forward to a liberatory textuality grants that Melanctha's "speaking voice and the dialogic narrative form she represents become nearly erased in the last pages," but it does not address the specifically racial essences that have such an appalling ring at this historical distance. One cannot know, of course, exactly the degree to which Stein either portrays or shares the attitudes she represents, and yet it matters that neither Melanctha nor her "wandering" represents the stereotype of the loose black woman since negative judgments on her come from social positions parodied as transparently self-serving. Yet it seems wrong to speak of Stein's later works as fulfilling the possibility and desire for narrative inherent in Melanctha's desire for Rose, since that desire stands so compromised by the internalization of racial constructions never integrated into the story of failed intimacy.

Much depends on the expressive difference between ironic narration that simulates social (and socially reductive) views and narration that provides a sense of an interiority different from constructedness. Narration that belongs either to a social world or to thought processes that internalize dominance betrays its transparent values with the piling on of adjectives of class and type, the iterative use of such verbal modifiers as "really," and the embedding of description in strong, and strongly asserted, moral and aesthetic judgments. Far from a "futuristic" or "surreal" absence of logic, such narration most often follows upon a character's articulating views identifiable as white, bourgeois, heterosexual, or all at once, as in the passage immediately following Rose's assertion that she, and Melanctha like her, "ain't no common nigger" (86):

> Why did the subtle, intelligent, attractive, half white girl Melanctha Herbert love and do for and demean herself in service to this coarse, decent, sullen, ordinary, black childish Rose, and why was this unmoral, promiscuous, shiftless Rose married, and that's not so common either, to a good man of the negroes, while Melanctha with her white blood and attraction and her desire for a right position had not yet been really married. (86)

The sheer density of stereotypical precision here, as well as such gossipy interjections as "and that's not so common either" (referring to black marriage), might argue against equating this narration with Stein's authorial consciousness. And structural logic does place next, immediately after this disturbing catalogue of oppositional values, a passage in which Melanctha's "thought" differs markedly from any concern for "right position" or what it means to be "really married":

> Sometimes the thought of how all her world was made, filled the complex, desiring Melanctha with despair. She wondered, often, how she could go on living when she was so blue. (87)

As elsewhere in the passages presenting Melanctha's interior affective life, no "really" and no lists of stereotypical association accentuate a clearly social discourse. Rather, an eloquently straightforward assertion captures the conflicted nature of self and world, often, as here, with explicit reference to a *made* world. In giving us a character "complex with desire," the narration of the first sentence affirms a thought of Melanctha's with straightforward, unironic assertion. But the second sentence returns to the only language available to Melanctha to express such complexity. Thus, rather than indirect affirmation, we have the exact language of Melanctha's thinking to herself: "How can I go on living when I am so blue." The language mimics the manner of any melodramatic heroine with hand clasped to brow.

The problem, that of how to suggest an unarticulated depth in characters whose own language participates in appalling social attitudes, resembles that in the realism of Flaubert and James that Stein thought of herself as upending. If Flaubert would substitute his own eloquence for its lack in Emma Bovary and if James would overtly manipulate ironic distances to express the inexpressible, Stein more radically suppresses authorial positioning by allowing only glimpses of internal qualities that neither the narration nor the characters articulate. The difficulty in reading Stein, and her availability to so many different modes of interpretation, has in part to do with her success in simulating the complicit, already encoded sociality of all telling. In this fictive world, some gestures, habits, and sounds belong to the characterization of a particular social milieu and some belong to the language itself, rather much in the way one may resist one dominant construction only to fall into reinscribing others. The sound of Melanctha's speech and the tic-like gestures of her reiterative phrasing reflect the soothingly reductive nature of values so cross-referential that phrases like "doing right" or "being proper" evade any explicit reference. Does Rose's laziness or Melanctha's wandering or narration's reference to "abundant black laughter" represent some view of essential traits, or do they, rather, represent internalized conceptions of identity, some false consciousness's linking of blood-essences and bourgeois values? Marianne DeKoven and others have discussed the readerly intimacy with narration in "Melanctha," yet that intimacy relies on a complicity with the social attitudes caught both in the figural consciousness of characters juxtaposed with Melanctha and in her own responsive, internalized language. Narration never focuses on more than two, Melanctha and some other, yet the others always invoke the more general social judgments of some absent but general authority. All the oppositional characters think they know "the right way to do," and in each case Melanctha tries first to please them and then, failing that, to resist negative social judgments even in the act of reiterating their entrapping language.

Successive characters reveal themselves in complicity with a plural but mimetic narration, a narration already constructed and speaking from the position of those who think they know themselves and therefore others. Narration judges such characters but does so from within the shared presumptions of this fictive world. Does narration share Rose's concern with propriety and decency in order to use her own standard to testify to her own insufficiency? Does Melanctha's restlessness and wandering accompany successive attempts to free herself from a prisonhouse of constructedness, only to find new variants of the old house?

I believe that the end of "Melanctha" provides telling evidence to the contrary because of its relation to melodrama and because it has nothing of the parodic tonalities that seem to structure so much earlier narration. Its last three paragraphs begin with language that invokes earlier repetitions and rhythms indicating an internalized social language, including the "really" signifier and a rhyming, sing-song syntax: "But Melanctha Herbert never really killed herself because she was so blue, though often she thought this would be really the best way for her to do" (235). But with an abrupt change, a bluntly prosodic syntax asserts an end more real than any "really" could represent:

Melanctha never killed herself, she only got a bad fever and went into the hospital where they took good care of her and cured her.

When Melanctha was well again, she took a place and began to work and to live regular. Then Melanctha got very sick again, she began to cough and sweat and be so weak she could not stand to do her work.

Melanctha went back to the hospital, and there the Doctor told her she had the consumption, and before long she would surely die. They sent her where she would be taken care of, a home for poor consumptives, and there Melanctha stayed until she died. (235–36)

The initial refrain about Melanctha's thinking herself so blue that she really would kill herself belongs to melodrama. The thought and its language belong to an internalized "scene" reenacted "often" without any referential reality. In contrast, the flatly assertive description of her actual death avoids any reference at all to how Melanctha feels beyond her clinical symptoms. From a perspective brutally outside Melanctha, it relates the action of melodrama without any of its characteristically affective layers.

This last paragraph resembles earlier narration in that it invokes the social view, even the social power, of a world indifferent to Melanctha's individuality. From whose perspective will Melanctha be "taken care of"? Who calls it "a home for poor consumptives"? In what kind of narrative does authority say so impersonally that a woman "stayed until she died"? Does it speak to a readerly audience supposed to care about her? No, it speaks into a gap of its own creation. In its opposition to melodrama, this sense of an ending obliquely alludes to—rather than taking up or fulfilling—something of the tragic in a character who never finds herself outside others' oppressive views of her. Narration in "Melanctha" has only make-believe reference to any contemporary realities of black life, and yet its negotiations with any number of genres, from a popular melodrama to the comic realism of Henry James, betray no felt difficulty with white access to the social discourse of black community. If blackness is foregrounded, it serves primarily to reveal the limitations of white imagining. To the degree that "Melanctha" fails to pass as a story in which race matters and chafes within a prison-house of constructedness, it reveals beneath the lesbian passing story the story of a white woman writer trying to write beyond stereotype and writing instead about her own complicity in white failures of imagining; it marks but does not interrogate racist discourse and fails even as melodrama because it cannot excite even condescending tears for the pitiable Melanctha. The mulatto tragedy hovering behind "Melanctha" as failed melodrama remains concealed and unmarked—in all probability as much from Stein herself as from readers who care more about gender, genre, or sexuality than about that classed, racial tragedy.

Mimicry and Masquerade

The distinction between *Ida*'s representation of a social lie and "Melanctha"'s reinscription of one rests neither on authorial consciousness nor on some easily referential mimesis (the argument that, since Stein has no experience of blackness, she had best leave it to others). Of course critics have long argued cases of authorial unconsciousness, but this case is harder because it deals with plural, split subjects and the liberatory gestures toward resisting dominant constuctions of gender or sexuality that may not even address the racial issues it raises.[14] Much that provokes in both texts suggests levels of authorial unconsciousness, yet "Melanctha"'s overtly important and constant invocations of race only reinscribe its invisibility, whereas *Ida*'s much more tangential concern with sexual, racial, and other marginalized difference does not. The occasional, interruptive role of social Others in *Ida* more closely resembles what Stein herself knew, a world in which dominance might conceal sexuality in code and only occasionally needed to acknowledge race or poverty at all. Formal, aesthetic judgments seem inseparable from the constraints of authorial positioning: Ida-Andrew's passing as a heterosexual couple does not so much lie as formally repress a form of cultural entrapment, whereas Melanctha, entrapped by any number of constructions, lives in a world where a specifically racial entrapment turns out to be formally irrelevant. That is, the overtly racial context of "Melanctha" has no meaningful relation to the project of reinventing genre, whereas *Ida*'s more concealed connections between sexuality, race, and class self-refer to social divisions *even when it leaves them out*. Whereas "Melanctha" traps readers in dialogue without any sense of the dialogical, *Ida* expressively abjures dialogue altogether.

Ida's ironic relation to any number of genres and sociocultural constructions does not belie the formal integrity of its own design. That is, the parodic mimicry of gendered entrapment, its corresponding generic entrapments, and the subsequent quasi-utopian liberation do not lie about other subjectivities in the same way that "Melanctha" lies about race. "Melanctha" 's formal interest belies its appropriated racial context because it cares primarily about developments it constructs as having nothing to do with race. In this, its racial lie differs from Melville's *Benito Cereno* or Faulkner's *Absalom, Absalom!* which, however white in their imagining, remain formally haunted by the racial horrors they depict. Babo's "voiceless end" may accompany his descent to social powerlessness, but it also remains a ghastly specter for his captors, an analogue to how Clytie's gaze and Jim Bond's howl haunt Quentin with a complicity he can neither embrace nor escape. In *Ida*, literary form captures something more about race and power relations than does "Melanctha," despite its similar entrapment in the white unconscious and despite a seemingly more tangential reference to race and class. And it does so in a way that does not lie about its place in the social unconsciousness of the United States. I do not mean to suggest that Stein showed any particular insights about the complexities of her own positioning, but rather that the form of *Ida* creates a utopia critical of its own binarisms, a hymn to indeterminacy still reliant on the determinate, and an intimacy acknowledging the distance of writer, narrator and reader from the earned, negotiated intimacy of Ida and her Andrew-gyne.

Readings of "Melanctha" as defiant anti-realism, sometimes comic in orientation and sometimes not, read its central character as though she teases with judgments about whether she acts well or badly, whether or not she has agency, and whether or not she has any socio-historical verity. If seen as a successful interrogation of comic realism, a postmodern "Melanctha" emerges as a study in the arbitrary nature of literary and social codes. Read thus, its comedy resembles the parodic comedy prized by much postmodernism; it never loses its distanced edge, even in the readerly/writerly distance from Melanctha's lonely demise. Because readers necessarily gaze on Melanctha from a distance made always self-conscious as such, it should not surprise that the distance has felt more arrogant to those few readers who focus on race and more artfully indeterminate to those who focus on gender or the play of linguistic surfaces.[15] The offensive racial story in "Melanctha" runs on like an enabling tic, with the verbal refrains about what comprises "negro fashion" or the ways of "the colored people" providing the context of a more interesting and developmental story about sexuality and class. Stein's own well-chosen epigraph from Jules Laforgue, "Donc je suis un malheureux et ce n'est ni ma faute ni celle de la vie," reminds us that it may not be salutary to chafe over the degree to which Stein shared in the "genial" racism of blood-essences, fixed natures, and familiar stereotypes.[16] In part, Melanctha resembles the characters described by Morrison in *Playing in the Dark*, black characters created by white writers to embody otherwise unrepresentable fears and desires. But "Melanctha" 's racial context positions writers and readers differently from the displacement afforded by *Absalom, Absalom!* in which racial mythology rests on ultimately indeterminate blood lines. Here Stein both attempts and risks more in taking black community as a fictive given and projecting both aesthetic and sexual risk onto a black surrogate. In a work carefully problematizing gender and genre, a mulatto's mixed blood becomes the abiding figure for mixed genres and mixed sexualities, alluding in code to a problematized sexuality; yet the work never interrogates the blood essences that define Melanctha's formal role.

Nothing in either *Ida* or "Melanctha" suggests that had Stein not had to sustain a masked lesbianism that she would have become more self-conscious about the racial context, yet *Ida* acknowledges what Judith Butler calls "convergent modalities of power" in the formal marking of its own ellipses.[17] Without even the vestiges of mimesis, *Ida* nonetheless moves from a mimicry of how social worlds construct categories and barriers to a critical utopia focused on resisting those same processes of construction. Ida-Ida-Andrew, the androgynous whole, must contain more of Ida and less of Andrew because of an initial asymmetry. The critically utopian ending of *Ida* reveals its complicity with what it resists more strongly in its feints to race and class than in the lesbian lie that enables Ida and Andrew to pass as the heterosexual couple of comic romance, despite its parodic edge. Yet here, the absence of any disturbing Others makes itself felt in the form of parable and digression, and the highest good (what is "there," "inside," not in language) stands explicitly outside the text's own boundaries. Unlike the romance's assertion of a symbolized good as simply "there," *Ida* makes it a matter of "why not," analogous to the identity-work undertaken by both Ida and Andrew as necessary to ongoing relationship. It would not take evidence of self-conscious authorial intent to read *Ida* as a dialogical response to the narrative problematics of "Melanctha." A writer cannot at will enter the problematics of representation through a merely willed intimacy with the internal and internalized processes of identification, and yet she can explore, as in *Ida*, how male-female relationship operates in social worlds constituted by the hovering injunctions and taboos belonging also to sexuality, race, and class.

The implications of narrative and social meanings in *Ida* and "Melanctha" contribute to ongoing dialogue about how critical masquerade differs from a mimicry that falls more readily into reinscription. Contrary to Stimpson's intuition that one kind of resistance necessarily helps inform others, the epigraph from Carole-Anne Tyler's "The Feminine Look" calls attention to how what has passed for "passing"—the parodic mimicry of femininity—may cover up certain unexamined notions of genuine femininity that are class-based and ethnocentric, and so too with race. Stimpson holds open the possibility of reading "a parable about the inexorably secretive powers of language" where others have found only "the lesbian lie" (163). But why does *Ida* seem more artful in passing as a comic masquerade of women's experience of both gender and sex roles than does "Melanctha" at passing for a comic masquerade of a mulatto's social anxieties?[18] As Houston Baker notes, "one is never 'incidentally,' 'adventurously,' or 'utopianly' mulatto," and, although none of the mulatto characters in "Melanctha" "pass" in the sense that Helga Crane, Clare Kendry, or Angela Murray do, they nevertheless live in a socio-textual world largely made of the language and values of a white bourgeoisie's take on what it means to be "really" married, decent, or proper.[19] Ida's progress from the social constrictions of heterosexual convention toward a more androgynous ideal takes place in a socio-textual world that never escapes from a dominant bipolarity, yet its cumulative paradoxes formally mark its own ellipses.

The racial lie of "Melanctha" does not depend on its central character lacking agency or a storytelling that "anesthetizes black history," though both are true enough. The method of characterization disallows any notions of individual agency, and narration quite purposefully sets about anaesthetizing most historical specificity. Nor does the ironic use of social discourse, including that of narration itself, necessarily help with distinguishing narrative stereotyping from Stein's own stereotyping. Rather, race alone among the social categories fails to become integral to narrative form, being the only part of social discourse that never becomes part of a story about stories. That is, the overt deployment of race has no part in the complexly self-referential connections among social and narrative processes, which explains in part why critics primarily concerned with those connections venture few suggestions about what all those mulattoes and blood-essences and observations about "the colored people" *mean.* "Melanctha" nevertheless has about it qualities that might explain the affirmative responses of both the black readers who came to its defense and feminist and/or postmodern critics. Read as a story about the deployment and diffusion of social power, particularly about how that power works in sexual relationships, or as one about storytelling in the twentieth century, Melanctha might well delight in how its necessarily defeated heroine shows tenacious resistance to coopted discourses, both her own and those of narration. But the confusion inheres in telling a racial story without ultimately caring about what race has to do with those other sides of the story.

The telling difference that marks "the lesbian lie" of *Ida* and the racial lie of "Melanctha," not tangentially, recommends the recursive view of modernity to which I turn in the Epilogue; that is, if even coded meanings have a formal artfulness, or not, then reading recursively from Walker and Bambara back to Stein, and from *Ida* back to "Melanctha," makes Stein appear less as *the* modern woman writer to advance the fictional parameters of social and cultural critique and more as the one to take up in *Ida* a revisioning begun by Jessie Fauset and Nella Larsen. The resistant paradox in *Ida* follows on works written a decade earlier in which a "splendid ambiguity" (Ann DuCille) about the material and metaphoric body "edged the discourse into another realm."[20] *Ida* has the integrity lacking in "Melanctha" to reveal a fearful critique of what the story leaves out: the tragically divided social world hovering behind a comically unfulfilled utopian mode. The intimacy the narrator shares with character ("Dear Ida") and reader ("They are there. Thank them") puts the lesbian coding in a nonjudgmental narrative context, so that "the lesbian lie" is less like an androgynous couple "passing" as straight than a form of coded reference of the kind identified by Amy Robinson as a "secret" play between passer and insider against a dupe (here, the "straight" reader or consciousness). Such a code refers, dramatically and in the expressive form of interruptus or digression, to those other kinds of "outsiderness" not allowed narrative development and to the identity-work across power relations necessary to any actual relationship. On the contrary, the "passing" in "Melanctha" allows a narrative authority about what is "decent" or "proper" or "real" to go unchallenged in reference to a black woman character who acts as a surrogate for a socio-sexual dis-ease. Instead of a secret encoding that hides the passing from a dominant dupe, the secret inheres in the duped character, the restless, wandering, and unfulfilled mulatto who does not even know the secrets shared by writer and reader. This play with race, its "lie," belongs to a presumptive whiteness that ultimately ignores its own appropriations and exclusions.

Chapter 6
World-Traveling as Modal Skid

Hurston and Vodou

There has never been a scholar who really, as a scholar, deals with ghosts. A traditional scholar does not believe in ghosts—nor in all that could be called the virtual space of spectrality. There has never been a scholar who, as such, does not believe in the sharp distinction between the real and the unreal, the actual and the inactual, the living and the non-living, being and non-being ("to be or not to be," in the conventional reading), in the opposition between what is present and what is not, for example in the form of objectivity.

—Jacques Derrida, *Specters of Marx*

I could not get upon the floor quickly enough for the others and was hurled before the altar. It got me there and I danced, I don't know how, but at any rate, when we sat about the table later, all agreed that Mother Kitty had done well to take me.

—Zora Neale Hurston, *Mules and Men*

Hazel Carby warns that Hurston's writing about her southward journeys, first to Eatonville and then to the Caribbean, appeal to contemporary readers in part because they displace the struggles of northward migration—and the devastating urban conflict that only intensifies in the present—with a celebratory view of rural folk culture.[1] And this *use* of stories with seemingly confused generic affiliations coincides with what has seemed wrong, even overtly reactionary, in work bearing the imprint of both romantic travelogue and anthropological fieldwork. Theorizing tragedy and comedy as modes that move expressively in and out of relation, both to each other and to other modes, allows a reading that finds in some modes a reinscription of particular dominances and in others a self-reflective critique. To this end, I want to focus on Hurston's conflicted engagements with Vodou—with what can be experienced and what can be told—and the dance of intimacy and distance that makes world-traveling both possible and dangerous. In its most intense form, possession becomes a sliding metonym for the most powerful and the most threatening aspects of otherness felt in a way both vicarious and yet beyond the vicarious. Although *Mules and Men* and *Tell My Horse* have a seemingly erratic hold on any self-conscious inquiry into Hurston's own subject positions, they nevertheless reveal a double consciousness with more than double resonance because its multiple voices and modes comprise a heteroglossia so ubiquitous that the "skid" among them constitutes its primary characteristic.[2] The artfulness of such a skid will not and should not assuage concerns like Carby's about what lies behind Hurston's literary reception, but—especially in relation to the modernisms in which these works find scant representation—it does reveal the aspects of Euro-American tradition against which she rebels and, therefore, the kind of resistance that may coexist with sundry cooptations. And it argues that one might at least recommend for Hurston what C. L. R. James argues for Shakespeare and Whitman, that their "actual politics" have little to do with the complexities of creative work able "to blow sky-high [their] commonplace conceptions of government and politics."[3]

Hurston's engagements with Vodou have everything to do with both her own multiple and conflicted subject positions and those of the audiences for whom she wrote. In writing that privileges the world of Vodou, she captures something of the dialogical production of the tragic and the comic (related to the Vodou priestess's possession by both terrible and funny spirits); and she does so in a paradoxical form of resistance that necessarily produces critical conflict about what to take as primary. Such conflict informs a literary reception that praises or blames in accordance with what it foregrounds, with the debate about voice that characterizes interpretive dialogue about Hurston's fiction becoming, in readings of the non-fiction, a dialogue about writerly positioning.[4] Later, in the Epilogue, I argue that intracultural dialogue about interpretation matters importantly to an intercultural dialogue with Euro-American theory.

In both *Mules and Men* and *Tell My Horse*, the "skid" between the tragic and the comic, the celebratory and the terrible, structures the skid among modes. For even while distancing herself from the black revolutionary experience that other African American writers found in Caribbean models, Hurston's art inheres in the complexity of her tonalities, in the inassimilable—rather than merely hybridized—nature of narrative affiliations, and in an ideal of cross-cultural world-traveling that compelled her but that she nowhere claims to represent in print.

Leveling and Literary Production

Neither all the stories in *Mules and Men* nor all the contexts for telling belong to the romance with folklore or to the comedy of folk humor. Both carnivalesque inversions of power and traditional healing rituals exist alongside sustained interrogations of personal interrelationship and social justice. Hurston may have added Part II of *Mules and Men* belatedly (Part I's ten chapters of folktales working up to Part II's six about her Vodou preparation and training), but Houston Baker, bell hooks, Susan Willis, and others have shown how her own well-documented social displacements give an ironic cast to a frame that begins with tributes to her white patron and to the mentor interested in the "objectivity" of the anthropologist's calling. *Mules and Men* works through different contexts for collecting and different kinds of telling only to end with the sustained and *silent* intimacies of her Vodou mentors.[5] The opening sentence has an already ironic ring: "I was glad when somebody told me, 'You may go and collect Negro folklore.'" "Somebody" depersonalizes the explicit reference to Mrs. Mason in the "Preface" and the later reference to "Dr. Boas," though biography suggests that Mrs. Mason's "permission" came at considerably more cost (literally enough) than that of her academic mentor. All available evidence suggests that Hurston felt both gratitude to Mrs. Mason for her support and also the constraints and condescension that such support represented.[6] Although Carby and others have seen the Introduction's hortatory praise of Mason and Boas as a sign of Hurston's inability to "query her anthropologist's role," any failures in self-conscious articulation of that role's tensions accompany a developmental progress toward intimate spirit-work with a woman named explicitly as "master," mentor, and friend, the Hoodoo priestess Kitty Brown. Boas and Mason have no presence at all in *Mules and Men* except in opening passages read most convincingly as self-referential irony. And that "lovable personality and revealing style" touted by Boas has multiple personae and exceedingly complex negotiations with intimacy and distance.

Comparing folk traditions to a chemise she "couldn't see for wearing it," Hurston asserts that Barnard, Boas, and anthropology allow her to "see myself like somebody else and stand off and look at my garment." This seeming mandate for social distancing, both from her own positioning and from that of those whom she studies, comes under increasing scrutiny and accumulates difficulties throughout Part I's overt placement of herself as a collector among storytellers. "Folklore is not as easy to collect as it sounds," Hurston asserts in describing the "feather-bed resistance" of those who put off researchers with "a lot of laughter and pleasantries": "I knew that even *I* was going to have some hindrance among strangers. But here in Eatonville I knew everybody was going to help me" (2–3). In a second-order success story told by someone who has just warned of a too-easy success, Hurston justifies the anthropologist's clear desire to describe the social contexts of folk culture in a way that foregrounds her own cultural knowledge, her insider's status. Yet the first chapters only *seem* to fulfill the optimistic sense of her own role: hometown friends greet her with immediate readiness to burst into storytelling, but with a loaded textual silence nonetheless. In the early Eatonville chapters, nobody asks about her life up north or comments on her clothes, her car, or her apparent financial ease.[7]

Thus, by Chapter 4 and beyond, a certain narrative tension accompanies the distance between the good times had by all and the social contexts of telling. In showing herself overcoming a skepticism and disbelief attributable to the "strangers" in Polk County and elsewhere, Hurston lies in a very different way than the "lyin'" celebrated by her companions:

I took occasion that night to impress the job with the fact that I was also a fugitive from justice, "bootlegging." They were hot behind me in Jacksonville and they wanted me in Miami. So I was hiding out. That sounded reasonable. Bootleggers always have cars. I was taken in. (61)

Always supported by her safe Eatonville allies (who know the truth but don't tell?), Hurston's participant-observation reveals the tension of sustained asymmetry: she herself neither tells stories nor risks relationships, and even an occasionally jocular, sexual interchange performs the rituals of intimacy without the social meanings they have in the lives of those about whom she writes. For the storytellers, the site of storytelling is also the site for workers' solidarity (as in the shared debunking of sway and swamp bosses), the ongoing rhythms of hard physical labor and cultural "play," and changing personal and sexual (heterosexual) liaisons. For instance, stories primarily about John and Ole Massa crowd themselves into the unusual circumstances of a holiday made by a boss's illness or a swamp gang's being out of work (reminiscent of "holiday" celebrations in *The Color Purple* and *The Salt Eaters*). Frequently, men tell the folktales that end with the slave John being lashed or put to work in the context of their own labor trouble. A tale ends with the white man saying, "you think I'm gointer pay you, but I ain't"; immediately following, the mill boss says, "Ah ain't got enough work for my own men. Git for home" (92). A cohesively communal point of view places the folktales in the context of oppressive black-white relations, even when, as Susan Willis explicates them, their "form, like the society in which they occur, denies transformation" (*Specifying* 122).

The story of Hurston's changing personal relations to those in Eaton-ville and elsewhere in Florida, and to her implied reading audiences, be-comes the anxious thread interwoven with the telling of these folktales. The tales incorporated by Hurston into her personal story all concern power differentials, but the behavior of those with less power and the outcomes of the tales differ markedly depending on the nature of social and historical reference. That is, although the figures on the under-side of power all evince trickster-like behavior, those involving animals pitted against each other, women against men, or the devil against God have a lightness of touch absent from the stories about John and Ole Massa. Resembling their African origin, the animal stories explain an ideal balance of power, as in God's providing the snake first with poi-son to compensate for his prone vulnerability and then with a rattle to avert those with no intent to harm.[8] Brer Fox or Gator may, like Ole Massa, lose the intended prey by falling for a vast repertoire of cunning, but even in the rare stories in which tricked animals "die," they emerge more as dupes than as either wicked or against nature. Similarly, the stories about women finagling power out of powerlessness most often refer back to stories about the origin of gender, and they customarily end not with the overt defeat or humiliation of the more powerful men, but with an artful solution to power struggles in some form of equitable balance (man's superior strength balanced by woman's power to "keep him from his generations," for example). The devil also plays his tricks on a relatively humorless and starchy God, one who speaks in the same vernacular as the devil and who often accommodates him. These stories predominate in the social context of Eatonville, a town proudly identi-fied as a black community with a school, a library, and a mayor.

The tales "skid" into one another rather much as Hurston's narrative and personal roles "skid," with the present duress of conflicted relation-ship providing the contexts for telling. The stories about John and Ole Massa, different in their intimate relation to history, further complicate the self-reference of tellers, eventually including Hurston herself, who identify with John's positioning. Importantly, Ole Massa brings himself down not simply by falling for John's tricks but by falling for them as a direct result of his own view of slave nature and the "naturalness" of slavery itself. When Ole Massa temporarily "succeeds" in turning the tables and fooling John, he nevertheless fails in his ultimate objective (as when he impersonates the Lord but John uses the ruse to escape [71]). The stories about John and Ole Massa, or any of those with specific ref-erence to lynching or violence, transform the context and the tonality of African trickster tales into African American tales with a tragic history already there behind the telling (what Willis might call "containment"). When folktales introduce Ole Massa and therefore invoke the legacy of slavery, they also move satire in the direction of the tragic, even within the comic frame of reference supplied by an often surly or petulant God. In wit that has only a self-repudiating surface (that "feather-bed resistance"), one tale parodies the white man's prayer in a first-person voice asking the Lord for rain and yet unable to drop either his arrogance or his cavilling complaint about the manner of a last year's rain that came "kicking up rackets like niggers at a barbeque" (89). Another has Ole Massa rewarding John for saving his children from drowning by promising a freedom which he then tries to avert with avowals of love, beginning with "de children love yuh" and "I love yuh" and only then progressing to "Missy *like* yuh" and "But 'member, John, youse a nigger" (90). John "answered Ole Massa every time he called 'im, but he consumed on wid his bag" to Canada. The extant Theories of comedy outlined earlier do not well explain the effect of John's silence, a silence that has both tragic and comic dimensions. John's perfunctory responses are actually nonresponses, and the direction of his feet represents his understanding of a history in which lynching and the fear of black men's sexuality coincide with sentimental white protestations of love. He is not fooled and only comically pretends to play the still obedient slave; but he is not free either, and Ole Massa's voice follows him, always intoning its tragic reduction of John's humanity.

So many of the folktales in the final chapters of Part I, especially the John and Ole Massa tales, have about them the feel of a mixed mode that slips from tragic to comic and back again in the context of a collecting that only partially reassimilates Hurston into a community. If the context of happy storytelling idealizes the interrelation between Hurston and her informants, the nature of the interaction here reveals that social distance cannot be as easily disavowed as the trick of attributing one's car to profits from bootlegging. In social contexts calling attention to how some folktales cope with damaging white stereotypes ("What Smells Worst," for example), the John the Conqueror stories reveal the soul-concerns of a hero who will never express them as such.[9] The hidden internal life of the folk hero corresponds to what remains hidden of Hurston's storytellers and Hurston herself, and a certain disease accompanies any ideal in which Ole Massa bears structural relation to bosses and white employers and in which those without power, even those who feel themselves powerless in love, actively seek alternative agency. As the interchange between Hurston and her informants becomes gradually more participation than observation, it leads ultimately to the dangerous fight with knives that Hurston flees at the end of Part I. The literary production of Part I's folktales disallows the social leveling to which Hurston has in theory committed herself. If she looks back, she will not do so here; instead, she will move to her own training in Vodou and intimacies impossible to tell, addressing precisely the issues raised by Part I's lost connections and partial acceptances.

Sis Cat and Vodou Justice

However self-conscious or not the ellipses and gaps of Part I, those of Part II emerge as climaxes in the narrative stages of Hurston's Vodou preparation and training; it cannot have been lost on her that in a book about how storytelling depends on relations of intimacy and trust the "story" she provides to Frank Boas and Mrs. Mason ends by replacing both mentor and patroness with Vodou doctors. Hurston begins Part II by asserting the secret mysteries of Hoodoo, its "profound silence," and her narration in Part II sustains a rule: the closer she gets to her teacher-mentors, the more distant her narrative relation to "unknowing" readers and the more tenacious her care in keeping the secrets of spirit-possession. The first chapter of Part II introduces New Orleans as the Hoodoo capital of America, rich in "rites that vie with those of Hayti in deeds that keep alive the powers of Africa" (183). From the outset, Hurston drops the voice of observing subjectivity and speaks of "the way we tell it," describing her own beginning study as getting in touch with a communal language also understood by Moses in God's "power-compelling words." Adopting a first-person voice to refer to cultural insiders (looking forward to her own reflections on black invocations of "my people" in *Dust Tracks on a Road*), she simultaneously creates a mystery about the experience of actual spirit possession. Hurston says "We talk it again" of "what the old ones said," referring to a "people's language" that believers must conceal because "Mouths don't empty themselves unless the ears are sympathetic and knowing." The story of her first study with Eulalia and then with Luke Turner, both Hoodoo doctors, acknowledges its own address to the unknowing, warning that "The profound silence of the initiated remains what it is" even as she tells of the first stages of her own initiation. The bulk of the description concerns the mechanics of the rites, but she also slips into the description of detail that "the details do not matter" (198), building to the first of several signifying narrative ellipses that stand for her own possession by spirits: "For sixty-nine hours I lay there. I had five psychic experiences and awoke at last with no feeling of hunger, only one of exaltation" (199).

Rejecting the invitation to stay on as a partner with Turner, she passes on to Anatol Pierre, the Hoodoo priest who oversees her next stage of initiation and a further removal from any unsympathetic, unknowing reader. After the appropriate rituals, her teacher tells her that she must read the third chapter of Job "night and morning for nine days." This third chapter immediately follows the opening frame of the Biblical folktale of Job with Job's first great lament. At the beginning of what many see as the tragic drama of Job, this chapter cries out the despair of injustice and the certainty that no preparation keeps it at bay:

Why is light given to a man whose way is hid, and whom God hath hedged in?
For my sighing cometh before I eat, and my roarings are poured out like the waters.
For the thing which I greatly feared is come upon me.
I was not in safety, neither had I rest, neither was I quiet; yet trouble came. (Job 3:23–26, King James)

In direct opposition to a hierarchial training that endows the initiated with authoritative understanding but not with any necessary empathy for others' suffering, this training teaches a kind of participatory vulnerability. Appropriate to the initiate's heightened understanding of felt suffering, both the chapter from Job and all aspects of the ritual inform the choice of "any kind of work I might want to perform." Hurston again marks the actual experience of communion with the spirits by an emphatic ellipsis, moving directly from what she was told about the ritual to her advanced status upon its completion:

I was told to burn the marked candle every day for two hours—from eleven till one, in the northeast corner of the room. While it is burning I must go into the silence and talk to the spirit through the candle.
On the fifth day Pierre called again and I resumed my studies, but now as an advanced pupil. (208)

An experience so strong that it obliterates individual character or personality, possession leaps the vicarious to a replete intersubjectivity undertaken in the interests of an alternative justice. Chapter II.4 takes Hurston to Father Watson, her next Vodou mentor, and training in rituals that end with two stories about a complementary leveling. The first acts to shore up "a weakish woman in her early thirties that looked like somebody had dropped a sack of something soft on a chair" and the second works against a popular preacher "too rich and big" and about to be a bishop (220). When her own ritual takes place "out of the sight of man," Hurston as initiate feels Death to be at hand. Consistent with prior narrative gaps for the secret of possession, Hurston ends this chapter with the "indescribable" experience of "unearthly" terrors and the strongest ellipsis yet: "Many times I have thought and felt, but I always have to say the same thing. I don't know. I don't know" (221).

The cumulative references to the indescribable and unrepresentable aspects of Vodou build to the penultimate chapter of *Mules and Men*, in which Hurston tells "conjure stories which illustrate the attitude of Negroes of the Deep South toward this subject" (231). All the stories deal with the sudden changes in fortune that can level human experience, yet the central, lengthy story about a wealthy Georgia planter illustrates how oppressive power relations hover behind the logic of Vodou. The story also illustrates the specifically white oppression that exerts a terrible and arbitrary authority over black labor and lives; it carries forward the problems and the revenge motifs of the earlier Ole Massa stories, except that the Vodou doctor becomes the means through which the planter ("very arrogant in his demeanor towards his Negro servants") is brought down. And the telling provides a finely drawn portrait of Vodou justice. The planter not only kills a servant daughter in a fit of pique, but he kills her with a sign of greedy plenty: an immense rib-roast. In a further act of cruelty, he flaunts the murder before the parents in asking them to remove "that sow" from where she has fallen. The family calls on a Vodou practitioner, who may be seen running from the house before each of several stages of the planter's downfall. First, a laughing hysteria captures his wife, whose subsequent attacks on her husband represent her primary symptom of madness. So the planter gathers up his great wealth and moves, only to be attacked by a suddenly demented son two years later, and after that by a similarly stricken daughter. In narration's present time, the planter skulks around in fear of Negroes, but he has more to fear from the children who attack him whenever unchecked. Not only does he lose his children in recompense for the daughter he killed, but he goes in constant fear of an arbitrary, all-powerful attack that comes always from within his own household and threatens not only his own life but the very fabric of family, precisely the circumstances formerly suffered by the household servants as part of their "normal" servitude. The Vodou doctor's surrogacy works to level and heal a social wound rather than to sacrifice, and yet it involves a complex alternative justice closely related to the malevolent power relations that give the Ole Massa stories their edge. No "happy and healthy" rural type appears here, for the historical legacy shows up everywhere in lives that must adopt both the slave's necessary response to injustice and the reason for turning to Vodou: "They knew better than to expect any justice. They knew better than to make too much fuss about what had happened."

In the last chapter, Hurston shares the greatest intimacy and humorous rapport with her final teacher, the one who—not coincidentally—explicitly takes Hurston's suffering upon herself. This root worker, in the manner of comedy, likes "to make marriages and put lovers together" (299), and she has a fondness for telling "funny stories." But she also works beyond a vicarious aesthetics, telling Hurston: "In order for you to reach the spirit somebody has got to suffer. I'll suffer for you because I'm strong. It might be the death of you."[10] The active engagements of II.7 completely supplant any notion of an "objective" perspective as Hurston's devotion to Kitty Brown becomes the basis for her intimate participation in Vodou ritual. Recognizing how other participants regard her with suspicion, Hurston recounts her first role as a Vodou dancer. To treat the betrayal of love and trust by a John Doe who has run off with his partner's savings in order to set up household with a much younger woman, Kitty calls for a ceremonial dance to Death. For the first time, she calls on Hurston:

A dispute arose about me. Some felt I had not gone far enough to dance. I could wait upon the altar, but not take the floor. Finally I was allowed to dance, as a delegate for my master who had a troublesome case of neuritis. (241)

As though an emblem for Vodou's larger bonds of surrogacy, Hurston takes upon herself this intimacy of surrogate dance for the "master" Vodou priestess she claims here as *primary* mentor. Abandoning herself completely to another spirit, Hurston finds herself "thrust" upon the altar to dance. She knows she danced but not how, her only sign of success being that the other dancers later affirm Kitty's prescience in taking her as surrogate dancer. When the man called to Death by their dancing returns to his former lover, Kitty sends Zora to the cemetery to undo Death's spell.

As anthropologist, Hurston would have been called on to explain the logic of Kitty's treatments, their social function and contexts. As storyteller, she leaves Vodou's social and psychological wisdom to illustrative stories about Kitty's ritual treatments, with repeated reference to mystery and to what she as an initiate cannot know. For example, Kitty has many home remedies for "bringing back a man or woman who had left his or her mate," illustrated by the case of Minnie Foster who wants "something for every little failing in her lover." In this case, the precision of Kitty's prescribed treatment depends upon her understanding that Minnie's constant insecurity about her love life indicates something "unsettled" in her. "You must be skeered of yourself with that man of yours," Kitty says in the act of prescribing an elaborate ritual, "but you ain't got no reason to be so unsettled with me behind you" (243). Through particular Vodou stories and the relationship with Kitty Brown, Hurston introduces possession as the embodied extension of an idea that in western tragic theory has only figurative validation: the dissolution of self-other boundaries in a state that connects human beings to their Others. Contemporary descriptions of the sacred in western tragic traditions reveal the distance between Hurston's Vodou surrogacy and the surrogacy taken up by choric witnesses confined to the status of observers and frequently praised for "the ritual standing aside of the tragic chorus, anticipating and mourning the terrible outcome" (300).[11] This praise for a communal "standing aside" involves an anticipation so fated that it includes mourning before the fact. By contrast, Hurston's treatment of Vodou surrogacy stands in recursive relation to the choric group in *Beloved*, who ritually act together rather than stand aside, and, just as important, act in concert toward a healing that only cathartic insight reveals as communal.

Both the spirit work with Kitty Brown and the work as a whole end with a clearly humorous vernacular parable, a story told directly to the reader and therefore of a very different kind than the "funny stories" shared with Kitty Brown that remain unwritten. Jumping without transition from Kitty's advice to Minnie Foster to her own telling, Hurston's tone in the parable about Sis Cat identifies her with the tellers of Part I, who comment on their tales' relation to their own experience, connect personal and storied contexts, and presume rough analogies among the tales about those with power (God, Ole Massa, the fox, men, and any outsiders come to watch or study) and those with resistant cunning (humankind, John the Conqueror, Br'er Rabbit, women, and any actual participants in the culture of storytelling). In Part I Hurston does not herself tell stories; in Part II she participates in Vodou rituals, but neither explicates their meaning nor claims conscious memory of her initiate's role. Only with the Sis Cat parable does she take up her role as teller of a tale, and only with this tale does Kitty Brown as "master" of the unrepresentable effectively replace Boas. The spiritual intimacies of Vodou supplant anthropology, and the folklorist turned participant tells a tale about social positioning.

Explicitly about respectability, manners, and a survival through wit, this final parable places Hurston self-referentially in relation to what has come before—the place of her several selves within the *heteroglossia* of *Mules and Men*—as an artful dodger practicing a double consciousness appropriate to a writer as aware of sundry white readers (from Boas to Mrs. Mason to the generalized white reader) as of the black worlds into which she seeks to gain acceptance (from Eatonville to other places in *Mules and Men* to a literary world already fraught with a sometimes bitter and tendentious struggle for reputation). Fooled once by a rat who convinces her that she should wash her hands before eating and thereby escapes, Sis Cat does not fall twice for the same ruse. Rather, she answers with a sure commitment to survival: "Ah eats mah dinner and washes mah face and uses mah manners afterwards." In humor with a sharp edge for the reader presuming any intimacy with this narrator, Hurston closes the tale and the book with both witty and disturbing self-reference: "I'm sitting here like Sis Cat, washing my face and usin' my manners." Even the quasi-vernacular "usin' my manners" sounds like somewhat stilted performance after the thrice-repeated "mah" in Sis Cat's last sentence, demonstrating that, even when telling the story most like the folktales of her informants, Hurston's telling belongs to the reader of the written text, not to those on the porch or at the party who share the oral tales and interactions that she wants to document and preserve.[12]

In a tonality that will become more strident and even self-repudiating in *Tell My Horse*, this humor with an edge self-refers *Mules and Men* to a power play having everything to do with social and cultural positioning; it is, after all, Hurston's second trip to Florida committed to collecting and writing about folklore, and an urgent instrumentality motivates her. The voice resembles that she used in writing to Hughes, in 1931, about their convoluted disagreements over their collaborative play *Mule Bone*.[13] Offering to take her share of the blame ("I am in fault in the end and you were in fault in the beginning"), Hurston conciliates, offering even to patch things up with Mrs. Mason "leaving you in a white light," and referring self-mockingly to her own "whitening" in the vernacular tones of someone well aware of the costs of patronage. She does so in a post-script responding to Hughes having written, "Let's not be niggers about the thing, and fall out before we've even gotten started":

How dare you use the word "nigger" to me. You know I don't use such a nasty word. I'm a refined lady and such a word simply upsets my conglomeration. What do you think I was doing in Washington all that time if not getting cultured. I got my foot in society just as well as the rest. Treat me refined.[14]

Demonstrating a wily doubleness toward Mrs. Mason as someone "who dotes so on our rock-bottom sincerity" (*Mule Bone* 223), a doubleness richly documented in Robert Hemenway's biography, this partly self-repudiating and partly rights-claiming voice has an almost perfect cynicism in its hostility toward both a smug propriety and the several contexts of her own exclusion. The self-mockery only calls attention to the distance of this humor from the comic vigor of Kitty Brown, for it points to the perpetual dislocations that make comedy as normalcy a very provisional mode, one always disturbed by the desire for the mutually exclusive acceptances that entail at least partial self-annihilation.

Hurston's penchant for ending cumulative dislocations with suggestively open-ended parable incites me, perhaps foolishly, to a real-life analogue with the feel of parable. Because of a partner's interest in Bruce Williams's work on the exploitation of workers in the catfish industry in Mississippi, which offers an interesting case of how racism may supersede even profit motives, we visited Indeanola and its environs. Once there, we could not resist a Catfish Museum heralded by downtown signs. A white attendant with familial ties to the industry—and cheerfully committed to the wonders of catfish technology—showed us around this industry-sponsored museum, whose exhibits included folk-artifacts depicting its development. One, a puzzle with three moving parts, asked what one needed to produce catfish and instructed us to lift the parts to discover the answer in land, water, and food (a production without workers). And a tableau lauded as folk art depicts a time before technology, when the bottom-feeding catfish had a muddy taste, presumably appropriate to the population (read black) who fed on them, but unappetizing to national and European (read white) markets. The single dark figure representing said catfish slurps off the depicted bottom in an image of uncouth, sensual feeding. In the scene after technology, a catfish couple en famille sit on the shore replete with silverware and napkins, in full dinner dress. Now humanized, gendered, and made respectable, their more refined table manners accompany a generally whitened appearance. The whole scenario, self-consciously and archly cute, emphasizes how the industry's technology has saved the catfish from its crude, muddy taste and made it clear enough for even the most refined palates. The museum's story moves the improved catfish away from its classed, racialized, sexualized predecessor, forever a hunkering scavenger-predator on muddy bottoms in search of grimy food (and with who knows what sexual proclivities). A subsequent video shows every aspect of technological ingenuity in growing and harvesting catfish, with no indication of black presence, yet stops before the catch ever makes it to Delta Pride (a name from Gede, surely).

These catfish minding their manners speak to me of Hurston's self-representation as Sis Cat, who apes the manners of bourgeois gentility but relegates them to show in favor of the clearly instrumental ends of survival. Hurston's ebullient tonality in the writerly identification with Sis Cat simulates that of the folk humor she so loved, but those manners-for-show have behind them the tragically hovering seductions of respectability, gentility, and a cunningly evasionary form of acceptance. The parable suggests that Hurston would have well understood both the tragic ellipsis of black people and towns from the catfish story, but also the humorous rapport necessary to make into comedy Sis Cat's opposite, the catfish who become civilized enough to be eaten by white folks.

"Rockatone at ribber bottom no know sun hot"

Hurston's translation of this Jamaican proverb, "rich in philosophy, irony, and humor," reads "The person in easy circumstances cannot appreciate the sufferings of the poor" (9). It aptly extends Janie Crawford's "you got tuh *go* there tuh *know* there" to the problem of positioning any reading in relation to a text's plural and often difficult, conflicted modes. Despite Ishmael Reed's certainty that *Tell My Horse* "is bound to be the postmodernist book of the nineties" ("Foreword" xv), few readings engage the conflicted qualities that seem to refuse to gel; and criticism finds confusions in political and social analysis mirrored in a confusion of tonalities and genres. Sometimes intimate and appreciative, sometimes exploratory and speculative, sometimes reactionary and dogmatic, Hurston's narration slips in and out of anthropology, history, autobiography, personal essay, hagiography, and more, seemingly ill-at-ease with any sustained narrative mode. Correspondingly, an often polarized critical reception may find it, on the one hand, "the first respectful treatment of Vodùn" (Hoffman 80) and "one of the most profound pictures of Haitian voodoo" (Baker, *Workings of the Spirit* 81) or, on the other hand, her poorest book (Hemenway), full of sundry chauvinisms and an ethnograpic point of view that "becomes a tool in the creation of her discourse of the rural folk that displaces the antagonistic relations of cultural transformation" (Carby, "The Politics of Fiction" 34).

Certainly Hurston tends to ignore the legacy of the Haitian occupation and a continuing exploitation by United States interests within and without, providing an historical account that lays Haiti's problems at the door of its own power-seeking politicians and the illiteracy rate (a phenomenon she refers to repeatedly without ever considering the anomaly of a literacy that means mastering an official French in a Creole-speaking country). She readily adopts both an insider's prescience about how Haitians themselves view their history and an outsider's presumption of superiority. When overviewing a general history, she frequently cites "new and thinking young Haitians," a minority not likely to view the occupation as the disaster even a public history now occasionally acknowledges, despite terrible ongoing formulations. (Much in the middle section named as "history" merges the outsider American's perspective with that of history "as the people tell it.") And yet conflicted texts have their own form of artfulness and that of *Tell My Horse* stands at least differently revealed in the tragic and comic modes of later African American women writers.

From its opening pages, *Tell My Horse* places Hurston's own conflicted positioning with regard to intimacy and distance as part of the dialogical production of tragic loss and comic rapport. That is, rather than the discrete elements of tragedy and comedy evident in Euro-American tragicomedy, the tonalities in *Tell My Horse* belong to narrative modes characterized by a pervasive, dynamic tension; they move, in Bambara's figure, like dancers for whom every movement creates responsive movements that are both part of the same movement and yet the beginning of new (like a call and response where each response is also a call). Moving from herself to her subject and back again, Hurston builds to the discussion of Vodou's possession, that state in which the subject and the object hang suspended in temporary merger. This ideal, much like that of the intersubjectivity described in Part I, derives from the structural logic of a work more conflicted than *Mules and Men* and with less overall sense of felt intimacy. In Hurston's descriptions of her own relations with social worlds in Jamaica and Haiti, an often comic self-assertion may seem forced in its energies and a tragic sense of loss may seem to slip too easily into the ritual lament of "Ah bo bo!" (as though appropriated from an absent chorus). And yet, in their very interrelation, tragic and comic modes both turn on a leveling at once personal and spiritual, a capacity for bringing intimacy, connection, and belonging "out of nothing." Far from explicating away the "rhetoric of division" Barbara Johnson and others have explicated in Hurston's fiction, critical attention to how these modes blend suggests that the intimacy felt by those linked in Vodou ceremony casts in relief the tragic character of social loss. Such loss means in relation to a resistant comedy less foregrounded than the self-consciously "witty" tonalities that do not seem so funny to many later readers. If the work has not seemed to many to assimilate its tonalities into some artful whole, then perhaps its art lies precisely there, in Hurston's own "skid" from disappointed desire to unrepresentable belonging, a rhythm elaborating the profound interconnections among the states represented by possession.

The first paragraph relates a sensuous Jamaican geography, a "bush" with more prolific plant variety that anywhere else on earth, to a richness of spirit and achievement. Note the expressive absence of transition between the island's prolific vegetation and its accomplished men of medicine and law; and note, too, the logic of passing from brilliant barristers, whose recognizable genius finds easy comparison to legal genius in the United States, to the very different genius of the Vodou leader Brother Levi, whose genius only *looks* as though "it might be translated into 'a little crazy'":

Jamaica, British West Indies, has something else besides its mountains of majesty and its quick, green valleys. Jamaica has its moments when the land, as in St. Mary's, thrusts out its sensuous bosom to the sea. Jamaica has its "bush." That is, the island has more usable plants for medicinal and edible purposes than any other spot on earth. Jamaica has its Norman W. Manley, that brilliant young barrister who looks like the younger Pitt in yellow skin, and who can do as much with a jury as Darrow or Liebowitz ever did. The island has its craze among the peasants known as Pocomania, which looks as if it might be translated into "a little crazy." But Brother Levi says it means "something out of nothing." It is important to a great number of people in Jamaica, so perhaps we ought to peep in on it a while. (3)

The language of these early pages reiterates authorial distance in almost every paragraph. The rite of Pocomania "boils down to a mixture of African obeah and Christianity enlivened by very beautiful singing" (4). As the "common language of slaves from different African tribes" (Reed, "Foreword" *Tell My Horse*, xiii), Vodou embodies processes explicitly in contradistinction to the Western "nothing will come from nothing," processes through which, in a *pocomania* Hurston identifies as common to all peasants, all that matters in life depends on "something out of nothing."

Although published three years after *Mules and Men*, the work's opening places Hurston herself "outside" Vodou as a merely curious peeper, one in complicity with readers' lack of both knowledge and familiarity. But if phrases like "barbarous rituals" and "peep in on it a while" place her in complicity with reader-outsiders, a corollary humility about places and customs "deep in the lives of the Jamaican peasants" honors the complexity of the connections between "voodoo and life," a complexity acknowledged in an awareness that what she discusses "certainly is not all of it." Although the Hurston of these early pages says that she derives her interest in Vodou from its "music and barbaric rituals," the processes of *Tell My Horse* will make of that "barbaric" an ironic foreshadowing of how the distance caught in the phrase "peep in on it a while" refers most forcefully, even self-referentially, to the prissy distancing of those who judge the efficacy of Vodou from within alien systems of belief and explanation—and, more tellingly, from outside the circumstances of material as well as spiritual need so characteristic of this Neo-African adaptation of African spirituality. By the work's end, no persona remains to "boil down" anything and spiritual possession by the loas becomes the measure of value for social as well as imaginative engagement. In a syntactical progression that invokes tragic circumstance within a comic frame, Hurston then reports an originary story that builds a spiritual practice on a humorous foundation: "Brother Levi said that this cult all started in a joke but worked on into something important. It was 'dry' Pocomania when it began. Then it got 'spirit' in it and 'wet'" (4). In an ethical position with specifically sexual reference, a joke's fertility depends on the moral seriousness of its consequences. Similarly, in describing a color line giving status to mulattoes "in order of their nearness to the source of whiteness," Hurston feigns having no opinion about "what is wise and best," yet compares such attitudes to an American generation immediately after slavery when distinctions between field hands and house servants still conferred status and still bore the imprint of "a left-hand kinship with the master" (7).[15]

Even in His Majesty's colony [Jamaica] it may work out to everybody's satisfaction in a few hundred years, if the majority of the population, which is black, can be persuaded to cease reproduction. That is the weak place in the scheme. The blacks keep on being black and reminding folk where mulattoes come from, thus conjuring up tragi-comic dramas that bedevil security of the Jamaican mixed bloods. (7)

Although the tonality here adopts a satiric view of an unlikely persuasion, it also invokes the tragedy of the originary rape. This tragicomedy names the site where the quasi-comic refusal to "cease reproduction" bears the current imprint of slavery's legacy. Tragedy may seem simply to have more global resonance than the local comedy, but by extension, "reminding folk where mulattoes come from" broadens most stories to include those of origin. The textual journey runs counter to the soul-journey, and, like those of Head and Bambara, involves tragic and comic modes hard for extant Theory to read as such because of their merger.

The "unctuous moral agency" present in African American women's storytelling often finds itself in *Tell My Horse* in the more conflicted context of mocking or self-mocking tones that come from a position superior to either Hurston's Caribbean subject-matter or her own formerly delimited understanding.[16] A mocking tonality may incorporate imperialist presumptions about nationhood, government, or misunderstood cultural practices, but the light self-mockery also portrays her moving from foolishness to camaraderie as she moves from cultural tourist to appreciative participant. When, for example, she tells of how she "kept on talking and begging and coaxing" her Maroon hosts to let her accompany them on a hunt for wild hogs, she tells the story with a lightly humorous regard for her own naive participation. The tale starts with a comic view of herself as the spoiled, soft American who first insists on the journey and then wants to turn back when it turns physically demanding. Yet the story itself, as so often, moves from the comedy of self-mockery (familiar to Western traditions) to a participatory humor, for when Hurston herself participates in the "high good humor" of those she describes, she loses the superior vantage point that makes of her readers a kind of in-group. The celebratory mood of the men after the hunt, in which they tell stories and sing songs, bears intimate relation to a social order deemed separate from differentials of power and wealth: "What was left of the wild pig was given to the families and friends of the hunters. They never sell it because they say they hunt for fun. We came marching in singing the Karamante' songs" (37).

Hurston turns from this jubilant singing to death, as often in *Tell My Horse*. where celebratory rituals alternate with fear of zombies and death rituals. Death the Leveler requires leveling responses, as here when the wife of the deceased cannot provide the lime and nutmeg necessary for rubbing the body and the woman in charge sends someone out to procure them "out of anybody's tree" (41). The role of humor in Vodou, especially its presence in Papa Gedé who also represents death, makes structural sense of many of Hurston's own quick tonal changes. Karen McCarthy Brown, herself an initiate in Vodou forms of possession, insightfully explains such shifts:

I have seen the quick transition between moods that marks Gede's comic sensibility hundreds of times in the marketplace, on the streets, and in homes. A tense situation is flipped on its back by a sudden laugh, a quick joke, or a bit of clowning. This kind of humor is never gratuitous, cruel, or untruthful, and it tends to work best when the stakes are high. "Some people got Ogou," said Alourdes. "Some got Papa Danbala . . . not everybody. But everybody got Gede. *Everybody!*" Everyone has Gede because death is a part of every human life. (Brown 376)

Later this same narrative rhythm occurs when she moves from a self-mockery directed at her own gender role (as a woman bringing presumption with her from the United States) to a treatment of gender and sexuality that has polarized readers, some finding in it the ur-form of a later black feminism and some offended by an exoticizing portrait.[17] Asserting that men in the United States view women as "born with the law in your mouth" (57), Hurston initially directs a mocking irony at an American female's penchant for considering oneself the center of the universe:

But now Miss America, World's champion woman, you take your promenading self down into the cobalt blue waters of the Caribbean and see what happens. You meet a lot of darkish men who make vociferous love to you, but otherwise pay you no mind. If you try to talk sense, they look at you right pitifully as if to say, "What a pity! That mouth was made to supply some man (and why not me) with kisses, is spoiling itself asking stupidities about banana production and wages!" . . . they flout your God-given right to be the most important in the universe and assume your prerogatives themselves. The usurpers! (57–58)

As before, Hurston turns from self-mockery about her own gender role as a woman from the United States to a more complex treatment of cultural tradition, describing how younger women learn from older ones about an affirmed sexuality (even if always a presumed heterosexuality).

In Chapter 5 of *Tell My Horse*, "Women in the Caribbean," Hurston describes virginity as a value primarily for females, with males gaining sexual experience through a trial and error particularly costly to women. Later feminist theory might argue that power relations and women's sexual pleasure have necessary interconnection, but Hurston clearly struggles within *Tell My Horse*, as elsewhere, to retain an enthusiasm for sexuality while providing a strong critique of gender relations. When Hurston writes of the unusual circumstance of a woman's being

allowed to witness a curry goat feed, she elaborates on how closely associated is the fun of the curry goat feed with its masculinist humor.
As accompaniment to a cock soup (no chicken allowed) comes "a storytelling contest, bits of song, reminiscences that were side splitting and
humorous pokes and jibes at each other" (13). Hurston affirms this
boisterous, tendentious, even aggressive play in all its masculine ritual:
phallic boiled bananas follow the soup, and by the time of the ram goat
course, "the place was on fire with life." But the rite celebrates a middle-
aged couple who, although they have raised grown children, have only
now gotten enough money to have a wedding.

In the context of her own debate with a young man about women's
capacities, Hurston places an admiring description of how older women
"who have lived with a great deal of subtlety themselves" prepare virgins
to meet their intended husbands with readiness and eagerness. Hurston
does not ask about men's preparatory experience, about whether or not
the joys of love-as-giving have primacy only for women, or about what
rituals might celebrate the female organs of generation and pleasure; yet
here and elsewhere she has for a model the female Erzli, Vodou spirits
who combine a robust sexuality with attributes of the Virgin Mary.[18]
She focuses on the care with which sexual tradition passes from older
women to younger and how that tradition creates glad, active engagement rather than some "nerve-wracked female" who approaches sexuality as a kind of doom. Not concerned here with gendered opposition,
the unspoken opposition is a western cult of virginity that leads young
women into marriage with a learned pride in having both suppressed
sexual feeling and staved off male advances. Convinced of the harm
done by images of female purity and passivity, Hurston negotiates the
profound tension between a condemnatory view of women's roles and
rights and an appreciation of a positively embraced sexuality. A tragically flawed social order provides the context for sexuality, yet Hurston
uses a tonality of "unctuous moral agency" to describe the conjunction
of personal energy, sexual openness, humor, and passion that Bambara
calls "wholesomeness."

Even a controversial passage about a mambo lifting her skirts and exposing herself may on one level seem a celebration of a sexuality somehow exotic in its very gesture; but on another its abrupt revelation joins
other intentionally "shocking" passages in *exposing* the prurient reader
to the taunt of such explicit gesture. On yet another level it protects in
ritual form a sexuality Hurston would never write about personally, as
though in foreboding of the later overtly humiliating accusation arising from the same nexus of oppressively linked marginalities.[19] In this
context, Hurston seems aware of what we now call reinscription: the
black woman's sexuality available to exposure because already exposed

in a history of abuse. Writing from above as the literate analyst, Hurston positions herself as personally outside the sexuality she describes, carefully contextualizing all affirmations of sexual expressiveness, as though taking into account the conflicted views of black female sexuality against which she places the mambo's dance. (Given that role of a racial and sexual identification commingled with the task of analyst, what genre of writing could imagine the sexuality of a poor, black, and female peasant "ridden" by the spirit, indeed *possessed* by it, without reinscription of some kind?) To read this passage as *either* an "exoticizing" of an explicitly sexual rite *or* as a laudably liberating moment participates in a binary logic that seems not to fit this case of multiple motivations asking for multiple readings.

Focused on the myriad forms of possession and its mysteries, Hurston is caught in positioning that strains against the structures of a spiritual world she trains to enter, caught in that distance between the logic of description and the intersubjectivity it cannot describe (quite literally, in Vodou, the falsity of any distance between the dancer and the dance). And the wealth of cultural certainties about what marks the exotic or the normative make it extremely hard to distinguish between scholarly argument and prior constructedness. (That commentators on Hurston's description of Vodou sexuality take strongly affirming or condemning positions surely reflects this constructedness.) Perhaps because Hurston's voice adopts tones neither monotonal nor consistent in their positioning, one may sense a presumption of intimacy with dominant readers (and therefore with their taste for judgments on the exotic and the bizarre), alongside a fervently admiring identification with those she describes. Certainly she frequently offers testimony conflicted enough that the irony cuts in several directions. The tonality that mocks in the context of seriousness often mixes self-mockery with judgments on cultural practices, yet it does not simply move between the anthropologist's distance and the folklorist's appreciation. Rather, as in passages distinguishing sex and gender roles, Hurston commingles disapproval and approbation. Contempt for the place and view of women may accompany admiration for an open acceptance of sexuality and its sacred role in ritual ceremony, a sacredness that includes both the tragic loss of misdirected love and the comic normalcy of mating and marriage.

Although most treatments of Vodou make its celebration of sexual mystery no less important than does Hurston, she bears the narrative burden of her own participation in a ritual that belies any pretense of a distancing intellection. As in the sexually inscribed dance in *Mules and Men*, Hurston admires a female straightforwardness in sexual expressiveness that from some perspectives might seem to exoticize in its Caribbean context a sexuality she could not write about in what was for her, even before the misaccusation of a later time, the more loaded context of a black woman's sexuality in the United States. Indeed, the richly figurative descriptions of Janie Crawford's developing and maturing sexuality seem relatively mild in comparison with the more boldly explicit language Hurston uses in *Tell My Horse* to describe the most positive aspects of a much freer sexuality. The mambo's raising of her skirts corresponds to many places in which sexual exhibition has an entirely positive connotation, as when she employs richly (hetero)sexual figures to describe a sunset:

> The sun was setting and I lifted my eyes as the father of worlds dropped towards the horizon. In the near distance a royal palm flaunted itself above the other foliage with its stiff rod of a new leaf making assignation with life. (255)

Such sexual "flaunting" occurs and reoccurs, sometimes with little contextual preparation, and seems at once an invocation of the natural and a writerly flaunting of a subject understood as transgressive. Such passages reinscribe Hurston's generative metaphor of Vodou as "creator of life," a religious form appropriate to a possession linked by the loas to both sexual and cultural possession. (For Hurston, of course, the personal tragedy of a false sexual allegation would ultimately silence that unctuous, liberatory case for an expressive sexuality.)

Passages found "exoticizing" or "romantic" in the context of ethnographic reference may in the context of a conflicted testimony belong to a comic mode struggling to be born in (and borne by) Hurston. Read thus, the question of "inappropriate" tonalities recedes and questions about a flexible centeredness and dynamic process emerge, all in the form of a resistance by definition paradoxical: Hurston wants to affirm values, sexuality primary among them, that she cannot write about personally, and she wants to represent the nature of liberatory release in those values without herself becoming the comic target of a very different kind of humor. In a world-traveling characterized by the value it places on intimacy and the relinquishing of personal subjectivity, and therefore very much in opposition to Boas's "objectivity," Hurston portrays any resistance to the sacred aspects of sexual pleasure as connected to a resistance to spirituality itself. Imbued with the ideological biases of Haiti's elite, Hurston nevertheless foregrounds a possession at once spiritual, cultural, and sexual, and therefore a possession resistant to the process of "getting cultured" with its facade of personal control, its smug respectability, and its sexual repressiveness. Hurston's other comic modes notwithstanding, this comic mode demonstrates how the absence of humor helps confine the story of suffering to either arbitrary acts of will and assertion or to deserved consequences (the always linked trials and guilts), whereas its presence places inequitable power relations in the context of vulnerabilities requiring rituals of healing and release. Hurston's most expressive moments as writer and as participant-observer have less to do with the backdrop of political power and upheavals than with the work and customs of the poor.

In *Tell My Horse*, tragedy often appears as it does in Faulkner or Stein, as an ellipsis or a loss marked in avoidances and therefore always vulnerable to sudden, intense reminders. But as the written story of Hurston's actual engagements with diverse groups, *Tell My Horse* elaborates her desire for approval and inclusion in mutually exclusive social worlds, both that of peasant ritual and that of a social or intellectual elite. Read under the influence of later African American women writers, it reveals a sense of the tragic made different by its cumulative, chronic rhythms of telling. Rather than the sudden eruptions of Quentin's passion or a textual narrator's social presumption, *Tell My Horse* accumulates paired disappointments: on the one hand, the alienation of the analyst whose participant-observation falls short of either intimate human connection or some ideal of analytic detachment, and on the other, the terror of not belonging among those whom Vodou protects. As in the rite from which Hurston takes her title, the *Parlay cheval ou* spoken by the loa through the mouth of the possessed mount or "horse," the words may represent an authentic possession or they may represent a possession feigned in order to manipulate others, in which case it must be revealed as fraudulent (related in difference to the surrogacy of the tragic *pharmakon* who enacts a ritual of catharsis meant to heal both the stage-audience and the actual audience, indeed, everyone left living *except* the *pharmakon*). The tragic mode surrounds the constraints on agency in a victimizing world.

Tellingly, Hurston's fascination with zombies links the terror of a living death to a tragic loss of agency. Many have stressed the levelling symbolism of the zombie's living death: neither worldly status nor the capacity to exploit the labor of others ensures any permanent protection from being oneself made into this ultimate figure of exploitation.[20] Hurston's explanation locates the fear and pity excited by zombies in an identification that imaginatively levels social distances, as though the lifestory has powers in the telling into which the audience knows it might be drawn:

The upper class Haitians fear too, but they do not talk about it so openly as do the poor. But to them also it is a horrible possibility. Think of the fiendishness of the thing. It is not good for a person who has lived all his life surrounded by a degree of fastidious culture, loved to his last breath by family and friends, to contemplate the probability of his resurrected body being dragged from the vault—the best that love and means could provide, and set to toiling ceaselessly in the banana fields, working like a beast, unclothed like a beast, and like a brute crouching in some foul den in the few hours allowed for rest and food.

From an educated, intelligent being to an unthinking, unknowing beast. Then there is the helplessness of the situation. Family and friends cannot rescue the victim because they do not know. They think the loved one is sleeping peacefully in his grave. They may motor past the plantation where the Zombie who was once dear to them is held captive often and again and its soulless eyes may have fallen upon them without thought or recognition. It is not to be wondered at that now and then when the rumor spreads that a Zombie has been found and recognized, that angry crowds gather and threaten violence to the persons alleged to be responsible for the crime. (181)

The relation to tragedy occurs here to Hurston in the particular configuration of circumstances: no worldly wealth or stature protects one against the radical contingency faced by Job, who did all that one might do "yet trouble came." No permanent security exists, the legacy of exploitation spreads beyond the grave, and the crime of robbing the grave for soulless labor is intimately related to treating human beings like animals.

Euro-American traditions may, of course, also play on the horror of the "living dead," witness Poe's fondness for postmortem erotica; and the contemporary horror story, filmic and otherwise, makes a cliché of rising from the dead. But as Slavoj Žižek has noted (*Looking Awry* 23), the "return of the living dead" typically reverses the pure symbolization of the funeral rite. Instead of acceptance and reconciliation with death, at one with the assurance that the dead will live symbolically, the make-believe horror of "the return of the living dead" signifies that they cannot "find their proper place in the text of tradition" (23). This horror appears as some "obscene leftover" returning in the form of the revengeful figure (split between cruel revenge and crazy laughter). The instructive difference of the actually living zombie reveals a very different kind of fear associated not just with the cruel, crazy, or vengeful, but with the embodiment of submission, the very form of negative agency. From positions of power and Western rationalism—even in its religious forms—the zombie appears as "the other of the Other," a case where those imagined without agency themselves imagine the horror of one without agency. Like imagining the paranoid's *actual* persecution, zombification terrifies because it brings an absolute spiritual justice from the afterworld to this one.

Hurston's own fear rested in part on a failure to understand the houngan as a kind of "public relations man" acting as a liaison between a necessarily secret society and the world at large, a function well described by Wade Davis. She therefore misconstrued the work of secret societies designed to mitigate the power of wealth and worldly authority. Michel Laguerre, a Haitian anthropologist, describes Vodou as an alternative system of justice for peasants, one that could provide the safety and security unavailable from the institutions granted state authority. In accordance with Karen McCarthy Brown's experience of Vodou, Laguerre and Davis show how excessive wealth and doing harm to others (virtues in the successful capitalist) carry within Voudou the severe sanctions of an elaborate legal and political system.[21] If her distance from peasant life was sometimes explained away yet always hovering, so too the connections forged through a rigorously difficult leveling always threatened foreclosure. Hurston *believed* the horror stories, and Hemenway, Dutton, and Rosaldo see her as caught in the fear of writing the book that would reveal the secrets as surely as she believed in the liberatory desire caught in states of possession. Looking for analogy, but also for a means of avoiding negative judgments on a religion she describes as creating life and beauty, Hurston constructs as "bad" the secret societies that remain closed to her. Replete with all the suggestions of cannibalism, baby-snatching, and arbitrarily random poisonings usually incumbent upon the demonic Other, Hurston's descriptions of the *secte rouge* make "bad" Vodou analogous to gangsters, criminals, and even the Ku Klux Klan in the United States.

A critical focus on *Tell My Horse* as evidence of an overall reactionary sensibility does not address the simultaneity of the terror and the desire of belief. For even in the act of conflicted description, Hurston's tonalities merge and divide only to regroup in changed but metonymic relation to prior positioning, always leaving traces of at least unconscious awareness that no equivalence exists between what she describes and her own methods of description. In this, she prefigures the problematics of aspiration and loss still at the heart of ethnography and literature, both tantalized by how far one can imagine otherness without losing one's grip on why one set about imagining in the first place, the positioning inherent in "where and when I enter."[22] Dutton tempts with the hypothesis that had she dared that leap of faith into less compromised belief, entered the fire to which she was so drawn, she might have better understood the function of the terror. But then, had she been able to surmount the terror enough to do that, she would probably have kept the secret and not have written *Tell My Horse*. In world-traveling, there is always some loss and it becomes tragic loss when it mandates even partial self-annihilation, here an annihilation-through-silence of those parts of oneself that cannot be spoken. The tragedy, then, inheres not so much in exile from two disparate worlds, the tragic mulatto about whom so much has been written, but in reinventing a self to fit a world in which one does not believe while fleeing from both the terrors and the joys of a believed world.

The Hour of Fire

The closing chapters of *Tell My Horse* make more structural sense when read as carrying within their resplendent affirmations both a joy resistant to print and the sorrow of Hurston's own distance from the ideal of possession. A comic self full of verve, style, energy, sexuality, and humor merges with the desire for a loss of self so complete that even talking about it can carry one off in the direction of a spiritualist world. With little extant critical explanation, the last two chapters might seem to conform to negatively judged Hurston types: the penultimate chapter on Dr. Reser as just one more paean to a cultivated white man gracing Haiti with that combination of folk character and scientific acumen she so admired and the story of the pintards as one more second-order folktale mediated through its narrator's romantic desire to demonstrate that "the Haitian people have a tremendous talent for getting themselves loved" (259). Yet the praise for Dr. Reser's character builds to his portrait of his own possession by the loa and provides an appropriate climax to the cumulative stories of possession structuring *Tell My Horse*. And the story of the pintards, the only rendering of a chapter as folk story in all of *Tell My Horse*, instructively links two kinds of world-traveling: that of Reser from hillbilly and scientist to Vodou practitioner and that of a kind of cosmic diaspora in which the story of black origins takes music and dance from God to Guinea and from Guinea to Haiti.

The good Dr. Reser's skill and personal capacity consists in treating his live-in patients' "mad" observations with the respectful answers that acknowledge their humanity while caring for their needs. Rejecting the logic of the color line and the status of doctor (a misnomer attached to his pharmacist's role in the navy), he answers Hurston's questions about his popularity among all Haitians with, "They are infinitely kind and gentle and all that I have ever done to earn their love is to return their unfailing courtesy" (248). Having stressed a vernacular humor appropriate to his "hillbilly" origins, Hurston creates a scene that does not so much romanticize the irrational as provide a critique of the claims of reason and "objectivity." Hurston could admire Dr. Reser's command of sources from Aristotle to modern science, but connected that admiration to his equal intimacy with areas in which relinquishing "command" signaled expertise. Hurston's awe attends his facility in moving so passionately among such diverse worlds:

He is a facile conversationalist on an amazing number of subjects. Philosophy, esoterics, erotica, travel, physics, psychology, chemistry, geology, religions, folk lore and many subjects I have heard him discuss in a single afternoon. (246)

Befitting such experiential range, Dr. Reser treats two patients engaged in a sexual encounter with respect, refusing to be scandalized.

In the chapter's climactic moment, Hurston describes a scene of Dr. Reser's possession, and yet not a scene conventional to Vodou possession. Although she says she has seen this possession in Dr. Reser often, she describes instead a possession that occurs as Dr. Reser himself *talks* about his experience of possession as world-traveling:

> Dr. Reser began to tell of his experiences while in the psychological state known as possession. Incident piled on incident. A new personality burned up the one that had eaten supper with us. His blue-gray eyes glowed, but at the same time they drew far back into his head as if they went inside to gaze on things kept in a secret place. After awhile he began to speak. He told of marvelous revelations of the Brave Guedé cult. And as he spoke, he moved farther and farther from known land and into the territory of myths and mists. Before our very eyes, he walked out of his Nordic body and changed. Whatever the stuff of which the soul of Haiti is made, he was that. You could see the snake god of Dahomey hovering about him. Africa was in his tones. He throbbed and glowed. He used English words but he talked to me from another continent. He was dancing before his gods and the fire of Shango played about him. (257)

In a possession through which the good doctor relinquishes all intellection and control, one described in sexual language and therefore invoking Dahomey, the doctor "throbbed and glowed" in a spiritual relation to Africa untroubled by "his Nordic body." Several readings of *Their Eyes Were Watching God* note that Tea Cake represents for a time an alternative, potentially feminist masculinity, and bell hooks notes that he falls from this oppositional manhood precisely when he becomes "obsessed by the desire to show others that he 'possesses' Janie." Importantly, Dr. Reser's "hour of fire" is not the same thing as Vodou possession, although that is his subject. Hurston chooses to focus not so much on the moment when ridden by the spirit as on the intimate *telling* about spirit possession, with its transformative power caught in narrating memory.

For the first time, the "Ah Bo Bo!!" following the description of the possessed Reser-Moses has none of the lamenting ring of earlier repetitions:

Then I knew how Moses felt when he beheld the burning bush. Moses had seen fires and he had seen bushes, but he had never seen a bush with a fiery ego and I had never seen a man who dwelt in flame, who was coldly afire in the pores. Perhaps some day I shall visit his roomy porch again and drink his orangeade and listen to him discourse on Aristotle, but even in the midst of it, I shall remember his hour of fire.
Ah Bo Bo!! (257)

While elaborating even here the connections between Damballa and Moses that would generate *Moses, Man of the Mountain,* Hurston uses "Ah Bo Bo!!" to signify a surplus of both awe and desire (with the two exclamation marks appropriate to its double reference). The refrain serves to name as unspeakable the causes behind the stories they succeed, such that this final use dramatizes the sameness-as-mystery belonging to both terrible and joyful possession. If it has earlier come precisely where Hurston cannot or will not reveal the secret, it comes now as a testimonial to the creative aspects of Vodou's possession.

Certainly, Aristotle has value in this scene about an American possessed by Haiti, and represents the pinnacle of a philosophic logic held in opposition to Vodou. At home in the world from which he travels, Reser's easy, front-porch "discourse" on Aristotle establishes his intellectual stature. But the narrative drama of the passage relies on its movement from the intimacy of the front porch to the spiritual intimacy about which the doctor speaks. Such intimacy involves a replete sexuality as well as the imaginative capacity to lose oneself in a telling that simulates possession itself, thus combining in a scene the several senses of "possession" that counter its meaning in descriptions of market economics. Far from a possession implying power or control over others, this possession involves a relinquishing of ego quite distinct from the "self-sacrifice" asked of anyone serving others, and especially distinct from that "sacrificing self" that Janie overcomes when she decides not to die for Tea Cake. Hurston likens herself to Moses beholding "a bush with a fiery ego"; to dwell in flame, to be "coldly afire in the pores" accompanies a world-traveling explicitly stepping out of both embodiment and ego and into "whatever the stuff of which the soul of Haiti is made." Dr. Reser does not have primacy of place here because he has experiential knowledge of possession; so had Hurston herself and she had witnessed any number of mambos and houngans in this state. Rather, she stands in awe of him because he could talk about that state, enter into it in the act of narrative and in so doing *become* the thing about which he spoke.

Because Hurston does not claim to represent the state of possession itself, the subject of *Tell My Horse* remains less the anthropological subject-object of the account named as "Voodoo and Life in Haiti and Jamaica" than the subjective desire to experience the intersubjectivity-as-possession that holds together the book's disparate and conflicted stories. The last chapter provides a story likening Haitians to the "pintards of God," the guinea-fowl who bring the cultural traditions of Africa, in the form of music and dance, from Guinea to Haiti. A petulant farmer tries to get the archangels to kill the rice-consuming pests that keep saving themselves with song and dance so compelling that those sent to kill end up participating. Finally, God himself, in all-too-human guise, falls under their spell and instead of shooting the pintards, as planned, sends them to earth "to take music and laughter so the world can forget its troubles." The surrogacy of archangels who fail to do God's will followed by God's failure to do his own will provides a comic resolution for the stories of surrogacy so central to Vodou justice.

Of course Hurston herself does not explicitly link either Vodou justice or the surrogacy of possession to the tragic, a word she would as often as not use pejoratively. Hurston declared that she was "not tragically colored," and in the conservative sense in which she understood it, she was not. Her proud self-identification as a woman of color supplied the impetus for her best work and her most joyous experiences. And yet she lived in a world in which to be black, female, intellectual, ambitious, traveling and "unctuous" implied a tragic entrapment nonetheless. Describing the shock of discovering herself to be "a little colored girl" rather than "Zora of Orange County," Hurston describes a transformation with tragic resonance: "In my heart as well as in the mirror, I became a fast brown—warranted not to rub nor run." Lest her reader mistake this sentiment, she begins her famous disavowal of the tragic with a "but":

> But I am not tragically colored. There is no great sorrow damned up in my soul, nor lurking behind my eyes. I do not mind at all. I do not belong to the sobbing school of Negrohood who hold that nature somehow has given them a lowdown dirty deal and whose feelings are all hurt about it. Even in the helter-skelter skirmish that is my life, I have seen that the world is to the strong regardless of a little pigmentation more or less. No, I do not weep at the world—I am too busy sharpening my oyster knife. ("How It Feels to Be Colored Me" 153)

Using the word in its most trivializing sense, Hurston connects tragedy to "the sobbing school of Negrohood," not to a social order in which people "knew better than to expect any justice." Similarly, she may make tragedy a matter of personal choice or attitude:

> I have been correlated to the world so that I know the indifference of the sun to human emotions. I know that destruction and construction are but two faces of Dame Nature, and that it is nothing to her if I choose to make personal tragedy out of her unbreakable laws. (*Dust Tracks in a Road* 347–48)

In such passages, nature takes on a cosmic necessity and selfhood the tone of the romantic sublime, both antithetical to the more conflicted relation to Vodou, as much a matter of structure and rhythmic alternation as of asserted belief.

Hurston actually lived in and experienced abundantly a diasporic world that many more politically astute knew much more superficially. To call her overall point of view "romantic" may capture something of her professional sense of calling, but it does not help with the difficulties of when she slides into a chauvinistic superiority to her subject and when her own positioning takes on greater complexity, if not always greater self-awareness. At cumulative climaxes in the work's structural rhythms and alternations, the very intersubjectivity of tragic and comic modes affirms resistant values, values that stand in difficult relation to the more overt chauvinisms that many take as the most representative feature of *Tell My Horse*. At these moments, a seemingly politically unconscious prescience values a leveling that includes not only undermining a reader's shared dominance (for example, as a United States citizen, a literate and sophisticated observer of backward cultural customs, or someone immune to debased status-mongering) but also traveling across the distance between herself and her subject. Hurston cannot ultimately displace either the tragic divisions of the racist social order or her own felt inability to both experience possession and write about it, both felt most forcefully in the tensions of intimacy and surrogacy with writerly distance. Unsurprisingly, interrelated tragic and comic intimacies center around those other great levelers, as in Vodou: sexuality and death.

In their structural alternation (slippage even), Hurston's descriptions of the way of Vodou sexuality and death make the connections also made by so many later African American women writers between a fear of sexuality, an internalized code of achievement and respectability, and a denial of aging and death (arguably the dominant features of dominance in the United States). Rather than praising authenticity, selfhood, or the origin of those who belong, Hurston's ending of *Tell My Horse* watches herself watching an expressive form of possession explicitly distant from her own case. That this ideal of possession belongs to a white American man living in Haiti may coincide with her political conservatism, but it does not disallow that only in the forever linked intersubjectivity of a profoundly shared laughter and suffering can tragedy, too, imply a resistant vision of wholeness, and comedy, too, provide a resistant critique of virtue.

Hurston's sundry audiences represent constraints always in conflict with the ethics and rituals of her Vodou training, with the goals of anthropology, history, autobiography, and more, always mitigating the deeply subversive justice and the deeply liberating transgressions of Vodou. She writes for herself, but also for the respect of a national culture whose avoidance of (and therefore titillating relation to) sexuality and death needs no argument. She wants to enlighten a world that sees in Vodou a savage and primitive darkness that it may also see in her. Certainly, she does not feel free to express any sexual enthusiasm with another person as the subject of desire, and subsequent personal history demonstrates the danger of even the forms of *possession* she attempted:

she would be accused of sexual transgression for crossing even narrative boundaries. Hurston's Vodou narratives are tragic, then, in the sense of someone trying to act upon the heaviest personal and cultural responsibilities without being free.[23]

The artfulness that captures these tensions suggests an inassimilable conflictedness in the "skid" of motivations, styles, and tonalities; and it recommends at least the complexity of conflicted readings in dialogue with each other. Caroline Rooney's description of Bessie Head's spiritual system fits Hurston's own spiritual story in its understanding that anyone can be brought low by a malignant, unsupportive community or by the sudden attack of spirits. In a "complexly contradictory" spiritual world, events happen that do not *literally* happen and even when they do not literally happen, "they are more than just metaphoric situations" (117). Hurston, like Head, both "understands the inexplicability of the experience—that is, the impossibility of the attempt to transcribe it further—and at once demonstrates that the process of writing, or writing up, is simultaneously one of speculative interpretation" (Rooney 118). Here, inexplicable experience and the impossibility of adequately writing it imply something about the process of writing, not something about the absence of experienced truths (a value more attuned to postmodern sensibility).

Hurston's possession relies only indirectly on any analogy to material or economic possession (the acquiring of power over territory, goods, or the labor of others); rather, it relies on a spiritual surrogacy in which the body relinquishes power to a loa who speaks through the mouth of its human "horse." In the chapter "Parlay Cheval Ou," Hurston provides telling reference for a work whose very title names both the surrogacy and the dual nature of the surrogacy, its potential to celebrate or relieve but also to threaten or exact sanction. The phrase "tell my horse" names the surrogacy itself, the spirit's voice commanding the mouth of the possessed in a role more literal than vicarious. To the extent that the apparatus remains visible, it only marks the artful totality of the possession. For this reason, as Hurston observes, the fraudulently possessed, those seeking the license of spiritual directive for pursuing their own ends, reveal themselves all too readily. It seems likely enough that although she could make possession the ideal representation of both belonging and surrogacy, Hurston could not make the leap of faith that might have released her from either the terror of reprisal or the ambition to write about the secret.

The interconnections of world-traveling—and its consequences—may mitigate some of its potential arrogances, for there is always something wrong at the end of travel and any arrival—the beginning of print—brings distance with it. *Mules and Men* and *Tell My Horse* need not be read *only* as romantic affirmations of folk cultures distanced from the horrors of urban black life, then and now, because they also speak to the dominant sensibilities that project a social order's tragedy onto cultural Others while finding entertainment in cultural forms stripped of any resistant—or even significant—meanings. Any vestiges of culture-envy disappear in the light of the severe sanctions against those unwilling to either suffer for others or come down from power or privilege to share the laughter, strong sanctions indeed for any Us clinging to an unproblematic social positioning (as when those aloof from the nature and implications of racial experience may exercise to rap, thrill to gospel, or watch—with no apparent discomfort—white officers arresting black men to a background music stemming from black traditions). The sense of an ending in both of these Vodou texts distances narration from any unbelieving audience, a paradoxical sign of resistance in a witnessing that makes vicarious witnessing impossible to some: one either participates or not, believes or does not. Related to the internal interrogations and healing in *A Question of Power, The Salt Eaters, Mama Day*, and other later works, in which healers and conjure-women have both great capacity for taking others' suffering upon themselves and great gifts of humorous rapport, the ethics of human relationship here has everything to do with the difficulty, even the simultaneity, of suffering *for* and laughing *with*. Modes that foreground the spiritual bonds of people with each other—both the painful, revelatory connectedness that grows from a prior presumption of separateness and the humorous rapport that sustains a "wholesome" vision of normalcy—find a place in modern American letters in the cumulatively expressive interstices of such narrative.

Epilogue

Critical (Post)modernity: At the Borders of Arrogance and Possibility

Modernist and high modernist forms, constructed in appropriate terror of the onto-logical, ecological and political instabilities of the twentieth century, have served to reconnect us with coefficients of what, with the dissolving of the Romantic glue, might have become vacant, lost sensibilities—our love of sound, language, color, texture, the play of ideas . . . and our capacity for the intelligent humor needed to moderate our odd predicament. Along with Gödel, Heisenberg, and Bohr modernist artists have engaged in paradoxical higher-order play that is nothing more or less than the making of those connections which can be made—both logically and juxta-positionally—in a post-Newtonian, non-Euclidian, even to some extent post-Einsteinian world.

        —Joan Retallack, "Post-Scriptum—High-Modern"

What is new in the contemporary metropolitan philosophies and the literary ideolo-gies which have arisen since the 1960's, in tandem with vastly novel restructurings of global capitalist investments, communication systems and information networks—not to speak of actual travelling facilities—is that the idea of belonging is itself being abandoned as antiquated false consciousness. The terrors of High Modernism at the prospect of inner fragmentation and social disconnection have now been stripped, in Derridean strands of postmodernism, of their tragic edge, pushing that experi-ence of loss, instead, in a celebratory direction; the idea of belonging is itself seen now as bad faith, a mere "myth of origins," a truth-effect produced by the Enlighten-ment's "metaphysic of presence." The truth of being, to the extent that truth is at all possible, resides now in occupying a multiplicity of subject positions and an excess of belonging; not only does the writer have all cultures available to him or her as re-source, for consumption, but he or she actually belongs in all of them, by virtue of belonging properly in none.

        —Aijaz Ahmad, *In Theory*

"Choose your cure, sweetheart. Decide what you want to do with wholeness."
        —Toni Cade Bambara, *The Salt Eaters*

What To Do with Wholeness

The epigraph from Retallack illustrates common assumptions about the passage from modernity to postmodernity, a concept often used not only to refer to a contemporary condition or to a period, but also to a range of ideas associated with a particular set of theorists and literary or cultural critics. When Toni Morrison says that black women in the nineteenth century experienced the postmodern long before the name, she refers to the embodied dislocations and decenterings of women denied the integrity of defining their own subjectivity. While perhaps loosely suggestive of the enforced dislocations and fragmented identities of contemporary life, this pejorative sense of the postmodern has only contingent relation to the theoretical idea, named postmodern, that subjectivity does not belong to unified, singular selves with autonomous control over their lives or their language. The play of subject positions and object positions within a multiple or fragmented self belongs to postmodern theory, as do conceptions of the Other as whatever slips through language, system, grid, or discourse (whatever supplements the structures of thought or resides in its gaps, ellipses, and absences). The theory of tragedy and comedy as resistant modes characterized by paradox uses the postmodern idea of subject positions, those variable and often cross-referential names for the ambivalences of social positioning, but it rejects the metaphor of Other for the indeterminate or the range of meanings that escape language or system. When postmodernism uses the "Big Other" as a metaphor, it gains a legitimacy and even a status that a tragedy and comedy of resistance belie. The abstract concept of alterity may even reinscribe a relationship that comes to seem like cultural necessity: how any belonging relies on a process of othering, seeing myself or my group as different in a bounded way that becomes tantamount to "better" even if the judgment remains implicit. In much academic writing, the social Other—capitalized here to suggest a reduced humanity—merges with the conceptual Other, that arena where one may enter into an abstracted alterity without ever changing one's own attitudes or social positioning.

Clearly no one set of explanatory terms—and no single definition of postmodernity—suffices, and some black feminist and postcolonial scholars talk of "late modernity" in order to avoid the implications of thinking about any Other(ed) people in abstracted, non-human ways. What I call here a critical (post)modernity acknowledges both the usefulness of many of the concepts brought forward by postmodern theory, particularly a postmodernism of resistance, as opposed to a ludic postmodernism, and the social fact of internal divisions in consciousness or selfhood. It does not, however, find in Otherness an appropriate metaphor for any transformative vision precisely because it retains a hopefulness about the human capacity to understand Othering as an evasionary, self-elevating process, a process unlike active negotiations with difference. Relationally, it values both coming to heal and coming to act in support of those who have seemed, prior to actual relationship, immoral, unnatural, extreme, foreign, marginal, dangerous, ugly, lazy, deceitful, or any of the words used for people whom one does not have to know in order to judge. Opposed to the positive, abstracted Other in conceptual schemes from Habermas to Lacan, the Medusa as social Other demands the maintenance of a tragic world order in which some project their worst fear and horror onto her; yet she shares the worldly stage with a Medusa made human by a healing comedy that looks with love on a woman whose ugliness or beauty depends entirely upon the observer's gaze.

Seen through the lens of "modernism's apartheid" (Wallace), Retallack's testament to modernism's making of "those connections which *can* be made" amounts to a postmodern evasion of any healing activism or social vision. Terror at the many instabilities has become so naturalized that it even appears as "appropriate" terror, presumably appropriate to an "odd" rather than dire predicament (and how terrible that merely "odd" to anyone for whom failures in connection carry life-threatening consequences). A formal delight displaces tragedy's more starkly incontrovertible terror, and an "intelligent" humor serves to "moderate" but cannot serve as either a stimulus to social desire or a call to social action. Play becomes a "higher-order play" as it surveys from its heights a post-everything world. And a logic and a juxtapositioning more intellectual than social makes paradox out of this "higher order," an ideal site where transgression loses its relation to either tragic loss or comic rapport.

In such a formally aestheticized world, resistance becomes so general that it has neither focus nor specific social reference. Ahmad's trenchant critique casts down the presumptions of a high modernism and the postmodernity he sees as its successor, but focuses on the dominant evasions characteristic of "the available metropolitan grids of modernism and postmodernism" (12). The writerly worlds that have been my subject here offer evidence that the urbane sophistication of metropolitan worlds has no more necessary stature than the tales of village, town, and neighborhood (even the symbolic neighborhood of a transplanted community in Brewster Place or the abstracted neighborhood to which Ida and Andrew retire after the failure of American cities to solve Ida's identity trouble). The dialogical interrelation of a tragedy inhering in the social order itself and a critically, comically utopian vision of healing suggest both the difficulty and the promise of reading against the grain of sundry modernisms' apartheid and against, too, the critical legacy of Euro-American Theory. Across sundry ideological predispositions, the asymmetries abound. A widespread enthusiasm for the postmodern games of imagining in *Absalom, Absalom!* may not address the work's incorporation of appalling social constructions or the social tragedy that provides their context. Praise of Stein's early and troubling "Melanctha" for its daring overturning of realism exists alongside readings of *Ida* that reduce its social critique to the play of language. And the reactionary aspects of Hurston's Vodou texts earn them (and their precursors) an invisibility justified by failures in writerly awareness, even while more overtly odious aspects of works by Eliot, Pound, or Hemingway, often in readings less self-conscious about readerly identification, do little to change the stories of literary modernity.

Although extant modernisms may make at least some room for feminist readings of modernism and even for the black modernism of the Harlem Renaissance, they tend not to do so in literary terms that grant the stature to reshape extant theory. Clearly, issues of focus and readerly relation do not divide up neatly in accordance with the social categories available to analysts or to the multiple and interconnected processes of self-identification.[1] Even if some dominant "we" were increasingly to recognize ourselves as having multiple subject positions, the fact of imagining a self as multiple does not necessarily avoid the constraints of positioning within system, grid, or discourse, any more than it represents a commitment to changing the inequities among actual people. The tragic and comic modes of black women writers foregrounded here rely on characters-in-process who retain their agency despite an ideal of intersubjectivity: the capacity to feel the strongest human connection with the suffering a community tries to cast out as Other and the capacity to share in the leveling labor that makes a healing laughter possible. These modes fit the testimony of many who have struggled with the processes of identity-formation and who therefore resist the idea of some universal multiplicity in favor of an ideal of integrated identity, some "wholeness" valuing traditions and yet committed to social transformation. Ideological predispositions from conservative to radical may well share commonly accepted texts or moments as sites where the modern reveals itself in the act of becoming the postmodern, yet the most hopeful and celebratory versions of this passage share with the most critical the absence of this vision of a "wholeness" born of intimacy and struggle.

Tragedy and comedy theorized in terms of a largely formal, generalized aesthetic resistance may have neither transformative focus nor any very specific social reference; and they often participate in popular (commercial) culture's reinscriptions of apathy, cynicism, and distancing. To read *Beloved* as though "rememory" were what any reader may acquire in the act of reading reduces it to a matter of supplying a chunk of once missing history in literary form (its frequent use in American history classes); and that too easy process of reading allows a fascination with how narrative involutions in *Absalom, Absolom!* become the history-making game of Chapter 8. On the contrary, the transformative possibility caught in the daily worlds of multiply positioned or processual characters, who understand their experience as neither unique nor universal, does not rely on any clear separation from dominance, even in resistance.

The wholeness described by Morrison, Walker, Head, Bambara, and others in Part I relies on an achieved belonging, an integrated self, and a whole panoply of values connected here to a resistant conception of tragic and comic modes. Such values remain primary even in a social world torn by divisions, fragmentations, and dislocations (including the world only recently named as "postmodern"). For such a critical (post)modernity, a healing comedy retains its profound relation to tragic loss, not of some essential identity but of the experience of wholeness; and in this, it practices what Gilroy calls "anti-anti-essentialism." As in Fanon and Freire, these tragic and comic modes see the conditions of living as always interrelated and never neatly divisible in accordance with the names for social categories that, when elevated to self-regulating categories of analysis, leave actual people "segmented into different social moments, made a victim of discrete determinations" (Bannerji 49).

If a postmodernism of resistance is a paradoxical rather than a hopelessly conflicted idea, then "wholeness" (and its corollary "wholesomeness") as an ideal leads toward choosing a course of social action that need represent no more a theoretical anathema than the values placed on shared physical labor, belonging, solidarity, intimacy, rapport, inter-subjectivity, spiritual relationship, and "unctuous moral agency" itself. In a more critical (post)modernity that includes the lived experience of dislocated or denied identity, there are specific uses for wholeness and for intracultural dialogue; and the intracultural negotiations characteristic of tragedy and comedy as dialogical modes have much to teach about the possibility and difficulties of intercultural dialogue, and about the social responsibility attendant upon bearing witness to suffering and desiring to share in laughter. Art and life are not the same thing, but art may further the felt relationships that inform the will and the ability to act. Karla Holloway (*Moorings and Metaphors*) describes within black women's fictions a telling that for some acts as "testimony that recenters the spirits of women, mythic and ancestral" (187); and yet such "creative convention of women's voices," referring to "passionate articulations" within fictions and outside them, belongs not to anyone who desires it, but only to those with lived relation to the community of women she describes. To presume a gendered belonging to such a community on the basis of literary experience misconstrues the nature of the telling, its paradoxical relation to lived struggle. In literary representations of this paradox of resistance, allied here with transformative ideologies, narrative catharsis and intersubjectivity serve to reveal the arrogances and complicities of those who presume themselves well in self-conceptions requiring separation from those they need to be sick.[2]

Collection Without Contagion

Most dominant description of social and cultural life in the twentieth century distinguishes between a contemporary period and what came immediately before, often called a difference between the modern and the postmodern. Different ways of linking the modern and the postmodern, though few would find them discrete historical periods, bear much socio-cultural weight.[3] The theory described in the Prologue as "transgressive" or "radical" comes closest to engaging the concerns (but not the literature) most important to me here, and so it may help to begin my own sense of an ending by distinguishing my sense of transformative theory from two uses within contemporary theory of tropes drawn from tragedy and comedy respectively, Daniel O'Hara's *Radical Parody: American Culture and Critical Agency After Foucault* and Jacques Derrida's *Specters of Marx: The State of the Debt, the Work of Mourning, and the New International* (the former more accurately "poststructuralist" than "postmodern," but sharing many similar concerns). Both works take up issues of intellectual lineage and both emerge with models of self-other relations rarely contaminated with cross-cultural (or even cross-gendered) contagion. Their difference from transformative vision is well glossed by James Snead's distinction between a metaphoric universality common to a Euro-American "collection" of textual frames of reference and an African universality implying "contagion," an actual touching of the human Other: "If *collection* exists as a guarantor of *pro*spective value, then *contagion* is a *retro*spective attempt to assess propinquity that seems to have always been present in latent form and has already erupted without cause or warning" (245). Taken together, O'Hara and Derrida reveal how profound the distance between much postmodern attention to social disorder and that furthered by the tragic and comic modes that have been my subject.

For O'Hara, the values of parody and its ascendant stature cross readily from literature to criticism. In a collection of essays that acts as both cultural history and critical Jeremiad, O'Hara undertakes to modify "the new orthodoxy" of deconstructed selves (Foucault, Derrida, Rorty) in the direction of an appreciative avowal of both the literary imagination and the socio-ethical consequences of theory itself. In readings that seek intriguing connections between critical theory, cultural context, and social consequences, O'Hara writes against the "opposing orthodoxies" of both those "against theory" and those practicing theory's supposedly most influential modes: "new historicism's weakly liberal poetics, neopragmatism's chilling professionalism unbound, [and] essentialist feminism's apocalyptic separatism" (269). O'Hara's own combinatory mode derives ideas from "imaginary fathers" that culminate in Lentricchia as the fulfilled "miglior fabbro."

O'Hara provides an imaginary genealogy of "our ancestral heritage" that lauds those felt to have a "strongly particular imaginative grasp of their actual historical situations." Yet for anyone who believes that only social action—actual changes in power and agency—links theory with its social and ethical consequences, such choices will seem weighted before the balancing, even when elegant in design and important as cultural and critical testimony. The critical consensus O'Hara characterizes as nihilistic, for example, might equally well represent a consensus that all language has ideology and all theory some originary belief. (Who would not, after all, prefer to come down on the side of hope over nihilism, imagination over determinism, and prophetic visions derived from a cultural past over narrow, reductive professionalism?) Yet frequent reference to cultural and social context aside, the terms of judgment here often fail to distinguish themselves from the old universals. Like their predecessors in universal-speak, such terms as "transhistory" and the "collective archive" all too easily select out influences from among the already influential, ignoring any of the theorist-critics who might have caught up more sharply the presumptions of value that so readily become "avowal." (As so often, Williams has prescience here: "We expect [people] brutally exploited and intolerably poor to rest and be patient in their misery, because if they act to end their condition it will involve the rest of us, and threaten our convenience or our lives" [*Modern Tragedy* 80].) Arguably, the most radical changes in critical agency after Foucault point to an American archive more hybrid than collective and to institutions more changed by those constructed as Other than "self-transforming."

With comic parody as a guide for ironic distancing, O'Hara's own American play of masks does not interrogate the conflicted nature of his own desire to have contingency and idealism too, to perform the self in multiple masks and worship at the feet of genius, to have—à la Hemingway—both the irony (self-parody) and the pity. *Radical Parody* does not ultimately spur the imagination towards more ethical or radical consequences than do many of the writers representing the "fashionable orthodoxies" accused here of professionalism, narcissism or essentialism. In the world O'Hara often aptly describes, where Stanley Fish represents the left in public scenes of "multiple misrecognition," his own language for value too often presumes some shared reference for "actual history" or "magnanimous" interpretation. Thus, his impressive, even formidable command of critical agency does not help to understand how an asserted "Over-Self" may, through parody alone, avoid the issue of its own complicity. The tragic and comic modes theorized by transformative ideologies take as part of theory the conflicted, paradoxical nature of social desire and they presume no totalizing referent for "shared" or "actual" history.

The sheer contingency of studying black women writers while reading Derrida's *Specters of Marx* presses home that their differences with regard to ghosts—their necessity and threat—is not merely a religious difference, nor even just about a secular postmodernity as opposed to one in spiritual opposition to the claims of a reason complicit with slavery and its forgetting. Rather, the difference lies in a tragic lack felt nowhere in Derrida *as* tragic, a lack reliant on some felt familiarity or intimacy with the condition of the Other, even the Other as specter (the spirit-world figured in the spirit-hauntings of Marx). Of course Derrida's use of the "Big Other" refers to largely textual hauntings and not to Marx personally or to a social other, and yet the attitude toward the "specters of Marx" undermines any ideal of human relationship between two figures made in necessarily human image: that of the scholar-analyst Horatio and that of *Hamlet*'s famous ghost.[4] In African American women's fictions, characters have intimate, familiar relations with spirit-figures, and those relations simulate successful, levelling and levelled relationships with the living. (The truism that conceptions of a spiritual world reflect real-world values applies here.) Despite political sympathies like those expressed in Derrida's Dedication to Chris Hani, the absence of any value on familiarity, intimacy, shared work, or supportive action matters, because without these values, no argument for either compassion or responsibility will seem efficacious (cost-effective). Here, even in a work expressly designed to answer charges that he has never come to terms with Marx, Derrida adopts a tonality resonant with the detachments such a failure implies.

The choice of *Hamlet*, the tragic intellect at antic play, well fits theoretical extrapolations about what the scholar might learn from the ghost of Marx. The scholar should

learn to live by learning not how to make conversation with the ghost but how to talk with him, with her, how to let them speak or how to give them back speech, even if it is in oneself, in the other, in the other in oneself: they are always *there*, specters, even if they do not exist, even if they are no longer, even if they are not yet. They give us to rethink the "there" as soon as we open our mouths, even at a colloquium and especially when one speaks there in a foreign language. (176)

One does not occupy hegemonic positions and escape the habits of dominance, of course, and the passage refers metaphorically to "discursive practices" rather than to people. And yet, the *even if they do not exist* clause has upon it the particular arrogance of the scholar-conjuror who finds in "Thou art a scholar; speak to it, Horatio" the validation for the final word on what must be done: *rethink*. When self-other relations are not a matter of positions taken but of intimacies sustained, then "the other of the other" as ongoing dialogue displaces unitary selves with a dynamic sense of oneself as a subject-becoming-object in the same present as those whom one has objectified take up subjectivity. The choice of the scene with Horatio and the ghost takes up the problem of the scholar's vicarious witnessing as *the* tragic problem, already a second-order relation to the suffering occasioned by a tragic world. Horatio becomes the admired figure for scholarly identification, and Horatio's speaking becomes the model for intellectual courage, an overt acceptance of the scholarly role as vicarious witness. For even in a work putting forward more concrete and engaged political ideas than any prior work, as though in answer to all the charges of ahistorical or apolitical evasion, Derrida's positioning represents only a more elaborately vicarious relation to social struggle, very different from hearing the call of tragedy to *bear witness* and to take action. (And Derrida seems to forget that the capacity of Horatio to communicate with a ghost in order to explain to others the mystery of Hamlet's death relies on his incapacity to understand that mystery.)

Derrida's work takes Horatio's interaction with the ghost in *Hamlet* as the guide for dealing with the "haunting" presence of Marx in a post-communist world and a dialogue among "avant-garde scholars" as its occasion. If Derrida's failure to come to terms with Marx emerges here in the New International, the New International itself bears only vicarious witness to social struggle. Derrida's consistent sense of genealogy (Hegel, Marx, Freud, Heidegger) reveals a lineage that can *only* end with the scholar-hero who braves speaking to the ghost, not with the awe of one struck to the marrow with ghostly presentness. This paradox has less to do with the contingencies of social positioning than with claiming both speculative distance and the capacity to speak to specters. The lack in both tragic and comic modes implies a supplemental fullness, a vision of wholesome living as the achievement of urgency, intimacy, agency, and action. The complexity and possibility of such vision has relevance to Hurston's belief in ghosts and Derrida's displaced enthusiasm for Horatio's manner of handling ghosts, a manner with as much scholarly and intellectual distance as his scholar-analyst successors. Derrida's focus on the scholar who must learn to speak to ghosts becomes a kind of deconstructionist's emblem for the repressed, the *revenant,* who in the act of asserting necessity, choice, belief, and engagement, must also add "even if they do not exist" and other gestures of rational distancing. Whatever the intensity of Derrida's own auto-critique and his engagements as an activist, behind the New International lies the analyst's dream of detachment.[5] That is, behind any amalgamation of political, media, and academic power lies the postmodern scholar's own unspoken desire: *I do not want to be hated, hurt, or killed. If only I get it right, I can show compassion at least. I can avoid being hated, hurt, or killed and still keep what I have.*

The emblem of the laugh, too, emerges in relation to the lack seen by Cavell and others at the center of comedy; it relies less on any necessary, dynamic interrelation to tragedy than on the willful exercise of analytical mind. See how quickly the healthy laugh turns to superior intellection:

> However alive, healthy, critical, and still necessary his burst of laughter may remain, and first of all in the face of the capital or paternal ghost, the *Hauptgespenst* that is the general essence of Man, Marx, *das Unheimliche,* perhaps should not have chased away so many ghosts too quickly. Not all of them at once or not so simply on the pretext that they did not exist (of course they do not exist, so what?)—or that all this was or ought to remain past ("Let the dead bury their dead," and so forth). (174)

How different the flippancy in "of course they do not exist, so what?" from Morrison's understanding that only when otherness becomes "familiar" do the spectral footprints match one's own. *They are so familiar. Should a child, an adult place his feet in them, they will fit. Take them out and they disappear again as though nobody ever walked there.* Transformative theory does better than to chafe away at the risks and arrogances embraced by Hurston (whose belief in ghosts does not allow such transparently privileged moves as "Who cares?" and "So what?")? The ghosts care, and if you believe they cannot get you for recording your most familiar interchanges in the context of scholarly performance, then you have placed yourself above any actual struggle for therapeutic relationship. However strongly you assert emancipatory desire (that New International that sounds in Derrida rather like a secret society), you must look at the something missing at the end of travel. World-travelers of the transformative kind never travel "in the line of" or with the security of vicarious "prior words," but always turn toward the something missing and something wrong, the *lack* of tragedy and comedy coupled with their desire for a world in which to belong. *In the beginning there were no words. In the beginning was the sound, and they all knew what that sound sounded like.* Nothing in Derrida values such a sound, and in this Derrida speaks as only one of many solo voices. Theory as either "radical" parody or as the "transgressive" desire to give back speech to ghost-Others regards its Others more as theorists in the academy than as people together in the world. It absents the scholar-analyst from social activism at the same time that it diminishes his world's tragedy.

Leaving the Story Unresolved

Bessie Head's appreciation for what she has learned from African American women asks that they, in turn, appreciate "the future greatness of Africa." And in a fictional world of 1974, her central character heralds a hopeful struggle toward normalcy with "She left the story like that, unresolved" (*A Question of Power* 201). In this, Head presages African American feminist theory's later investment in tales that leave specifically unresolved the issue of "whether the insiders' acknowledgement of the other is symbolic or transformative" (Valerie Smith, "Black Feminist Theory" 56). Black feminist and postcolonial theories, in both their storied and unstoried forms, have understood that the metaphor of "intersection" for social categories does not, ultimately, serve the interests of social transformation. The idea that oppressions intersect like roads coming to a traffic circle, on the same plane, suggests that any approach leads to a single intersection where one meets others having come to the same place.[6] (As Brackette Williams has put it, "Only a fool stands in the middle of an intersection.")[7]

The dialogue among feminists spurred by black feminist criticism has revealed repeatedly that women neither start from nor arrive at the same intersections, but that a fear of difference among women should not disallow a conception of a common struggle. This sense of difference differs from the standpoint of epistemology in that subject positioning depends not on some chosen approach but rather on one's social roles, paradoxically contingent and yet chosen. Recursivity is a better (but not unproblematic) figure, since it implies that once having conceived of a dialogical relation formerly unthought, something very different emerges on the other side and, further, changes how the landscape just traversed now looks.[8]

The paradox of social positioning—always part of the paradox of resistance—acknowledges the contingent, constructed character of experience but also the need for change, the agency behind actions responsible even when not free. Valerie Smith argues that a defining characteristic of black feminist theory is that "it seeks to explore representations of black women's lives through techniques of analysis which suspend the variables of race, class, and gender in mutually interrogative relation" ("Black Feminist Theory" 45). Such "mutually interrogative relation" takes into account differences in positioning, but also relies on the intra-cultural sense that "the circumstances of race and gender alone protect no one from the seductions of reading her own experience as normative and fetishizing the experience of the other" (57). Ideas informing the conception of resistant tragic and comic modes find in black feminist, African American, and postcolonial theory some alternative ways of fig-uring the tensions in self-other relations, alternatives that also refigure the (post)modern as no longer a post-European (post)modernity.

Building on earlier critiques of postmodernist indifference to black culture by Robert Storr and Cornel West, bell hooks's "Postmodern Blackness" provides a critique of how an abstracted postmodern interest in "Otherness and difference" has coincided with indifference to both black feminism and black women (explaining black women's disinterest in debates about the postmodern). Although reflecting on those aspects of postmodernism that might be useful to black women intellectuals, she knows that the knowledge of intellectuals is not the only knowledge and that it has no sacrosanct position in thinking about self-other rela-tions. In reviewing a postmodernist critique of essentialism that evades black yearning for empowered subjectivity, hooks articulates the desire "to critique essentialism while emphasizing the significance of 'the au-thority of experience'" (29). Later works by hooks elaborate how "re-sisting representation" means differently across social positions, never far from Bambara's or Head's charity toward any who act in the direc-tion of recovery to undo who they have been and what they have done. Patricia Hill Collins, too, sees the application of terms like "deconstruc-tion" to black feminist thought as justified by the legacy of women like Sojourner Truth (equally important to hooks) whose

actions demonstrate the process of deconstruction—namely, exposing a concept as ideological or culturally constructed rather than as natural or a simple reflec-tion of reality [Alcoff 1988]. By deconstructing the concept *woman*, Truth proved herself to be a formidable intellectual. (15)

When Gayatri Spivak asks the useful question "Can the subaltern speak?" her analysis of the complex and multiple subject positions of women in postcolonial situations informs an argument that anyone must "risk essentialism" in order to act in alliance or solidarity with others. And yet, it also spurs the sense that anyone concerned about such "risk" may have posed for themselves the wrong questions, questions that avoid actual relationship (*In Other Worlds*). Similarly, Homi Bhabha uses a postmodern focus on indeterminacy to explore the subaltern subject's quest for identity and freedom.

The intracultural processes that provide the lens to see (post)modernity through black women's fictions and the black feminist dialogue framing their traditions also provide enough of cultural wisdom to imagine boundary crossings across the gulf that separates not only the white and the black, the dominant and subaltern engagements in debates about the (post)modernisms, but also Theory and theory (theory and antitheory in some formulations). The white, often progressive feminisms promoted by Seyla Benhabib, Judith Butler, Julia Kristeva, Donna Haraway, and others stands on one side of Theory, enmeshed in abstract language (subject positioning, gaps, ellipses, absences, difference, supplementation, indeterminacy, and so on) and debates with (inter)textual authority (even when trying to pay attention to actual women's lives). The black, usually progressive feminisms promoted by Katie Cannon, Patricia Hill Collins, Kimberlé Williams Crenshaw, bell hooks, Wahneema Lubiano, Valerie Smith, Hortense Spillers, Patricia Williams, and others stands on the side of more eclectic theory based on experiential as well as *merely* textual authority. (Crenshaw cites as characteristics of critical race theory its insistence on experiential knowledge, its eclectic nature, and its social action toward ending racist oppression.) Very few, Houston Baker, Henry Louis Gates, Jr., bell hooks, Wahneema Lubiano, and Hortense Spillers among them, have tried to reconcile the concerns of black feminism and African American women writers with those of postmodern consciousness or sensibility. And white Theory, with white feminisms perhaps foremost, has only begun the revisioning of its own categories implied in this latter body of thought.

Here, I have used many metaphors considered anathema to postmodern sensibility: the concern for an organic link to black life; the womanist focus on ancestors, lineage, and a felt sense of tradition; spirituality (the sign in Euro-American Theory for a despised metaphysics); and above all, the value placed on coming to a subjectivity felt as wholeness. Yet in each of these areas, both imaginative testimony and the theory of black feminists themselves suggests no very necessary distance from a postmodernism of resistance's concerns with subject positioning (representing unrepresentable, negotiated identities) and the arbitrary boundaries of genres, forms, and the "literary" itself. In many areas, the theoretical problems important for reimagining tragic and comic modes importantly mesh with the concerns that black feminist theory has made primary. Yet in a work about the paradox of resistance, this paradox remains: only if no longer at the margins does black feminism have relevance to formulations about the postmodern's relation in difference to the modernity that precedes it.[9]

Michelle Gellrich's sense of the (post)modern invokes Kermode, Habermas, Foucault, and others as "addressing the exclusionary biases that necessarily attend theory's claim to authority and coherence" (xi–xii).

Yet recent theories of black feminism and modernism open the possibility of theory with a lowercase "t," that is, theory with no claims to
Grand Theory or the exclusions conventionally signified by such values
as "authority and coherence." Rather, they are theories about cultural
and intellectual interaction and an ideal for which "dialogical" only
roughly stands, unless as defined in one of Bakhtin's last notes in its difference from the dialectical:

Dialogue and dialectics. Take a dialogue and remove the voices (the partitioning
of voices), remove the intonations (emotional and individualizing ones), carve
out abstract concepts and judgments from living words and responses, cram
everything into one abstract consciousness—and that's how you get dialectics.
(*Speech Genres* 147)

I have coupled here this notion of the "dialogical" and that of the
"intersubjective," chosen despite its problematic variants in Habermas
and Lacan (and resembling "the dialogic correlation between identity
and non-identity" [Bakhtin, *Speech Genres* 159]). Taken together, they
suggest processes of both intracultural and intercultural exchange and
a focus on more complex selves (subject positions, multiple identities,
fragmented or split selfhood) and more problematic (as opposed to the
already problematized) relations both between writers and readers and
between worlds named too readily as fictional and worlds named too
easily as real. The disjunct literary boundary between tragic and comic
clearly touches many presumed oppositions in addition to bipolar social
categories, between metaphysical and physical, spiritual and material,
individual and social, self and Other, theory and praxis, literature and
criticism, and, yes, modernity and postmodernity. A necessarily more
distanced mediation of experience than Cherrie Moraga's "theory in
the flesh," this theorizing nonetheless both mandates full engagement
of readers from quite different positioning and calls for actions outside
of writerly/readerly ones.

What stands as resistance in Euro-American traditions does not well
address conflicted, hidden, or relational resistances, resistances that
when they take the shape of art do not necessarily mean in the same
way to all readers, and may, in fact, matter more importantly to some
readers than to others. Very specific cultural parameters and traditions
delimit the distance between relational interpretation and misreading,
especially in situations where deploying a fixed map of misreading or
extending intertextual play, especially with culturally dominant modes
of play, may well imply serious consequences for some. Resistant relations—both resistant to power and resistant to too-easy identification
or presumed relationship—suggest no particular set of ideologies which
appeal or do not, but rather much more complex and relational ways

of thinking about modes of resistance and how they have integrity, or do not, in the variously postioned problematics of representing cultural contexts. Jacqui Alexander and Chandra Mohanty have compelingly argued that for dominant Theory, the theories of women of color "are plausible and carry explanatory weight only in relation to our *specific* experiences, but that they have no use value in relation to the rest of the world" (Introduction xvii). Unless read as relevant to a critique of dominant ideas about both tragedy and comedy, the works in Part I lose strong relevance to what it means to categorize works and how those categories reinscribe, or do not, specific social and moral attitudes.

Readings informed by generic distinctions have commonly found violations of generic rules and boundaries (sometimes masked as charges of superficiality, confusion, or incoherence) in writers on the margin. The traditional boundaries between tragedy and comedy—central to Theory from Aristotle to Cavell—make sense primarily in conceptions that take as foundational the bounded nature of social groups and the ultimate defeat of resistance from below. To accept the generic terms applied to works *as a whole*—even if as mixed genres or self-conscious boundary crossing—means to slight the subtlety with which works may rely on more fluid and overlapping modes, modes better described in terms of an implied relation between fictional and actual worlds (and therefore a negotiation involving social relations) than as formal characteristics belonging to texts (and therefore seemingly abstracted from social relations). Since condescension toward a kind of writing often becomes difficult to separate from condescension toward a writer herself, the charge of generic "confusion" may signal a literary process of a more difficult modal order, one that acknowledges and addresses how the paradoxes of writerly resistances must necessarily enter into dialogue with the paradoxes of readerly resistance. Yet a theory of tragedy and comedy as modes of resistance does not pretend to be a "theory in the flesh" of the kind put forward by Cherríe Moraga for women of color, but rather a mediated theory about writing and reading that takes seriously the distance between "theory in the flesh" and the processes of reading and experiencing put into motion by texts.

The case of black women writers' relevance to a large body of Theory should bring to mind the intracultural experience explored by others whose self-identifications mandate both negotiating sundry dominances and writing from the margins, a combination that necessarily involves stories in paradoxical relation to consequential action. For however contingent multiple self-identifications and however nonessential cultural affiliations, individual and communal experiences with different kinds of difference must all negotiate the inequitable and asymmetrical power relations that belong not only to writers and their written worlds but also to their multiply positioned readers. The resistant modes of tragedy and comedy examined here provide readerly imperatives far from any loose sense of paradox. These paradoxes of resistance recommend rather precisely positioned responses that resist, for readers, either a too easy identification or a too easy appropriation, both reliant on that "excess of belonging" of which Ahmad Aijaz speaks. When the tragic and comic theory read through black women's fiction becomes central rather than marginal, its dialogical modes reveal both the tragedy of an oppressive social order *that can be resisted* and the comedy of a marginalized healing *that can achieve normalcy.* Both resist the scapegoating common to tragic sacrifice and comic attack as traditionally conceived, and both recommend alternatives to the nicely symmetrical typologies of dominant versions of (post)modernity with Euro-American texts at the center. Those dominant versions represent a kind of culture-tax on works that necessarily deal with conflictedness, a tax not levied on those works most amenable to that "excess of belonging" for which such conflicts do not exist; and such a tax skews how (post)modern "collection" works for even domiant fictions. Put otherwise, inequity rules work with both more complexity and more sophistication than do systems of analysis and their always troubling categories. I have tried to show that this does not merely entail exclusion, a history characterized by self-perpetuating ellipses, but also the maintenance of relatively fixed parameters for how to read even those works commonly associated with American modernism. And thus, I have tried to do more here than pay attention to black women's fiction as necessary to transforming Theory; that is, I have tried to articulate particular ways in which the social negotiations of narrative voices or fictional characters require differently placed readers to negotiate the relationality of their responses, that is, their own distinctive relation to narrated worlds that refer (and often self-refer) to actual experience.

The stakes of literary discussion may not seem very high, but they relate to social meanings with much at stake. Many women of color, including black feminists, have argued that as long as white women and women of color are content with living separately in a state of psychic social apartheid, racism will not change. If women allow racist/sexist systems to control our relationships with one another, we cannot blame patriarchy for keeping us apart.

But you said there was no defense.
"There ain't."
Then what do I do?
"Know it, and go on out the yard. Go on." (Morrison, *Beloved* 244)

Many women carry on the dialogue almost by definition, since the conditions of identity-formation may disallow any independent or "free" self-definition; but dominant theories of genre, the formal categories of literary study, or readings of texts may ignore or suppress negotiations carried on as a condition of survival or membership. As bell hooks puts it, interrogating female xenophobia (fear of difference) must be a significant part of future struggles to end racism and sexism:

At this point in time we need to build a body of literature that will both acknowledge the political significance of bonds between white and black women as well as document the process in which those ties influence the direction of progressive politics, particularly the struggle to end racism. (hooks, *Killing Rage* 224)

Many examples within these pages cite two common postures of criticism that avoid such active engagement, the one turning away from black women's writing and the critical and theoretical problems it raises for fear of "speaking for others," and the other embracing generalizations that "collect" African American women writers into existing categories, canons, and judgments. Warnings about totalizing and universalizing argue a needed specificity, a closer attention to differences, but they should not discourage serious engagement on the grounds of not wanting to "speak for others." Attempts to avoid the possibility of appropriation may universalize precisely because they do not engage differences-in-relation and do not advance "readings" from one's own positioning as informed by one's own appearance as Other (something those in marginalized positions must do by definition). That avoidance disallows making needed distinctions between Stein's use of race as a contingent backdrop in "Melanctha" and Faulkner's more artful self-reference—not the same thing as his limited socio-political views—in leaving black characters without individualized consciousness as part of a social tragedy both lived and written.[10] Too often, the critical choice seems between, on the one hand, a wholescale appropriation of texts into critical designs with no regard for intracultural frames of reference, its self-identifications, and, on the other hand, a bending over backward to avoid "colonizing" or appropriation of any kind, resulting in a principled silence difficult to tell from other altruism in the presumption of its good intentions. Oppositely, the tragedy and comedy of resistance place a tragic emphasis on witnessing that ultimately reveals a complicity that requires social redress (even for generalized societal constructions) and a comic emphasis on the familiarity, relationship, intimacy (the shared energy of shared work) that makes a shared laughter possible. A (post)modern apartheid inheres in precisely the opposition of a too

easy belonging and a self-repudiating withdrawal.[11] The paradox of resistance applies to dominant subject positions too, for if one takes the
advice "Let black women speak for themselves" to imply others' silence,
then the burdens of social transformation become impossibly, unbear-
ably heavy.

Rereading and Rememory

Although discussions about black modernism have characterized African American studies for over a decade, they have had relatively little
place in debates about which modernity informs which postmodernity.
The "metropolitan philosophies" cited by Ahmad have largely failed to
include views "from elsewhere," and least of all views less metropolitan
or less celebratory of a formalist avant-garde. The concerns that link
black women writers and critics suggest the probable reasons why black
feminists have provided no global overviews of (post)modernity and
have instead focussed on the tasks of "(re)constructing womanhood"
(the title of Hazel Carby's study of nineteenth-century black women's
writing) and explicating the black women's traditions that inform ongoing social struggle. Spiritualism, ancestral mothers, healing, and the
often conflicted quest for wholeness have little stature in a modernity
perceived as dependent upon a man "who is completely modern only
when he has come to the very edge of the world leaving behind him
all that has been discarded and outgrown and acknowledging that he
stands before a void out of which all things may grow."[12]

Although only tangentially concerned with women writers as modernists (Fauset, Larsen, or Hurston receive scant mention, for example),
Paul Gilroy's *Black Atlantic: Modernity and Double Consciousness* has argued
that the concerns linking the traditions of the black diaspora all stem
from a resistance to the Western myth of progress, with its forward-
looking teleology and its excitement in newness. What Gilroy describes
as a countermodernity, I call here a critical modernity in order to as-
sure the "contagion" of dialogical interrelation for all those writers who
in some way resist both bourgeois values and the myth of progress in
favor of a "community without unity" (Corlett), one capable of accepting difference without fearing it and of acting on a felt relationship to
those outside its own constructions of normalcy. The dominant myth of
progress now has its postmodern successor in the newness praised by
Retallack and described critically by Ahmad: "an excess of belonging;
not only does the writer have all cultures available to him or her as re-
source, for consumption, but he or she actually belongs in all of them,
by virtue of belonging properly in none" (44). A modernity conceived
against "the grand narrative of Euro-American progress" also resists any

postmodern successor that values the urbane spectacle of apocalypse, parody, and an omnipresent ironic distance. I have argued that Bessie Head's "gesture of belonging," Toni Morrison's waiting footprints, and Toni Cade Bambara's "wholesomeness" do not recommend some essentialist or ultimately romantic view of identity, but worlds in which power always affects how anyone comes to self-definition. However conflicted the dialogic responses to these worlds, they rely on referential hook-ups to actual worlds where differences in power demand constant negotiation and where spiritual life and the integrity of intimacy and relationship demand ongoing social struggle. Characters within these fictional worlds, usually characters-in-process and in-merger, share in the condition often described as "postmodern," but they share in it critically and without relinquishing a sense of loss in a tragic social order or a sense of joy in the forms of intersubjectivity.

Critical focus on the modernism of the twenties, in all its fast paced urbanity, has seemed all about the Euro-American myth of progress, technological and otherwise, caught in a normative enthusiasm for experiments with language and form. Described in either apocalyptic or celebratory mode, this modernism has little room for either black women writers or a white working class; and it has no room at all for the transnational struggles that may appear in conflicted or as yet "non-literary" modes.[13] Ann Douglas's *Terrible Honesty* provides the most relevant example here, in its monumental survey of "mongrel Manhattan" as the center of 1920s modernism, with the "intersection" of social identities spurring forays across races, ethnicities, genders, sexualities, and the high and low forms of art. In this impressively researched story, the players take up and cast off roles upon the urban "scene" with theater, spectacle, and media always providing the backdrop. In a book with the Harlem Renaissance writ large, Hurston finds only cursory mention and the Stein of *Three Lives* has primacy over that of the later *Ida*. (Despite a 1906 letter in which Stein laments that "I have to content myself with niggers and servant girls and the foreign population generally," Douglas shares in Carl Van Vechten's and James Weldon Johnson's praise for her making black characters "crucial to her artistic enterprise.")[14] Since "wit, drama, and role-playing" signal the excitement of the times, this story of modernity foregrounds a common "struggle for self-definition" that tends to diminish differences in social positioning while making self-consciously aesthetic experiment the basis of boundary-crossing, a new art appropriate to the newest excitements of the new world.

A liberatory, forward-looking modernism, such as that in Ann Douglas's recent portrait, exists as surely as the high modernism described by earlier critics, but neither has room for the critical modernism of those who did not see the 20s, and certainly the 30s and 40s, as a time for either breaking with the past or producing the thrill of instincts for "the dangers attendant on liberation and exile from past illusions and constraints" (Douglas 483). At one time, Hugh Kenner's sense that modernism raised the question "what the written word might be good for" produced a witty panorama of the American modernist world:

> So here it was at last, the distinguished thing: an immense panorama of futility and anarchy, together with some hope of articulating it through myth. Scott Fitzgerald by 1924 was working from a pervasive local myth, vast as the continent: the myth of Promise. That myth was not homemade. It had helped propel the Renaissance. It was one of those foreign things, long naturalized, long reduced to the bare authority of a diagram. The bitter European books which the Society for the Suppression of Vice so disliked said that promise was deceit, and promise was American now. Even in Europe they thought so. (Kenner 19)

Now, a once exclusively high and exclusively white and male American modernism has at least broadened into an inclusion of both some women writers and some black modernists. But neither a black, transatlantic (or even transnational) modernism nor a black feminist one have yet influenced conceptions of the postmodern, those connections to later writers that might inform a critical (post)modernity not understood as a discrete period.[15] African American women writers undertook (and undertake) their own narrative traditions, beginning with the slave narrative and moving through Frances Harper and Pauline Hopkins to not only Hurston, but also Lucille Boehm, Marita Bonner, Anna Julia Cooper, Jessie Fauset, Nella Larsen, Ann Petry, Dorothy West, and others.[16] As black feminist criticism has observed, most of these writers have at least ambivalent relation to the pressures of dominance and its narrative forms, and most differ from the later writers that Barbara Christian identifies as undergoing internal struggles with self-identification as well as the struggles with an external world more characteristic of modern writers.[17] But a literary complexity that ought to produce a dialogue among readings has still a largely unexplored relation to such modern writers as Josephine Herbst, Josephine Johnson, Meridel Le Sueur, Tillie Olsen, Maimie Pinzer, Muriel Rukeyser, and Agnes Smedley. And although multiply positioned feminisms provide a ready context for intercultural dialogue, that dialogue would spur increased attention to the artfulness with which male writers also transform conflicted subject positions into paradoxically resistant tragic and comic modes; it would, for example, examine with greater interest the still devalued Langston Hughes of the 1930s, the expatriot writing of Richard Wright, and James Baldwin's fiction.

In addition to Gilroy's *Black Atlantic*, several recent works have begun a shift in emphasis that makes more possible the intercultural dialogue recommended by the critical (post)modernity of black women writers. Sandra Adell provides a self-reflective inquiry into how attempts to reconcile black and postmodern critical projects risk a contemporary form of the "double consciousness/double bind" that she explicates in a black modernity's paradoxical relation to "the social myth that literary criticism can somehow speak for the absent and unrepresented other" (118). Houston A. Baker's *Modernism and the Harlem Renaissance* argues effectively against a standard for "modernism" that precludes writers of the Harlem Renaissance from a vital and effective modernity (with "conjure" stories among those providing "*tricky* or transformative" signs). James De Jongh's *Vicious Modernism: Black Harlem and the Literary Imagination* traces the role of Harlem in both the writing of black modernists and a later beat generation (Allen Ginsberg and Kenneth Rexroth, for example). Philip Brian Harper's *Framing the Margins: The Social Logic of Postmodern Culture* explores "modernist alienation/postmodern fragmentation" in writers across the periods, races, and ethnicities. Charlotte Nekola's and Paula Rabinowitz's *Writing Red: An Anthology of American Women Writers, 1930–1940* evinces the shared social concerns of black and white women writers of the depression era. In addition, many cultural critics have provided exemplary vision of intercultural exchange, among them Michael Awkward's *Negotiating Difference: Race, Gender, and the Politics of Positionality*; Karen McCarthy Brown's *Mama Lola: A Vodou Priestess in Brooklyn*; Angela Davis's *Blues Legacies and Black Feminism* (which takes up the blues as "an important elaboration of black working-class social consciousness" (42); Ruth Frankenberg's *White Women, Race Matters: The Social Construction of Whiteness* and *Displacing Whiteness*; bell hooks's *Yearning: Race, Gender, and Cultural Politics*; *Talking Back: Thinking Feminist, Thinking Black*; and *Killing Rage, Ending Racism*; Toni Morrison's *Playing in the Dark*; and Susan Willis's *A Primer for Daily Life*.

The dialogue already begun among black and white feminists (female and male) finds no more eloquent expression than in Alice Walker's appreciation of both Hurston and Agnes Smedley and in Toni Morrison's Foreword to *Writing Red*; both presume a critical (post)modernity's connections and both understand literary values as also ethical ones:

Agnes Smedley never forgot the hunger and humiliations of her childhood, the oppression of her parents, the snuffing out of her brothers by the exploitation of the American capitalist system, or her own struggle to remember and to affirm them, even as she fought against falling victim to the poverty that had eradicated them, herself. Everywhere she went she saw herself, her family, her class, her own people's *condition*. Her spirit was darkened at times by all the light in others she saw blotted out. Yet poverty in Chinese or Hindi or black folk speech was recognized as the same language by her; she spoke (and understood) it fluently. This ability then, so far from the capacity of most white women and men, became for her the gift concealed in the wrappings of pain.

She was a citizen of the planet. (Walker, Foreword, Smedley 3–4)

When women take noncompetitive notice of other women, when their sensitivity to the plight of each other traverses the lines that separate them—class, race, religion, nationality—extraordinary things can happen: poor women see through the bars rich women are caged in; black women understand the 'privileges' of light skin as destructive to the whole race; mothers recognize the dependence of capitalist bosses on prolific child-bearing; female office workers perceive the oppressive complexities of gender and power at the workplace; middle-class women respond to strikers with compassion and intelligence. (Morrison, Foreword, Nekola and Rabinowitz, *Writing Red* ix)

Many of those Spivak names as "subaltern" evince the charity of inter-category relationship that carries less risk of arrogance or appropriation than do the attempts at world-traveling among those accustomed to dominance. And yet, if subject positions used to sundry dominances go in fear of arrogance and complicity, then they will be unlikely either to embrace those moments when former presumptions stand revealed as such or to seek the "mutually interrogative relation," Valerie Smith's phrase, that occur when arguments about the primacy of race, class, gender, or sexuality become dialogues about the implications and consequences of particularly positioned power. And therein lies the need to abjure the modern apartheid that leads to postmodern avoidance in favor of a dialogical, critical modernity leading to a negotiational, critical postmodernity, one as firmly relevant to area studies, cultural studies, subaltern studies, women's studies, and all studies of identity and representation as to any narrowly conceived literary or genre theory.

If the contingencies of classed, gendered, racialized, sexualized experience "protect no one from the seductions of reading her own experience as normative and fetishizing the experience of the other" (Valerie Smith), then how to read becomes a matter of creating possibilities for engagement, for which "the desire for transformation" is a better trope than "transcendence." Critical postmodern supplementation, as opposed to figures for competitive territory, might well encourage intercultural dialogue that turns on understanding how the conflicted positioning of modern writers, texts, and worlds corresponds to that of contemporary readers, who come from some social positioning and some habitual set of power relations however they name their methodologies. If the tragic and comic in literature necessarily involve some take on the tragic and comic in life, then their interrelated concerns arise inseparably from those of any active engagement with difference.

Tragedy as a projective identification with another's difference-in-sameness and comedy as a projective identification with another's sameness-in-difference not only resist the confinement of either to strictly literary genres; such focus also engages the problematics of how to forge connections across socio-cultural boundaries, even when those boundaries have marked out contested territories within a self. Susan Willis expresses the historical parameters of such social desire in the act of noting how the folktales within *Mules and Men* "affirm race, but they do not then transcend racial prejudice. That is, instead, the project for our time" (*Specifying* 45). Such a view implies changes in both what and how to read, with much greater emphasis not only a black modernism, but also on Chicano/a, Asian American, and Native American traditions (among others); on the art of proletarian fiction; on the interrelation of only seemingly discrete categories (like "black modernism" or "proletarian fiction"); indeed, on the intra- and intercultural relations-in-difference of all those who have felt themselves on the underside of power or privilege; on transnational (or postnational) cultural interconnections; on works and modes with literary value but not written as literature; and on connections to orature, folk, and popular culture (blues genres, industrial folklore, and song forms, for example). It does not imply debunking the long-standing stature of such a modernist as Faulkner on the grounds of his own positioning or the voice he gives to social constructions now found offensive; rather, it implies rereadings that search out the tensions that make his work still one of the most provocative sites for intercultural dialogue.[18]

What I recommend here with reference to theorizing about the tragic and the comic may imply a restructuring of any hierarchy of genres and opening the boundaries of extant genres, but more importantly, it calls for more nuanced examination of the modes within written worlds that provoke moral and social judgments about whether characters in fictions—or even writerly personae—appear as better or worse than particularly positioned readers presume themselves. Rather than playing into the Medusa's demands for some normative modernity, these modes have more to do with furthering a supplemental understanding of the dialogical nature of literary modes themselves and what they do or do not have to do with the complexities of both writers' and readers' social positioning. The turn away from formal generic categories does not give up on aesthetic evaluation or substitute some set of ideological or identity categories in their place, a widely expressed fear. But the willingness to find literary value in the artfulness with which conflicted positions themselves find paradoxical expression, or to find an artful resistance of one kind linked to habitual dominance of another, corresponds to the willingness to engage in dialogue across the categories and positions. Intercultural dialogue must resist the demand for consensus (usually a veiled desire for lost or never possessed authority) in favor of the felt relationship capable of sparking both the desire for a just social order and the impetus to act on such desire. Such dialogue acknowledges that actual worlds pre-exist written texts, that knowing passes through gates of horn, not ivory, and that how to read always means how to live in the world.

The critical tragic and comic modes examined here address from different positions, even if as loss or absence, the possibility of leveling social transformations that might bring some to a newly empowering subjectivity and some to a confrontation with themselves as complicit in the processes of others' objectification. As critical modes, their interdependence—simultaneity even—imagines a better world's more just relationships (not kindler or gentler, but infinitely more tenacious in valuing the intersubjectivity of changing power relations). They imagine, too, how to get there from here, how to resist reproducing the old relations of power caught in both the vicarious thrill of scapegoating and the heady, distancing intellection of merely Theory. *Instantly the kneelers and the standers joined her.* And only then, by acting, how to keep one's gaze from turning another to stone or how to comb the snakes out of one's own hair.

Notes

Prologue

1. The names given to ideologies have, of course, only provisional status; to label characteristic tendencies as conservative, liberal, transgressive, or transformative does not disallow the overlapping subject positions of writers, texts, and readers. In a more technical sense of ideology, I examine here the "nodal points" around which scholarly practice "structures floating signifiers into an identifiable ideological field" (Žižek, *The Sublime Object* 67). Thus, generalizations about a conservative use of Greek drama do not locate something conservative "in" Greek drama that might negate the importance of Euripides (spurned by Aristotle) to more transgressive theory. Nevertheless, the naming usually implies some conflation of meanings negotiated by writers, readers, and works. The project of this chapter suggests strong interconnections, even while taking the social implications of how to read tragedy and comedy as primary.

2. Among others cited both in chapters on specific texts and in the Epilogue, see Sandra Adell, Homi Bhabha, Patricia Hill Collins, Karen Fields, bell hooks, Françoise Lionnet, and Obioma Nnaemeka, all of whom address Theory's failure to engage in dialogue with its constructed Others. Barbara Christian's "The Race for Theory" and Roxanne Rimstead's "Between Theories and Anti-Theories: Moving Toward Marginal Women's Subjectivities" make complementary arguments against Theory in the act of recommending the theory implicit in black women's and other marginalized women's narratives respectively.

3. A note on my own positioning in a work all about relational readings that aspires also to deal with what constitutes misreading. Ever since Carlene Young, then president of the African American Studies Association, complained to me of the plethora of loose women, incest victims, prostitutes, and Aunt Jemimas in black women's contemporary fictions, in the summer of 1984–85, I have worried over my own responses to characters who seem to risk strong relation to stereotype, yet show their differences most forcefully at precisely those moments of strongest resemblance. In dialogue with Carlene about how fictional representations both do and do not work, I realized that I had interpretive responses that felt to me validated by textual evidence, but that did not even attempt to negotiate either intracultural debate about what is hurtful or not to black women as readers or about what aspects of texts particularly positioned readers foreground. At the time, I mostly wanted to avoid the role of the white critic making her way through a profession by writing about black women writers (an understandable source of complaint among black women ignored by the academy),

even though everything I wrote seemed to be in some way about the positioning of the reader, both ideologically and in terms of subject position. Gradually, with the benefit of many conversations cited in the Acknowledgments and with tragic and comic theory my chosen focus, I began to focus on how some of the most overtly controversial texts in debates about race, gender, nations, and sexualities artfully manipulated writerly gestures of inclusion and exclusion such that readers, too, must negotiate when they can and cannot identify with characters in fictional contexts that take the hurtful nature of marked categories as part of the problem. So many black feminist (and Africana womanist) critics, many cited throughout, have specifically addressed relational and critical difference among readers, yet relatively few white feminist readers have ventured into readerly responses to this multivocal writerly art (with Barbara Johnson's "Metaphor, Metonymy, and Voice in *Their Eyes Were Watching God*" standing as a well-known exception). So I offer here criticism that I hope will be of interest to all readers of these works and traditions, but which I understand as furthering an intercultural dialogue about which I speak more fully in the Epilogue.

4. Rather than reiterating "dominant forms of Euro-American theory," the capitalized Theory will represent this somewhat crude generalization across difference (as in those Theories of tragedy and comedy surveyed here) and the lower-case theory will represent theory either marginalized or not yet construed *as* theory (as in the black feminist or postcolonial theory that has not yet, even if well-known, significantly altered generic classification or description). Exemplifying the universalizing tendency of Euro-American Theory, tragic theorists may claim tragedy as the most profound and universal of forms and yet conceive it as a specifically Western genre comprised of works by those representing a fairly narrow range of sociocultural positions. The masterworks of Euro-American tradition conventionally inform debates about the death of tragedy, its dying, its rebirth, or its reinvention as something else (the sublime, the absurd, the apocalyptic), just as they inform the neat division of the tragic into such oppositions as "tragedy" versus "anti-tragedy" and "post-tragedy." For example, Ekbert Faas recommends such categories in the act of constructing tragedy as a uniquely Western genre, and David Lenson names tragedy as the most profound treatment of human suffering, "the most prestigious form of art" (140), despite a strictly Western, strictly canonical frame of reference.

5. I do not mean to suggest that all aspects of the texts in Part I are recuperable to some aesthetic coherence implied through reference to tragic or comic modes.

6. Here and elsewhere, I capitalize "Other" when I take it to mean an unrepresentable category that resists the objectification the naming implies. Homi Bhabha explicates it in this sense in "Interrogating Identity: The Postcolonial Prerogative."

7. See George Steiner's *Antigones, After Babel*, " 'Critic'/'Reader'," *Real Presences*, and "A Note on Absolute Tragedy."

8. Bergson as cited and translated by Avner Ziv (76).

9. Avner Ziv (42). As here, psychoanalytical perspectives frequently adopt conservative ideology, perhaps because theories that foreground the play of conscious and unconscious mind, even when used as an analogy for socio-political or economic tensions, always refer back to individual or subjective psychic space. Because psychoanalysis dedicates itself to avoiding the despotism of the passions, not the despotism of dominant social power, it generally pays little attention to either the suffering or the humor of the oppressed except as internalized

self-disparagement or aggressive, inversionary backlash. I address here what Jane Flax has called the "adaptive and conformist tendencies" of psychoanalysis (*Thinking Fragments* 91). There are, of course, psychoanalysts who work in the direction of a possible, sustained social criticism, taking up suggestions in Fanon.

10. Theoretical dispositions as diverse as those of Suzanne Langer, Wayne Booth, Norman Holland, Paul Cantor, Christopher Nash, and Helen Vendler all view genre as formally defined and therefore presumably free of "ideology" in ways that those who explicitly address ideological constructions do not. Fortunately, the journal taking *Genre* as its name has no such blindspot, and invites problematizing the power relations implicit in all generic constructions.

11. Frye understands, of course, that much comedy presents ambivalent modes and encourages ambivalence in how to play or read, as in the choice of whether to foreground a comic expulsion of Shylock as scapegoat or to play Shylock as a tragic figure within a comic frame. But his unproblematic contrast between tragedy and comedy preserves the separations of fictive worlds that insist on the purity of their own make-belief. Jameson (*The Political Unconscious*) usefully explicates how Frye's reversal of the last two levels of medieval exegesis works to contain any collective energy within an ideology of individual desire.

12. Dolf Zillman (100) refers to this process as allowing dominance "to be malicious with dignity."

13. This sense of a literary evasion of power is consistent with such general critiques of liberalism as those provided by Michael Sandel, Martha Minow, Ron Scaap, and Iris Marion Young. The black critique of white liberalism will receive more attention in the Epilogue, but argues generally, in the words of bell hooks: "While in some ways true, a construction of political solidarity that is rooted in a narrative of shared victimization not only acts to recenter whites, it risks obscuring the particular ways racist domination impacts on the lives of marginalized groups" (hooks, *Killing Rage* 152).

14. This formulation is the basis of Snyder's explication of tragedy and its difference from other genres.

15. See my "Ideologies of the Funny" for the range of humor theorists with connections to particular ideological predispositions.

16. Accordingly, at the height of fashionable postmodern transgression, Lillian Robinson once described the academy as the place where radical talk takes the place of radical action (in a lecture at Bates College in May 1992 entitled "Waving the Flag at Racism and Sexism: The Semiotics and Politics of the Political Correctness Flap").

17. Thus modern societies are "continually behind or ahead of themselves": "The social axiomatic of modern societies is caught between two poles, and is constantly oscillating from one pole to the other. Born of decoding and deterritorialization, on the ruins of the despotic machine, these societies are caught between the Urstaat that they would like to resuscitate as an overcoding and reterritorializing unity, and the unfettered flows that carry them toward an absolute threshold" (Deleuze and Guattari, *Anti-Oedipus* 260).

18. Bakhtin's sense of carnival has, of course, received criticism from both the right and the left. Given my framework, only the critiques from the left delimit the relevance of Bakhtin's carnival to positive social change.

19. David Patterson compares and contrasts Bakhtin's emphasis on the carnivalizing forces that oppose institutional or "official" discourse and Foucault's emphasis on the complexly dynamic sites of institutional power.

20. Umberto Eco, a trenchant disbeliever, argues that carnival does not feed

some revisionary view of how the world should be, but rather acts as a release generally consonant with accommodation.

21. Understandably, Lacanian psychoanalysis frequently contributes to transgressive ideology, since transgression always involves some repressed "law," and feminist revisions of psychoanalytic theory often adopt extreme laughter as the chosen figure for transgression. For many psychoanalytically informed studies of humor in life or comedy in art, women laughing remain either invisible (because women laughing together stand outside the family romance), necessarily hidden behind veils (Luce Irigaray names her "La Mystérique"), or over the edge like the hysteric or the madwoman, whose laughter speaks in riddles and who always risks the mastery of newly author(iz)ed masculine exegesis. For Irigaray, the male speculum functions as a distorted mirror for women's self-observation or self-representation. Thus, a woman writes in "a masquerade, the mimesis of mimicry, the textual *enactment* (not just articulation) of hysteria." Similarly, Julia Kristeva's negative portrait of the woman writer outside "legitimized" language posits a neurotic doomed to reminiscence: "if no paternal 'legitimation' comes along to dam up the inexhaustible non-symbolized impulse, she collapses into psychosis and suicide" (*About Chinese Women* 41). The only protest available to women remains a staged miming separate from, yet mysteriously related to, her real "self," a role well-figured in the hysteric's repetition of the language and role ascribed to her.

22. Slipping between Western constructions of the "Oriental" woman and those of the "African" woman, Cixous's explication locates in Cleopatra's inscrutable intelligence the "slippage" in literary and philosophical tradition that allows revisioning Cleopatra at all. In a more general way, Cixous's own slippage from one kind of "otherness" (the Oriental or African female Other) to another (the condition of women at large) has much to do with her metaphoric sweep, those largely undifferentiated, uncritical metaphors for imagining difference. Although Cixous seeks an imaginative "out" from originary Western myths, that is, from explicitly *written* constructions of "the dark continent," her "liberatory" adoption of the imperialist's language remains troubling.

23. Much feminist critique has sensed the danger in theoretical affirmations of women over the edge and has understood both Cixous and Irigaray as in some measure informed by a Lacan ambivalently situated as both "an archphallocrat" and "the prick who dares to speak its name" (Elizabeth Grosz 187).

24. Irving Howe's use of "postmodern" in his 1959 essay "Mass Society and Postmodern Fiction" began the practice of distinguishing fictions as "postmodern" in their specific difference from a modernism exemplified by Joyce, Mann, Kafka, Beckett, Hemingway, Fitzgerald, and others. The subsequent use of the term to signify a more generalized condition, as in David Harvey's *Condition of Postmodernity*, has provoked widespread, ongoing debates about its often conflicting frames of reference. See *Universal Abandon? The Politics of Postmodernism* (ed. Andrew Ross); *Feminism/Postmodernism* (ed. Linda J. Nicholson); *Zeitgeist in Babel: The Postmodernist Controversy* (Ingeborg Hoesterey); *Postmodernism and the Re-Reading of Modernity* (ed. Francis Barker et al.); and *Modernity: An Introduction to Modern Societies* (ed. Stuart Hall et al.).

25. C. Fred Alford hits on the tragic premise behind this transformative impulse in his definition of the tragic: "Tragedy means, above all else, that people are responsible without being free" (115).

26. I take "diaspora" here, as do Rosalyn Terborg-Penn and others, to refer to women of African descent traveling, voluntarily or involuntarily, away from local

kinship networks to places with customs and environments, if not languages, foreign to them. Thus Bessie Head moving from her native South Africa to Botswana as an exile represents a diasporic move within Africa.

27. Gilroy (*Black Atlantic* 218) names it "an intense and ambivalent negotiation of the novel form that is associated with their various critiques of modernity and enlightenment."

28. All such texts, for instance, have found themselves at the center of debates about the primacy of gender, race, class, or sexuality, especially in the context of felt distances between feminisms accused of desiring very limited transformations (e.g., acquiring for some white women the power of some white men) and either black feminism or what Clenora Hudson-Weems calls "Africana womanism," with a focus on fighting all oppressions that deny people equal human dignity, power, and rights. For the complex positioning of diverse black women writers among these debates, see the recent essays collected by Obioma Nnaemeka in *Sisterhood, Feminisms, and Power: From Africa to the Diaspora*.

29. For the parameters of debate about specifically aesthetic formulations, see Rita Felski (*Beyond Feminist Aesthetics* and *The Gender of Modernity*), Fredric Jameson (*The Political Unconscious, Postmodernism*, and *The Seeds of Time*), Stuart Hall, and Mas'ud Zavarzadeh and Thomas Morton.

30. See in particular Simon During's "Literature—Nationalism's Other? The Case for Revision." Paul Gilroy's *Black Atlantic: Modernity and Double Consciousness*, and Geneviève Fabre's and Robert O'Meally's edited *History and Memory in African-American Culture* provide overviews of a cultural history linking contemporary crises to those of black modernism.

31. The phrase comes from William Corlett's *Community Without Unity: A Politics of Derridian Extravagance*.

Chapter 1. The Tragedy of Slavery and the Footprints' Fit

1. See Morrison's *Playing in the Dark: Whiteness and the Literary Imagination*.

2. My "Positioning Subjects and Objects: Agency, Narration, Relationality" offers a critique of arguments implicitly suggesting or explicitly confirming the superior agency of subject positions other than those of victims, particularly that of the "philosopher-observer."

3. *Paradise* appeared after the bulk of my work here, but supplements the tragic mode found in *Beloved*.

4. For a sustained explanation of "signifyin[g]" within African American literary traditions, see Henry Louis Gates, Jr.'s *The Signifying Monkey: A Theory of African-American Literary Criticism*.

5. Michael Awkward usefully criticizes an example of this transcendent claim, often generalized beyond tragic empathy, in his discussion of Donald Wesling's "Writing as Power in the Slave Narratives of the Early Republic" in which Wesling regards the slave narrative's literariness as belonging to a "narrative of the realized self that enables the reader to live in the skin of another" (cited in Awkward 71).

6. Raymond Williams cites this passage from Hegel's *Aesthetics* (*Modern Tragedy* 33).

7. Hegel 1.212.

8. This passage from Nietzsche's *The Birth of Tragedy* is cited by Silk and Stearn 72.

9. I remember as a child thrilling to Robert Burns's "Wha sae base to be a slave?" with its responsive, "Let us do or die!" One cannot, probably, entirely exorcise this legacy of arrogant heroism.

10. Relevantly, Spillers ("Changing the Letter") cites Girard in her explication of Stowe's sacrifice of Little Eva in a kind of vicarious punishment for a dominant culture's "interdicted desire." As the embodiment of an elaborate "disguise and substitution" for an inarticulable desire that links the white woman and the black man, Little Eva becomes "the *expendable* item of culture whose dying will not release the dynamics of a violent reprisal" (45).

11. As variants of such theory, see also Eva Figes's *Tragedy and Social Evolution*, Ian Kott's *The Eating of the Gods*, and Eli Sagan's *The Lust to Annihilate: A Psychoanalytic Study of Violence in Ancient Greek Culture*.

12. In a chapter of a work forthcoming from Rutgers University Press ("The Dundes and the Nation," *Postnationalism Refigured*), my friend Charles Carnegie, an anthropologist, discusses with relevant insight his own experience as a black albino in Jamaica. For black Jamaicans, as well as for white historians, white albinos do not threaten in the way black albinos do, precisely because black albinoism threatens to expose the myth of racial difference. That is, by taking away the most culturally accepted marker of racial difference, it threatens *sameness*, which collective experience associates with what happens when cultural order breaks down. White albinos merely represent a different white, but blacks with white skin threaten something more foundational in how people differentiate each other.

13. Although this characterization of Girard's thought belongs to Guy Lefort, he articulates it as such in a dialogue-question to which Girard answers, "That is indeed my view" (*Things Hidden Since the Foundation of the World* 134).

14. Žižek uses this phrase in reference to his Lacanian analysis of the detective novel in "Two Ways to Avoid the Real of Desire" (*Looking Awry*).

15. Most notably, see Frances S. Foster's *Witnessing Slavery: The Development of Ante-Bellum Slave Narratives* and *Written by Herself: Literary Production by African American Women, 1746–1892*; Charles T. Davis's and Henry L. Gates's edited *The Slave's Narrative*; Houston Baker's *Blues, Ideology, and Afro-American Literature: A Vernacular Theory* and *Workings of the Spirit: The Poetics of Afro-American Women's Writing*; Robert B. Stepto's *From Behind the Veil: A Study of Afro-American Narrative*; Bernard W. Bell's *The Afro-American Novel and Its Tradition*; Valerie Smith's *Self-Discovery and Authority in Afro-American Narrative*; Deborah E. McDowell's and Arnold Rampersad's edited *Slavery and the Literary Imagination*; and Paul Gilroy's *The Black Atlantic: Modernity and Double Consciousness*.

16. So self-reflexive is African American scholarship about this relationship between the oral and the written that Ronald Judy's *(Dis)Forming the American Canon: African-Arabic Slave Narratives and the Vernacular* can convincingly argue that the use of African American slave narratives as a material foundation for cultural history runs the risk of reinscribing a Western modernity's association of literacy with self-reflective cognition. Relatedly, Hazel Carby ("Ideologies of Black Folk") warns that contemporary critical theory has displaced treatment of both historical and urban consciousness by foregrounding (and often romanticizing) the rural and folk traditions connected with slavery, so that a literary, constructed slavery paradoxically takes the place of slavery "as a mode of production and as a particular social order" (125). And Paul Gilroy locates the neo-slave narratives of the twentieth century in a more general "scepticism about the value of trying to revisit the sites of ineffable terror in the imagination" (218).

17. Harryette Mullen also pursues instances of this connection.

18. See Rosalyn Terborg-Penn's "Slavery and Women in Africa and the Diaspora" (here 217–18) for both differentiation and cross-cultural similarity among enslaved women in Africa, Europe, and the Western Hemisphere.

19. Cited by Foster, *Witnessing Slavery* xxxiii.

20. Valerie Smith's *Self-Discovery and Authority in Afro-American Narrative* contrasts the male narrator's story of "the triumph of the individual will" to the female narrator's "story of a triumphant self-in-relation." In "'Loopholes of Retreat': Architecture and Ideology in Harriet Jacobs's *Incidents in the Life of a Slave Girl*," Smith also uses Harriet Jacobs's metaphor of "loopholes of retreat" to refer to all the gaps, spaces, silences, and ironies through which Jacobs demonstrates the inadequacies of the forms available to her.

21. Black feminist theory and criticism continues to deconstruct and reconstruct these terms in ways that matter to both fictions and lived experience. In addition to Spillers, see Hazel Carby (*Reconstructing Womanhood*), Carole Boyce Davies, Patricia Hill Collins, bell hooks, and Gloria Joseph.

22. Ronald Judy 30.

23. Readings of *Beloved* achieve little consensus in either what they take as primary or in how, ultimately, to value its power. Most helpful to me here are those readings that place myth in the context of history, both a diasporic history of the slave crossing and the American history of slavery as an institution built on the rupturing of familial and communal ties. See in particular Mae Henderson ("Toni Morrison's *Beloved*"), but also Sally Keenan, Satya Mohanty, and Ashraf Rushdy. Although I appreciate Marianne Hirsch's suggestion that *Beloved* demands a psychoanalysis that begins with mothers rather than with children, a conception envisioning "a culturally variable form of interconnection" (428), readings confined to psychoanalytic explanation, while helpful with the coherence of the personal narratives, help less with the interrelation of Sethe's story and that of communal witnesses. In reading *Beloved* as a story about the "psychic trauma of infantile abandonment" or the "maternal semiotic," psychoanalytic treatments make entirely gendered distinctions between a maternal rememory and the traumatic rememory experienced by Stamp Paid and Paul D. Although convincing enough as particularly positioned explanation, such readings bypass issues of surrogacy and witnessing—its multivocality—in order to return to a story most relevant to "African Americans [who] can learn to mother themselves through reciprocal self-love" (Fitzgerald 685). Clearly, my own positioning foregrounds, instead, the intercultural implications of Morrison's fictional representation of an intracultural witnessing (how characters come to bear witness after only vicarious witnessing).

24. Valerie Smith (*Self-Discovery and Authority*) focuses on this aspect of Morrison's fictions even before the publication of *Beloved* in her chapter on "Toni Morrison's Narratives of Community."

25. In addition to Henderson, Satya Mohanty ("The Epistemic Status") and Homi Bhabha ("Freedom's Basis") consider the explicitly epistemic problems of cultural identity in *Beloved*. For important sustained readings of *Beloved*, see also Susan Bowers, Carole Boyce Davies (*Black Women*), Brian Finney, Anne Goldman, Marianne Hirsch, Karla Holloway (*Moorings and Metaphors*), and Ashraf Rushdy.

26. Jacqueline Trace (15) cites this phrase of Morrison's from Bessie W. Jones and Audrey Vinson (142).

27. Thus Stanley Crouch's snide explication of Sethe as a failed "Aunt Medea" shows as little attention to difference as to similarity.

28. Richard H. Palmer's *Tragedy and Tragic Theory: An Analytical Guide* offers a useful summation of theories criticizing the tragic response as a form of self-indulgence and of theories affirming the value of identification followed by distance.

29. Marianne Hirsch 428. The view that Sethe possesses the novel's "dominant voice" somewhat devalues the smoothness and the frequency with which narration passes among figural perspectives, thus focusing on the interrelation between so many binary oppositions (or, in Mae Henderson's terms, between the psychoanalytic story and the historical one). Hirsch, for example, in locating Sethe as *Beloved*'s dominant narrative presence, deemphasizes both the cathartic crises of others and the communal power behind the exorcism.

30. Henderson discusses these poetic chapters and how they inform the symbolism of Beloved as a character (75 and following).

31. The phrase comes from McDowell's "Negotiating the Tenses: Witnessing Slavery After Freedom—*Dessa Rose*." See also Bhabha ("Freedom's Basis") and Finney.

32. For an overview of diverse views of catharsis, see Michelle Gellrich or Richard H. Palmer.

33. Both slave narratives and critical explanations of them often stress the power of animal analogies and slave resistance to them.

34. Among readings that explicate away the paradox implicit in *Beloved* as "not a story to pass on," some find that characters within the story tell it (e.g., Barbara Hill Rigney) and others that the work itself "speaks the unspeakable; it is 'a story to pass on'" (e.g., Karla Holloway).

35. For a psychoanalytic analysis of the Bacchanalian (and psychoanalytic) resonance of this figure, see Ian Kott's *The Eating of the Gods*.

36. Madelyn Jablon and Gina Wisker explicate it in this way in making connections between these two works.

37. Davies, for example, focuses on the lack in Sethe, whereas Henderson's reading answers questions about the work's "final legacy to us as readers" by stressing its open-endedness, seeing what Rushdy describes as Morrison's "ambivalence" (569) as instead "draw[ing] out the paradoxes and ambiguities of 'this perfect dilemma'" (82).

38. See Anne E. Goldman's tracing of this figure.

39. Susan Wendell provides a replete outline of the victim's "perspective" from the implicitly superior position of the analyst in her "Oppression and Victimization: Choice and Responsibility." My "Positioning Subjects and Objects: Agency, Narration, Relationality" offers a critique of such analytical changes in perspective, and suggests that even "standpoint epistemology," preferable to the fixed kind, may yet disguise the superiority of she who gets to choose.

40. Carole Boyce Davies's (*Black Women*) reading of *Beloved* usefully invokes the Yoruba *abiku* and the Igbo *ogbanje*, children "who die and are reborn repeatedly to plague their mothers and are marked so that they can be identified when they return" (139), as analogues to the bodily marks of slavery borne by black women (witness the mark of the saw on Beloved's neck). With a focus on specifically maternal agency, she agrees with Paul D.'s negative judgment about Sethe's "too thick" love, contrasting the failures of both Sethe and Baby Suggs to the more "empowering" gestures in Sherley Anne Williams's *Dessa Rose*, where Dessa moves "from being the-mother-as-she-is-written to being the-mother-as-she-writes" (147). Thus she does not place any emphasis on the communal nature of the exorcism, its dependence on a collective solidarity nevertheless

born of personal, interior crisis. I am grateful to Charles Nero for discussions about how the Morrison works he loves and finds prescient on the grounds of race and gender may also represent consistently heterosexist vantage points.

41. The formulation of the power relations implicit in tragedy as "win, lose, or draw" belongs to John Snyder's *Prospects of Power: Tragedy, Satire, the Essay, and the Theory of Genre.*

42. Žižek phrases it thus: "Essentially it is this unknown element in the alterity of the other which characterizes the speech relation on the level on which it is spoken to the other" (*For They Know Not What They Do* 199).

43. Joy James's essay as a whole suggests why *Beloved*'s vision of tragedy could not be more pressing in an era when the lives of many are in constant and recurring crisis and where any desire to think of slavery as a thing of the past must confront what Leonard Harris has described as "an era that has created a slave quarter without creating structural malfunction" (51). Indeed, many contemporary writers have followed W.E.B. DuBois's postulation of a "neo-slavery" after the emancipation, well explicated in Arnold Rampersad's "Slavery and the Literary Imagination: DuBois's *The Souls of Black Folk*," by understanding contemporary social crisis as both legacy and extension of the slavery system.

44. The quoted phrase refers to one of the epigraphs for Chapter 4, Žižek's observation that "*[Social] fantasy is a means for an ideology to take its own failure into account in advance*" (*The Sublime Object* 126).

45. Cornel West explains a contemporary culture's penchant for this danger-plus-distance as an "addiction to stimulation [that] becomes the only means by which a vitality is preserved by a self in a society that promotes spectatorial passivity and evasive banality. The culture of consumption generates a passivity by means of spectatorial enactment" ("Philosophy and the Urban Underclass" 195–96).

Chapter 2. Humor, Subjectivity, Unctuousness

1. Both Calvin Hernton and Jacqueline Bobo provide useful overviews of the critical controversies surrounding *The Color Purple*. Specific to my purposes, Susan Willis (*Specifying*) will serve as an example of a critic treating *The Color Purple* as resistance literature and Molly Hite, Priscilla Walton, and Margaret Walsh as examples of critics who read in the direction of comic romance. Trudier Harris is among those who register frustration with Celie's "passivity," a charge to which Michael Awkward responds by placing Celie's development in an intertextual context provided not only by African American women writers but also by the narratives connecting literacy and freedom (Frederick Douglass's *Narrative* and Richard Wright's *Black Boy*, for example).

2. Perhaps those explicating colonial and postcolonial/post-independent literary resistance have argued this most strongly. Jenny Sharpe's "Figures of Colonial Resistance" finds an emphasis on the partial, complicit nature of literary resistance common to such theorists as Gayatri Spivak, Homi Bhabha, Abdul JanMohamad, and Benita Parry; and Stephen Slemon uses the "double, necessarily mediated" location of literary resistance to argue for the inclusion of "second world" texts by white Australian, New Zealander, Southern African, and Canadian writers in "postcolonial literary studies."

3. Jameson (*The Ideology of Theory* 2) refers to something like the possibility of an alternative realism in theory, though he has not generally explicated it in

texts, when he postulates a collective subject and the "obligation to reinvent" a conception of realism that holds onto the aporia "which contains within its structure the crux of a history beyond which we have not yet passed" (147).

4. This sense of intersubjectivity differs from that of Habermas because it dialectically negotiates among complexly plural and overlapping subject positions, not among subject individuals. Although concerned here with the meaning of a humorous rapport among characters-in-process, I see both laughter and play as signs of a rapport capable of becoming intersubjective.

5. I do not mean to imply that the nature of humorous rapport in *The Color Purple* is unprecedented, but rather that dominant theories of how to read the comic have precluded paying attention to the kind of humorous rapport so important here, and have thereby tamed at least this kind of resistance out of reading. Katie Geneva Cannon well explicates "unctuousness" in Hurston and in black "womanist" traditions as a "steadfastness akin to fortitude" that achieves a "balance of complexities" through the sustained struggle that "creatively strain[s] against external constraints" (*Katie's Canon* 92).

6. Although Henry Louis Gates's reading (*The Signifying Monkey*) requires that he foreground Celie's "control" of others' language so that we have only Celie's and "Celie-cum-characters'" speech, his explication relies on conceptualizing different characters as such, perhaps most significantly in discovering Shug as a (re)writing of Hurston herself. The distinction between speakerly and writerly texts originates with Roland Barthes, who uses it in *S/Z* to oppose an older realism (readerly texts) to a modern ideal (writerly text) corresponding to the plural, ambiguous properties of language; when Gates refers to Zora Neale Hurston's *Their Eyes Were Watching God* as a speakerly text "(re)written" by Walker in *The Color Purple*, he strangely allies Hurston's passionate grounding in oral and folk traditions with the singular, imperialist language and authority Barthes identifies as readerly characteristics. Nevertheless, Gates's attention to the "simultaneous, inseparable, bonded" nature of voices suggests a resistant laughter here.

7. While brilliantly disclosing the transformative use Walker makes of both Zora Neale Hurston and Rebecca Cox Jackson, Gates (*The Signifying Monkey*) foregrounds a resisting agency belonging to Celie's use of free indirect discourse (246–47). Humor, since it erases boundaries between individual "selves," appropriately figures some mediation between those who argue that any attention to characters-as-speakers suggests some unitary, regressively-situated subject, and those who, like Homi Bhabha ("Interrogating Identity"), argue that some fluid, "evolving cultural agent" must connect agency with victims' capacity for resistance.

8. Deborah E. McDowell ("Boundaries") finds in Morrison's *Sula* a model for thinking about "self-worlds" that "can and do impinge on one another" in "multiple, fluid, relational" ways (70). She calls for a dialogical relation between a fictional characterization-as-process and analogous reading strategies provoked by Morrison and African American women writers more generally. Responding to her suggestion, I find analogical links in addition to "identification" between characters with fluid identities and implied reading processes, differentiated in relation to readers for whom selfhood has more fixed assumptions than for either Morrison or McDowell.

9. See Angela Davis on the "blues legacies" that link a specifically sorrowful laughter with active protest and resistance.

10. Significantly, Wahneema Lubiano uses Sofia's invocation of "how the col-

ored live"—an antidote to Eleanor Jane's presumption—as evidence that "the styles of living as well as the material conditions under which 'colored' live" become through Sofia "a means to historicize love and ownership" (76).

11. Importantly, this description does not suggest any totalizing gesture toward understanding the rich number of humorous kinds used by both male and female African American writers. Carlene Young, Valerie Smith, Leslie Hill, Beverly Guy-Sheftall, and other black feminist scholars have agreed in informal discussion that qualitative difference does exist between African American men's and women's forms of humor, both in fictions and in life, but that the subject still awaits its researchers.

12. Stanley Cavell (*In Quest of the Ordinary*), in his sustained refusal to ally his own skepticism with the more absolute absences of deconstruction, explicates this distinction in "The Uncanniness of the Ordinary" (174).

13. Despite my own conflictual invocations of Walker as author, whether or not Walker intended Nettie's voice as painfully devoid of humor and her situation as inimical to humorous rapport matters only if one reduces issues of resistance to issues of intentionality.

14. Trudier Harris's explication of religion and community in several of the writers that matter to me here usefully focuses on spiritual relationship that "restructur[es] the process of salvation" (161).

15. Mae Henderson ("Speaking in Tongues") aptly formulates how Celie and Mary Agnes as well as Sofia and Shug act initially as doubles, complemented by successive triadic relationships. My point here is that any "new paradigm for relationships" relies more on resisting relations of dominance than on moving from dyads to triads (but one exemplary model of symbolic dismantling and reconstructing).

16. Although hooks ("Writing the Subject" 468) has a less positive sense of Walker's success in differentiating *The Color Purple* from its sentimental frames of reference, her phrase well expresses the difficulty of an ending within the conventions of happy endings but also *not* itself simply the generic equivalent of such an ending.

17. Cheryl Wall (*Changing Our Own Words*) usefully relates "the persistent tension between fragmentation and unity" in the book's closure to related tensions between Anglo-American and French feminisms.

18. In this emphasis, I agree with Susan Willis (*Specifying*) that "Walker's affirmation of blackness uses racially specific traits not to define a form of Black racism but to delineate the look of a class. Black is the color of the underclass" (126). Willis's explication of *Meridian* rightly distinguishes Walker's sense of revolutionary praxis from anything resembling "the politics of counterculture" (128).

19. Kimberly Benston's ("Facing Tradition") description of Celie's and Nettie's meeting as a "melting" that poses "a radical challenge to our own liminal stance as interpreters, as negotiating judges between distanced parties" (106) has particular relevance to what I have called "intersubjectivity." In his context of facing traditions (here, effacing) in African American literature, the scene captures a revision "divested of the coercive powers of a specifically positioned look" (106). Taking laughter, not the mutually reflective gaze, as trope, my reading also differs in its sense that readers' subject positions affect responses to a laughter inseparable from intersubjectivity.

20. While focusing on the autobiographical strategies that may subvert narrative expectation, Valerie Smith (*Self-Discovery and Authority*) significantly theo-

rizes the persistence of hybrid forms in African American literature as derived from "their alienation from the ideological content of received literary conventions" (153).

21. Margaret Walsh 100.

22. This seems closely related to Karla Holloway's ("Revision and [Re]membrance") theorizing of African-American women writers' "polysignant" or "multiplied" texts that demand something she calls "shift," further explicated in *Moorings and Metaphors.* As "a necessary mediation between the reader and the text," shift "encourages a dialogue among critical postures within the interpretive community" (625).

23. Deborah McDowell (*"The Changing Same"*) finds affirmation in an implied intimacy between Walker and the black women readers invoked by "sisterhood," whereas bell hooks ("Writing the Subject") finds a voyeuristic, even pornographic presumption of a white, privileged female audience.

24. This sense of intersubjectivity differs from that of Habermas because it dialectically negotiates among complexly plural and overlapping subject-positions, not among subject-individuals. Although concerned here with the meaning of a humorous rapport among characters-in-process, I see both laughter and play as signs of a rapport capable of becoming intersubjective. For further discussion of "other-aligning" humor, see both Sheldon Ungar and my "Ideologies of the Funny."

25. Jane Flax (*Thinking Fragments*), among others, has commented on the implicit elitism of those in love with activities of solitary mind as the route to social change, noting the difficulty of imagining childraising, say, as a figure for postmoderns. In naming the incommensurable, noncoherent positions their thinking entails, Gayatri Chakravorty Spivak (*In Other Worlds* and *The Post-Colonial Critic*) and Anthony Appiah ("Tolerable Falsehoods"), for example, succeed better in acknowledging the overlapping, dialectical nature of academic theory and social praxis.

26. Although generally read as a work about what Karla Holloway calls "spiritual dislocation" (139), several have found something disturbing in its portrayals of characters either close to stereotype or somehow inauthentic. Barbara Smith, for example, appreciates much about the book but from a black lesbian perspective finds the last story, "The Two," flawed by "how utterly hopeless Naylor's view of Lesbian existence is" (230).

27. Farah Jasmine Griffin offers an extended reading that foregrounds the novel as a migration narrative. See also Barbara Christian's "Gloria Naylor's Geography" in *Black Feminist Criticism.*

28. Stanley Cavell (*In Quest of the Ordinary*), in his sustained refusal to ally his own skepticism with the more absolute absences of deconstruction, puts this distinction as follows:

> So let me say here that differences between what I do and what deconstruction does seem to me registered in my speaking of presentness (which is about me and my world) instead of (meaning what?) presence (which is about Being, not something I will ever be in a position, so far as I can judge, to judge); and in my criticism of "philosophy" (by which I take myself to mean a way human beings have of being led to think about themselves, instead of something I can spell "Western metaphysics") which is not, anyway not at first, that it originates in a domineering construction of (false) absence for which it falsely offers compensations. (174)

29. Homi Bhabha ("Interrogating Identity") uses this phrase in an eloquent, appreciative "interrogation" of Fanon, while, at the same time, himself interrogating how the Black presence defeats narratives of Western personhood (205).

30. I refer to a note in which Suleiman counters the possibility of considering Toni Morrison or Ntozake Shange "black women feminist postmodernists" with: "But the question of priorities (race or gender?) remains" (248). Calvin C. Hernton's focus on critical, largely male responses to *The Color Purple* understandably responds with a female-centered reading in the direction of romance where, "The promise in the beginning is fulfilled in the end. The ending is the beginning. The dismembered tree, the broken family, is back together again" (26). This pastoral vision overlooks the radical change in subjectivity and the fact that the "broken" family at the beginning is not the same as the "us" at the end. Even the paradigm of the "female symbol" of the porch with its "diamond of women in sisterhood" (Celie, Mary Agnes, and Shug) ignores how Albert is foregrounded in the geography of the porch.

31. This point, that reading from different subject positions implies different interpretive responses, does not suggest some imprecise or amorphous relativity (parallel, again, to Karla Holloway's [*Moorings and Metaphors*] "plurisignant" or shifting text). That texts may be chastening to some and discouraging to others demands rigorous examination of how and why readings separate, conflict, or overlap. Barbara Smith's reasoning and tonality captures this sense of relation-in-difference when she speculates on the different effects of Naylor's "The Two" for heterosexual and lesbian women readers in the context of an argument that fictional representation of black lesbians "has crucial implications for all women's political liberation" (243).

32. The engagement of any text outside the cultural traditions that engender it perhaps necessarily risks appropriation; yet, as I try to suggest here, some forms of cross-cultural engagement may act as a critique of dominant presumptions and some merely reinscribe those presumptions.

Chapter 3. Tragedy and Comedy Reborn(e)

1. Although much of this chapter appeared in *Genre* in 1993 and grew from earlier work, I both cite and recursively use some of the important expressions of related ideas that have since appeared on the forms of resistance in African women's writing, most notably the new essay by Andrea Benton Rushing included in the second edition of *Women in Africa and the African Diaspora* (1996) and those collected by Obioma Nnaemeka in *The Politics of (M)Othering: Womanhood, Identity, and Resistance in African Literature* (1997) and in *Sisterhood, Feminisms and Power: From Africa to the Diaspora* (1998). David Lenson usefully posits the paradox that makes tragedy theoretically compatible with any group or ideology, significantly ending his case for Hegel's and Nietzsche's primacy in theory (as opposed to Aristotle's) with the words: "If tragedy is to be taken as a conflict of orders, it is very hard to restrict what these orders can be. If the tragic hero is to be understood as extreme, there is no way to prescribe what extremity will be his [hers]. In many ways, that theory of tragedy is best which specifies least" (171).

2. Froma Zeitlin, for example, considers the ways notions of gender in Greek tragedy ultimately mandate "closures that generally reassert male, often paternal, structures of authority" even though the drama may "open up the masculine view of the universe" (81). More extensively, Michelle Gellrich traces a history of interacting exclusions which she juxtaposes to her own readings of ca-

nonical tragedies. Focusing on how theory's penchant for a totalizing order has interacted with interpretation's reluctance to see the "destabilizing, unsystematic features of tragic conflict" (267), she explicates resistances she finds within tragic dramas themselves to theoretical traditions that "tam[e] conflict, when it finally surfaces in critical discussion, and reduc[es] it to terms of philosophical order" (266).

3. James Snead ("European Pedigrees") has demonstrated how the concept of universality itself may confine and dominate, as when critics use it to accumulate as many texts as possible under one rubric in a kind of "mammoth power play" (244).

4. This formulation comes from Morrison's Nobel Prize Lecture (12).

5. The difficulty of genre inheres, for example, in using conventions drawn from "realism" for interpreting Head's work. Even the modified term "mythic realism" suggests a combinatory or supplemental genre for a mode characterizd by no felt separations between the mythic and the real.

6. Other works by African women writers that suggest alternative forms of the tragic, in addition to others by Bessie Head, are TsiTsi Dangarembga's *Nervous Conditions* and Ama Ata Aidoo's *Anowa*.

7. These oppositional terms are worked out by Paul Gordon, who elaborates the typological association of Antigone with Dionysus, or the conflict of male with female, culture with nature, and Pentheus with Dionysus (213).

8. Michelle Gellrich uses this phrase in explicating how Euripides's *Bacchae* insists that both social hierarchy and violence inhere in the polis, thus undermining the Aristotelian notion of *spoudaiotes* (goodness). Important for my analogy to Euripidean precedent, she also locates in Plato's anxiety about tragedy a more insightful understanding of "the ways in which tragedy questions the unity of values, the efficacy of reason in settling dilemmas, and the normative role of the *spoudaios* in deliberation and action" (158).

9. The foremost theorist of this sense of the tragic remains Alisdair MacIntyre, who takes diversity more seriously than many, yet starts from the assumption of the breakdown of moral discourse itself, a position derived from his overview of Western moral discourses. Such a view of "the new dark ages" in moral life has only tangential relation to tragic paradox as Lenson, for example, describes it, reasonably enough since MacIntyre's answer to "Nietzsche or Aristotle?" is, predominantly, Aristotle, and Lenson's answer to which tragedy, Nietzsche's or Aristotle's, is, predominantly, Nietzsche's in balance with Hegel's. Jeffrey Stout undertakes a broad critique of MacIntyre, and an approving synthesis of other critical responses.

10. The phrase belongs to John Barbour 173.

11. See also Susan Andrade's "Rewriting History, Motherhood, and Rebellion."

12. These self-interrogations should not be confused with the constructions of identity called into question by Susan Gardner. Teresa Dovey rightly criticizes the presumptions behind Gardner's article, whose "true" story purports to reveal how Head constructed an elaborate fiction upon the only known "facts" of her birth.

13. Though not my focus here, Head's paradoxical will to both particularity and abstraction provides interesting dialogical response to Abdul JanMohamed's general argument that writers in postcolonial African contexts must ironically use the English that destroys oral cultures to record the advent of historical con-

sciousness (as distinct from an earlier mythic consciousness). In complex ways, Head's work could be said to explore the collusion or complicity of historic and mythic consciousness in ways that affirm orality even within an alien, written "English as a foreign anguish" (Marlene Nourbese Philip xi). Cynthia Ward explores the rejection of fixed meanings in African oral traditions. In any case, the problem of whether myth necessarily becomes history as oral becomes literate stands in this text in metonymic relation to "a question of power," an abstracted question that clearly includes the panoply of economic, social, and political questions addressed in JanMohamed's readings, but a question that nevertheless links a whole series of questions in what Barthes (*S/Z*) calls "metonymic skid."

14. Readings of Head's works frequently hit on evidence from narrative assertion (dramatic rather than authoritative, in my view) for a Manichaean contest between good and evil as the primary frame for interpretation (see, e.g., Goddard, Gover, and Ola), perhaps due to Abdul JanMohamed's strong readings of both colonial and African writers' works as related-but-different responses to the "Manichaean allegories" of the colonialist world. Huma Ibrahim's important book on Head appeared after this chapter was written, but it usefully situates the Medusa as a feminized figure of exile, appropriate here as she prevents Elizabeth from any sense of belonging in the exile of Botswana. Ibrahim's readings of Head focus on "exilic consciousness" and she elaborates well how the "act of re-envisioning becomes a simultaneous act of redefining and reclaiming one's identity within spaces determined by the imperialist intervention and then equally successfully by other patriarchal discourses which replaced them" (201).

15. As images of compromised love, the homophobic nightmares Elizabeth suffers necessarily derive from specifically African views of sexuality. John S. Mbiti observes that "African peoples are very sensitive to any departure from the accepted norm concerning all aspects of sex. This is a fundamentally religious attitude, since any offence upsets the smooth relationships of the community which includes those who have already departed" (148).

16. For extended discussion of the particular forms of women's resistance in Africa, see the Introduction and the essay by Amina Mama in *Feminist Genealogies, Colonial Legacies, Democratic Futures*, ed. M. Jacqui Alexander and Chandra Talpade Mohanty; essays by Rosalyn Terborg-Penn and Andrea Benton Rushing in *Women in Africa and the African Diaspora: A Reader*, ed. by Rosalyn Terborg-Penn and Andrea Benton Rushing); Introduction and essays by Uzo Esonwanne, Huma Ibrahim, and Obioma Nnaemeka in *The Politics of (M)othering: Womanhood, Identity, and Resistance in African Literature* ed. Obioma Nnaemeka; the essay by Filomena Chioma Steady in *Theorizing Black Feminisms*, ed. Stanlie M. James and Abena P. A. Abusia, and essays by Clenora Hudson-Weems and Angela Miles in *Sisterhood, Feminisms and Power: From Africa to the Diaspora*, ed. Obioma Nnaemeka.

17. Charles Sugnet provides a useful overview of how Tsitsi Dangarembga's *Nervous Conditions*, and by extension other African women's novels written in times of national struggle and transition, both suggest "hazy parallels" between national and women's struggles (with the "inspirational atmosphere" of one relevant to the other) and at the same time do not "subordinat[e] women's politics to a masculine, national master narrative" (46).

18. This connection between Africa as "mother," or mother-tongue, and "(m)othering" has been well explicated by others. See, for example, both Obioma Nnaemeka's Introduction and Cynthia Ward's "Bound to Matter: The Father's Pen and Mother Tongues" in *The Politics of (M)othering*.

19. This paradoxical position does not disallow critical emphasis on either how Elizabeth "conquers the psychopathology of the colonial encounter" or how powerful is her vision of wholeness, aspects explicated variously in Roger A. Berger, Kolawole Ogungbesan, and Adetokunbo Pearse. The affirmation of Elizabeth's final vision becomes no less affirmative when seen in the context of necessarily ongoing struggle that implies cosmic as well as worldly critique.

20. See Goddard, "Imagery in Bessie Head's Work." Daniel Gover suggests that Head retains a gendered ambivalence in this last scene and Head herself, in her interviews, never addressed Western feminisms' concern for the implications of language making maleness the sign of the universal. Both "humanity" and the "brotherhood of man" seem without conscious verbal irony, but a structural irony remains since Sello and Dan have both invoked the imagery of domination in their torturing visions. Her sense of a resistant irresolution to match a "slippery resolution" grows out of prior scenes where Sello-Dan's language and "performances" set up extreme dissonances with Elizabeth's daily sense of the ordinary virtue in work, belonging, nurturing, and loving.

21. See note 16 above.

22. Cherry Clayton and Adetokunbo Pearse give the last paragraph a straightforwardly autobiographical reading, associating the soul-journeys with Head's earlier experience of apartheid in South Africa and the final affirmation with her "hopeful" arrival in Botswana. Yet both Head's fictional worlds and her own sense of personal history conjoin concerns and contexts:

> All my work had Botswana settings but the range and reach of my preoccupations became very wide. People, black people, white people, loomed large on my horizon. I began to answer some of the questions aroused by my South African experience. (Head, *A Woman Alone* 15)

Sara Chetin sees Head as a "mediator among timeless paradoxes" who "never lets herself or her audience get too involved to the point of forgetting they are outsiders, excluded from this world while at the same time part of its reconstruction" (116).

23. Although directly related to Africana explanations of the conflicted role of women in postcolonial, nationalist ideologies (Amina Mama), this focus on interconnected systems of power also brings to mind the stages of Western feminisms, where, for example, initial hypotheses about women's language and genres subsequently gave way to theorizing about language and genres characteristic of all those on the underside of power relations.

24. Zeitlin considers in some depth the implications for Greek tragedy of the fact that the boundaries crossed by the tragic so often invoke the feminine by way of madness, the irrational, or the emotional: "The boundaries of women's bodies are perceived as more fluid, more permeable, more open to affect and entry from the outside, less easily controlled by intellectual and rational means. This perceived physical and cultural instability renders them weaker than men; it is also the more a source of disturbing power over them" (65). Here I mean the blurring of the distinction between the gendered and the cross-cultural Other to reflect only how often theorizing about women's roles has given way to theorizing about powerlessness and how it works. Head's own work blurs the pain she feels as liminal to cultural presumptions about gender, sexuality, nation, and race, all caught together in her title.

25. Euripides's interest in women characters had as corollary a greater emphasis on private, internal states of being that explode the assumptions of public history, and his women characters, as Claire Nancy has explicated them, both expose the injustice of the social order and create a felt dissonance between questions of good and evil and those of social justice. Zeitlin describes Euripides's much-mocked sympathy toward women as necessarily entailing greater emphasis on "interior states of mind as well as on the private emotional life of the individual" (81).

26. One would hate to reinscribe the ancient mockery of a feminized Euripides through such an analogy between the concerns of a contemporary feminist reading of Euripides and those of Bessie Head. The point is to see how the cross-period analogies so commonly used in discussing Euro-American tragedy as value also ascribe value here.

27. Barbara Harlow's *Resistance Literature* provides a specifically literary treatment of revisionary models of resistance emerging across the social sciences. Bhabha's "Interrogating Identity: The Postcolonial Prerogative" places "a form of power that is exercised at the very limits of identity and authority" in the context of contemporary theoretical discourse. Certainly, those explicating colonial and postcolonial/post-independent literary resistance have argued the partial, complicit nature of resistance most strongly. Jenny Sharpe's "Figures of Colonial Resistance" finds such an emphasis common to such theorists as Gayatri Spivak, Homi Bhabha, Abdul JanMohamed, and Benita Parry.

28. Susan Andrade traces the dialogism (from Bakhtin) of competing discourses in Flora Nwapa's *Efuru* and Buchi Emecheta's *The Joys of Motherhood* as a form of written resistance to particular historical conditions, despite ideological "blindspots" about power relations evident in both works. So here, although Elizabeth cannot conceptualize how to change the world, she commits herself to a resisting irresolution among the competing terms of economic independence, sexual and maternal love, and spiritual imagination.

29. Although overused, the Derridean "always already" formulation works well here to describe a paradoxical choice that has none of its usual suggestion of control or instrumentality; Elizabeth lives in a world where she has always already chosen what she specifically desires *not* to choose, yet evinces agency in both her resistant thought-processes and her joy in daily work and relationship (however vulnerable).

30. Françoise Lionnet elaborates a thematic focus on just such conflicted positioning in her "Geographies of Pain: Captive Bodies and Violent Acts in the Fictions of Gayl Jones, Bessie Head, and Myriam Warner-Vieyra."

31. For an extended analysis of issues of "presence" in relation to African literatures, see James Comas's "The Presence of Theory/Theorizing the Present."

32. Katie Cannon applies this phrase to Hurston in *Black Womanist Ethics.*

33. Perhaps postmodernism has most egregiously erred in its attempt to counter Western metaphysics and hegemony on the level of discourse, not in relation to actual suffering; Elizabeth's desire to leave the story unresolved while engaging in actual relationships has suggestive resonance for attempts to negotiate multiply complex relations of subordination. Paul Gilroy (*The Black Atlantic*) observes that "the concept [of postmodernism] may have some value as a purely heuristic device, but it seems often simply to serve to validate another equally Eurocentric master narrative from which the history and experiences of blacks remain emphatically absent" (278). Jeffrey Stout describes an analogous reli-

gious chauvinism: "'Fallacy' and 'superstition' are modern moral philosophy's derogatory names for the religious 'other' against which it defines itself as rational and secular" (5).

34. The risk of cultural appropriation always exists, but may primarily inhere in any implicit suggestion that discussing Head's work in the context of tragedy has any necessary primacy, and I do not believe it does. Inclusionary risk at least invites revisionary conceptions, and such risks of engagement seem vastly preferable to the consoling presumptions of exclusion. This said, any pat opposition between Western and "indigenous" traditions seems not only exclusionary but ahistorical. As Gayatri Spivak has put it, addressing the issue of "using what one has" as opposed to choosing between "first world" theory, "indigenous" theory or "synthesized" theory:

> I cannot understand what indigenous theory there might be that can ignore the reality of nineteenth-century history. As for syntheses: syntheses have more problems than answers to offer. To construct indigenous theories one must ignore the last few centuries of historical involvement. I would rather use what history has written for me. (Spivak, *The Post-Colonial Critic* 69)

35. Martin Bernal's *Black Athena: The Afroasiatic Roots of Classical Civilization* relies heavily on the work of scholars of the black diaspora.

Chapter 4. Who Owns the Terror in *Absalom, Absalom!*?

1. I do not mean to suggest that a substantial body of criticism does not address social issues in Faulkner, only that my own reading addresses the particular problems of readings that either evade the social implications of affirming an abstracted narrativity or render it as primarily relevant to the historical overview of Southern history. For treatments of race and gender in Faulkner, see particularly essays in *Faulkner and Ideology*, ed. Donald M. Kartiganer and Ann J. Abadie; essays in *Faulkner and Race*, ed. Doreen Fowler and Ann J. Abadie; James Snead's *Figures of Division: William Faulkner's Major Novels*; Eric J. Sundquist's *Faulkner: The House Divided*; Sally Page's *Faulkner's Women: Characterization and Meaning*; Deborah Clarke's *Robbing the Mother: Women in Faulkner*; and commentary in James Baldwin's *No Name in the Street* and Toni Morrison's *Playing in the Dark*.

2. The phrase belongs to Brian McHale (10). I think it possible to speak of gendered "character" and "voice" without denying Judith Butler's insight that gender coherence depends on "the interests and the power relations that establish that identity in its reified mode to begin with" (339). The reification of gender relations that allows us to talk of men's and women's roles can still be understood as a "regulatory fiction," not some "interior origin" for character. Susan Winnet considers how masculinist understandings of pleasure affect narratology, though she focuses less on reading from a male point of view than on critical expectations of women writers.

3. The phrase is Zender's (*The Crossing of the Ways* 20).

4. In this regard, Phillip M. Weinstein's (*What Else But Love?*) reading seems a kind of new, new criticism, in which the author's willingness to locate himself as a reader—identifying with the writer more than with characters in the text—takes into account a broad social and historical context, but primarily viewed from the perspective of similarity rather than of difference.

5. These readings tend to foreground romantic and epic genres in ways that lend themselves to critical representations of both ludic postmodernity and a kind of historical-cultural determinism.

6. Weinstein, *What Else But Love?* 148. Throughout a work devoted to often rich similarities-in-difference between Faulkner and Morrison, Weinstein's explication starts and ends with a Southern white man's sharing the nanny-tradition with Faulkner and finds some universalized relationality (Faulkner to his world, Morrison to hers) in value that "resides in the text that creatively disturbs such axes [as race or gender], making us realize afresh. . .that we carry our culture's raced and gendered arrangements (the brutal as well as the most beneficent) inside ourselves" (183). Although largely written before Weinstein's work appeared, my reading resists both *Absalom, Absalom!* as "a tragic repudiation of the nonnormative" and the primacy of "the monumentality of the culture that has been lost," arguing that Faulkner read under the influence of Morrison—as opposed to Morrison read under the influence of Faulkner—yields a much more resistant sense of modern tragedy's relation to its readers. Barbara Foley (*Radical Representations*) traces the origins of readings of *Absalom, Absalom!* as effete aesthetics, beginning with Philip Rahv's characterization of it as "[e]ndless, ideologically barren experimentation and superficial cleverness, esthetic and intellectual dandyism without a breath of life" (cited in *Radical Representations* 59). She attributes to Mike Gold and other radicals of the period a more sophisticated view of form-content relations and refers elsewhere to "Faulkner's undifferentiated blending of the voices of Quentin and Shrevc," implying "an equivalence in the subjects of perception" (*Telling the Truth* 213–14).

7. Peter Brooks uses "the reader freed to speak the text" along with the "empty center" and other decentering phrases in his projection of Miss Rosa's "incredulous narration" onto *Absalom, Absalom!*'s narration at large; and Stephen M. Ross speaks of "engraving the power of *was* in the silence of voices" in a work that "displays—and finally celebrates—history-making and story-telling as fundamental human acts" (135).

8. The fact that Faulkner frequently adjusted the text from quasi-omniscience to the voices of narrators by merely changing around quotation marks does not disallow the presence of a perspective outside all the work's characters.

9. The only essay to trace the complexity of the Haiti connection in *Absalom, Absalom!* appeared after this chapter was written, but it affirms with biographical and dating detail the nature of Faulkner's linkage of black characters with the fear of Haitian revolt. See Barbara Ladd's " 'The Direction of the Howling': Nationalism and the Color Line in *Absalom, Absalom!*"

10. Here and in the analysis that follows, I do not mean "feminization" to suggest the feeling as sentiment so easily ascribed to heterosexual men—described by Eve Kosofsky Sedgwick as the "vast national wash of masculine self-pity"—but rather the affective range more appropriate to forms of resistance "feminized" in symptoms ranging from monosyllabic acquiescence to passional outburst.

11. Warwick Wadlington explicates the performative mode in *Absalom, Absalom!* in great detail, but compromises his insights about an oracular, internal audition by privileging observations on language and narrativity themselves compromised by narrative context. Like Brooks, Wadlington cites Mr. Compson's and Miss Rosa's aphoristic lessons as though they carry textual authority. More tellingly, he insists on Sutpen as a "hero of literary tragedy," a tragedy based on classical models where catharsis "of already existing perceived pollution" (177) includes Clytie's burning of Sutpen's Hundred. Thus Clytie becomes "one of

Sutpen's proxies in the novel" (177), not a character whose name bears ironic relation to Sutpen's design. Most significantly, he makes Quentin's "audience-oriented impulse" into a positive value while minimizing the progressive narrative entrapment of Quentin. Correspondingly, Wadlington sees the work's narrative accommodations as a good thing, where the "ghost" voices assimilated into narrative voice represent "our human accommodation, our human being" (194).

12. The phrase belongs to John Duvall 115.

13. James Snead (*Figures of Division*) comes close to my emphasis here in noting how narrators "learn and tactfully transmit the secret sleight of hand upon which racial classifications are based"; but, although he makes useful distinctions between written and oral transmission, Snead nevertheless credits Shreve with something like moral and imaginative prescience and locates the primary moral failure in *Absalom, Absalom!* in Quentin's failure as a narrator.

14. Brooks and Matthews, among others, provide excellent analysis of the narrative effect of the palindrome, but take that effect as *Absalom, Absalom!*'s primary concern rather than seeing it in the dramatic context of Chapter 9 as a whole.

15. Thus Weinstein takes his title for *What Else But Love?* from the juxtaposition of Guitar's words about love, later rethought by Milkman, in *Song of Solomon* and those in Chapter 8's description of love as posited by Shreve-Quentin's "transcendent" union. In considering Faulkner's legacy *to* Morrison, Weinstein works toward an aesthetic argument more relativist than relational (with relativism's relentless symmetries), and one that makes of tragedy a fated past leaving out any spur to extra-textual action (and therefore belonging to a dominant way of reading Faulkner rather than to Faulkner as read under the influence of Morrison).

16. An exception is David Ragan's article on the ending of *Absalom, Absalom!*

17. John Irwin's *Doubling and Incest/Repetition and Revenge: A Speculative Reading of Faulkner* remains the most lucid account of the intertextual relations between *The Sound and the Fury* and *Absalom, Absalom!* Psychoanalytic in orientation, Irwin necessarily internalizes the significance of incest and miscegenation; rather than seeing them as issues of a social world where morality inheres in attitudes that do more or less harm, he, in keeping with Brooks and Matthews, reads the text's "outraged recapitulations" as an authorial doubling in which "the author's self is reconstituted within the realm of language as the Other, a narcissistic mirroring of the self to which the author's reaction is at once a fascinated self-love and an equally fascinated self-hatred" (159). His emphasis on the work of art as "the feminine aspect of the masculine self," on writing as an act of "autoerotic self-destruction," inundates analysis in the Oedipal triangle and necessarily obscures *Absalom, Absalom!*'s criticism of intellectual/aesthetic detachment.

18. James D. Gray attributes a "lesson of love" to Shreve and Brooks gives Miss Rosa the "last word." Unlike Larry Allums, Gray acknowledges how a "framing punctuation" interrupts the "marriage of speaking and hearing" that is "primarily Shreve's to tell and Quentin's to hear" (30), yet he moves easily from "Shreve's analysis" to "Shreve's (Quentin's) analysis." He sees Shreve's "lesson of love" figured in the "altruistic self-sacrifice" of Bon's gesture of replacing the portrait, despite Shreve's easy reference to Bon as "the black son of a bitch," his trashing of women, and his cumulatively crude treatment of Quentin ("the imperfect and doomed listener"). Seeing Shreve as "a realist who endeavors to distinguish myths from facts" ignores the Canadian's imaginative collaboration in an adolescent, idealizing narrative accommodation.

19. Carolyn Porter has sensed the connections between narratology and readerly relation to Quentin, but she does so in the act of finding Faulkner's self-

imposed task impossible on those grounds: "We cannot avoid resisting the implications of Quentin's position at the novel's end, for the simple reason that the implications are suicidal" (73).

20. Most know this experientially, as when feminists distinguish between those who only use socially self-conscious language and those actively and emotionally engaged in issues of social justice whose social positions may or may not reflect self-conscious language use.

21. Put otherwise, *Absalom, Absalom!* addresses as tragic lack precisely what Judith Butler names as the delimitation of Foucault's account of the "subject" of desire. Because Foucault's abstracted, discursive subject defines itself in relation to domination, Foucault "may well give us an account of how the 'subject' is generated, but he cannot tell us which subjects are generated in the way that he describes, *and at whose expense*" (Butler, *Bodies that Matter* 137, my emphasis).

22. Wadlington, among others, offers a largely psychoanalytic treatment of Judith as tragic heroine.

23. Accordingly, Weinstein's explication ends on a note of perfect fatalism: "Quentin may or may not manage to hate that culture (the text ends in perfect suspense), but the one thing he cannot do is change its racial politics" (151). And Sandra Adell, theorizing from the perspective of black modernity, comes closer by articulating the paradox in a nostalgia for a world in which "life could be lived as a symbolic re-enactment" (Adell 139).

Chapter 5. Literary Passing

1. For a description of how Stein's triangular love-relationship with May Bookstaver turned into "Melanctha," see Leon Katz's Introduction to Stein's *Fernhurst, Q.E.D., and Other Early Writings*.

2. Among exceptions are Marianne DeKoven, Sonia Saldívar-Hull, and Catherine Stimpson. In addition, Michael North usefully considers the Stein-Picasso fascination with African masks. North explicates Stein's remarkable assertion that she believes "in reality as Cézanne and Caliban believe in it," by pointing to the collaborative similarities in "Melanctha"'s vicarious treatment of conventions of the senses and Picasso's vicarious use of African masks as cover to sexual ambiguity in *Les Desmoiselles*. He, too, notes the tendency "to concentrate on aesthetics, as critics of *Three Lives* have for so long, or to demolish the racism of 'Melanctha'" (64).

3. The phrase comes from Patricia Wald, who aptly demonstrates this process for *The Making of Americans*. Catherine Stimpson dubs the distinction between the older focus on indeterminate meaning and the newer focus on gender and genre one between the "Old Stein" and the "New Stein" ("Gertrude Stein and the Transposition") and Randa Dubnick traces Stein's changing styles in terms of their relational forms of obscurity and lyricism. See Ann Douglas's bibliographical essay in *Terrible Honesty: Mongrel Manhattan in the 1920s* (514–15) for an overview of critical work on Stein.

4. Hull usefully considers these consequences for Alice Dunbar-Nelson, Angelina Weld Grimké, and Georgia Douglas Johnson in particular. For an historical overview of the historical connections between a conception of miscegenation that makes black-white marriage illegal until 1967 and a conception of homosexuality that continues to make same-sex marriage illegal, see Jonathan Goldberg's "Sodometries."

5. Randa Dubnick argues that *Ida* provides only very superficial, general information about characters, and only generalized summaries of events or actions. She refers the work's level of abstraction to "freedom from fidelity to the external world as referent" (71). More generally, a focus on Stein's use of language as arbitrary or on period and genre has tended to use both her pronouncements and her works to document the break from 19th-century realism and her connections to later avant-garde writers from Ionesco to Robbe-Grillet.

6. Leigh Gilmore extends this insight about a subtextual lesbianism in her reading of how the lesbian signature "Gertrice/Altrude" informs Stein's indirection in telling her own story as that of Alice in *The Autobiography of Alice B. Toklas*, where she creates a lesbian couple that exists in a discursive practice always undermining any unified self in favor of "a linguistic 'shifter' that does not properly refer" (59–60).

7. The phrase is from William Corlett's "Containing Indeterminacy: Problems of Representation and Determination in Marx and Althusser," 469. Patricia Wald explicates Stein's related experiments with "preperception" and its importance to attention and character (260–72).

8. Dubnick refers to a six-page "digression" about dogs.

9. The most predictable course of any contemporary talk-show's attention to race allies a white audience around a troubled superiority to differences in race, a superiority in tolerance implicitly or explicitly opposed to the "hypersensitive" or "racist" distinctions made by people of color. It always starts "I don't care what race you are." For a critique of the genre of standpoint epistemology that "imagines" from different positions in order to analyze the possibilities and limitations of each, see my "Positioning Subjects and Objects."

10. Quoted with permission from an unpublished paper.

11. John M. Brinnin cites not only the famous approbation of Richard Wright, but also of Nella Larsen and James Weldon Johnson as black writers who appreciated "Melanctha" "because of its uncommon assumption that Negro characters and themes associated with Negro life were matters as naturally available for imaginative fiction as for sociological tract" (120), with Claude McKay arguing that the story contained "nothing striking and informative about Negro life" (121). Any "appreciation" belongs in the context of the constraints for writers of color in depicting any explicit sexuality; for the asymmetrical experience of such constraints on black women writers, see Cheryl A. Wall's "Poets and Versifiers, Singers and Signifiers: Women of the Harlem Renaissance." Representative of feminist readings, Harriet Chessman reads "Melanctha" as a self-referential experiment with alternative forms of narrative; with useful insight into Melanctha's resistance to intimacy, she foregrounds gender in her explication of narrative subjectivity.

12. As suggested by this phrase, Chessman traces a "double narrative impulse" in "Melanctha," which consists of an oppositional tension between knowing and feeling, telling and not telling.

13. Stephen Scobie collects these adjectives from Marianne DeKoven's *A Different Language: Gertrude Stein's Experimental Writing* as descriptive of Stein's experimental style (100).

14. Marianne DeKoven argues that "conventional assumptions about the impact of class overtly endorsed by the text are overthrown" (74).

15. Thus, in my view, Marianne DeKoven or Michael North has stronger insight into the "complex, undecidable concatenations" (DeKoven) of stereotypes

and counterstereotypes within this text than do those who focus primarily on gender and genre.

16. I take the word from Catherine Stimpson's ("Gertrude Stein and the Lesbian Lie") observation: "Her [Stein's] comments on American blacks, for example, can be genial. They are also patronizing, inept, and foolish."

17. Edward Said generalizes this point beyond racial difference to Eurocentrism:

> if it is embarrassing for us to remark that those elements of a society we have long considered to be progressive were, so far as empire was concerned, uniformly retrograde, we still must not be afraid to say it. Advanced writers and artists, the working class, and women—groups marginal in the West—showed an imperialist fervor that increased in intensity and perfervid enthusiasm as the competition among various European and American powers increased in brutality and senseless, even profitless, control. Eurocentrism penetrated to the core of the workers' movement, the women's movement, the avant-garde arts movement, leaving no one of significance untouched. (*Culture and Imperialism* 222)

18. Wright offerred the example of black stockyard workers' responses to his oral rendering of "Melanctha" ("they slapped their thighs, howled, laughed, stomped, and interrupted me constantly to comment upon the characters" [quoted by John M. Brinnin 121]) as evidence of its successful comic realism, but their approval was no doubt gendered in its humorous focus on female characters constraining men both in and out of marriage.

19. In contrast to reading Melanctha as a "sign," Debra B. Silverman reads Melanctha as a realistic character and contrasts Nella Larsen's granting Helga Crane agency in *Quicksand* to Stein's denying it to a stereotyped Melanctha. This seems a somewhat unliterary contrast because, as Judith Butler's reading of Larsen's *Passing* makes clear, Larsen's works, too, mean beyond realist conventions. Using psychoanalytic assumptions to argue for *Passing* as a paradigmatic site for "the convergent modalities of power by which sexual difference is articulated and assumed" (*Bodies That Matter* 168), Butler implicitly relates Larsen to a Stein who negotiates sexual boundaries through grammar itself.

20. This revisionary literary story relates to my earlier premise that multiply-positioned and variously resistant forms of written subjectivity/intersubjectivity characterize writing under duress for audiences felt as also variously positioned and frequently hostile. And it explains why works by Fauset and Larsen should also be at the center of important black feminist debate about interpretation, with Claudia Tate acknowledging that how one reads the ending of *Passing* depends on who one takes to be the central character. Deborah McDowell argues that the ending "punish[es] the very values the novel implicitly affirms," whereas Ann DuCille argues for reading *Passing* as "artistically complex beyond the limits of any particular reading or any single rhythm" (108).

Chapter 6. World-Traveling as Modal Skid

1. Hazel Carby ("Politics of Fiction") understandably prefers the perspectives of black intellectuals of the period who have a clearly progressive relation to

Caribbean revolutionary history, such as C. L. R. James, Hughes, and DuBois; see also Farah Jasmine Griffin's *The African-American Migration Narrative.*

2. Roland Barthes coined the term "metonymic skid" in *S/Z.* John Lowe has written the only sustained analysis of Hurston's "cosmic comedy" and provides much insight into both her use of folk humor and her own comic personae. He does not, however, explicate either *Mules and Men* or *Tell My Horse,* perhaps because these texts lie so much more problematically within extant comic theory, precisely my interest here. Cheryl Wall ("*Mules and Men* and Women") and Houston Baker (*Workings of the Spirit*), to whom I am generally indebted, both provide more positive readings than Carby's of Hurston's narrative strategies in *Mules and Men* and their relation to female empowerment.

3. *C.L.R. James Reader* 246. Janet Wolff (*Resident Alien*), Carole Boyce Davies (*Black Women*), and others have documented the gendered nature of travel. Yet if, as their work suggests, what it means to travel depends on constructions of race, class, and sexuality, as well as gender, then the case of a black American woman's travel to the Caribbean—a 1930's transgression even in conception—complicates the negotiations with Boas and Mrs. Mason (a patroness with a penchant for measuring the accomplishments of "her Negroes" against each other).

4. Carby ("Politics of Fiction"), for example, believes that Hurston's assertion of an autonomous personal pleasure in *Mules and Men* and *Tell My Horse* "displaces the folk community utterly and irrevocably" (39), a contrast to Houston Baker's explication of the Vodou texts as rich in a spiritual legacy intimately connected to the folk cultures about which Hurston wrote. Identifying the value of conjure with Hurston's "bright words," Baker cites with approval the works' most resplendent passages. And Susan Willis (*Specifying*) adjudicates the tensions thus: "Most often, Hurston remains locked into the motif of wandering, trapped in a geography of spirit that is independent of property relationships and domination, but unable to transform the metaphoric geography into an alternative notion of daily life" (38). Ann DuCille relates interpretive emphasis to whether Hurston appears, rightly, as a writer among others, including such precursors as Frances Harper and Pauline Hopkins and such contemporaries as Jessie Fauset, Nella Larsen, Alice Dunbar-Nelson, and Marita Bonner.

5. For diverse discussion of Hurston's relationships with Mrs. Mason and Frank Boas, see Robert Hemenway, Hazel Carby ("Politics of Fiction"), bell hooks's *Yearning,* George Houston Bass's and Henry Louis Gates, Jr.'s Introductions to Hughes's and Hurston's *Mule Bone: A Comedy of Negro Life,* and Arnold Rampersad's Introduction to *Mules and Men.*

6. For my purposes, the harshest criticism of Mrs. Mason (as in bell hooks's portrait of her as "the colonizer who masks her desire to control by assuming the role of caretaker," analogous to "the plantation owner") does not disallow her necessary role as outlined by Rampersad in his Introduction: "Volatile in personality, contemptuous of European rationalism and radically devoted to the idea of extrasensory communication, and a champion of the notion of the artistic and spiritual superiority of the darker races, Mrs. Mason, more than any of Hurston's academic advisers, paved the way for Hurston's plunging not simply into the Eatonville community of her childhood but, far more radically, into voodoo and black magic in Louisiana" (xx).

7. Perceptive readings have in common an attention to the complexity of implied relations among speaker, hearer, reader, and writer in Hurston's first-person works, the strategic, artful manipulation of any "specific interlocution-

ary situation" (Barbara Johnson, "Thresholds of Difference" 172–83). See also Françoise Lionnet's *Autobiographical Voices* and bell hooks's essay in *Yearning*, which elaborate some of the strategies used by Hurston to manipulate "conventional power dynamics" to serve her own ends.

8. John W. Roberts usefully examines how the African American trickster-tale tradition relates to but differs from African trickster tales, most notably with a common grounding in material shortages and rigid social hierarchy but also with profound differences between the African shortages and those endemic to slavery.

9. Both Roberts and Beulah S. Hemmingway examine the characteristics of John as a culture hero.

10. Houston Baker's reading of the final section of *Mules and Men* as the achievement of an intimate spiritual space helps to relate the professional practice of vicarious suffering to the intimacy that nurtures humorous rapport:

> Hurston's camaraderie with the vernacular community represented by inhabitants of the Florida sawmill seems to come to fullness in her final hoodoo partnership. Having made her way in the first three-quarters of *Mules and Men* through various spaces of the Afro-American vernacular, she at last achieves the power of a two-headed doctor. Her final appearance as a hoodoo healer locates [her] within a *community of women* who have the powers on their side. (*Workings of the Spirit* 299)

Far from a regressive or "superstitious" practice, the practice of Vodou consolidates both spiritual and worldly power in those most energetically and actively resistant to oppressive white power.

11. This language comes from Cesáreo Bandera's *The Sacred Game: The Role of the Sacred in the Genesis of Modern Literary Fiction* (300), a work that as a whole postulates a "fundamental, primitive fear of the open society," with "open society" meaning one that might altogether renounce the search for a victim. Making the victim an historical, naturalized necessity, Palmer affirmatively explicates the "equilibrium" of Greek tragedy.

12. Pearlie Peters calls what Hurston values in black women's expression of character and spunk "the assertive voice": "The assertive voice, be it in the narrative or basic conversational mode that draws upon various manifestations of Black speech styles, is the yardstick by which Hurston stresses the significance of the Black oral tradition in determining the individualism of folk women" (102).

13. *Mule Bone: A Comedy of Negro Life* invaluably chronicles all sides of the controversy that ended Hurston's and Hughes's collaboration. It includes all primary sources as well as important accounts by Gates ("A Tragedy of Negro Life"), Robert Hemenway (from his biography of Hurston), and Arnold Rampersad (from his biography of Hughes). It also documents the complexity of both writers' relationship with Mrs. Mason, a relationship so damaging that it left Hughes in a state of physical and emotional breakdown and Hurston in isolation from any black community of writers and artists.

14. Letter to Langston Hughes, 20 January 1931, *Mule Bone* 223.

15. Speaking of her initiate's attempt to joke with Papa Gede, the Vodou spirit linking death and humor, Karen McCarthy Brown describes his necessary truthtelling. I quote the passage in full because it so well captures the integrity of humorous belief:

I once learned an important lesson about Papa Gede's comic sensibility. Early on, when I was still feeling my way at Alourdes's Vodou parties, I risked joking with Ti Malis. "I like your hat," I said. "Do you like my *zozo* [penis]?" he asked, and everyone laughed. "I don't know your *zozo*," I responded. People laughed again. "Oh, yes, you know it," said Gede. "If you know any man's *zozo*, you know my *zozo!*" More laughter. "Oh, Papa Gede," I said, feigning great earnestness, "maybe you did not know. I am a virgin." This time no one laughed, and Gede simply looked confused. Then someone leaned over and whispered in my ear, "You know, Papa Gede does not lie." Gede's humor denies no reality; he is funny precisely because he tells the truth. He is powerful because he works an alchemical change, not on the facts of life, but on our attitude toward them. (*Mama Lola* 375–76)

16. Katie Cannon's *Black Womanist Ethics* introduces Hurston's "unctuous moral agency" in a passage worth quoting in full:

Hurston, like Black people generally, understood suffering not as a moral norm nor as a desirable ethical quality, but rather as the typical state of affairs. Virtue is not the experiencing of suffering, nor in the survival techniques for enduring. Rather, the quality of moral good is that which allows Black people to maintain a feistiness about life that nobody can wipe out, no matter how hard they try.

Some of Hurston's critics charged her with writing shallow, romantic, naive counter-revolutionary literature because she portrayed a sense of psychic and physical pleasure amidst desperation and tragedy. She portrayed the humor and good times among people who lived, day in and day out, with pathetic and inarticulate needs. Hurston reminded individuals that they were a part of the communal kinship within the Black cultural heritage.

The result of this type of moral agency in Hurston culminates in a quality that Alice Walker identifies as "unctuousness." (105)

17. Positively, Sandra Adell sees feminism as "much more strongly articulated and cleverly rendered in Part 1 of *Tell My Horse*" (111) than in *Their Eyes Were Watching God*, whereas, negatively, J. Michael Dash puts the Vodou priestess's sexual dance in scandalizing quotation as appropriate to Hurston's "nightmare" vision of Haiti. Both Sandra Adell and Houston Baker (*Workings of the Spirit*) view Hurston's depiction of female sexuality in *Tell My Horse* as consistent with later black feminism. This view finds its opposition not only in Hazel Carby but also in Dash's work on stereotypes of Haitians and the literary imagination. In the context of praising the superior insight of African American and Haitian male writers focusing on the "dream" of a black diasporic identity, Dash condemns Hurston's description as reinscribing exoticism. (Dash tends to ignore Hurston's affirming lyricism, as when she describes La Gonave, an island off the Haitian shore, as possessing "a peace I have never known anywhere else on earth.")

18. Leslie G. Desmangles describes the Erzli (Erzulie), female Vodou spirts who combine the attributes of the Virgin Mary and Aphrodite, as being as relevant to the virginal preparation for love as to erotic sexuality and childbearing.

19. Hemenway describes the ravages of the incident in his Chapter 12, appropriately entitled "The Pots in Sorrow's Kitchen."

20. See Wade Davis's *Passage of Darkness: The Ethnobiology of the Haitian Zombie.*

21. Ironically, the phrase "voodoo economics," intending to undermine

supply-side economic theory, participates in the continued misconstruction of Vodou, in which a levelling spiritualism has integral ties to anti-capitalist economics.

22. Insightfully, Renato Rosaldo uses Hurston's reference to herself at Barnard as a "sacred black cow" as an example of how "wit," along with any number of other expressive or playful uses of language, can lend a literary complexity to an ethnographer's self-other conceptions: "Hurston's ironic self-portrait enables her to depict the two-sidedness of her status elevation without losing its critical edge" (193). Others who usefully explore the fluid boundaries of ethnographic and literary analysis are Sydney Mintz, Greg Sarris, Arnold Krupat, and Judith Oakley.

23. This relates in difference to Alford's view of the tragic as "responsibility without freedom" (115).

Epilogue

1. Satya Mohanty's ("Colonial Legacies") distinctions among the mediations of experience and theory help clarify these interrelations.

2. Paula M. L. Moya offers a cogent warning about how easily white feminist Theory can slip into arrogance by idealizing women of color in the act of readings where " 'difference' is magically subverted and we find out that we really are all the same after all" (Moya 114).

3. Of the many edited collections surveying ways of differentiating postmodernity from the modernity that comes before it, see especially essays in *Modernity and Its Discontents* (ed. James Marsh et al.), *Universal Abandon? The Politics of Postmodernism* (ed. Andrew Ross); *Feminism/Postmodernism* (ed. Linda J. Nicholson); *Zeitgeist in Babel: The Postmodernist Controversy* (ed. Ingeborg Hoesterey); *Postmodernism and the Re-Reading of Modernity* (ed. Francis Barker et al.); and *Modernity: An Introduction to Modern Societies* (ed. Stuart Hall et al.).

4. Fredric Jameson provides a largely sympathetic reading of *Specters of Marx* in "Marx's Purloined Letter."

5. My colleague David Kolb usefully comments here that "detachment" may be another name for the postmodern scholar's fear of being ridiculed, the fear of finding someone with an even more radical position "under" or "behind" you trying to reveal your naiveté.

6. Kimberlé Williams Crenshaw ("Color Blindness, History, and the Law") usefully explicates some legal implications of such fraudulent symmetry.

7. Cited from opening remarks at the Race Matters Conference (Princeton, 28–30 April 1994) by Kimberlé Williams Crenshaw in "Color Blindness" (280).

8. This point is related to a dominant model of interdisciplinarity and to one form of multiculturalism: an American Studies conceived as an intersection of what discrete disciplines do, and which therefore rarely disturbs their methods. In literary history, conceiving of literary traditions conceived as discrete entities ignores how very literate in Euro-American traditions those Other to them— always negotiating them—have always been.

9. Wahneema Lubiano puts this relatedly when she warns of how recent interest in African American literature on the part of dominant culture has historically coincided with "a contemporary dismissal of the discourse of African Americans around their own production" ("Mapping the Interstices" 76). And Sandra Adell's intracultural negotiations in her chapter "Seeking the Other

Women of (Black) Feminist Literary Critical and Theoretical Discourses" warns of the paradoxical risks of criticism representing academic expertise, citing Michelle Wallace's "Inevitably, we silence others that we may speak at all" (quoted 115 from Wallace, "Variations on Negation" 59).

10. As argued in the chapter on *Absalom, Absalom!* this does not assume any particular prescience on social issues in Faulkner, just some aesthetic sense of tragic loss in what could *not* be represented. And the distinction enables differentiation useful for dominant writers, as between Fitzgerald's antisemitism in *The Great Gatsby*, which focuses with marked identification on its major character's trying to get rid of ethnic markers, and Hemingway's in *The Sun Also Rises*, which uses an unmarked antisemitic portrayal to elevate in difference its affirmed characters.

11. Examples of such readerly gestures are too ubiquitous to document, but range from the passing reference to more sustained gestures of avoidance. As an example of passing reference, Deleuze and Guattari wax rhapsodic in an unreflecting and reinscriptive affirmation of "Ol' Man River" ("as they say about old man river" introduces the most familiar stanza), clearly accepting the Broadway version of blackness as having some cultural resonance (*A Thousand Plateaus* 25). In a more sustained divigation on how well suited Morrison's works are to her own critical premise, Catherine Belsey's discussion of "Postmodern Love: Questioning the Metaphysics of Desire" ends by deferentially omitting any attention to Morrison's texts because "I have a fear of appearing to colonize her work, or at least of seeming to preempt the work of African American critics" (702). We should, I think, be always receptive to charges of colonization, but not worry about "seeming" or "appearing" to do so (a language revealing one's own status as still central); and seriously engaging the work of African American feminist critics, I have come over many years to feel, respects work that cannot be preempted unless ignored or unacknowledged (a critical variant of a belief in "separate but equal" status). Another common move simply names and justifies an ellipsis on the grounds of a liberal dislike for "speaking for others," as when Lori Gruen undertakes a feminist analysis of figures linking the oppression of women and animals: "A similar analysis could be done for oppression of all kinds, but it would be more appropriately accomplished by people of color, the infirm, the colonized, and so on, who are undoubtedly more able than I am to speak of their own oppression" (84).

12. Carl G. Jung, *Modern Man in Search of a Soul* (197). Partly at stake is a canon with more flexible boundaries but also how to read (post)modern works without taming either their tragic edge or what Jameson calls "vestiges of mimesis." Perhaps expectedly, critics of African American, black feminist, postcolonial, and working class studies have most forcefully resisted this image of modern man leaving his traditions behind him with anticipation before the void rather than a sense of loss. The archival work of Maryemma Graham, Janet Zandy, and others pushes at the boundaries of expanding rather than reducing the linkages to sundry nondominant traditions.

13. Douglas, despite the attention to hybridity, follows Kenner and others in foregrounding a modernism with the American 1920s at its inception and a self-conceived avant-garde as its successor.

14. Douglas cites from an unpublished letter (116–17).

15. Because the term "postmodern" may suggest a discrete period or characteristics, some, like Stuart Hall, prefer "late modern" to "postmodern," cor-

responding to Jameson's preference for "late capitalism" as the socio-economic system underlying postmodernity.

16. Jean Rhys's Creole extraction might make her for some a dubious entry in the African American canon, which underscores the problematics of conflicted social positioning. *Wide Sargasso Sea* has nevertheless become one of the most read works of Caribbean literature that takes up racial and racist mythologies from a positioning self-identified as Other to both Euro-American and "native." The business of naming, while by no means trivial, founders somewhat when notions of blood and lineage replace those of self-identification, and there is perhaps some asymmetry here across the genders. Readings of Jean Toomer's *Cane*, for example, often relate narrative trouble to the author's white appearance and his own claims to whiteness, but never exclude him from the African American canon on such grounds.

17. Sandra Adell, Michael Awkward, Houston Baker, Hazel Carby, Frances Smith Foster, Henry Louis Gates, Karla Holloway, bell hooks, Trudier Harris, Valerie Smith, Hortense Spillers, Mary Helen Washington, and others have all explicated the shifting or indeterminacy in black women writers' relation to dominant forms and traditions, yet this indeterminacy (like Head's "leaving the story unresolved") implies more about an ongoing process of becoming than about indeterminate *values*.

18. Craig H. Werner puts this well when he asserts that "the Afro-American literary response to Faulkner, like Faulkner's greatest works themselves, pushes us to excavate the premises of our history, to focus not on the 'eternal verities' that can be carved on the walls of libraries but on those aspects of our experience that we least understand" (35).

Bibliography

Abrahams, Cecil, ed. *The Tragic Life: Bessie Head and Literature in Southern Africa.* Trenton, N. J.: Africa World Press, 1990.

Adell, Sandra. *Double Consciousness/Double Bind: Theoretical Issus in Twentieth-Century Black Literature.* Urbana: University of Illinois Press, 1994.

Aijaz, Ahmad. *In Theory: Classes, Nations, Literatures.* London: Verso, 1992.

Alexander, M. Jacqui and Chandra Talpade Mohanty, eds. *Feminist Genealogies, Colonial Legacies, Democratic Futures.* New York: Routledge, 1997.

Alford, C. Fred *The Psychoanalytic Theory of Greek Tragedy.* New Haven, Conn.: Yale University Press, 1992.

Allums, Larry. "Overpassing to Love: Dialogue and Play in *Absalom, Absalom!*" *New Orleans Review* 14, 4 (1987): 36–41.

Andrade, Susan. "Rewriting History, Motherhood, and Rebellion." *Research in African Literatures* 21,1 (1990): 91–110.

Appiah, Anthony. "Tolerable Falsehoods: Agency and the Interests of Theory." *Consequences of Theory,* ed. Jonathan Arac and Barbara Johnson. Baltimore: Johns Hopkins University Press, 1991. 63–90.

Awkward, Michael. *Inspiriting Influences: Tradition, Revision, and Afro-American Women's Novels.* New York: Columbia University Press, 1989.

———. *Negotiating Difference: Race, Gender, and the Politics of Positionality.* Chicago and London: University of Chicago Press, 1995.

———. *New Essays on* Their Eyes Were Watching God. Cambridge: Cambridge University Press, 1990.

Baker, Houston A. *Blues, Ideology, and Afro-American Literature: A Vernacular Theory.* Chicago: University of Chicago Press, 1984.

———. *Modernism and the Harlem Renaissance.* Chicago: University of Chicago Press, 1987.

———. *Workings of the Spirit: The Poetics of Afro-American Women's Writing.* Chicago and London: University of Chicago Press, 1991.

Bakhtin, Mikhail M. *The Dialogical Imagination: Four Essays.* Ed. Michael Holquist, trans. Caryl Emerson and Michael Holquist. Austin: University of Texas Press, 1981.

———. *Speech Genres and Other Late Essays.* Ed. Caryl Emerson and Michael Holquist, trans. Vern M. McGee. Austin: University of Texas Press, 1986.

Baldwin, James. *No Name in the Street.* London: Michael Joseph, 1972.

Bambara, Toni Cade. *Deep Sightings and Rescue Missions: Fiction, Essays, and Conversations.* Ed. and Preface Toni Morrison. New York: Pantheon, 1996.

———. *The Salt Eaters.* 1980. New York: Vintage, 1992.

Bandera, Cesáreo. *The Sacred Game: The Role of the Sacred in the Genesis of Modern Literary Fiction*. University Park: Penn State University Press, 1994.

Bannerji, Himani. *Thinking Through: Essays on Feminism, Marxism, and Anti-Racism*. Toronto: Women's Press, 1995.

Barbour, John D. *Tragedy as a Critique of Virtue: The Novel and Ethical Reflections*. Atlanta: Scholars Press, 1984.

Barker, Francis, Peter Hulme, and Margaret Iverson, eds. *Postmodernism and the Re-Reading of Modernity*. Manchester and New York: Manchester University Press, 1992.

Barthes, Roland. *S/Z*. Paris: Editions du Seuil, 1970.

Bell, Bernard W. *The Afro-American Novel and Its Tradition*. Amherst: University of Massachusetts Press, 1985.

Belsey, Catherine. "Postmodern Love: Questioning the Metaphysics of Desire." *New Literary History* 25, 3 (1994): 683–705.

Bentson, Kimberly. "Facing Tradition: Revisionary Scenes in African American Literature." *PMLA* 105, 1 (1990): 98–109.

Berger, Roger A. "The Politics of Madness in Bessie Head's *A Question of Power*." Abrahams, *The Tragic Life*. 31–44.

Berke, Bradley. *Tragic Thought and the Grammar of Tragic Myth*. Bloomington: Indiana University Press, 1982.

Bernal, Martin. *Black Athena: The Afroasiatic Roots of Classical Civilization*. New Brunswick, N.J.: Rutgers University Press, 1987.

Berry, Ellen. *Curved Thought and Textual Wandering: Gertrude Stein's Postmodernism*. Ann Arbor: University of Michigan Press, 1992.

Bhabha, Homi K. "Freedom's Basis in the Indeterminate." *October* 61 (1992): 46–57.

———. "Interrogating Identity: The Postcolonial Prerogative." *Anatomy of Racism*, ed. David Theo Goldberg. Minneapolis: University of Minnesota Press, 1990. 183–209.

———, ed. *Nation and Narration*. London and New York: Routledge, 1990.

Blau. Herbert. *The Eye of the Prey: Subversions of the Postmodern*. Bloomington: Indiana University Press, 1987.

Bobo, Jacqueline. "Sifting Through the Controversy: Reading *The Color Purple*." *Callaloo* 12, 2 (1989): 332–42.

Bowers, Susan. "*Beloved* and the New Apocalypse." *Toni Morrison's Fiction: Contemporary Criticism*, ed. David L. Middleton. New York: Garland, 1997. 209–30.

Brinnin, John M. *The Third Rose: Gertrude Stein and Her World*. Radcliffe Biography Series. Reading, Mass.: Merloyd Lawrence, 1987.

Broe, Mary Lynn and Angela Ingram, eds. *Women's Writing in Exile*. Chapel Hill: University of North Carolina Press, 1989.

Brooks, Peter. *Reading for the Plot: Design and Intention in Narrative*. New York: Knopf, 1984.

Brown, Karen McCarthy. *Mama Lola: A Vodou Priestess in Brooklyn*. Berkeley: University of California Press, 1991.

Burkert, Walter, René Girard, and Jonathan Smith. *Violent Origins: Ritual Killing and Cultural Formation*, ed. Robert G. Hamerton-Kelly. Stanford, Calif.: Stanford University Press, 1987.

Butler, Judith. *Bodies That Matter: On the Discursive Limits of "Sex."* New York: Routledge, 1993.

———. *The Psychic Life of Power: Theories in Subjection*. Stanford, Calif.: Stanford University Press, 1997.

Cannon, Katie Geneva. *Black Womanist Ethics*. Atlanta, Ga.: Scholars Press, 1988.
———. *Katie's Canon: Womanism and the Soul of the Black Community*. Foreword Sara Lawrence-Lightfoot. New York: Continuum, 1996.
Carby, Hazel. "Ideologies of Black Folk: The Historical Novel of Slavery." McDowell and Rampersad, *Slavery and the Literary Imagination*. 125–43.
———. "The Politics of Fiction, Anthropology, and the Folk: Zora Neale Hurston." *History and Memory in African-American Culture*, ed. Geneviève Fabre and Robert O'Meally. New York: Oxford University Press, 1994. 28–44.
———. *Reconstructing Womanhood: The Emergence of the Afro-American Woman Novelist*. New York: Oxford University Press, 1987.
Carnegie, Charles. "The Dundes and the Nation." *Postnationalism Refigured*. New Brunswick, N.J.: Rutgers University Press, forthcoming.
Cavell, Stanley. *The Claim of Reason: Wittgenstein, Skepticism, Morality, and Tragedy*. New York: Oxford University Press, 1982.
———. *In Quest of the Ordinary: Lines of Skepticism and Romanticism*. Chicago: University of Chicago Press, 1988.
———. *Must We Mean What We Say?: A Book of Essays*. New York: Cambridge University Press, 1976.
Chessman, Harriet. *The Public Is Invited to Dance: Representation, the Body, and Dialogue in Gertrude Stein*. Stanford, Calif.: Stanford University Press, 1989.
Chetin, Sara. "Myth, Exile, and the Female Condition: Bessie Head's *A Collector of Treasures*." *Journal of Commonwealth Literature* 24,1 (1989): 114–37.
Christian, Barbara. *Black Feminist Criticism: Perspectives on Black Women Writers*. New York: Pergamon Press, 1985.
———. "The Race for Theory." *Cultural Critique* 6 (1987): 51–64.
Cixous, Hélène. "The Laugh of the Medusa." Trans. Keith and Paula Cohen. *Signs* 1, 4 (1976): 875–93.
———. *Sorties*. Trans. Betsy Wing. New York: Routledge, 1997.
Clarke, Deborah. *Robbing the Mother: Women in Faulkner*. Jackson: University Press of Mississippi, 1994.
Clayton, Cherry. "'A World Elsewhere': Bessie Head as Historian." *English in Africa* 15,1 (1988): 55–69.
Collins, Patricia Hill. *Black Feminist Thought: Knowledge, Consciousness, and the Politics of Empowerment*. Perspectives on Gender 2. Boston: Unwin Hyman, 1990.
Comas, James. "The Presence of Theory/Theorizing the Present." *Research in African Literatures* 21, 1 (1990): 5–31.
Cooey, Paula M. *Religious Imagination and the Body: A Feminist Analysis*. New York: Oxford University Press, 1994.
Corlett, William. *Community Without Unity: A Politics of Derridian Extravagance*. Durham, N.C.: Duke University Press, 1989.
———. "Containing Indeterminacy: Problems of Representation and Determination in Marx and Althusser." *Political Theory* 24, 3 (1996): 463–92.
Crenshaw, Kimberlé Williams. "Color Blindness, History, and the Law." Lubiano, *The House That Race Built*. 280–88.
Crouch, Stanley. "Aunt Medea." Review of *Beloved* by Toni Morrison. *New Republic*, 19 October 1987: 38–43.
Dash, J. Michael. *Haiti and the United States: National Stereotypes and the Literary Imagination*. New York: St. Martin's Press, 1988.
Davies, Carole Boyce. *Black Women, Writing and Identity: Migrations of the Subject*. London: Routledge, 1994.

————. "Private Selves and Public Spaces: Autobiography and the African Woman Writer." *CLA Journal* 34, 3 (1991): 267–89.

Davis, Angela Y. *Blues Legacies and Black Feminism: Gertrude "Ma" "Rainey, Bessie Smith, and Billie Holiday.* New York: Pantheon, 1998.

Davis, Charles T. and Henry Louis Gates, Jr., eds. *The Slave's Narrative.* Oxford: Oxford University Press, 1985.

Davis, Thadious M. *Faulkner's "Negro": Art and the Southern Context.* Baton Rouge: Louisiana State University Press, 1983.

————. "Reading Faulkner's Compson Appendix: Writing History from the Margins." Kartiganer and Abadie, *Faulkner and Ideology.* 238–52.

Davis, Wade. *Passage of Darkness: The Ethnobiology of the Haitian Zombie.* Chapel Hill: University of North Carolina Press, 1988.

————. *The Serpent and the Rainbow.* New York: Simon and Schuster, 1985.

De Jongh, James. *Vicious Modernism: Black Harlem and the Literary Imagination.* Cambridge: Cambridge University Press, 1990.

DeKoven, Marianne. *Rich and Strange: Gender, History, Modernism.* Princeton, N.J.: Princeton University Press, 1991.

Deleuze, Gilles and Félix Guattari. *Anti-Oedipus: Capitalism and Schizophrenia.* Preface Michel Foucault. Minneapolis: University of Minnesota Press, 1983.

————. *A Thousand Plateaus: Capitalism and Schizophrenia.* Trans. and Foreword Brian Massumi. Minneapolis: University of Minnesota Press, 1987.

Derrida, Jacques. *Specters of Marx: The State of the Debt, the Work of Mourning, and the New International.* Trans. Peggy Kamuf, Intro. Bernd Magnus and Stephen Cullenberg. New York: Routledge, 1994.

Desmangles, Leslie G. *The Faces of the Gods: Vodou and Roman Catholicism in Haiti.* Chapel Hill: University of North Carolina Press, 1992.

Douglas, Ann. *Terrible Honesty: Mongrel Manhattan in the 1920s.* New York: Farrar, Straus and Giroux, 1995.

Dovey, Teresa. "A Question of Power: Susan Gardner's Biography Versus Bessie Head's Autobiography." *English in Africa* 16, 1 (1989): 29–38.

DuCille, Ann. *The Coupling Convention: Sex, Text, and Tradition in Black Women's Fiction.* New York: Oxford University Press, 1993.

Dubnick, Randa K. *The Structure of Obscurity: Gertrude Stein, Language, and Cubism.* Urbana: University of Illinois Press, 1984.

During, Simon. "Literature—Nationalism's Other? The Case for Revision." Bhabha, *Nation and Narration.* 138–53.

————. "Postmodernism or Post-Colonialism Today." *Textual Practice* 1, 1 (1987): 32–47.

Duvall, John. *Faulkner's Marginal Couple: Invisible Outlaw and Unspeakable Communities.* Austin: University of Texas Press, 1990.

Eco, Umberto. "The Frames of Comic Freedom." *Carnival!,* ed. Thomas A. Sebeok. Berlin: Mouton, 1984. 1–9.

Esonwanne, Uzo. "Enlightenment Epistemology and 'Aesthetic Cognition': Mariama Bâ's *So Long a Letter.*" Nnaemeka, *The Politics of (M)Othering.* 82–100.

Fabre, Geneviève and Robert O'Meally, eds. *History and Memory in African-American Culture.* New York: Oxford University Press, 1994.

Faulkner, William. *Absalom, Absalom!* 1936. New York: Random House, 1964.

Felski, Rita. *Beyond Feminist Aesthetics: Feminist Literature and Social Change.* Cambridge, Mass.: Harvard University Press, 1989.

————. *The Gender of Modernity.* Cambridge, Mass.: Harvard University Press, 1995.

Figes, Eva. *Tragedy and Social Evolution.* New York: Persea Books, 1976.

Finney, Brian. "Temporal Defamiliarization in Toni Morrison's *Beloved.*" *Obsidian II* 5, 1 (1990): 20–36.

Fitzgerald, Jennifer. "Selfhood and Community: Psychoanalysis and Discourse in *Beloved.*" *Modern Fiction Studies* 39, 3/4 (1993): 669–87.

Flax, Jane. *Thinking Fragments: Psychoanalysis, Feminism, and Postmodernism in the Contemporary West.* Berkeley: University of California Press, 1990.

Foley, Barbara. *Radical Representations: Politics and Form in U.S. Proletarian Fiction, 1920–1961.* Durham, N.C.: Duke University Press, 1993.

———. *Telling the Truth: The Theory and Practice of Documentary Fiction.* Ithaca, N.Y.: Cornell University Press, 1986.

Foster, Frances Smith. *Witnessing Slavery: The Development of Ante-Bellum Slave Narratives.* Westport, Conn.: Greenwood Press, 1979.

———. *Written by Herself: Literary Production by African American Women, 1746–1892.* Bloomington: Indiana University Press, 1993.

Frankenberg, Ruth. *White Women, Race Matters: The Social Construction of Whiteness.* Minneapolis: University of Minnesota Press, 1993.

———, ed. *Displacing Whiteness: Essays in Social and Cultural Truth.* Durham, N.C.: Duke University Press, 1997

Frazer, James George. 1913. *The Golden Bough: A Study in Magic and Religion.* London: Macmillan, 1980.

Frye, Northrop. *Anatomy of Criticism: Four Essays.* 3rd ed. Princeton, N.J.: Princeton University Press, 1973.

Gardner, Susan "'Don't Ask for the True Story': A Memoire of Bessie Head." *Hecate* 13, 2 (1986): 110–29.

Gates, Henry Louis, Jr., ed. *Black Literature and Literary Theory.* New York: Methuen, 1984.

———, ed. *Reading Black, Reading Feminist.* New York: Penguin, 1990.

———. *The Signifying Monkey: A Theory of African-American Literary Criticism.* New York: Oxford University Press, 1988.

Gellrich, Michelle. *Tragedy and Theory: The Problem of Conflict Since Aristotle.* Princeton, N.J.: Princeton University Press, 1988.

Gilmore, Leigh. "A Signature of Lesbian Autobiography: 'Gertrice/Altrude.'" *Autobiography and Questions of Gender,* ed. Shirley Neuman. London: Frank Cass, 1991.

Gilroy, Paul. *The Black Atlantic: Modernity and Double Consciousness.* Cambridge, Mass.: Harvard University Press, 1994.

———. *Small Acts: Thoughts on the Politics of Black Cultures.* London: Serpent's Tail, 1993.

Girard, René. *The Scapegoat.* Trans. Yvonne Freccero. Baltimore: Johns Hopkins University Press, 1986.

———. *Things Hidden Since the Foundation of the World.* Coll. Jean-Michel Oughourlian and Guy Lefort, trans. Stephen Bann and Michael Metteer. Stanford, Calif.: Stanford University Press, 1987.

———. *Violence and the Sacred.* Trans. Patrick Gregory. Baltimore: Johns Hopkins University Press, 1977.

Goddard, Horace I. "Imagery in Bessie Head's Work." Abrahams, *The Tragic Life.* 105–10.

Goldberg, Jonathan. "Sodometries." *English Inside and Out: The Places of Literary Criticism,* ed. Susan Gubar and Jonathan Kamholz. New York: Routledge, 1993. 68–86.

Goldman, Anne E. "'I Made the Ink': (Literary) Production and Reproduction in *Dessa Rose* and *Beloved.*" *Feminist Studies* 16, 2 (1990): 313–30.

Goodman, Nelson. *Languages of Art: An Approach to a Theory of Symbols.* Indianapolis: Hackett, 1976.

Gordon, Paul. "Misogyny, Dionysianism and a New Model of Greek Tragedy." *Women's Studies* 17 (1990): 211–18.

Gover, Daniel. "The Fairy Tale and the Nightmare." Abrahams, *The Tragic Life.* 111–22.

Gray, James D. "Shreve's Lesson of Love: Power of the Unsaid in *Absalom, Absalom!*" *New Orleans Review* (Winter 1987): 24–35.

Griffin, Farah Jasmine. *"Who Set You Flowin?": The African-American Migration Narrative.* New York: Oxford University Press, 1995.

Grossberg, Lawrence. *We Gotta Get Out of This Place: Popular Conservatism and Postmodern Culture.* New York: Routledge, 1992.

Grosz, Elizabeth. *Jacques Lacan: A Feminist Introduction.* London: Routledge, 1990.

Gruen. Lori. "Dismantling Oppression: An Analysis of the Connection Between Women and Animals." *Ecofeminism: Women, Animals, Nature,* ed. Greta Gaard. Philadelphia: Temple University Press, 1993. 60–90.

Hall, Stuart et al., eds. *Modernity: An Introduction to Modern Societies.* Oxford: Blackwell, 1996.

Harlow, Barbara. *Resistance Literature.* New York: Methuen, 1987.

Harper, Philip Brian. *Framing the Margins: The Social Logic of Postmodern Culture.* New York: Oxford University Press, 1994.

Harris, Leonard. "Agency and the Concept of the Underclass." Lawson, *The Underclass Question.* 33–54.

Harris, Trudier. "From Exile to Asylum: Religion and Community in the Writings of Contemporary Black Women." Broe and Ingram, *Women's Writing in Exile.* 151–69.

Harvey, David. *The Condition of Postmodernity: An Enquiry into the Origins of Cultural Change.* Oxford: Blackwell, 1989.

Head, Bessie. *The Collector of Treasures.* Oxford: Heinemann, 1977.

———. *A Gesture of Belonging: Letters from Bessie Head, 1965–1979.* Ed. Randolph Vigne. Oxford: Heinemann, 1991.

———. *A Question of Power.* Oxford: Heinemann, 1974.

———. *A Woman Alone: Autobiographical Writings.* Oxford: Heinemann, 1990.

Hegel, Georg Wilhelm. *Aesthetics: Lectures on Fine Art,* vol. 1. Trans. T. M. Knox. Oxford: Clarendon Press, 1975.

Hemenway, Robert E. *Zora Neale Hurston: A Literary Biography.* Urbana: University of Illinois Press, 1977.

Hemmingway, Beulah S. "Through the Prism of Africanity: A Preliminary Investigation of Zora Neale Hurston's *Mules and Men.*" *Zora in Florida,* ed. Steve Glassman and Kathryn Lee Seidel. Orlando: University of Central Florida Press. 38–45.

Henderson, Mae Gwendolyn. "Speaking in Tongues: Dialogics, Dialectics, and the Black Woman Writer's Literary Tradition." Gates, *Reading Black.* 116–42.

———. "Toni Morrison's *Beloved*: Re-Membering the Body as Historical Text." Spillers, *Comparative American Identities.* 62–86.

Hernton, Calvin C. *The Sexual Mountain and Black Women Writers: Adventures in Sex, Literature, and Real Life.* Foreword Gloria Wade-Gayles. New York: Anchor Books, 1990.

Hirsch, Marianne. "Maternal Narratives: 'Cruel Enough to Stop the Blood.'" Gates, *Reading Black*. 415–30.

Hite, Molly. *The Other Side of the Story: Structures and Strategies of Contemporary Feminist Narrative*. Ithaca, N.Y.: Cornell University Press, 1989.

Hoesterey, Ingeborg, ed. *Zeitgeist in Babel: The Postmodernist Controversy*. Bloomington: Indiana University Press, 1991.

Hoffmann, Léon-François. 1984. *Essays on Haitian Literature*. Pueblo, Colo: Passigiata, 1999.

Holloway, Karla F. C. *The Character of the Word: The Texts of Zora Neale Hurston*. New York: Greenwood Press, 1987.

———. *Moorings and Metaphors: Figures of Culture and Gender in Black Women's Literature*. New Brunswick, N. J.: Rutgers University Press, 1992.

Holloway, Karla F. C. and Stephanie A. Demetrokopoulos. *New Dimensions of Spirituality: A Biracial and Bicultural Reading of the Novels of Toni Morrison*. Westport, Conn.: Greenwood Press, 1987.

———. "Revision and [Re]membrance: A Theory of Literary Structure in African American Women's Writing." *African American Review* 24, 4 (1990): 617–31.

hooks, bell. *Ain't I a Woman: Black Women and Feminism*. Boston: South End Press, 1981.

———. *Feminist Theory: From Margin to Center*. Boston: South End Press, 1984.

———. *Killing Rage, Ending Racism*. New York: Henry Holt, 1995.

———. *Outlaw Culture: Resisting Representations*. New York and London: Routledge, 1994.

———. *Talking Back: Thinking Feminist, Thinking Black*. Boston: South End Press, 1989.

———. *Teaching to Transgress: Education as the Practice of Freedom*. New York and London: Routledge, 1994.

———. "Writing the Subject: Reading *The Color Purple*." Gates, *Reading Black* 454–70.

———. *Yearning: Race, Gender, and Cultural Politics*. Boston: South End Press, 1990.

Howe, Irving. "Mass Society and Postmodern Fiction." *Partisan Review* 26 (1959): 426–36.

Hudson-Weems, Clenora. "Africana Womanism." Nnaemeka, *Sisterhood*. 149–62.

Hughes, Langston and Zora Neale Hurston. *Mule Bone: A Comedy of Negro Life*. Ed. George Houston Bass and Henry Louis Gates, Jr. New York: HarperCollins, 1991.

Hull, Gloria T. *Color, Sex, and Poetry: Three Women Writers of the Harlem Renaissance*. Bloomington: Indiana University Press, 1987.

———. "'What Is It I Think She's Doing Anyhow?': A Reading of Toni Cade Bambara's *The Salt Eaters*." *Conjuring: Black Women, Fiction, and Literary Tradition*, ed. Marjorie Pryse and Hortense J. Spillers. Bloomington: Indiana University Press, 1985. 216–32.

Hurston, Zora Neale. *I Love Myself When I Am Laughing . . . And Then Again When I Am Looking Mean and Serious: A Zora Neale Hurston Reader*. Ed. Alice Walker, Intro. Mary Helen Washington. Old Westbury, N. Y.: Feminist Press, 1979.

———. *Dust Tracks on a Road*. 1942. Foreword Maya Angelou. New York: Harper-Perennial, 1991.

———. *Mules and Men*. 1935. Ed. Henry Louis Gates, Jr., Preface Franz Boas, Foreword Arnold Rampersad. New York: Harper and Row, 1990.

————. *Tell My Horse: Voodoo and Life in Haiti and Jamaica.* 1938. Ed. Henry Louis Gates, Jr. Foreword Ishmael Reed. New York: Harper and Row, 1990.

————. *Their Eyes Were Watching God.* 1937. Foreword Sherley Anne Williams. Urbana: University of Illinois Press, 1978.

Ibrahim, Huma. *Bessie Head: Subversive Identities in Exile.* Charlottesville: University Press of Virginia, 1996.

————. "Ontological Victimhood: 'Other' Bodies in Madness and Exile—Toward a Third World Feminist Epistemology." Nnaemeka, *The Politics of (M)Othering.* 147–61.

Irigaray, Luce. *Speculum of the Other Woman.* Trans. Gillian C. Gill. Ithaca, N.Y.: Cornell University Press, 1985.

Irwin, John T. *Doubling and Incest, Repetition and Revenge: A Speculative Reading of Faulkner.* Baltimore: Johns Hopkins University Press, 1975.

Jablon, Madelyn. "Rememory, Dream History, and Revision in Toni Morrison's *Beloved* and Alice Walker's *The Temple of My Familiar.*" *College Language Association Journal* 37, 2 (1993): 136–44.

James, C. L. R. *The C.L.R. James Reader.* Ed. Anna Grimshaw. Oxford: Blackwell, 1992.

James, Joy. "Racism, Genocide, and Resistance: The Politics of Language and International Law." *Marxism in the Postmodern Age: Confronting the New World Order,* ed. Antonio Callari, Stephen Cullenberg, and Carole Biewener. London and New York: Guilford Press, 1995. 115–25.

Jameson, Fredric. *The Ideology of Theory: Essays 1971–1986.* 2 vols. Theory and Literature 48–49. Minneapolis: University of Minnesota Press, 1988.

————. "Marx's Purloined Letter." *New Left Review* 209 (1995): 75–110.

————. *The Political Unconscious: Narrative as a Socially Symbolic Act.* Ithaca, N.Y.: Cornell University Press, 1981.

————. *Postmodernism: Or, The Cultural Logic of Late Capitalism.* Durham, N.C.: Duke University Press, 1991.

————. *The Seeds of Time.* New York: Columbia University Press, 1994.

JanMohamed, Abdul R. *Manichaean Aesthetics: The Politics of Literature in Colonial Africa.* Amherst: University of Massachusetts Press, 1983.

Johnson, Barbara. "Metaphor, Metonymy, and Voice in *Their Eyes Were Watching God.*" Gates, *Black Literature.* 205–19.

————. "Thresholds of Difference: Structures of Address in Zora Neale Hurston." *A World of Difference.* Baltimore: Johns Hopkins University Press, 1987. 172–83.

Jones, Anne Goodwyn. "Desire and Dismemberment: Faulkner and the Ideology of Penetration." Kartiganer and Abadie, *Faulkner and Ideology.* 129–71.

Jones, Bessie W. and Audrey Vinson. "An Interview with Toni Morrison." *Conversations with Toni Morrison,* ed. Danielle Taylor-Guthrie. Jackson: University Press of Mississippi, 1994. 171–87.

Joseph, Gloria. *Common Differences: Conflicts in Black and White Feminist Perspectives.* Garden City, N.Y.: Anchor Books, 1981.

Judy, Ronald A. T. *(Dis)Forming the American Canon: African-Arabic Slave Narratives and the Vernacular.* London and New York: Verso, 1992.

Jung, Carl G. *Modern Man in Search of a Soul.* New York: Harcourt, Brace and World, 1934.

Kartiganer, Donald M. and Ann J. Abadie, eds. *Faulkner and Ideology: Faulkner and Yoknapatawpha, 1992.* Jackson: University Press of Mississippi, 1995.

Keenan, Sally. "Myth, History, and Motherhood in Toni Morrison's *Beloved*." White, *Recasting the World*. 45–79.

Kenner, Hugh. *A Homemade World: The American Modernist Writers*. New York: William Morrow, 1975.

Kott, Ian. *The Eating of the Gods: An Interpretation of Greek Tragedy*. Trans. Boleslaw Taborski and Edward J. Czerwinski. New York: Random House, 1973,

Kristeva, Julia. *About Chinese Women*. New York: Urizen Books, 1977.

Krupat, Arnold. *Ethnocriticism: Ethnography/History/Literature*. Berkeley: University of California Press, 1992.

Ladd, Barbara. " 'The Direction of the Howling': Nationalism and the Color Line in *Absalom, Absalom!*" *Subjects and Citizens: Nation, Race, and Gender from Oroonoko to Anita Hill*, ed. Michael Moon and Cathy N. Davidson. Durham, N.C.: Duke University Press, 1995. 345–72.

Laguerre, Michel S. *Voodoo and Politics in Haiti*. New York: St. Martin's Press, 1989.

Lawson, Bill E., ed. *The Underclass Question*. Philadelphia: Temple University Press, 1992.

Lenson, David. *Achilles' Choice: Examples of Modern Tragedy*. Princeton, N.J.: Princeton University Press, 1975.

Lionnet, Françoise. *Autobiographical Voices: Race, Gender, Self-Portraiture*. Ithaca, N.Y.: Cornell University Press, 1989.

———. "Geographies of Pain: Captive Bodies and Violent Acts in the Fictions of Gayl Jones, Bessie Head, and Myriam Warner-Vieyra." Nnaemeka, *The Politics of (M)Othering*. 205–27.

———. *Postcolonial Representations: Women, Literature, Identity*. Ithaca, N.Y.: Cornell University Press, 1995.

Lowe, John. *Jump at the Sun: Zora Neale Hurston's Cosmic Comedy*. Urbana: University of Illinois Press, 1994.

Lubiano, Wahneema. "Henry Louis Gates, Jr., and African-American Literary Discourse." *New England Quarterly* 62,4 (1989): 561–72.

———. "Mapping the Interstices Between Afro-American Cultural Discourse and Cultural Studies: A Prolegomenon." *Callaloo* 19,1 (1996): 68–77.

———, ed. *The House That Race Built: Black Americans, U.S. Terrain*. New York: Pantheon, 1997.

MacIntyre, Alisdair. *After Virtue: A Study in Moral Theory*. London: Duckworth, 1981.

Mama, Amina. "Sheroes and Villains: Conceptualizing Colonial and Contemporary Violence Against Women in Africa." Alexander and Mohanty, *Feminist Genealogies*. 46–62.

Marsh, James L., Merold Westphal, and John D. Caputo, eds. *Modernity and Its Discontents*. New York: Fordham University Press, 1992.

Matthews, John T. *The Play of Faulkner's Language*. Ithaca, N.Y.: Cornell University Press, 1982.

Mbiti, John S. *African Religions and Philosophy*. Rev. ed. Oxford: Heinemann, 1990.

McDowell, Deborah E. "Boundaries: Or Distant Relations and Close Kin." *Afro-American Literary Study in the 1990s*, ed. Houston A. Baker, Jr. and Patricia Redmond. Chicago: University of Chicago Press, 1989.

———. *"The Changing Same": Black Women's Literature, Criticism, and Theory*. Bloomington: Indiana University Press, 1995.

———. "Negotiating the Tenses: Witnessing Slavery After Freedom—*Dessa Rose*." McDowell and Rampersad, *Slavery and the Literary Imagination*. 144–64.

McDowell, Deborah E. and Arnold Rampersad, eds. *Slavery and the Literary Imagination.* Baltimore and London: Johns Hopkins University Press, 1989.

———. "'That nameless . . . shameless impulse': Sexuality in Nella Larsen's *Quicksand* and *Passing.*" *Black Feminist Criticism and Critical Theory,* ed. Joe Weixlmann and Houston A. Baker, Jr. Greenwood, Fla.: Penkevill, 1988. 139–67.

McHale, Brian. *Postmodernist Fiction.* New York: Methuen, 1987.

Braxton, Joanne M. and Andrée Nicola McLaughlin, eds. *Wild Women in the Whirlwind: Afra-American Culture and the Contemporary Literary Renaissance.* New Brunswick, N.J.: Rutgers University Press, 1990.

Miles, Angela. "North American Feminisms/Global Feminisms: Contradictory or Complementary?" Nnaemeka, *Sisterhood.* 163–82.

Miller, J. Hillis. "Ideology and Topography in Faulkner's *Absalom, Absalom!*" Kartiganer and Abadie, *Faulkner and Ideology.* 253–76.

Mohanty, Satya P. "Colonial Legacies, Multicultural Futures: Relativism, Objectivity, and the Challenge of Otherness." *PMLA* 110,19 (1995): 108–18.

———. "The Epistemic Status of Cultural Identity: On *Beloved* and the Postcolonial Position." *Cultural Critique* 24 (1993): 41–80.

Morrison, Toni. *Beloved.* New York: New American Library, 1988.

———. "A Conversation with Sheldon Hackney." *Humanities* (March/April 1996): 4–9, 48–50.

———. *Conversations with Toni Morrison.* Ed. Danielle Taylor-Guthrie. Jackson: University Press of Mississippi, 1994.

———. "Home." Lubiano, *The House That Race Built.* 3–12.

———. "Living Memory: Meeting Toni Morrison." Interview. Gilroy, *Small Acts: Thoughts on the Politics of Black Cultures.* 175–82.

———. "Nobel Prize Lecture, 1993." *Humanities* (March/April 1996): 14–17.

———. *Paradise.* New York: Knopf, 1997.

———. *Playing in the Dark: Whiteness and the Literary Imagination.* New York: Vintage, 1992.

———. "Unspeakable Things Unspoken. The Afro-American Presence in American Literature." *Michigan Quarterly Review* 28,1 (1989): 1–34.

Moya, Paula M. L. "Postmodernism, 'Realism,' and the Politics of Identity." Alexander and Mohanty, *Feminist Genealogies.* 125–50.

Mullen, Harryette. "Runaway Tongue: Resistant Orality in *Uncle Tom's Cabin, Our Nig, Incidents in the Life of a Slave Girl,* and *Beloved.*" *The Culture of Sentiment: Race, Gender, and Sentimentality in Nineteenth-Century America,* ed. Shirley Samuels. New York: Oxford University Press, 1992. 244–64.

Nancy, Claire. "Euripide et le parti des femmes." *Quaderni Urbinati de Cultura Classica* 17 (1984): 111–36.

Napora, Joseph. "The Story and the Living: Meridel Le Sueur's *The Girl.*" Meridel Le Sueur, *The Girl,* rev. ed. Albuquerque, N. M.: West End Press, 1990. 147–58.

Nasta, Susheila, ed. *Motherlands: Black Women's Writing from Africa, the Caribbean and South Asia.*" New Brunswick, N. J.: Rutgers University Press, 1992.

Naylor, Gloria. *The Women of Brewster Place.* New York: Penguin, 1983.

———. *Mama Day.* New York: Vintage, 1989.

Nekola, Charlotte and Paula Rabinowitz, eds. *Writing Red: An Anthology of American Women Writers, 1930–1940.* Foreword Toni Morrison. New York: Feminist Press, 1987.

Nelson, T. G. A. *Comedy: An Introduction to Comedy in Literature, Drama, and Cinema.* New York: Oxford University Press, 1990.

Nicholson, Linda J., ed. *Feminism/Postmodernism.* New York: Routledge, 1990.

Nietzsche, Friedrich Wilhelm. *The Birth of Tragedy: or, Hellenism and Pessimism.* The Complete Works of Friedrich Nietzsche, vol.1. Trans. William A. Haussman. New York: Russell and Russell, 1964.

Nnaemeka, Obioma, ed. *The Politics of (M)Othering: Womanhood, Identity, and Resistance in African Literature.* London: Routledge, 1997.

————. "Introduction: Imag(in)ing Knowledge, Power, and Subversion in the Margins." Nnaemeka, *The Politics of (M)Othering.* 1–25.

————, ed. *Sisterhood, Feminisms and Power: From Africa to the Diaspora.* Trenton, N.J. and Amara, Eritrea: Africa World Press, 1998.

————. "Urban Spaces, Women's Places: Polygamy as Sign in Mariama Bâ's Novels." Nnaemeka, *The Politics of (M)Othering,* 162–91.

North, Michael. *The Dialect of Modernism: Race, Language and Twentieth-Century Literature.* New York: Oxford University Press, 1994.

Ogungbesan, Kolawole. "The Cape Gooseberry Also Grows in Botswana: Alienation and Commitment in the Writings of Bessie Head." *Journal of African Studies* 6 (1979–80): 206–12.

O'Hara, Daniel T. *Radical Parody: American Culture and Critical Agency After Foucault.* New York: Columbia University Press, 1992.

Ola, Virginia Uzoma. *The Life and Works of Bessie Head.* Lewiston, N.Y.: E. Mellen Press, 1994.

Omolade, Barbara. *The Rising Song of African American Women.* London and New York: Routledge, 1994.

O'Neill, Patrick. *The Comedy of Entropy: Humour, Narrative, Reading.* Toronto, Buffalo, and London: University of Toronto Press, 1990.

Page, Sally R. *Faulkner's Women: Characterization and Meaning.* Deland, Fla.: Everett/Edwards, 1972.

Palmer, Richard H. *Tragedy and Tragic Theory: An Analytical Guide.* Westport, Conn.: Greenwood Press, 1992.

Parker, Andrew et al., eds. *Nationalisms and Sexualities.* New York and London: Routledge, 1992.

Parry, Benita. *Conrad and Imperialism: Ideological Boundaries and Visionary Frontiers.* London: Macmillan, 1983.

Patterson, David. *Literature and Spirit: Essays on Bakhtin and His Contemporaries.* Lexington: University Press of Kentucky, 1988.

Pavel, Thomas. "Tragedy and the Sacred: Notes Towards a Semantic Characterization of a Fictional Genre." *Poetics* 10, 2/3 (1981): 231–42.

Pearse, Adetokunbo. "Apartheid and Madness: Bessie Head's *A Question of Power.*" *Kunapipi* 5,2 (1983): 81–93.

Peters, Pearlie. "Women and Assertive Voice in Hurston's Fiction and Folklore." *Literary Griot* 4, 1–2 (1992): 100–110.

Philip, Marlene Nourbese. "An Extract from 'Discourse on the Logic of Language.'" Preface, Nasta, *Motherlands.*

Porter, Carolyn. "William Faulkner: Innocence Historicized." *William Faulkner's Absalom, Absalom!*, ed. Harold Bloom. New York: Chelsea House, 1987.

Ragan, David Paul. *William Faulkner's Absalom, Absalom!: A Critical Study.* Studies in Modern Literature 85. Ann Arbor, Mich.: UMI Research Press, 1987.

Retallack, Joan. "Post-Scriptum—High Modern." *Postmodern Genres,* ed. Marjorie Perloff. Forewords Robert Con Davis and Ronald Schleifer. Norman: University of Oklahoma Press, 1989.

Rigney, Barbara Hill. "'A Story to Pass On': Ghosts and the Significance of History in Toni Morrison's *Beloved.*" *Haunting the House of Fiction: Feminist Perspec-*

tives on Ghost Stories by American Women, ed. Lynette Carpenter and Wendy K. Kolmar. Knoxville: University of Tennessee Press, 1991. 229–35.

Rimstead, Roxanne. "Between Theories and Anti-Theories: Moving Toward Marginal Women's Subjectivities." *Women's Studies Quarterly* 23, 1/2 (1995): 199–218.

Roberts, John W. "The African American Animal Trickster as Hero." *Redefining American Literary History,* ed. A. LaVonne Brown Ruoff and Jerry W. Ward, Jr. New York: Modern Language Association, 1990. 97–114.

Robinson, Amy. "It Takes One to Know One: Passing and Communities of Common Interest." *Critical Inquiry* 20 (1994): 715–36.

Robinson, Lillian S. "At Play in the Mind-Fields." *Women's Review of Books* 7, 10–11 (1990): 32–33.

———. *Sex, Class, and Culture.* Bloomington: Indiana University Press, 1978.

———. "Waving the Flag at Racism and Sexism: The Semiotics and Politics of the Political Correctness Flap." Lecture, Bates College, May 1992.

Rooney, Caroline. "'Dangerous Knowledge' and the Poetics of Survival: A Reading of *Our Sister Killjoy* and *A Question of Power.*" Nasta, *Motherlands.* 99–128.

Rosaldo, Renato. *Culture and Truth: The Remaking of Social Analysis.* Boston: Beacon Press, 1989.

Ross, Andrew, ed. *Universal Abandon: The Politics of Postmodernism.* Minneapolis: University of Minnesota Press, 1988.

Ross, Stephen M. *Fiction's Inexhaustible Voice: Speech and Writing in Faulkner.* Athens: University of Georgia Press, 1989.

Rushdy, Ashraf H. A. "Daughters Signfyin(g) History: The Example of Toni Morrison's *Beloved.*" *American Literature* 64, 3 (1992): 567–97.

———. "'Rememory': Primal Scenes and Constructions in Toni Morrison's Novels." *Toni Morrison's Fiction: Contemporary Criticism,* ed. David Middleton. New York and London: Garland, 1997. 135–64.

Rushing, Andrea Benton. "On Becoming a Feminist: Learning from Africa." Terborg-Penn and Rushing, *Women in Africa.* 121–34.

Sagan, Eli. *The Lust to Annihilate: A Psychoanalytic Study of Violence in Ancient Greek Culture.* New York: Psychohistory Press, 1979.

Said, Edward W. *Culture and Imperialism.* New York: Vintage, 1993.

———. *The World, the Text, and the Critic.* Cambridge, Mass.: Harvard University Press, 1983.

Saldívar-Hull, Sonia. "Wrestling Your Ally: Stein, Racism, and Feminist Critical Practice." Broe and Ingram, *Women's Writing in Exile.* 181–98.

Schenck, Celeste M. "Exiled by Genre: Modernism, Canonicity, and the Politics of Literary Revision." Broe and Ingram, *Women's Writing in Exile.* 225–50.

Scobie, Stephen. "The Allure of Multiplicity: Metaphor and Metonymy in Cubism and Gertrude Stein." *Gertrude Stein and the Making of Literature,* ed. Shirley Neuman and Ira B. Nadel. Boston: Northeastern University Press, 1988. 98–118.

Sedgwick, Eve Kosofsky. *Epistemology of the Closet.* Berkeley: University of California Press, 1990.

———. "Socratic Raptures, Socratic Ruptures: Notes Toward Queer Performativity." *English Inside and Out: The Places of Literary Criticism,* ed. Susan Gubar and Jonathan Kamholz. New York: Routledge, 1993. 122–36.

Sharpe, Jenny. "Figures of Colonial Resistance." *Modern Fiction Studies* 35, 1 (1989): 137–55.

Shulman, George. "American Political Culture, Prophetic Narration, and Toni Morrison's *Beloved.*" *Political Theory* 24, 2 (1996): 295–314.

Silk, M. S. and J. P. Stern. *Nietzsche on Tragedy.* Cambridge: Cambridge University Press, 1981.

Silverman, Debra B. "Nella Larsen's *Quicksand*: Untangling the Webs of Exoticism." *African American Review* 27, 4 (1993): 599–614.

Slemon, Stephen. "Unsettling the Empire: Resistance Theory for the Second World." *World Literature Written in English* 30, 2 (1990): 30–41.

Smedley, Agnes. *Daughter of Earth.* Foreword Alice Walker. New York: Feminist Press, 1987.

Smith, Barbara. "The Truth That Never Hurts: Black Lesbians in Fiction in the 1980's." Braxton and McLaughlin, *Wild Women in the Whirlwind.* 213–45.

Smith, Valerie. "Black Feminist Theory and Representations of the 'Other.' " Wall, *Changing Our Own Words.* 38–57.

———. " 'Loopholes of Retreat': Architecture and Ideology in Harriet Jacobs's *Incidents in the Life of a Slave Girl.*" Gates, *Reading Black.* 212–26.

———. *Self-Discovery and Authority in Afro-American Narrative.* Cambridge, Mass.: Harvard University Press, 1987.

Snead, James. "European Pedigrees/African Contagion: Nationality, Narrative, and Communality in Tutuola, Achebe, and Reed." Bhabha, *Nation and Narration.* 231–49.

———. *Figures of Division: William Faulkner's Major Novels.* New York: Methuen, 1986.

———. "Repetition as a Figure of Black Culture." Gates, *Black Literature.* 59–80.

Spillers, Hortense J. "Changing the Letter: The Yokes, the Jokes of Discourse, or, Mrs. Stowe, Mr. Reed." McDowell and Rampersad, *Slavery and the Literary Imagination.* 26–61.

———, ed. *Comparative American Identities: Race, Sex, and Nationality in the Modern Text.* Essays from the English Institute. New York and London: Routledge, 1991. 1–25.

———. "Mama's Baby, Papa's Maybe: An American Grammar Book." *Diacritics* 17, 2 (1987): 65–81.

Snyder, John. *Prospects of Power: Tragedy, Satire, the Essay, and the Theory of Genre.* Louisville: University Press of Kentucky, 1991.

Spivak, Gayatri Chakravorty. *In Other Worlds: Essays in Cultural Politics.* New York: Methuen, 1987.

———. *The Post-Colonial Critic: Interviews, Strategies, Dialogues.* Ed. Sarah Harasym. New York and London: Routledge, 1990.

Steady, Filomena Chioma. "Women and Collective Action: Female Models in Transition." *Theorizing Black Feminisms: The Visionary Pragmatism of Black Women,* ed. Stanlie M. James and Abena P. A. Abusia. London: Routledge, 1993.

Stein, Gertrude. *Fernhurst, Q.E.D., and Other Early Writings.* New York: Liveright, 1971.

———. *Ida: A Novel.* 3rd ed. New York: Vintage, 1972.

———. *Three Lives.* 2nd ed. New York: Vintage, 1936.

Steiner, George. *After Babel: Aspects of Language and Translation.* New York: Oxford University Press, 1975.

———. *Antigones.* New York: Oxford University Press, 1984.

———. " 'Critic'/'Reader.' " *Real Voices: On Reading,* ed. Philip Davis. New York: St. Martin's Press, 1997. 3–37.

———. *The Death of Tragedy.* New York: Knopf, 1961.

———. "A Note on Absolute Tragedy." *Journal of Literature and Theology* 4, 2 (1990): 147–56.

———. *Real Presences.* Chicago: University of Chicago Press, 1989.

Stepto, Robert B. *From Behind the Veil: A Study of Afro-American Narrative.* Urbana: University of Illinois Press, 1979.

Stimpson, Catherine. "Gertrude Stein and the Transposition of Gender." *The Poetics of Gender,* ed. Nancy K. Miller. New York: Columbia University Press, 1998. 1–18.

———. "Gertrude Stein and the Lesbian Lie." *American Women's Autobiography: Fea(s)ts of Memory,* ed. Margo Culley. Madison: University of Wisconsin Press, 1992. 152–66.

Stout, Jeffrey. *Ethics After Babel: The Languages of Morals and Their Discontents.* Boston: Beacon Press, 1988.

Sugnet, Charles. "*Nervous Conditions*: Dangarembga's Feminist Reinvention of Fanon." Nnaemeka, *The Politics of M(O)thering.* 33–49.

Suleiman, Susan Rubin. *Subversive Intent: Gender, Politics, and the Avant-Garde.* Cambridge, Mass.: Harvard University Press, 1990.

Sundquist, Eric J. *Faulkner: The House Divided.* Baltimore: Johns Hopkins University Press, 1983.

Taylor, Carole Anne. "Ideologies of the Funny." *Centennial Review* 36, 2 (1992): 265–96.

———. "Positioning Subjects and Objects: Agency, Narration, Relationality." *Hypatia: A Journal of Feminist Philosophy* 8,1 (1993): 55–80.

Terborg-Penn, Rosalyn. "Slavery and Women in Africa and the Diaspora." Terborg-Penn and Rushing, *Women in Africa.* 217–30.

Terborg-Penn, Rosalyn and Andrea Benton Rushing, eds. *Women in Africa and the African Diaspora: A Reader.* Washington D.C.: Howard University Press, 1996.

Thurman, Judith. "A House Divided." *New Yorker,* 21 November 1987: 175–90.

Trace, Jacqueline. "Dark Goddess: Black Feminist Theology in Morrison's *Beloved*." *Obsidian II* 5, 3 (1991): 14–30.

Tyler, Carole-Anne. "The Feminine Look." *Theory Between the Disciplines: Authority/Vision/Politics,* ed. Martin Kreiswirth and Mark A. Cheetham. Ann Arbor: University of Michigan Press, 1990.

Ungar, Sheldon. "Self-Mockery: An Alternative Form of Self-Presentation." *Symbolic Interaction* 7, 1 (1984): 121–33.

Wadlington, Warwick. *Reading Faulknerian Tragedy.* Ithaca, N.Y.: Cornell University Press, 1987.

Wald, Priscilla. "A 'Losing Self-Sense': *The Making of Americans* and the Anxiety of Identity." *Constituting Americans: Cultural Anxiety and Narrative Form.* Durham, N.C.: Duke University Press, 1995. 237–98.

Walker, Alice. *Her Blue Body Everything We Know: Earthling Poems, 1965–90 Complete.* San Diego: Harcourt Brace Jovanovich, 1991.

———. *The Color Purple: A Novel.* New York: Harcourt Brace Jovanovich, 1982.

———. *In Search of Our Mothers' Gardens: Womanist Prose by Alice Walker.* San Diego: Harcourt Brace Jovanovich, 1983.

———. *The Temple of My Familiar.* San Diego: Harcourt Brace Jovanovich, 1989.

Wall, Cheryl A., ed. *Changing Our Own Words: Essays on Criticism, Theory, and Writing by Black Women.* New Brunswick, N.J.: Rutgers University Press, 1989.

———. "*Mules and Men* and Women: Zora Neale Hurston's Strategies of Narration and Visions of Female Empowerment." *Black American Literature Forum* 23 (1989): 661–80.

————. "Passing for What? Aspects of Identity in Nella Larsen's Novels." *Black American Literature Forum* 20 (1986): 97–111.

————. "Poets and Versifiers, Singers and Signifiers: Women of the Harlem Renaissance." *Women, the Arts, and the 1920s in Paris and New York*, ed. Kenneth W. Wheeler and Virginia Lee Lussier. New Brunswick, N. J.: Transaction Books, 1982. 74–98.

————. "Zora Neale Hurston: Changing Her Own Words." *American Novelists Revisited: Essays in Feminist Criticism*, ed. Fritz Fleischmann. Boston: G. K. Hall, 1982. 371–93.

Wallace, Michelle. "Modernism, Postmodernism, and the Problem of the Visual in Afro-American Culture." *Out There: Marginalization and Contemporary Cultures*, ed. Russell Ferguson et al. Cambridge, Mass.: MIT Press, 1990. 39–50.

————. "Variations on Negation and the Heresy of Black Feminist Creativity." Gates, *Reading Black.* 52–67.

Walsh, Margaret. "The Enchanted World of *The Color Purple.*" *Southern Quarterly* 25, 2 (1987): 89–101.

Walton, Priscilla. " 'What She Got To Sing About?' Comedy and *The Color Purple.*" *Ariel: A Review of International English Literature* 21, 2 (1990): 59–74.

Ward, Cynthia. "Bound to Matter: The Father's Pen and Mother Tongues." Nnaemeka, *The Politics of (M)Othering.* 114–29.

Weinstein, Phillip M. *Faulkner's Subject: A Cosmos No One Owns.* New York: Cambridge University Press, 1992.

————. *What Else But Love?: The Ordeal of Race in Faulkner and Morrison.* New York: Columbia University Press, 1996.

Wendell, Susan. "Oppression and Victimization: Choice and Responsibility." *Hypatia: A Journal of Feminist Philosophy* 5, 3 (1990): 15–46.

Werner, Craig H. *Playing the Changes: From Afro-Modernism to the Jazz Impulse.* Urbana: University of Illinois Press, 1994.

West, Cornel. "Philosophy and the Urban Underclass." Lawson, *The Underclass Question.* 191–201.

White, Jonathan, ed. *Recasting the World: Writing after Colonialism.* Baltimore and London: Johns Hopkins University Press, 1993.

Williams, Patricia, "The Ethnic Scarring of American Whiteness." Lubiano, *The House That Race Built.* 253–63.

Williams, Raymond. *Modern Tragedy.* London: Chatto and Windus, 1966.

Winnett, Susan. "Coming Unstrung: Women, Men, Narrative, and Principles of Pleasure." *PMLA* 105, 3 (1990): 505–18.

Wisker, Gina. " 'Disremembered and Unaccounted For': Reading Toni Morrison's *Beloved* and Alice Walker's *The Temple of My Familiar.*" *Black Women's Writing*, ed. Wisker. New York: St. Martin's Press, 1993. 78–95.

Willis, Susan. *A Primer for Daily Life.* London and New York: Routledge, 1991.

————. "Eruptions of Funk: Historicizing Toni Morrison." Gates, *Black Literature.* 263–84.

————. *Specifying: Black Women Writing the American Experience.* Madison: University of Wisconsin Press, 1987.

Wolff, Janet. *Resident Alien: Feminist Cultural Criticism.* New Haven, Conn.: Yale University Press, 1995.

Woodfield, Malcolm J. "Tragedy and Modernity in Sophocles, Shakespeare and Hardy." *Journal of Literature and Theology* 4, 2 (1990): 194–218.

Zavarzadeh, Mas'ud and Donald Morton. *Theory, (Post)Modernity, Opposition: An*

"Other" Introduction to Literary and Cultural Theory. Washington D.C.: Maisonneuve, 1991.

Zeitlin, Froma I. "Playing the Other: Theater, Theatricality, and the Feminine in Greek Drama." *Representations* 11 (1985): 63–94.

Zender, Karl. *The Crossing of the Ways: William Faulkner, the South, and the Modern World.* New Brunswick and London: Rutgers University Press, 1989.

Zillman, Dolf. "Disparagement Humor." *Handbook of Humor Research,* vol. 1. New York: Springer-Verlag, 1983. 85–107.

Ziv, Avner. *Personality and Sense of Humor.* New York: Springer, 1984.

Žižek, Slavoj. *For They Know Not What They Do: Enjoyment as a Political Factor.* London: Verso, 1991.

———. *The Sublime Object of Ideology.* London: Verso, 1989.

———. "Two Ways to Avoid the Real of Desire." *Looking Awry: An Introduction to Jacques Lacan Through Popular Culture.* Cambridge, Mass.: MIT Press, 1991.

Index

Acknowledgments

In the belief that people rather than institutions need acknowledgment, I want to pass directly to them, even though the necessary convention of the list belies the nature of the gratitude. Appropriate to a work about suffering and laughter, and about how present understanding requires recursive change in any past, I start with gratitude to Maria Escobar, Juana Quiroa, and Andrea Rodriguez, *mujeres de fuerza* whose courageous energy in organizing at DeCoster Egg Farms in Maine demonstrates amazingly prinipled good will, both toward those tempted into cooptation and toward those whose privilege allows an activism with minimal personal risk; their critical kinship, both intellectual and social, brings more sharply forward the black women in church basements in the 1960s, who practiced an activism that disallowed any of the easier solidarities of the next thirty years and who tempered feminism with a clear vision of ongoing, communal struggle; such political and spirit-work found celebration in the work of Toni Cade Bambara in the 1970s long before I met her in the '80s, and therefore to Toni (now in spirit) not just for the art and the Medusa-figure as impetus for this work, but also for the tough charity of her engagements; to Edward Said for first introducing me, more than twenty years ago now, to how both forms and theories of resistance adapt to their positioning; to Joseph Boskin, Ronald Schleifer, and Kenneth Surin for significant encouragement at crucial stages; to Janet Zandy for exceedingly generous overall support, both personal and intellectual; to bell hooks for her admonitions about the courage of engagement, and for a model of teaching that so well theorizes a critical activism; to Maryemma Graham, Evelyn Hawthorne, Wahneema Lubiano, Soyini Madison, Carlene Young, and Karl Zender for generously constructive suggestions about particular ideas or chapters; to Jerome Singerman, Humanities Editor of the University of Pennsylvania Press, for wit and wisdom, patience and encouragement; to Eugenia DeLamotte for the close attentions of an extraordinary reader and critic; to Freida High W. Tesfagiorgis for creating the art that captures the spiritual dimensions of black women's "interventions in this world," and for allowing me to use "Transformation" on my cover even though it has personal significance for her; to instrumental friends, colleagues, and, of course, readers: William Corlett, Sanford Freedman, David Kolb, Yvette LaChapelle, Christina Malcolmson, Laura Malloy, Liz Muether, William Pope L., Lavina and Rajiv Shankar, Charlotte Templin, and Anne Thompson; to Carolyn Chute, Yvonne DiBuffalo, and John Mohawk, who act as worthy guides for changing both institutions and "structures of feeling"; to President Don Harward of Bates College for important support, and to those in the Community-ERA, the Maine Rural Workers Coalition, and the Maine People's Alliance for that "steadfastness akin to fortitude" (Katie Cannon) of those who, among so many others, live the paradoxes of resistance.

In the bolder print of long-term kinship and indebtedness, I want to thank: Charles (Val) and Barbara Carnegie, Timothy Chin, Elizabeth Eames, Eloisa Gordon-Mora, Irv Kurki, Francesca Lopez, Cynthia Snow, Elizabeth Szöke, and Anne Thompson for the sustaining kindness of tried-and-true friends; Leslie Hill and Walter Cade III for the numberless hours of intensely personal and revelatory discussions about intercultural negotiations and much else, discussions that perhaps only happen in the context of friendship characterized by a highly serious intimacy and hilarity; Eliot King Smith for the radical soul of a pianoman and scholar who fought long with dominance before he came, formally, to the study of cultural resistance; Eric Taylor for the energy and enthusiasm of his support, the moral integrity of his commitments, and for keeping the banter always loving; and my partner William Corlett for the *extra-vagance* of all his surpassingly free and daily gifts.

Portions of several chapters come (reprinted by permission) from articles originally appearing, in different form, as the following: "Humor, Subjectivity, Resistance: The Case of Laughter in *The Color Purple*," *Texas Studies in Literature and Language* 36, 4 (1994): 462–82; "Tragedy Reborn(e): *A Question of Power* and the Soul-Journeys of Bessie Head," *Genre: Forms of Discourse and Culture* 26, 2/3 (1993): 331–52; "Positioning Subjects and Objects: Agency, Narration, Relationality," *Hypatia: A Feminist Journal of Philosophy* 8, 1 (1993): 55–80; "Ideologies of the Funny," *Centennial Review* 36, 2 (1992): 265–96.